YOUR NAVY

PREPARED BY
STANDARDS AND CURRICULUM DIVISION
TRAINING
BUREAU OF NAVAL PERSONNEL

NAVY TRAINING COURSES

EDITION OF 1946

UNITED
GOVERNMENT PR.
WASHINGTON: 1946

Preface

This book is written for all enlisted men of the U. S. Navy. As part of the Navy training courses program it is intended to give men an understanding of the history and development of the Navy and an appreciation of the Navy's role in our national history.

Beginning with a chapter on old world navies, the book quickly takes the reader to the beginning of the American Navy in the Revolutionary War. Succeeding chapters carry through the campaigns of the Barbary Coast, the War of 1812, and up to the Civil War. The Civil War chapters cover fully the actions of both Union Navy and Confederate Navy and show how the lessons of the Industrial Revolution affected sea power during that war. A brief chapter on the Spanish American War and a longer chapter on the Navy's part in the First World War brings the reader to the concluding chapters covering World War II. Throughout the book, the story of your Navy is told in a colorful and dynamic style that makes this history exceptionally readable.

Acknowledgement is accorded Mr. Theodore Roscoe, author of the major part of the book, which, as one of the NAVY TRAINING COURSES, was prepared by the Training Courses Section; and many original illustrations were prepared by the Illustrators' Unit, Standards and Curriculum Division of the Bureau of Naval Personnel. Credit and thanks for many other illustrations are due to the following agencies and collections: Bureau of Aeronautics, Coast Guard Official Photographs, Franklin Institute, Historial Society of New York City, Marine Corps Official Photographs, Mariners' Museum of Newport News, National Archives, National Park Service, Naval Records and Library, *New York Times*, and Official Navy Photographs.

YOUR NAVY

TABLE OF CONTENTS

Anchors Aweigh

This is the story of the United States Navy, and every sailor ought to know it. To begin with, it's a bang-up, thundering good story.

Some may call it a history, but don't let that word dismay you. History after all, is only a story—a true story of the past. And just as truth can be stranger than fiction, it is often five times as interesting.

Some folks say that history is "dry," and then they tell you an exciting incident that happened yesterday, and so become historians themselves. You've heard Joe down at the lunch car go over last year's batting averages—well, that's history. Your grandad's recollections of the first automobile, your Dad's recollections of World War I, your brother's or your pal's descriptions of the fighting at Omaha Beach or Iwo—you've been hearing American history all the time. What's more, as a bluejacket today in the Navy, you are making history. And when you go home and relate your own experiences, you (but stick to the facts!) will be a historian in your own right. So, first hand, you know that history can be interesting. And certainly the story of the Navy won't be dry.

Why Study History?

But aside from the fact that it's a whale of an interesting story, why bother with past history? What's the good of going back

to the old days, or even yesterday, when you've got your hands
full as a bluejacket in the present? You're kept jumping by
what's going on around you here and now. You're busy with
what you're doing here today.

Well, look at it this way—what you do today depends largely
on what was done yesterday. And yesterday's doing depended
on the day before that, and so on back through the months
and years, yes, and centuries. So you're not so far removed
from the old days, after all. Past events are linked up together
like a chain, and the present you're in is at this end of it. For
instance, you're in the Navy now. But there wouldn't have been
any U. S. Navy for you to be in, or any U. S., for that matter,
if it weren't for things that were done in the past.

People are likely to associate the word "past" with the phrase
"past and done"—meaning, "It's all over." They may consider
history in that light. The trouble here is with the time element.
Go back 150 years, for example. But that was "long ago," someone will say. Long ago? Not so long when scentists figure the
world is several billion years old! That brings 150 years a

little closer to home. It shaves the whiskers off American history
and brings it up to date. Yes, that goes back to the time of
George Washington; but historically speaking, it's in your time.
Actually there are men alive today who have shaken hands with
men who shook the hand of George Washington. You can figure
that one out on your abacus, if you want, but the point is that
Washington wasn't some old fogey in a time of long ago that's
"past and done."

The past, then, is closer to the present than people sometimes
think. And the things done in the past are not "all over with."
For another simple illustration, there was World War I. Many

Americans thought it was all over with. But in World War II America faced the same enemy, Germany—in some places on exactly the same front. In many respects it was the same war, fought for the same reasons. Only the faces of those in the line had changed. Time marches on, but it doesn't leave the past behind.

You can see, then, how the things you're doing now result from, and are a continuation of, things done in the past. History can tell you about some of those past things, and give you a better understanding of "what it's all about" and what you're doing today.

As a bluejacket making history in the American Navy you want a clear idea of what America is, to begin with, and just why you are an American. You want to know what kind of history you're making, why you're making it, the reason for making it at all. Past history gives you a blueprint of the job you're working on, a design of the vital events you're helping to shape. The story of the American Navy—as a part of American history—can tell you why you're aboard, and make you sure of your objective.

There's another reason for taking a bearing on the past. History can be a guide for the future. Like a navigational chart, it can show you where you've been, how you arrived at where you are, and it can also give you an idea of where you're heading. People who waste money on fortune tellers to find out what may happen tomorrow could learn more from yesterday's newspapers. You've heard the old axiom, "History repeats itself." If you want to know what may and can happen, look back and judge accordingly.

So you have four good reasons for acquiring a little knowledge of your Navy's history: it's a whacking good story—it can give you an idea of what today is all about—it can tell you some things about the service you're in and why you're in it—it can serve as a reference bearing on your objective.

But these are broad generalities, and you want to learn something you can apply to your immediate job. You're out for something specific. You're Seaman First, perhaps, striking for Gunner's Mate 3/c. Or you're a Bosun's Mate, a Signalman aboard a BB, a Chief Fire Controlman on a flat top, a Motor

3

Machinist's Mate. What's there in this story of the Navy for your practical use?

Well, this manual can't tell you how to break down and repair a 5″38 gun. Or how to pipe the watch, or execute flag signals, or maintain a Mark 51 director, or change an oil filter on a Diesel engine. It won't even show you how to stow your seabag. You have other manuals for such specific instruction.

This manual is designed to teach you something about Navy life, about Navy ways, about the Navy as a fighting organization. It is a story to be read as a story, giving you something to think about, to get excited about, to form opinions on, perhaps to chuckle over. For this is chiefly the story of the Navy's men, the officers and bluejackets of the past, the things they thought and did, and why.

On The Record

Some episodes in this human story you may find hard to believe—such as the long odds in some of the battles. But you won't find anything stated as fact that isn't down somewhere in the records. The early sailors kept their log books, the captains turned in their reports, documents were filed, letters written, and events recorded which can be checked just as you can check the Declaration of Independence by going to the Library of Congress in Washington and looking at it today. Sometimes uncertainty may arise over an episode in history, and where such uncertainty exists it will be indicated. When something is quoted as having been written or said, and the exact words are given, the quotation is in *italics*.

Yes, yesterday's Navy is "on the record," and its men left marks for you to shoot at. Targets at which any modern bluejacket can profitably aim. You'll find some challenging scores in their story—scores in skill, resolution, and "guts" that in some cases have never been equalled.

Incidentally, as a member of the American Navy—YOUR Navy— you should become acquainted with its manners, customs, and traditions. Do you know why, in the Navy, you honor your ship's quarterdeck? Why a visiting officer is piped over the side? Do you know the origin of the American flag that you salute?

You can brush up on the answers in this story as you read

along. And perhaps you can find the answers to some other, more basic questions concerning your Navy. Such as the importance of sea power in modern warfare. The development of American naval strategy. The vital necessity for Navy training.

Watch how that factor, TRAINING, particularly influences the whole story. How naval victories depend, as many instances have proved, on a welded combination of brains, discipline, and target practice. For though forces are often even, and courage can often be equalled, victory comes to the side that has the better discipline, that does the better thinking and the better shooting.

But draw your own conclusions—they're up to you. And now push aside those heavy words—training—education—indoctrination—instruction—history. Think of this manual as an introduction (the handshaking kind) to old comrades you'd like to meet. A chance to see some of the great American Naval leaders, to be in on some of the greatest sea battles of all time, to become personally acquainted with the captains and crews who served before you in the U. S. Navy.

Would you like to walk the deck with John Paul Jones? Go pirate-hunting with Stephen Decatur? Catch a glimpse of Farragut at Mobile? Serve one of the old guns under Dewey? Believe it or not, you are serving under those leaders.

Old John Adams once shocked his stiff-necked neighbors by announcing (when he was eighty) that he was never going to die.

He didn't.

He lives today in the Navy Department in Washington, and you can hear him (if you listen sharp) still urging stout ships, a good set of Navy Regs, and top pay for the enlisted man.

John Paul Jones still roams the sea, and you can see him (if you have the eye) all over your warship from stern to forepeak, on her gun decks, in the wardroom, on the bridge.

Who can say the old captains and crews are gone when their words still echo through the Navy, their actions go on influencing the present, their personalities continue making history? Meet them, and they'll give you a hand on deck. Make friends with them, and they'll serve alongside you in the Navy as it puts out for the future.

Now to go on with the story—

Civilization and Sea Power

The American Revolution, called the War for Independence, did not explode all at once like a powder mine. Like the Navy, it was a long time building before it went into action. The forces which set it off were long at work under the surface.

The American War for Independence was a part of something taking place all over the globe, a revolution that began long before America was discovered—before Britain was discovered, for that matter. For centuries men had been struggling to win their independence. And man had to think of independence before he could aspire to fight for it. He had to work it out in his head, had to learn to reason. In other words, before he could free himself from tyranny he had to become educated. As H. G. Wells, the historian, has put it, *"History is a race between education and disaster."*

As soon as man reasons, he begins to ask why. And as soon as he learns the answer, he starts becoming educated. One occupation at least led to a broadened outlook and independent thinking—seafaring. From the first the ancient mariner had to use his head. Fishing, sailing, exploring, seafaring men were among the best educated of early times.

You can see how civilization followed the sea. First, fishermen. Then explorers. Then sailors of commerce. Then sea fighters to protect that commerce. Sea power and civilization (or call it education, or man's advancement) went hand in hand.

Go back to the island of Crete. Two thousand years before Christ the Egyptians had a war fleet of some 400 ships. But Crete was carrying on commerce with Egypt centuries before that. Her warships in the Mediterranean are the earliest on record, and Crete is regarded as the world's first great sea power.

Phoenicia followed Crete as sea power No. 2. The Phoenicians were a maritime people, and they developed an alphabet as an aid to keeping track of commercial deals. Phoenicia grew up on sea power. Her cargo carriers, known as "round ships," were all over the Mediterranean. Her warships, called "long ships," set the model for the Greek and Roman "bireme" and "trireme"—oar galleys with double and triple banks of rowers, high bulwarks to protect the men, and a beak-nosed ram on the bow. Early records indicate that a Phoenician naval squadron circumnavigated Africa some seven hundred years before Christ.

The early Greek sailors were the most advanced in ancient history. They employed astronomy and mathematics in naviga-

tion. They were aware of the earth's magnetic influence, and invented a primitive form of compass. Their warships used strategy and tactics to fight sea battles that rank as historic classics. They drew charts. And they studied geography.

The early Romans had brains, too, and they conquered and developed a mighty empire. Their legions conquered southern Europe, North Africa, and the Near East, and had voyaged by sea in triremes to Britain.

Slaves pulled at the oars of the Roman warships heading for Britain, and the captains did some remarkable navigating considering they mixed navigation with advice from pagan idols and their sailors were always on the verge of mutiny. They found no gold in Britain, so they let the colony go to seed. The last legionnaires were called home to fight the invasion by northern tribes.

Swarming out of the north, these ferocious barbarians—Goths,

Visigoths, and Vandals—fell on Rome like an avalanche of tigers. They found the Romans fat, juicy, pickled in alcohol, and to their taste. When the barbarians returned to their northern homelands, the Roman Empire lay in fragments, and even the culture which Rome had borrowed from the Greeks was buried in the ruins.

Europe plunged into an age of darkness that set it backward a thousand years. Tyranny was rampant as individual fuedal lords gained control, robber barons pillaged the continent, and the average man became a dull-witted serf living in want, fear, voiceless humility, and hobgoblin superstition. Only the Christian Church struggled to keep alive a spark of culture.

Then came the Moslem invasion of Europe. The Arabians were rallying to the call of Mohammed, who called himself the "Prophet of Allah," and preached a religion of fire and sword. *We Arabians are destined to rule the world,"* they cried. This was some eleven hundred years ago, and they nearly succeeded.

For three hundred years the struggle against the Mohammedans lasted. The Christian armies, referred to as the Crusaders, played an important part in stopping the threat to Europe. And upon returning home, they brought back into Europe a renewed knowledge of reading, writing, arithmetic, and geography that had been all but lost to Europe's people since the fall of Rome.

Commerce started up again, ships put to sea again, people began thinking again, and Europe woke up to enter that period of history known as the "Rebirth"—the Renaissance. And? And a bright, new page was turned in the story of man's struggle for freedom.

Then an amazing event took place. In England a group of barons and knights cornered King John at a place called Runnymede and forced him to sign a document guaranteeing them certain rights. Just which ones doesn't matter. What matters is that a group of men were demanding their rights from a king, a being hitherto considered unapproachable on this subject. And you can see this document today—the Magna Carta, or "Great Charter"—man's first big step toward a constitutional form of government.

The Magna Carta fired the minds of all who heard of it back there in the year 1215. It showed how power could be used to obtain rights as well as to withhold them. And this revelation made an echo. In France, the Netherlands, Italy, Spain—the maritime countries in contact with England—the idea grew.

Other people—the Netherlanders and Italians, for example— kept in step with the English and wrenched a little liberty from their sovereigns. Venice set up a sort of republic that became one of the most progressive in Medieval Europe. It was Marco Polo, a Venetian merchant, who explored all the way across Asia to China, and brought back vivid tales of the Far East.

These tales of the rich Far East, magnified by a wealth of imagination, started a treasure-hunt for gold. Eager faces turned toward Damascus and Bagdad; adventurers embarked on the long overland journey for India and China. If they came back with little gold, they did return with cloth, porcelain, drugs, and spices which they could sell for gold.

But the fierce followers of Allah's Prophet straddled Asia Minor, and made overland travel deadly dangerous. If only another route to the Orient could be found—a sea-route around the dark coast of Africa.

The idea came to Prince Henry of Portugal, a maritime country whose people were learning to think. This prince distinguished himself by setting up a school of navigation and sending out expeditions to explore the western coast of Africa. So he came to be called Prince Henry the Navigator. Although he died in 1460 his project was carried out in 1487 when Bartholomew Diaz rounded the Cape of Good Hope.

Eleven years later Vasco da Gama followed this lead and

continued on across the Indian Ocean to reach India. The first all-water route to the Orient had been found.

But meantime the world had been rocked by the discoveries of another mariner, who added two new continents to mankind's knowledge.

Columbus Sails the Ocean Blue

Some time around 1470, rich stories of the Orient and golden tales of India reached the ears of a young Genoese dress-goods salesman named Christopher Columbus. He began to dream of India and gold. He didn't have enough of the latter to start a search, but he had plenty of the dream.

It seems that this visionary Italian, sailing to Spain with a bundle of dress-goods, fell into the hands of Mohammedan pirates off North Africa, then was rescued from the corsairs by a Spanish warship. The Spanish captain took a liking to Christopher. Probably it was this mariner who told him the earth was round and gave him rudimentary lessons in seamanship and navigation.

As the idea of finding a western passage to India and Zipangu (Japan) percolated in the brain of Columbus, he studied maps, pored over and drew charts, and went to Portugal with his project. Failing to interest the Portuguese, he spent several years in Spain and finally won the support of King Ferdinand and Queen Isabella.

Even so they didn't back him with much—three tiny vessels, a crew of about 100 men, a promise to promote him to Admiral of the Ocean if he made good, plus one-tenth of *"all the pearls, precious stones, gold, silver, spices, and other merchandise,"* he might find. Obviously, they were counting on his hitting the jackpot.

They did lend him a Spanish officer, Martin Pinzon, who was an experienced sailor. It was this Spanish mariner who handled most of the navigating.

Now think of the project—sailing into an unknown, uncharted ocean where no man to your knowledge had been before and the boundary was only a myth. Would it pour off somewhere into empty space as many men continued to believe? If India was there somewhere to the west, what chance was there to reach it? What rations to take? Would the casks of drinking water last?

These questions might disturb Martin Pinzon, but they deterred Columbus not at all. The expedition set sail on August 3, 1492, and every schoolboy today knows how the *Pinta, Nina,* and *Santa Maria* fared.

Halfway across the crews grew terrified and wanted to turn back. Columbus put down the mutiny. He himself must have been uneasy aboard his flagship, *Santa Maria,* a caravel that

you wouldn't dare sail on a canal today, with its top-heavy poop, its rotted timbering, and its rats. But Columbus was one of those strange idea-men who wouldn't be stopped by fear. One part of him was as dreamy as a cloud, the other as down-to-earth as granite. You can see this in his famous journal, his log-book on the voyage. One day he imagines giant sea serpents on the horizon, or sees a palatial mirage in the sky. The next day he makes a firm decision with the men. Nothing can swerve him. He sails on.

October 11, after sixty-nine days in space, the *Santa Maria* sighted land. Probably it was an island in the Bahamas (historians calculate Watling's Island) but Columbus believed he had found India. He sailed on to explore Cuba and the island of Haiti, and he called the peaceful natives he found there "Indians." In his imagination he also saw a lot of gold on these islands, and so reported in his journal. Doubtless this was just the shine of sunlight on the sand, for gold was not one of the things Columbus took back with him to Spain.

He returned to Spain with Martin Pinzon. Little *Santa Maria* had been wrecked off the coast of Haiti, and the sailors had dismantled her and used her timbers and guns to build a blockhouse.

Ferdinand and Isabella were disappointed in a cargo of parrots, cocoanuts, and brown Indians, but they still had hopes; and Columbus was showered with honors. In 1493, given another ship, Columbus set out again. Revisiting Haiti, he could not find a single trace of the blockhouse and men he had left there. He pushed on across the Caribbean, and on this and two more trans-Atlantic voyages he discovered the coast of Central America and the northern tip of South America, claiming these lands for Spain.

To his dying day he believed he had discovered Asia. And it remained for another Italian explorer, Amerigo Vespucci, sailing under Portuguese colors three years later, to proclaim

the discovery of a "new world." European mapmakers gave the new continents Vespucci's name — Amerigo, or America.

Columbus received poor reward for his great exploit. Because he failed to find gold on his ensuing voyages, the Spanish rulers turned their backs on him, the crowds forgot him. Impoverished by his efforts, he ended up in debtor's prison. He died in 1506 in such poverty and obscurity that his burial place is still in doubt.

The Gold Rush

Indeed, Columbus was shabbily rewarded, for he had discovered the richest land of all. It wasn't long before Balboa, Cortez, Pizarro, and Ponce de Leon, following the trail Columbus blazed, were conquering the New World in the name of Spain.

In the short space of two decades, Spain became the world's richest and most powerful nation.

In 1540, Hernando De Soto landed in Florida, and pushing cross-country, he discovered the Mississippi. Around 1542, Coronado, another Spaniard, explored as far as present-day Kansas. In 1565 the first permanent white settlement in North America was established —St. Augustine, Florida.

Meanwhile stories of the New World had gone galloping around Europe, and the French king decided to enter the exciting treasure hunt. Presently Verranzo, flying the French flag, was probing along the wilderness-wooded shores of North America. In 1535 Jacques Cartier, seeking a northern passage to India, explored the St. Lawrence. These territories were claimed by the French crown. and in 1603 Champlain was setting up trading posts in Nova Scotia and scouting around eastern Canada.

The English had been even quicker to follow Columbus. As early as 1497, the Italian navigator John Cabot had carried the flag of England to the North American coast. It was not until 1577 that England sent another adventurer to America— Sir Francis Drake.

Drake ran into the Spanish, with bad results for the latter. After a cruise around the world (which had first been circumnavigated by Magellan for Portugal in 1522) he returned to England, where Queen Elizabeth knighted him on his vessel's quarterdeck.

Queen Elizabeth was an unusual woman. Sometimes referred to (perhaps dryly) as "Good Queen Bess," she was the daughter of Henry VIII, from whom she inherited a temper and a royal talent for treachery. But she also had a lot of business sense.

13

Under her driving influence, England went in for trade and shop-keeping in a big way. She wasn't the woman to overlook a gold mine like the New World.

In 1578 she sent out Sir Humphrey Gilbert, an energetic navigator, to lay claim to the territory discovered by Cabot. When Gilbert went down in a storm at sea, she sent his half-brother, Sir Walter Raleigh, to do the job. Raleigh set out in 1584, and landed in America in the region he called Virginia in honor of his "virgin queen."

And now began a race to stake out claims and establish New World colonies—Portugal and Spain in South and Central America, France and England in North America, and later the Dutch, with Hendrick Hudson founding New Amsterdam, the grandfather of New York. And then? Then began wars to hold these colonies from competing power-rivals. Wars, you might say, fought for the power of kings. And next, wars to free the colonials, themselves, from Old World tyranny—wars fought for the rights of men.

And of necessity these became sea wars, demanding battle-ships and fighting crews.

Spanish Armada

Drake might be considered the first great admiral in the modern sense of the word. In 1588 the Spanish, under the fanatical rule of Philip II, launched a sea attack against England, intending to sink Queen Elizabeth and all her works. Queen Elizabeth's spies informed her of this invasion plan, and she promptly assigned the island's defense to Drake.

The Spanish fleet was the mightiest yet assembled. The war-ships were galleons—stubby vessels, three and four-deckers with square sails—a big advance over the one-deck caravels of Columbus' time. They were armed with the newest weapons—guns. The brass carronades firing iron and stone cannon balls might appear toy-like today, but in 1588 they were the deadliest thing on earth, and had already put an end to knightly lances and chain armor.

The English had guns, too—in fact, they had used cannon against France in the Battle of Crecy, long before. However, the English fleet in size or fire power didn't hold a candle to

14

Spain's, and things looked dark for the "tight little isle." But the Spanish hadn't counted on the weather or Sir Francis Drake.

They were no match for either. Drake's ships out-navigated, out-fought, and out-maneuvered the slower, heavier Spanish

galleons. And a great storm drove through the English Channel and completed the destruction of Philip's fleet. The Spanish Armada was wrecked, and England became the world's No. 1 maritime power.

These Elizabethan Britons took to the sea like schools of salmon. Shipyards mushroomed along the Thames in company with a hurly-burly of wharves, warehouses, and docks. As the thriving merchant service opened sea lanes to the Caribbean, the British Navy developed as a protective arm.

Seamen were early impressed into the service—meaning Jack had to go whether he liked it or not. A drummer might appear on the public square. As a crowd thronged around to learn the news, the royal officers would pounce. And Jack would be carried off kicking and cussing—he was now in the Royal Navy.

The Royal Navy of old-time England was no bed of roses. Jack lived pretty much on hard-tack and hopes. If he survived a few voyages, he might escape in the New World. Or, if lucky, he might become a Navy Boatswain.

BOATSWAIN (you call it bosu'n) is one of the oldest titles in the Navy. It comes from the Anglo-Saxon word, *batsuen*, meaning "boat swain," or boat's servant.

The boatswain of Elizabethan days was in charge of the seamen's work on deck and aloft, and he was quite an individual. As symbols of authority he carried a rattan cane and a silver whistle. The bosun's pipe makes music in the Navy to this day, as every bluejacket knows. Well, there it was, piping away in the days of Shakespeare. The rattan cane was an article less popular among the men. If Jack so much as stooped to buckle a shoe, he regretted it.

COXSWAIN (you call it cox'n)—originally "Cocksu'n"—is another of the oldest titles. It was the cox'n's job to take charge of small boats (called cockboats) and rowing parties working from ship to shore. The cox'n also had a whistle which he used, according to one reporter of the time, *"to cheer up and direct his gang of rowers, and to keep them together while waiting."*

These Petty Officers also officiated at floggings, keel-haulings, and other deck sports to be discussed later. The quality of mercy, as described by Shakespeare, did not drop "like the gentle rain from heaven" on the early Royal Navy.

GUNNER'S MATE is still another naval title that goes way back. In the early days he served under the Master-Gunner, who corresponded to today's Gunnery Officer. The Gunner's Mate's job

16

was much as it is today—serving and maintaining the weapons aboard ship.

QUARTERMASTER is a rate as old as Gunner's Mate, the title deriving from the quarterdeck of the old galleon-type sailing ship. Stationed on this deck, the Quarter-Master relayed orders from the Captain aft to the forecastle, and served as assistant to the Officer of the Watch. Eventually the business of running orders forward was detailed to ship's boys, called "the King's Letter Boys"—nimble lads who raced fore and aft with messages and so came to be known as "midshipmen." The Quarter-Master gave his time to steering and keeping records. He was also in charge of the ship's hourglass, ancestor of your modern chronometers.

CARPENTER and SAIL MAKER are other ancient titles that still survive. Carpenter's Mates seem to have been on deck in 1300, which apparently gives "Chips" the record. Sail makers still work with marlinspike and palm aboard "rag wagons," although the rate is now extinct in the Navy along with a host of other quaint ratings such as Armourer's Mate, Gunner's Tailor, Cooper (ship's barrel maker), and Swabber (Petty Officer in charge of swabbing decks). Meanwhile, the Navy man today who serves as Gunner's Mate, Bosun's Mate, Quartermaster, Carpenter, or Cox'n can take pride in the fact that he carries on in one of the oldest known rates at sea.

Jack of the Elizabethan Navy led a dog's life, and in the warship's foc's'le he was in the dog's house. His pay was a pittance, his food was miserable, and his life in battle wasn't worth a farthing. And he had over him a top-heavy leadership of officers drawn from the nobility and landed gentry. Many of these "gold braids" were hopeless nincompoops who got their commissions through family connections. It gave poor Jack, no matter how hard-working and intelligent, little chance to get ahead. He might work up to Boatswain, Gunner's Mate, or Quartermaster, but there he stopped.

How, then, with this caste system of upper-crust leadership and down-trodden Jack-tars, did the Navy of old England become the world's greatest sea power? How did England become *Great Britain?*

The answer is that the Royal Navy succeeded in spite of

the system, and because the competing navies of the time were even more straight-jacketed by "nobility" rule. This was also true of the nations themselves in those days. The England of four hundred years ago was an "absolute monarchy" in which the king supposedly ruled by "divine right." Even so England was out in front of her neighbors. England had her Magna Charta, and Englishmen had a few rights. And precisely as Englishmen forged ahead in that respect, the nation held a lead over backward competitors.

But the Old World back in the 17th Century seethed with fierce intolerance. In France, where fanaticism had gained the upper hand, the Protestant Huguenots had been massacred. Throughout Europe the Jews were being driven from pillar to post (sound familiar?). In England the Catholics had been ruthlessly treated. And then, in the reign of King James, a little band of non-conformists, who wanted to worship God according to their lights, were furiously set upon.

The little band was ordered to conform or else—so the Separ-

atists, as they were called, left England for more liberal Holland. In Holland they finally obtained a land grant from the Virginia Company. With 7000 pounds ($35,000) to finance them, they chartered the *Mayflower* and embarked to found a settlement in the New World. You recognize this band, of course, as the Pilgrims. They were not all religiously motivated—a number of them being gentleman adventurers—but all were determined to find freedom.

On November 11, 1620, they reached the tip of Cape Cod, anchored off shore, and drew up a compact aboard the *Mayflower*. This compact, called the Mayflower Compact, included a pledge to obey, *"such just and equal laws as shall be thought most meet and convenient for ye general good of the colony."*

Here was a government of the people, by the people, and for the people! The first true Democracy had been founded in America.

The Thirteen Colonies

The Pilgrims were not the original American colonials. In 1606 King James of England had granted the famous Virginia Charter establishing the London Company and the Plymouth Company to open up trade in America. In 1607 a party of 140 colonists, including Captain John Smith, sailed into Chesapeake Bay and founded the settlement of Jamestown on the James River.

Next to settle were the Dutch, opening a trading post on Manhattan Island in 1614.

Ten years after the Pilgrims landed, some two thousand Puritans arrived to found a "Bible Commonwealth" in Massachusetts under John Winthrop. The stern Puritans, having broken with the Church of England, now refused to acknowledge anyone's right to differ with their own religious beliefs. They banished the pastor, Roger Williams, for declaring that the State had no right to dictate a man's religion, and exiled Mrs. Anne Hutchinson for holding independent views. Rhode Island, Maine, and New Hampshire were settled by many later exiles from the Puritan commonwealth.

In 1632 Charles I gave Lord Baltimore a grant to the land

of present-day Maryland, and there 300 settlers came the following year.

In 1637 another group of English immigrants settled in Connecticut.

About the same time a group of Swedes founded a colony in the vicinity of Delaware which they later lost to the Dutch in 1655.

The Carolinas were opened for colonization by Charles II in 1663. (They separated into North and South Carolina in 1729.)

New Jersey was parceled out as a land grant in 1664 by the Duke of York, whose fleet in the same year forced the Dutch to cede New Amsterdam to England. New York State resulted from this real-estate deal.

In 1681, to pay his military debts, Charles II granted to the Penn family the wilderness between Delaware and Jersey; and William Penn founded there a Quaker colony called Pennsylvania, which means Penn's Woods.

Georgia, last of the thirteen colonies, was set up as a buffer state between the Carolinas and Spanish Florida. It was settled in 1733 under the influence of James Oglethorpe, who desired to open a refuge for English debtors.

You don't need to memorize these facts. They merely indicate how America's seaboard was chartered, leased, donated, or sold to the settlers by the English Government, and how early America became colonized in a little over 100 years.

Well, the immigrants came over. A few at first, then crowded shiploads. Farmers and townsfolk, woodchoppers and weavers, tinkers, tailors, and traders. Many were indentured servants with debts to work off. Some were gentlemen adventurers with sword and snuffbox handy. Some were righteous men, some were rogues, some were scholars, and some were fools. But the majority were hard-working, common-sense, save-spend-and-lend-a-little human beings such as you find today on any street. By 1770 or thereabouts, there were almost 4,000,000 of them in the colonies.

And these were the early Americans. But remember, all these people were originally immigrants. Prior to the Revolution, all had considered themselves British subjects. At the same time, all had undergone a process of Americanization.

The type of men who left the Old World because of tyranny certainly would not put up with it for long in the New.

In Virginia the poor farmers and field hands, led by Nathaniel Bacon, rose in revolt against Governor Berkeley and set up a government of the people. Berkeley managed to crush the revolt with a savage come-back, but the Virginians later won a more liberal government. Bacon's Rebellion in 1676 against the authority of the Crown was the first big straw in the American wind.

A few years later, in New England, tyrannical Governor Andros was thrown out of office. William of Orange, at that time King of England, agreed to restore a measure of home rule to these colonies.

Throughout the early 1700's, the American colonials, raising their families, working their farms, building their towns, were less and less willing to accept regulations imposed by the Mother Country.

Here was the English point of view: The colonies were territories to be exploited for the benefit of the Mother Country. Therefore the colonies must be subordinate to the Mother Country.

And here was the American colonial point of view: "We colonials are just as good as the folks back home. Why should we be exploited for the benefit of anybody? We're a God-fearing, hard-fighting bunch who've had to make our own way out here."

Yet they tried to remain loyal to the Crown. From 1700 to 1776 England was engaged in a series of wars with France and Spain. These power-struggles echoed to the New World, and border warfare in America was constant. Agents of all the contesting powers kept stirring up the Indians, and the colonists usually bore the brunt.

When the French and Indian War broke out in 1754, the colonials marched with the Red Coats sent over from England. One of the colonial officers under the Red Coats was young George Washington of Virginia. New England colonials joined the British Army in the campaigns by which England finally won control of Canada.

But the English leadership was often clumsy. The red-coated troops were shot down in the forest like scarlet tanagers; the officers floundered; and the colonials frequently had to carry the ball.

The colonists blamed England for the slipshod conduct of these Indian fights. The very summer the French and Indian War broke out, 1754, seven colonies sent delegates to Albany, New York, to discuss common action against the hostile tribes. A Pennsylvania publisher, Benjamin Franklin, proposed a political union of these colonies whereby they might raise taxes to maintain a frontier army for their mutual protection. This proposition, the Albany Plan, was scowled upon by the Crown. And the colonies, themselves, couldn't get together. But it was an idea.

The Americans were becoming full of ideas. Roger Williams, William Penn, and Nathaniel Bacon were long-since gone, but they had planted seeds which had taken root. A great tree was growing in America. Thomas Jefferson called it the "Tree of Liberty."

The King of England at this time was George III. Of German descent, he was stubborn, rather thick of neck and head. His advisers told him of this tree in America, and he determined to nip it in the bud. To put down smuggling, he garrisoned a standing army in the colonies. He set British battleships to patrol the coast. He put his seal on a lot of tax laws to raise money to pay for England's war with France. He ordered stern punishments for talk of rebellion.

Some of the laws were carried out and some of them weren't enforced. No matter, it was too late to stop what came. For the colonists had become self-reliant. And self-reliant people don't need other people to do things for them—even rule them. In fact, they prefer to do such things for themselves. Self-reliance, you might say, is first cousin to independence.

And so the battle for independence was underway. From a skirmish at a small bridge the fighting was to spread all up and down the coast of America. Every colonist would soon be involved—and many Britishers, too.

The Revolution had begun.

LIBERTY OR DEATH

The Revolutionary War (Part 1)

The Revolutionary War may seem a long time ago. And perhaps you think of colonial America in terms of candlelight and cobblestones, the early Americans quaint figures wearing knee-breeches, lace cuffs, powdered wigs, and three-cornered hats. But the war was something more than a pageant of muskets, Minute Men, Mount Vernon, and minuets. George Washington and his colleagues weren't cold marble figures posturing around in heroic attitudes. Ben Franklin and the others who met in the little brick building in Philadelphia weren't faces on postage stamps.

They were living Americans, those who met in Philadelphia on May 10, 1775, to open the Second Continental Congress. And they were dealing with the lives of many other living Americans—men who, like you today, loved their homes and families, took pride in their work, admired a pretty girl, liked dogs and horses, enjoyed a pipe or a glass of cheer.

It was *"Liberty or Death!"* as Patrick Henry had challenged, and those early Americans chose to fight for liberty. The men at Philadelphia voted for a Continental Army, and George Washington was unanimously chosen Commander-in-Chief. Still it was hoped the fighting at Boston would not spread, and the king would back down. Many members of the Continental Congress were against a complete break with Great Britain.

27

As late as January, 1776, New Jersey, New York, Maryland, and Pennsylvania were voting to remain within the Empire.

However, events and George III decided the issue. On May 10, '75, Ticonderoga on Lake Champlain was the scene of one of the events when Ethan Allen and a band of Vermonters calling themselves "The Green Mountain Boys" captured old Fort Ti. On June 16, the Massachusetts militia seized Breed's Hill commanding Boston Harbor, and dug in. Gage sent his Red Coats to regain the height, and a violent battle exploded. The British captured the height, but it cost them over 1,000 casualties. As the original British objective was neighboring Bunker Hill, the engagement became famous as the Battle of Bunker Hill.

Although the Red Coats remained in control of Boston, the battle was a shot in the arm to the Americans. Everywhere in New England heartened patriots were unlimbering Old Betsy from the fireplace mantel and taking the road to Boston. General Washington, arriving at the scene on July 3, found a first-class seige going on, and realized at once it meant a full-dress war.

America Builds a Navy

It was going to mean a long war, and it was going to mean a sea war—Washington was aware of that. He had a keen mind, this Virginia planter who had been a frontier surveyor as a youth, had won high rank in the Colonial Army, and whose recognized ability and integrity had caused his neighbors to appoint him their military leader in this fateful hour. What were his thoughts as he took command at Boston? Personally, as one of the wealthiest men in America, he had much to lose. His Virginia plantation, his future, his life, his family were at stake. Tremendous responsibility lay ahead of him—perhaps a nation was in the balance. If he failed? George Washington set his jaw. He wouldn't fail! Other men had risked their lives here for liberty. Without hesitation he pledged his own life and fortune to the cause.

Yet his heart must have sunk as he surveyed the fight ahead—this long war, this sea war. At Boston the patriots were low on powder. They had no artillery. England had carefully confined the manufacture of arms and munitions to her own shores. And the colonists were untrained, lacking in discipline. They weren't going to want training, either, for twice they'd defeated the Red Coats in skirmishes—why train?

But the war coming up wasn't going to be a skirmish, and Washington knew from experience that in the long run trained soldiers would beat undisciplined troops. George III would soon send a great army to invade the colonies. And the colonies were still acting like individual countries; in Philadelphia the repre-

sentatives were bickering. Where were trained soldiers, powder, guns, money coming from? As for war at sea—

George Washington saw the problem as you can see it from today in retrospect. Colonial America was largely engaged in agriculture and fur trapping. The towns—Boston, Providence, New York, Philadelphia, Alexandria, Charleston—were mainly trading centers where British merchandise was exchanged for American produce. A few muddy turnpikes connected these towns, the roads were generally impassable in winter, and transportation depended largely on river traffic and coastal shipping. Britain would blockade the seaports, seize the waterways, bottle up the shipping if she could, then land troops at will. What was to stop her?

The king boasted the world's biggest navy. Recent victory over the French had sent its morale higher than its topsails. Already there were warships off the coast—frigates and sloops. Examine these vessels for a moment. They may seem antique compared to today's, but in those days they were the mightiest things afloat and a big advance over the waddling galleons of Drake's time.

During the Revolutionary period (and they were standard until the Civil War) there were three main classes of naval vessels —the sloop-of-war, the frigate, the ship of the line.

All three types were "ship-rigged," meaning they were square-rigged with three masts called the fore, main, and mizzen. The topmost deck of the ship was called the "spar-deck." The after part of this deck, the quarter-deck, was sacred to the commissioned officers. The men were quartered up forward. Between main and foremast there was generally a well-deck with gangways leading from forecastle to quarter-deck aft.

The sloop-of-war (also called a "corvette") carried all her guns on the spar-deck. Smaller vessels of this class were designated as brigs and schooners. The average sloop carried around 20 guns.

The frigate, next in size, was the cruiser of that day. She had one gun-deck below her spar-deck, and generally carried from 28 to 44 guns.

The ship of the line was the battleship of sailing days, distinguished by having two or more gun-decks below her spar-deck. These gun-decks were indicated by broad bands of white or yellow painted on the ship's side. These big sailing ships carried from 74 to 120 guns and were the "terror of the seas."

Aboard these vessels there were powder and munition holds,

great tanks for storing water, supply holds for food and gear, a cockpit where the surgeon cared for the wounded. The officers' quarters were miserable, and the men were packed in like sardines. And imagine the fire hazard on a wooden ship topped by clouds of billowing canvas. "Hot shot" to fire the enemy's rigging was a standard projectile.

The cannon on these vessels were cast iron, mounted on wooden carriages which recoiled on wheels. All were muzzle loaded, and fired by the simple application of a slow match to a vent drilled in the breech. Flint-locks were sometimes used, but were unreliable. The gunners thrust a bag of powder into the muzzle, rammed home with a ramrod, then rammed in the cannon ball. The gun was run out through the port by hand, the crew backed off, and the match was applied. Wham! Training was done by hauling on tackle to move the gun around. Elevation was a matter of jacking up the breech with a handspike. More detail on these naval cannon later.

The cannon balls of the Revolution period were solid "round shot," classed by weight—5-pound, 10-pound, and so on. Sometimes they were hitched together on a short piece of chain to make "chain shot." Or they were heated red hot on a forge to make blazing firebrands. One hundred yards was good range for such guns, but the fighting at sea was largely close work, beam to beam, and ships locked together with grappling hooks were won by "boarding" and bloody work with pike and cutlass. Trained for this hand-to-hand fighting, large crews were aboard each naval vessel, plus extra hands to man captured prizes.

No American knew the number of ships in England's Navy, but they floated in the hundreds, and they ranged the seas from India to the Caribbean. THE COLONIES DID NOT POSSESS A SINGLE WARSHIP! What were the thoughts of George Washington?

He sent appeal by special delivery to the Congress in Philadelphia. Sailors must be recruited immediately. Ships must be sent to Boston to break the King's blockade. An expedition should be rushed to Bermuda where large stores of powder—the immediate necessity—could be seized. In short, the Americans must organize a Navy! At once!

Congress was startled. Fight the British on the sea? Why, the Royal Navy was invincible! A cold chill invaded the little hall in Philadelphia, and the representatives, who were mostly lawyers, began to argue.

There was talk of appeasement and conciliating the King. But that mulish monarch had already issued a proclamation declaring the Americans rebels. In September, '75, his envoys hired 20,000 German Hessians to fight in America. And the Royal Navy was on the way.

Early in October British warships descended upon Falmouth, Maine, and burned the fishing village to a cinder. Congress woke up with a shock. George Washington was right.

On October 13, Congress voted to establish a committee to handle naval affairs. This body, called The Marine Committee, was the great-great-granddaddy of the present Navy Department. It began with three members—John Adams of Massachusetts, John Langdon of New Hampshire, Silas Deane of Connecticut.

Imagine that—three men setting out to construct a navy from scratch and send it into action against the world's greatest sea power. But one of those members made up for a hundred ordinary. This was doughty John Adams, a nutmeg of a character with a blue spark to his eye and the fire of independence in his soul. He was a lawyer, but he knew how to stick to the point—the point now was an American Navy. He drove the committee into action, and he launched the project on the same day the committee was formed. Historians put him on the book as the founder of the American Navy.

It is common in the naval service to refer to Congress as the "Father of the American Navy." It was Congress that had to legalize this fledgling and provide it with food, weapons, and clothes.

Certainly it was an infant on that October 13th, 1775, when Mr. Deane, prodded by John Adams, stood up to propose that the colonies equip, *"a swift sailing vessel to carry ten guns, for intercepting such transports as may be laden with warlike stores for the enemy."*

Did Congress take kindly to the infant? Well, hands were raised in alarm. A Pennsylvania delegate said he didn't like it at all. Such naval force, he said, would be sure to anger King George. The Royal Navy would blockade the entire American seaboard. *"I am clearly against any proposition to threaten,"* said Pennsylvania's Dr. Zubly. *"The people of England will take it we design to break off or separate."*

At this, Mr. Chase of Maryland wanted to know if it was any more threatening to fight the enemy at sea than on land? Many members of Congress thought it was—the King would declare that sea war was piracy. This aroused John Adams, whose sarcasm could rasp like rosin on a string. Why mince matters? The fight for Freedom was on. And with a few warships of their own the Americans could force Great Britain to keep a large fleet on the job and expend much to gain little.

So in truly democratic fashion—all sides being heard—the Navy was born.

1776—!

The year opened grimly with the British burning Norfolk, Virginia, while late news arrived to further dishearten Philadelphia—a campaign under Generals Montgomery and Benedict Arnold had failed at Quebec.

Pro-British Tories were deriding the patriots and there was talk of appeasement again. But George Washington was holding his ground. In March, 1776, his troops broke the British line and forced the Red Coats to evacuate Boston.

America cheered the news. Fife and drum sounded on the village greens where recruits tramped, singing "The Girl I Left Behind Me," and the new tune, "Yankee Doodle." It was this fellow in the song that popularized the nickname for the New Englanders— Yankees.

And throughout t h i s spring of 1776, the Americans were getting some

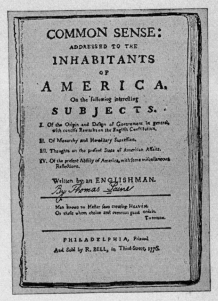

COMMON SENSE:
ADDRESSED TO THE
INHABITANTS
OF
AMERICA,
On the following interesting
SUBJECTS.

I. Of the Origin and Design of Government in general, with concise Remarks on the English Constitution.

II. Of Monarchy and Hereditary Succession.

III. Thoughts on the present State of American Affairs.

IV. Of the present Ability of America, with some miscellaneous Reflections.

Written by an ENGLISHMAN.
By Thomas Paine

Man knows no Master save creating HEAVEN,
Or those whom choice and common good ordain.
THOMSON.

PHILADELPHIA, Printed.
And Sold by R. BELL, in Third Street. 1776.

more encouragement—encouragement in the form of an extraordinary little book entitled *Common Sense*. This book was written by a recent comer from London, an Englishman named Thomas Paine. Though called radical and atheistic, Paine sounded the keynote for American Independence. His book, discussing such subjects as the "Origin of Government" and "Monarchy and Hereditary Succession," made mincemeat of royalty in all its aspects. As an argument for democracy, it still stands like a granite monument.

Paine called on the colonies to unite and break from England. *"Everything that is right or reasonable pleads for separation!"* He urged all Americans to stick to their posts in the fight for Liberty and not lay down on the job. His book brought Americans everywhere to their feet. George Washington expressed gratitude for its publication. John Adams wrote to Jefferson, *"History is to ascribe to Paine the Revolution."*

Spurred by such thinkers as Paine and Benjamin Franklin and the valor of such patriots as young Nathan Hale, the Congress moved to separate from England. On July 4, 1776, it was presented a soul-stirring document which was drawn up by Thomas Jefferson.

"When, in the course of human events—"

THE DECLARATION OF INDEPENDENCE announced the founding of a nation dedicated to the proposition that all men were created equal and that *"governments derive their just powers from the consent of the governed."* Its signing marked a milestone in the progressive history of mankind. It was the birth certificate of the United States of America.

First Sea Battle

The first sea battle of the American Revolution had already been fought by a crew of lumberjacks. And they made it a symbolic fight. To Jeremiah O'Brien and his wood-choppers goes the honor of waging and winning the earliest American naval engagement.

The fight took place off Machias, Maine, a few weeks after the Battle of Lexington. In May, 1775, British General Gage sent two sloops and an armed schooner to Machias to commandeer a load of lumber for the Red Coat garrison in Boston.

Instead of lumber, the British got a load of O'Brien—a fighting Scotch-Irishman with hair as red as their coats.

Entering the harbor of Machias, the British war-schooner, under command of a haughty young midshipman, was surprised to find this O'Brien and a crowd of some forty-odd loggers waiting on the wharf. The young mid directed his two sloops to tie up, and then, holding His Majesty's schooner off-shore, he hailed to learn what the crowd on the wharf wanted.

For answer there came a bellow from O'Brien, "Surrender!" and the lumberjacks brandished muskets, axes, and pitchforks.

The English sailors had to laugh. His Majesty's schooner was armed with three 3-pounders and four swivel-guns—enough to blow the whole village of Machias to match-wood. With a sneer for the rabble on the wharf, the Britons simply turned their backs on the scene and sailed out to the harbor entrance to stand by. So a knight might have refused to do battle with a serf, considering the fellow unworthy of his steel.

This irritated O'Brien and his boys into seizing one of the

lumber sloops and giving chase. Piling up lumber along the gunwales for protection, the loggers worked furiously while O'Brien steered the craft straight for the enemy. In the harbor mouth, the schooner turned to fight, her guns roaring out, like a lion wheeling on a small and annoying badger. The Americans replied with a rattle of musketfire and sharp marksmanship that, at first volley, didn't strike the Royal Navy men as so funny.

Cannon balls vs. bullets, the one-sided battle raged for over half an hour—one-sided for the Americans who riddled the British gunners at their gunports, shot the daylights out of the crewmen, and dropped the young midshipman on his quarterdeck. The sloop, protected by its jerry-built bulwarks, closed in. Swinging axes, rifle butts, and pitchforks, and led by indomitable O'Brien, the lumberjacks swarmed aboard the Englishman like timber wolves, and down came King George's flag.

Up went a strange new flag—a fitting flag for valiant lumberjacks—a white flag on which a green pine tree stood above the legend, *"An Appeal to Heaven."* The first American naval encounter had ended in victory for the Americans.

Considering the odds, it was something to be proud of. And it was symbolical, this victory achieved by "made in America" valor, sharpshooting, and New England pine. The lumberjacks of Maine had felled a long-standing giant—the tradition that the King's Navy was invincible—and reared in its stead the Tree of Liberty.

Washington's Raiders

Six months later, while the three-man Marine Committee was struggling in Philadelphia to bring a tiny navy into existence, George Washington was pacing his headquarters in anxiety. There at Cambridge, Massachusetts, where he'd taken command of the American Army, the situation was desperate. His troops were out of powder and military stores. Boston (this was in the autumn of 1775) was in the hands of the British, and they were using the port as a base for unloading transports and military supplies. Munitions must be obtained and those transports must be stopped. This called for naval action, and the infant navy in Philadelphia was slow a-borning. The Father of his Country couldn't wait.

"It is not in the pages of history to furnish a case like ours," he wrote to Congress. *"To maintain a post within musket shot of the enemy, for six months together, without powder, is probably more than was ever attempted."*

While his men rigged up phoney cannon to fool enemy scouts, he set out to organize a fleet on his own initiative. Early in August he'd requested the Governor of Rhode Island to send an armed ship to Bermuda where the people were sympathetic to the colonies and military stores might be obtained. Delay—delay—delay. In September, combing the Massachusetts fishing villages, he recruited a few small vessels to go out as privateers and raid enemy shipping in Massachusetts Bay. Finally six little schooners were fitted out, manned with officers and soldiers. Carrying four to six small guns apiece, and flying the Pine Tree Flag, they were contemptuously referred to by royalist Tories as "Washington's fleet." Bouncing over the waves, they sailed out to do battle with the whole Royal Navy.

In command of this squadron Washington placed John Manley, a Marblehead fisherman, one-time boatswain mate in the Royal Navy and now flaming to fight the King.

Obstinate, high-handed, and imperious as the King he wanted to fight, Manley was also an able schooner captain and the best commodore available in emergency. Pounding through wintry November gales, he took the miniature fleet down the New England coast and promptly captured the British supply ship, *Nancy,* a lucky bag of military stores including a brass mortar reported as *"the noblest piece of ordnance ever landed in America."*

This exploit made Manley a legend overnight, and when his "fleet" followed through by capturing thirteen more small enemy transports, the colonies cheered him from Maine to Georgia. All in all, the little mosquito fleet accomplished much. Washington had a cannon and enough munitions to bluff through the winter and mount his spring offensive which won Boston. Equally important, the fleet showed a dubious Congress what an ounce of sea power could do, thereby convincing the members they should buy a pound. And patriotic fishermen, schooner skippers, and sailors of America's seaboard made a rush to enter the service as privateers. Dozens of little smacks and brigs put out from

American ports carrying small arms and "letters of marque," empowering them to harry British shipping.

This last was not so good, for the Revolutionary privateers, although government-commissioned, were allowed to operate "on their own." The vessels remained under private ownership; and there were endless squabbles between government agent and privateer, arguing the value of "prizes." Finally, the privateers competed with and sometimes fought each other over prizes, and the system, lacking central leadership, became a free-for-all with every captain for himself. Washington himself could not hold them in line.

"The plague, trouble, and vexation I have had with the crews of all the armed vessels is inexpressible," he wrote. *"I do believe there is not on earth a more disorderly set."*

In justice to the privateers of the Revolution, they did hound the British up and down the Atlantic. They captured many valuable merchant ships and supply vessels, and they served to scout the sea lanes and bring in much information. Among their captains were such valiant patriots as John Barry, Gustavus Conyngham, and the incredible Joshua Barney. But these great sea fighters, serving as raiders, were individualists who operated as "lone wolves," more like the knights of old on private mission. It could be called only a makeshift.

The need was a national Navy, an organization of fighting ships with centralized leadership, unity of purpose, and standard regulations—ships with crews of military, fighting sailors who had uniform discipline, training, and pay.

Such a navy was in the mind of John Adams in December, 1775, when, steering the Marine Committee, he helped put a bill through Congress calling for thirteen American warships and "the Navy of the United Colonies."

Such a navy was also in the mind of a young sailor from the West Indies, an unknown, seafaring exile, who had come to Philadelphia to volunteer his services in the now fast-growing fight for Democracy.

His name was John Paul Jones, though we meet him in our story first as John Paul.

JOHN PAUL JONES

The Adventures of John Paul

The story of John Paul is right up any Navy man's alley. Adventure, romance, mystery, action, all blended with seafaring to make his career one of the saltiest on record and livelier than anything in fiction. And no character in naval history better exemplifies the qualities of leadership, the fighting spirit, the combination of brains, training, and discipline that go to make up a real American Navy man.

Records show that John Paul was born on July 6, 1747, in a rough stone cottage in Kirkbean, Scotland, where his father was a gardener, his mother a Highland maid. They also show he left school at twelve to ship before the mast. But, lacking much book learning, John Paul seems to have embarked on his nautical career with a cargo of native intelligence remarkable for his or any year and time.

He went through the school of hard knocks without skipping a day, and graduated from the college of practical experience with a master's papers in capability. And he emerged as a man who could do everything from handle a naval squadron to write poetry, debate with statesmen, design ships, quote Shakespeare, outwit some of the craftiest plotters in Europe, win one of the greatest sea battles in history, and leave a name that still burns as bright as Liberty's torch, a living inspiration to the world's greatest navy. Pretty good for a penniless boy who left home at twelve to ship out. Symbolic of Democracy, that this small, smudged figure could end up as the U. S. Navy's greatest hero. Any sailor who strikes for a rating can remember this. John Paul was strictly a mustang.

Sailing on some collier or coastal schooner, pint-sized John Paul got his sea legs. Then he signed aboard the sailing vessel *Friendship*, bound from Scotland for America, where his older brother had gone ahead of him to the Virginia Colony.

Aboard a sailing vessel in those days you learned your ropes at rope's end. Crack! across the knuckles, and you'd bend a sheet at double time. Whack! across the shoulders, and you'd go up the shrouds as if the devil were after you, as he usually was. In his first and later voyages to Virginia, John Paul learned his ropes—hundreds of them—and he also learned something of America.

"My favorite country from the age of thirteen when I first saw it," he wrote afterwards.

He made a number of these trans-Atlantic crossings as a ship-boy; then, seeking better service, he joined the Royal Navy. Apparently he served out an enlistment as midshipman, but he did not reenlist. The Royal Navy was too royal for his Highland blood.

In the early days, as you know, each warship carried a number of young lads who acted as messengers, rushing orders from the officers aft to the men up forward. These "midshipmen," as they were called, were generally regarded as officer material and treated with a trifle more consideration than were the unfortunate mess boys and powder monkeys. But Midshipman John Paul must have endured plenty; and if he wasn't flogged,

he saw other sailors stripped to the waist, bound to a cannon or net, and lashed by the lead-tipped cat-o'-nine-tails until their spine-bones gleamed through the welter. Thirty lashes —fifty lashes — sometimes a hundred. Death by flogging was not uncommon in the early navies.

Perhaps he saw some sailor "keel-hauled"— that barbarous punishment in which the victim was lowered overside on a rope and hauled underneath the ship to the opposite side to come up drowned, as often as not, or with his back sliced to ribbons by the jagged barnacles on the keel.

But with these cruelties commonplace, regard it all the more remarkable that John Paul never became calloused, never brutalized his own crews. To the end he remained a defender of the men's rights, often paying them out of pocket when their money failed to arrive, always sparing of their lives in battle. Strict discipline was necessary in the Navy, yes. But note the distinguishing thing about his idea of discipline. It applied to officers as well as men—to those in authority as well as those below. He demanded top performance from those on top, an unusual idea in that day.

In 1766 he was out of uniform, and sailing as chief mate aboard the brigantine *Two Friends*, plying between Africa and Jamaica in the West Indies. The *Two Friends* was a slaver, and John Paul couldn't take much of that, either. At that time the slave trade paid the highest wages on the sea. Credit John Paul for washing his hands of this filthy money, and, with nothing in his ditty bag save character, going ashore in Jamaica to try his hand at any better enterprise. He had the courage of his convictions, this lad of nineteen!

Kingston, Jamaica, was the gem of the West Indies, a rich, colonial seaport with all the glamor and color of the tropics. With indolence in the air and rum a penny a glass, it was just the place for a nobody to stay on the beach. John Paul, who was already somebody, didn't stay on it—he caught a brigantine bound for Scotland.

There was drama at sea before he was a week out. The captain and first officer died of fever. The crew and other passengers voted John Paul the best mariner aboard and urged him to take command. Nine years before, he had sailed to America as a shipboy. Now he sailed into his home port as a captain.

The owners of the ship made it a permanent appointment, and the following year Captain Paul sailed her back to the West Indies to Tobago. Here the curtain rose on a grim drama, with John Paul as the central character. Only in recent years have historians managed to unravel conflicting accounts and bring to light what seem to be the facts.

Ship's carpenter aboard the brigantine was a Scotchman from John Paul's home county, a fellow named Mungo Maxwell. Lazy and incompetent, he apparently gave the young captain a bit of his lip, and John Paul had him whipped as insubordinate.

When the ship reached Tobago the carpenter went ashore and complained to the Court of Vice-Admiralty. It couldn't have been much of a flogging for the Judge Surrogate found only several "stripes" on Maxwell's shoulders, and adjudged the punishment not only slight but warranted. Growling and scowling, Maxwell went across the wharf and signed aboard a Barcelona packet bound north up the Caribbean.

Doubtless John Paul was glad to be rid of the fellow. But six months later word came from Scotland that Maxwell had died aboard the Barcelona packet as a result of the flogging dealt him aboard John Paul's ship. As Maxwell had left Tobago under his own power, the accusation hardly appeared well founded. But the rumor grew. "John Paul flogged a man to death unjustly." And when John Paul made the return voyage to Scotland, he found a warrant out for his arrest. He reported to the authorities at once, and was charged with murder.

John Paul stood by six months awaiting trial, then sailed under bail bond, once more heading for Tobago. While there, in September 1772, he received word that his name had been cleared by the captain of the Barcelona packet, who testified that Mungo Maxwell had died of the fever.

This Maxwell affair was hardly over when the drama quickened into dark melodrama—one that almost cost John Paul his life. Having saved his earnings, he was able to buy the schooner *Betsy*, which he took to the Caribbean as an independent trader. Oddly enough, the scene was again Tobago—moonless night—the harbor black in silhouette—men moving catfoot on the *Betsy's* quarterdeck—mutiny!

Possibly it was inspired by the rumors lingering over the Maxwell affair. Unquestionably it was fired by shore leave and Caribbean rum. The first John Paul knew of it was when he discovered an open cabin hatch and a figure lunged out of the pitchy dark, swinging a bludgeon. Quick as light John Paul whipped out his sword. There was gleam of steel in the midnight, a grunt, a crash, and the mutineer was down.

John Paul wheeled in time to see shadows retreating forward. Bare feet whispered, running across the wharf, and the *Betsy's* deck was cleared. Only the dead man, a ruffian who had towered head and shoulders above the captain, remained in open-mouthed testimonial of mutiny.

John Paul knew when the odds were all against him. On top of the Maxwell affair, this mutineer, slain without witnesses, would stand to ruin him. Strange quirk of fate that a man so humane should, at the outset of his career, have his name overclouded with rumors of murder. He must have been sick at heart when he went ashore to put his case in the hands of the Tobago authorities.

He had friends in Tobago—the Judge Surrogate who acted in the Maxwell case, and the Lieutenant Governor. They told him the Admiralty Court would not convene until the following season, and it would not be necessary to surrender himself until the court was in session. They advised him to leave the island until such time as the rumor-mongering would blow over and he could return to stand fair trial. Why didn't he go north to the American colonies, take another name for a while?

He did. The name he took was John Paul Jones.

The Adventures of John Paul Jones

John Paul Jones arrived in Fredericksburg, Virginia, late in 1773 (or early in 1774) apparently in time to settle the estate

of his older brother, William. Try to put yourself in his place
—a man who had climbed the hard way to find the top of the
ladder treacherous—who had fallen to the bottom, and now must
climb all over again, with a way to make and a name to clear.

He must have learned, then, that old, exacting law of the sea
that accidents permit a captain no excuse. It must have been
bitter medicine, for he contemplated leaving the sea and farming
a plantation. But winds were blowing in Virginia—winds that
stung the cheek and quickened the blood, that soon rose to the
height of a gale, stirring the hearts of liberty-loving seamen and
making it impossible for John Paul Jones to "swallow the anchor."

The Revolution. And suddenly it was April, 1775. The "shot
heard 'round the world" had been fired. The Minute Men had
stood at Lexington. The Red Coats were coming.

There was no chance now for John Paul Jones to return to
Tobago and stand trial for a crime of which he was innocent.
For eighteen months, as he wrote a friend, he had waited for
word from the West Indies. Now the word that came was war
with England and the closing of American ports to West Indies
merchantmen.

John Paul Jones had made friends among the colonists. Among
others he'd become acquainted with Joseph Hewes, an enterprising shipper in the West India trade, a patriot and a delegate
from North Carolina to the Continental Congress. You can see
Hewes' signature today on the Declaration of Independence.

Hewes invited Jones to accompany him to Philadelphia that
summer of 1775. America was going to be in need of good sailors.
Would Jones be willing to join a Revolutionary navy and help
fight a War of Independence? But his seabag was already packed.
America had befriended him, and serving her, as he said later,
was an obligation of *"gratitude and honor."*

At Philadelphia, John Paul Jones bided his time, listening and
observing. Sponsored by Hewes, he was probably introduced to
Franklin, Adams, Jefferson, and other statesmen on the scene.
He was also introduced to the workings of Democracy, that state
of affairs in which all points of view are freely aired. With all
his sailor's love of order and direction, he saw that this method
of government, seemingly hurly-burly, was a government of, by,
and for the people, dedicated to individual freedom and men's

rights. It was a government he could believe in, a government he could fight for. He didn't have long to wait.

The Marine Committee, beginning with three members on October 13, 1775, had by the end of October grown to seven. Along with John Adams, Langdon, and Deane, it now included Christopher Gadsden, the South Carolina financial expert, Richard Henry Lee of Virginia, Stephen Hopkins of Rhode Island, and Hewes, the North Carolinian. Originally granted an ounce of authority, it now was awarded a pound—$100,000 to spend on four warships.

A Marine Committee of seven, four warships, and $100,000— so the American Navy, christened "The Navy of the United Colonies," was launched. Great oaks from little acorns grow. Regard your Navy Department of today, the world-ocean battle fleet, and the $100,000 cost of a single modern Navy plane.

But there in colonial Philadelphia men wondered if the little acorn could sprout at all. The four warships were on paper. The $100,000 had to be raised. Not a single sailing ship was under construction in America, nor was any shipyard equipped to build one.

The Marine Committee got to work. And those seven members worked a lot harder than portraits of them sitting around might suggest. They had to argue, dig, and sweat it out just as you do when you're up against a tough problem. Like Hewes, who wrote that he worked *"from six in the morning until five or six in the evening, without eating or drinking,"* they stayed on the job.

Gadsden raised some money. John Adams devised naval laws and regulations. Congress was persuaded to add nine more warships to the original four, making, in all, five 32-gun frigates, five 28-gunners, and three sloops. All very fine, but still on paper, and the Red Coats were on the way. You can't fight an enemy with paper ships, but if you're a desperate committee, you can use the wooden ones at hand. Luckily there were a number of stalwart merchant vessels right there in Philadelphia, including a salty, tea-carrying Indiaman titled *Black Prince*. The committee jumped to convert these cargo carriers into warships.

They found the ordnance somewhere. Old cannon from the French and Indian War, new cannon from a rustic foundry, a battery picked up here, another there. *Black Prince* became the flagship *Alfred*, with 30 assorted guns. The other redecorated merchantmen became *Columbus*, with 28 guns, *Andrew Doria* and *Cabot*, 16 and 14 guns respectively, little *Providence*, with 12 guns, and three armed craft not much bigger than their names, *Hornet*, *Wasp*, and *Fly*.

In December, 1775, they were ready to sail—four warships and four escort vessels—the original American Navy. Against them stood the Royal Navy of Great Britain, the world's champion sea power. Talk about odds!

"The first beginning of our Navy," John Paul Jones wrote later, *"was, as navies rank, so singularly small that I am of the opinion it has no precedence in history."*

Nor did John Paul Jones, himself, have any precedent in history. The Marine Committee, at the urging of Hewes, offered to make the unknown volunteer the captain of *Providence*. John Paul Jones declined the commission. He lacked military experience, he said, and asked no more than a chance for training aboard the flagship *Alfred*. This from a man who'd held master's papers at twenty! John Paul Jones entered the Navy as a first lieutenant, asking nothing of the service but a chance to serve.

The fleet must have a Commander in Chief, so Stephen Hopkins, the Rhode Islander, put forward the name of his brother, Esek, a retired sea captain. Nobody bothered to find out whether the old skipper had acquired any barnacles during his retirement. Rhode Island carried a lot of weight, so Esek Hopkins became Commander in Chief of the Navy of the United Colonies.

Command of the flagship *Alfred* was given to Dudley Saltonstall, a brother-in-law of Silas Deane.

Captaincy of *Columbus*, the next biggest ship, went to Abraham Whipple, a robust mariner who, three years before, had led a raiding party across Narragansett Bay to burn a British revenue vessel.

Nicholas Biddle, a young patriot of twenty-five who had been seasoned as a midshipman in the Royal Navy, was made captain of *Andrew Doria*.

John B. Hopkins, the commodore's son, was given command of *Cabot*.

And command of the armed sloop *Providence* went to one Tom

Hazard, nicknamed "Sailor Tom" to distinguish him from the two dozen other Tom Hazards in the colonies.

With the exception of young Biddle, who hailed from Pennsylvania, all these top commissions went to New Englanders, and the majority was obviously "political." Little *Hornet* and *Wasp* came up from Baltimore with Southerners aboard, but the Navy was largely Yankee—an example of the "sectionalism" and favoritism that almost beached the Ship of State at the outset.

Now you can notice that John Paul Jones, a favorite son of none, was not helped by any political backing. A stranger on his own, he stepped into the Navy picture with no personal axe to grind save the bright, clean battle-axe of Freedom.

Don't Tread on Me!

As a lieutenant he boarded the flagship at Philadelphia early in December. With Saltonstall absent, he found himself the senior officer aboard. Lying in midstream, *Alfred* was taking on men and supplies. Jones set immediately to work and began putting the men through gunnery exercises. In a few days he had them trained so well that he could write at a later date, *"They went through the motions of broadsides and rounds as exactly as soldiers generally perform the manual exercise."* He saw to the vessel's stowage and the enlistment of volunteers. There were Marines aboard, Congress having established the Marine Corps on November 10, 1775, and he drilled them on the double. The men knew they had an officer in this little Scotch lieutenant.

Since Captain Saltonstall was still absent from Philadelphia, the honor of raising the flag aboard *Alfred* fell to John Paul Jones. The exact date is blurred in the records, but it was probably December 3, 1775, when he rowed out to *Alfred* with the new American flag in his hands.

The flag that John Paul Jones hoisted aboard *Alfred* has been described as "a Union flag with thirteen stripes in the field emblematical of the Thirteen United Colonies." In the upper left corner, however, it retained the crosses of St. George and St. Andrew as a sort of last, lingering tie to the mother country. George Washington raised a similar Grand Union flag a few days later at the front at Boston. The canton of the British

CONTINENTAL FLAGS

PINE TREE FLAG
(WASHINGTON'S NAVY)

RATTLESNAKE FLAG
(GADSDEN'S FLAG)

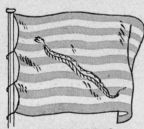

RATTLESNAKE FLAG
(FLOWN BY MANY PRIVATEERS)
FIRST NAVY JACK

BEDFORD FLAG
(ONE OF FIRST IN
NEW ENGLAND)

FORT MOULTRIE FLAG
(FLOWN AT CHARLESTON
IN 1775)

GRAND UNION FLAG
(WASHINGTON AND PAUL JONES)
FIRST NAVY ENSIGN

Union was soon to fade out under a haze of battlesmoke, to be replaced by thirteen stars. But the flag hoisted by John Paul Jones was the Mark I original with the thirteen red and white stripes—the first American flag bearing a resemblance to Uncle Sam's.

Some historians believe the flag hoisted aboard *Alfred* was a combination Union Flag and Rattlesnake Flag with the snake rippling diagonally across the stripes. However, the Gadsden design of the Rattlesnake Flag—yellow flag with coiled snake— was the personal standard of Commander-in-Chief Hopkins. Probably both flags were flown, the Grand Union at the hoist of honor, and Hopkins' standard hoisted later.

The sailors stood at attention, the Marines on the quarterdeck fired a salute, one of *Alfred's* guns boomed, and the red and white stripes fluttered in the wind above the icy river. A crowd massed on shore gave a resounding cheer. The American Navy was launched.

"I hoisted with my own hands the flag of freedom the first time it was displayed on board the Alfred in the Delaware."

Leave it up to John Paul Jones.

He never liked the Rattlesnake Flag. *"For my part,"* he wrote, *"I could never see how or why a venomous serpent could be the combatant emblem of a brave and honest folk, fighting to be free. I abhorred the device."*

He was soon to raise another flag—the one you salute today. But, although he disliked the Rattlesnake Flag, its motto was certainly a good one for Jones. For he, perhaps more than any Revolutionary warrior, personified the warning, *"Don't Tread on Me!"*

No man in the Navy was more frequently stepped on. Fate, itself, tried to tread him under at the last. And each time he came up fighting—for the Navy.

The Navy Learns A Lesson

Down in Virginia, the Tory governor, Dunmore, had remained loyal to the king. He favored hanging these revolutionists who talked about men's rights and a democratic government. Liberty or death? All right, he'd give them death; and he mobilized a flotilla of small warships to deal it out.

So the first orders given to Commander-in-Chief Hopkins were to proceed to Chesapeake Bay in Virginia and seek out and fight Dunmore's flotilla. After which he was to go without delay to Rhode Island to *"attack, take, and destroy"* all the enemy's naval force he might find there. This was the first battle-order given to the American Navy. For a newborn Navy just starting out to get its sea legs in a fight with a giant, it sounds like a large order.

As a matter of fact, it wasn't so large. The giant wasn't awake as yet. A few British warships had started across the Atlantic, including the 28-gunner *H.M.S. Liverpool* on its way to head up Dunmore's little fleet. But Hopkins' squadron had a good chance to deal Dunmore a hard blow before reinforcements arrived.

However, Hopkins was given permission to use his own judgment, and he judged that the ice in the river was too thick for the squadron to start out. He received the orders to move on January 5, 1776, and he didn't get under way until February 18th.

Then he judged that the squadron could round Cape Henlopen in a nor'east gale, with the result that the small craft *Hornet* and *Fly,* collided in the storm and had to leave the squadron, disabled.

His next judgment was that the waters off the Virginia Capes were too rough for action, so he headed south for the balmier Gulf Stream on a plan to attack the Bahamas. This was a daring enough plan, calling for an attack on the Bahaman forts, Nassau and Montague, known to contain large stores of powder. And powder, you'll remember, was Washington's rush order.

But it was up to Hopkins' judgment again, so he sailed in to attack by daytime instead of night, and lost the advantage of surprise. He also wanted to attack Fort Nassau first while his officers pointed out that it would be better to first take small Fort Montague, which would provide extra munitions for attacking the larger citadel. But Hopkins said that in his judgment the approaches to Fort Montague were too shallow for safe navigation.

Meantime, John Paul Jones aboard Hopkins' flagship had been doing some judging. He judged that Esek Hopkins was something of a fuddy-duddy.

"*Mr. Hopkins displayed neither zeal nor talents,*" he wrote of the campaign later. "*He lost so much time that his squadron was frozen in the Delaware.*"

Now he went to Hopkins to urge that the Bahama attack should begin against Fort Montague. As for the shallow approaches to this fort, he offered to pilot the squadron himself.

He did pilot the squadron, and he was aloft in the crosstrees of *Alfred,* directing navigation, when the ships moved in to the attack.

Had Hopkins not waited for daylight it could have been a brilliant surprise. As it was, the British were alerted, and the fort's batteries were ready. Guns boomed in the dawn, and cannon

balls splashed the peacock waters of the bay, throwing up fountains around the American ships.

But the British gunners were poorly trained, and two hundred Marines under Captain Nicholas plus fifty sailors under Lieutenant Weaver stormed the fort with great valor and took it handily.

This was the Navy's first amphibious action, and the first battle fought by the American Marines.

Then Hopkins delayed again, and it wasn't until the following morning that the jubilant Marines swept across to take Fort Nassau. The fort surrendered without a shot, and the Americans captured eighty-seven guns, some military stores, and a few casks of gunpowder.

But where was the main powder supply? Well, during the night the Bahamans had loaded a merchant ship with all the powder they could rush from the arsenal, and sent her kiting away in the darkness to race down the West Indies and warn the British that the Americans were coming. Hopkins hadn't judged it necessary to guard the western side of the island.

So the enemy scored a "safety" on the winning team. Hopkins consoled himself on the powder loss by taking the governor of the Bahamas and a number of prisoners as hostages. On March 17, 1776, the squadron started north for Rhode Island.

Three weeks later, passing Block Island, the Americans ran into the schooner *Hawk* and the bomb-brig *Bolton*, convoying two small supply ships under the British flag. The outnumbered Britons surrendered, and the two supply ships were found to contain liquor stores for an English squadron reportedly operating off Newport, Rhode Island.

Hopkins accordingly judged it best to head for New London, Connecticut. Prizes in tow, the squadron tacked westerly in the night.

Now it seems there was some celebrating with the captured liquor cargo. And the early Americans were soon to learn that basic military lesson—there's many a slip twixt the cup and the ship.

Sometime around 0100, *Andrew Doria* spied a sail in the moonlight off to starboard, and Captain Biddle signaled the alert to *Alfred*. By 0200 the stranger, coming on, was recognizable as an enemy warship. Evidently she took the Americans for British.

Esek Hopkins signaled the squadron to clear for action, and rubbed his hands in prospect of another easy prize. His son's brig, *Cabot*, was nearest the enemy ship which now identified herself as H. M. S. *Glasgow*, 20 guns, under Captain Howe.

Aboard *Cabot*, Captain John Hopkins hung out his battle lanterns and opened fire with a hasty broadside. *Glasgow* replied with a furious blast, and immediately the American brig found itself no match for the heavier British vessel. Young Hopkins went down, badly wounded. Another blast swept *Cabot*, smashing through her rigging and killing her navigator. A third blast brought down a tumble of canvas, and sent her off listing and disabled.

Enraged at this disaster, Old Esek crowded on sail and brought *Alfred* beam to beam with the Britisher. Exchanging broadsides, the two ships rolled along, while the remaining American vessels jockeyed for position.

John Paul Jones, aboard *Alfred*, was in charge of the main battery, and he directed his fire with telling effect. But he was short-handed. There was smallpox in the squadron, and a number of his gunners were in sick bay. Also a number of *Alfred's* crew were in sick bay with something not as serious as smallpox, but you can't fight a battle with a hangover.

The fact is the Yankee crew had done too much celebrating off Block Island, and the seamanship wasn't what it should have been. Jones' gunnery gave the enemy warship a pounding, but *Alfred* got a savage hammering in return. She also got in the way of *Columbus*, veering in to her support.

Young Captain Biddle maneuvered *Andrew Doria* smartly, but *Doria's* guns were outranged although she did score several hits. Finally *Providence*, opening fire at even longer range, missed the enemy entirely.

For three hours the clumsy battle went on, one British corvette standing off the four-ship American squadron. At dawn the Britons punched a shot through *Alfred's* quarter and wrecked her steering cables. Another broadside raked the American flagship, killing twenty of Hopkins' men. *Alfred* drifted, her rudder helpless. *Columbus*, unable to close in, fell back, winded. *Providence* hung far astern. *Cabot* was out of it, and *Andrew Doria*, despite Biddle's smart handling, was too small to carry on single-handed. So H. M. S. *Glasgow* got away.

When Hopkins reached New London with his battered squadron, he found news of the sea fight ahead of him. The town cheered the Americans, home from the Navy's first cruise. Then, at sight of the damaged flagship, the cheers soured somewhat. They died out entirely when it was learned the enemy warship had escaped. And when the report reached the Continental Congress that Hopkins had missed the powder in the Bahamas, there was demand for an investigation.

It was a stiff investigation. Commander-in-Chief Hopkins was censured for not proceeding on his orders to destroy Dunmore's Virginia flotilla. Captain Whipple of *Columbus* was criticized for being lackadaisical in the Block Island battle. Whipple angrily countered by placing the blame for the lost battle on Hopkins' seamanship, and for himself demanded a court martial. He was exonerated, with John Paul Jones testifying in his defense. Finally Captain Saltonstall was also criticized, and "Sailor" Tom Hazard was dismissed for faint-heartedness aboard *Providence*.

All in all, it might seem as if the Navy's first cruise ended in a fiasco. But even a fledgling eagle must learn how to fly. The Navy was learning discipline was necessary, that politics and salt water didn't mix, and that it was responsible to a higher authority than itself.

Two names emerged as stars on the Navy's horizon.

Nicholas Biddle was lauded for his good work in the squadron.

John Paul Jones was made captain of *Providence*.

The Navy Changes Strategy

Now, to understand the events coming up, you'll need an overall picture of the war. At this point you've reached summertime, 1776. The Declaration of Independence has been signed —the Liberty Bell is ringing—Americans are fighting on land and sea to win their rights.

So far the battles have been little more than skirmishes—brief bonfires on the edge of towns—mere match-flares in the vast, wooded wilderness. The Red Coats have been cleared out of Boston. The Americans have been thrown back from Canada. The Thirteen Colonies, loosely held together by the Continental Congress at Philadelphia, are by no means united in the war effort. The Army is small, untrained, lacking in ammunition. The Navy is jerry-built, amateur, untried. These soldiers and

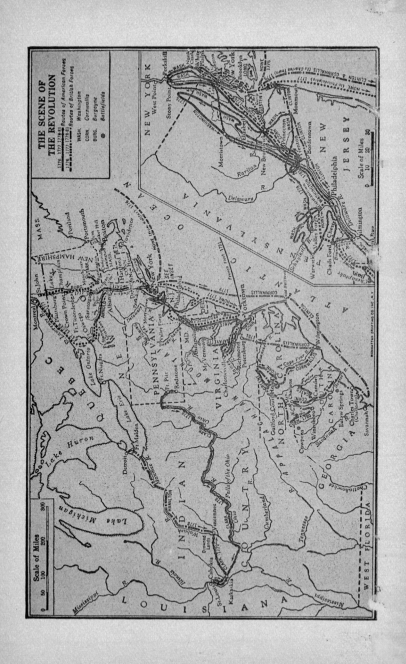

THE SCENE OF
THE REVOLUTION

1776, 1777, 1778-81 Routes of American Forces
1776, 1777, 1778-81 Routes of British Forces
WASH. Washington
CORN. Cornwallis
BURG. Burgoyne
⊛ Battlefields

Scale of Miles
0   50   100   200   300

Scale of Miles
0   10   20   30

sailors number only a handful compared to the mighty forces of Great Britain. In America, too, there are thousands of Tories and royalist sympathizers, openly joining the British or working underground as saboteurs. It is the moment for Great Britain to strike.

The Lion struck. Struck hard. But not hard enough. The British high command underestimated the difficulties of land fighting in frontier America. These newly united States were very different then from the same States today. Colonial America was just a thin strip of seaboard—its front exposed to the Atlantic, its rear backed up against Appalachian Mountains and against a whole unexplored continent of dark wilderness. And much of the seaboard strip was thickly wooded, with villages huddled in clearings. Mountains, streams, and woods made overland travel exceedingly slow and tedious. Farms in the North and large plantations in the South supplied such towns as Boston, New York and Philadelphia with food. Roads were few and in bad condition, and transportation was mainly by water—along the coast and by way of inland rivers.

The British strategists planned to blockade the seaports and rivers to cut off transport and communication. But their main blows were launched at the centers of population—New York, the Jersey flats, Philadelphia—in an effort to capture big towns. This was typical European military strategy, but it failed to recognize the fact that the American population was largely rural, widely distributed, and the pioneers were self-supporting. The loss of New York, for instance, meant little to the homespun frontiersman of Pennsylvania.

So George III, aiming his biggest blows at the towns, was to miss the mark. And strategically speaking, the Americans missed it, too. Actually they spent too much effort defending the big towns, and too little defending the waterways. A strong navy, for example, could have stopped the enemy from landing in the first place. And you'll see how the enemy was stopped when naval force finally came into the picture. But in the early part of the war naval ordnance was neglected while land artillery got a high priority. Had the English been less involved with "chess game" military tradition at this time, they might have captured armies rather than towns, and won the war.

However, the Red Coats arrived to take the field (walking targets in those scarlet jackets, too.) Down from Quebec came British General Carleton, pushing Benedict Arnold's ragged army along the shore of Lake Champlain in weary retreat.

On Carleton's flank came Sir John Burgoyne—"Gentleman Johnny," with fresh regiments and baggage wagons loaded with champagne and finery for his Lady—driving ahead of him the tattered troops of American General Sullivan.

Down from Halifax came General William Howe and his brother, Lord Howe, by-passing Boston with an invasion fleet to attack New York.

Over from England came Lord Cornwallis with his batch of German Hessians to reinforce Howe.

Over from England came General Sir Henry Clinton and Admiral Sir Peter Parker to attack Charleston, South Carolina, with two battleships, three frigates, and a large landing force.

And behind these forces, and bent on blocking the American coast, came the mighty Royal Navy.

In the face of all this land and sea power, how could the Americans hold out?

Well, down at Charleston, where the harbor was treacherous with sandbars, there was a tight little fort made of palmetto logs banked with sand. In this fort, which controlled the harbor entrance, there was a handful of Carolina patriots under the never-say-die leadership of Colonel Moultrie.

Morning, June 28th, General Clinton and Admiral Parker sailed in to attack the fort. Nightfall, June 28th, they sailed out again. Aboard the battleship the casualties were close to 50%. One of the frigates was badly damaged, the other afire and ready to blow up. Charleston remained untaken. Colonel Moultrie and his little fort were altogether too much for Sir Henry Clinton and Sir Peter Parker.

In the fall of that year of 1776, Benedict Arnold stopped General Carleton at Ticonderoga. Then he swung up Lake Champlain with a fleet of barges and row-galleys built out of pine trees and thin air, and delayed Burgoyne long enough to save General Sullivan.

Meantime George Washington (against his better judgment) had marched his troops from Boston to New York to protect

Manhattan and Long Island. The Howe Brothers landed in August with 20,000 men, and slowly drove Washington along Brooklyn Heights, over to Harlem, up into Westchester.

Now what of the American Navy at this time? Not much, for Commander-in-Chief Esek Hopkins had decided to hole in at Newport, Rhode Island.

Not so John Paul Jones with his sloop-of-war, *Providence*. While Hopkins dilly-dallied, anchoring the main portion of the little fleet, Jones obtained permission to operate on his own.

Patrolling Long Island was *H.M.S. Cerebus*, a big frigate carrying 32 guns. One day in July she sighted a Yankee sloop named *Providence*, and tried to chase. *Providence* ran rings around her, thanks to the seamanship of John Paul Jones.

Off New York a merchantman from San Domingo was trying to slip through with supplies for Washington's army. A sloop appeared from nowhere, and convoyed the big merchantman safely through the blockade. Jones, again.

When Washington wanted a company of specialists brought down from Rhode Island, they were brought by *Providence* and Captain Jones.

Presently, somewhere near Bermuda, *H.M.S. Solebay* sighted a sloop, and set out in chase. *Solebay* got a saucy shot in her bows for her pains, but she never got her hooks or her shots into *Providence* or John Paul Jones.

A month or so later in the vicinity of Nova Scotia, *H.M.S. Milford* sighted a Yankee sloop cooly enjoying the offshore fishing. *Milford* rushed at the American, and *Providence* waltzed around her for eight straight hours, making a monkey of the British helmsmen and causing His Majestry's gunners to throw away round after round of shot. A single Marine stood on the Yankee's afterdeck, answering each salvo with a taunting musket-shot while the Yankee crew uttered gales of laughter. The fish that got away again was John Paul Jones.

A few nights later he was in the Canadian Bay of Canso where he secured fresh water, burned an English schooner, sank another, and captured a third.

From there he swung to attack the fisheries of Ile Madame, where he captured nine fishing smacks. These were lost on the way home in a rip-roaring gale, but he had done all right, at that. In less than seven weeks little *Providence* had captured eight enemy vessels, sunk eight more, played ring-around-the-rosy with two British frigates, destroyed the Ile Madame fishing fleet, and avenged the burning of Falmouth. He was writing his name on the sea with indelible seamanship.

With these successes to his credit, Jones sailed into Newport to rejoin Hopkins' fleet. He found Hopkins and the fleet sitting

like bumps on a log. Everywhere he saw rust, tangled cordage, and barnacles. Desertion and smallpox had thinned the crews. The few sailors on hand were sullen and disorderly.

To a seaman of Jones' caliber, this was a hellish state of affairs, and he didn't hesitate to report the same to the Marine Committee. With characteristic punch, he asked the committee to let him take three ships on a cruise to Africa where he proposed to smash up British merchantmen on the sea lanes to India. This daring plan burst like a bombshell in Philadelphia, scattering paper-work all over the place. Who *was* this John Paul Jones?

Then, still thinking in terms of local favoritism, the committee began to wrangle. If such a cruise did start out, it would have to be commanded by one of the senior captains, Whipple or

Saltonstall. However, recognizing seamanship and leadership, t committee voted to give Jones a three-ship squadron on a mission to Canada to release American prisoners in the Cape Breton coal mines.

Rescue prisoners? John Paul Jones went whole-heartedly for such a project. And Hopkins concurred, anxious to get the sandy-haired firebrand out of Newport as soon as possible. So he willingly consigned to Jones the old flagship *Alfred*, the brig *Hampden*, and the sloop *Providence*.

But ships and crews were in such poor condition that the start was delayed. Jones had to tramp up and down Newport's water-front, doing his own recruiting. Where were patriots? Where were fighting Americans? Everywhere he found down-hearted-ness, indifference, or self-interest. Worse, he found the Navy's reputation bedraggled. Heard Hopkins was a flogger. Sailors were never paid. Why should Johnny risk his life in the Navy for nothing when he could board a privateer and make a fortune in prize money? Hopkins, himself, had invested in privateers. Newport was hostile, and Jones had to scrape the bottom of the manpower barrel.

He scraped. He took a Marine patrol through the clutter of privateers in the bay, rounding up deserters. He enlisted a few new volunteers. Still his ships were short-handed, and he had to leave *Providence* behind for lack of a crew. But the Yankee prisoners in the coal pits couldn't wait. John Paul Jones put out.

Bungle at the take-off. Captain of *Hampden* was a shabby old shellback named Hoysted Hacker, appointed by Hopkins. Hacker was no sailor. The squadron was hardly out of Newport before he ran *Hampden* aground on a reef, rupturing her keel. The ships had to put in at the port of Providence, where Jones wrote a red-headed letter to Hopkins demanding to know why he'd elevated Hacker to a captaincy.

Hopkins replied by merely transferring Hacker to command of the old sloop *Providence*, and ordering Jones to start afresh for Cape Breton.

It was now November 2nd, bad weather coming up, but Jones could only obey. Short of men and stores, he took *Alfred* and *Providence* around Cape Cod in the teeth of high seas and mutiny. Ten days out he captured the enemy vessel, *Active*, and shortly afterward the big British transport, *Mellish,* with a valuable cargo of military supplies.

The weather thickened. Hacker's ship, lagging, signalled for permission to turn back. John Paul Jones signalled, *"Stay on course."* Northward he drove stubbornly into night and foggy storm. In the morning—no Hacker!

Realizing the weak-kneed Hacker had run for home, John Paul Jones hit the cabin overhead. Alone, he drove *Alfred* to Cape Breton, found the harbor frozen over with no chance to break through, and was forced to head south with fire in his heart.

Home-bound, he captured four fishing boats, a big 10-gun raider, and had a close shave with the frigate *Milford,* which had almost caught him the previous summer. Signalling his prizes to scatter, he put a light at *Alfred's* masthead and decoyed the frigate on a wild-goose-chase through the night. At midnight he blacked out, leaving Milford playing blind-man's-buff off St. George's Bank. Safe with his prizes, Jones made home base in December.

Only to find that Hopkins and his wire-pullers had done it again. While John Paul Jones had been fighting at sea, the Continental Congress had been muddling on land. Three new battleships, six frigates, and a score of smaller warships had been ordered. But, under pressure, the Marine Committee had been reshuffled and forced to play favorites in assigning captains to these vessels.

In a line-up of twenty-four captains, John Paul Jones was No. 18 down the list, and reassigned to the old sloop, *Providence.* Ahead of him were Nicholson, McNeil, Thompson, Alexander—captains he'd never heard of. Manley, the former boatswain, had a battleship. Hopkins junior had a frigate—after mishandling *Cabot* off Block Island! Why, Jones was even outranked by that jellyfish, Hoysted Hacker!

John Paul Jones was served with a $50,000 law suit brought against him by the deserters he had taken from the privateers in Newport. Hopkins refused to quash the suit, agreeing that Jones had done his recruiting without official recommendation.

Eighteenth down the list of captains, and a law suit for $50,000! John Paul Jones blew up like a cannon.

When the smoke and fire died away, he had bombarded

Congress and the Marine Committee with letters that landed in Philadelphia like cannon balls. Esek Hopkins, he declared, was a *"petty genius."* Manley's appointment, he said, was typical of blind-fold commissioning—he had served well as a privateer, but you couldn't jump a boatswain's mate to captaincy of a big man-o'-war. *"He is altogether unfit to command a frigate of 32-guns."*

Having spoken his mind on paper, John Paul Jones took the stage to Philadelphia to speak it in person.

Then, rattling across country, he did some hard thinking. Destructive criticism was too easy. What was needed was constructive criticism. The Navy must have a plan, a basic template to build on. The fundamental necessity was leadership—good leadership—trained officers with high character and patriotic motives to inspire the men. Given good leaders, the men would follow. And Education was a requirement for good leadership.

So John Paul Jones sat down and wrote a letter which remains as a blueprint for Navy leadership to this day.

"I have sat on a Court Martial where the President of the court could not read the orders that appointed him, and a Captain of Marines had to make his mark in signing a report. As long as you have such characters for officers the Navy will never rise above contempt. IT IS BY NO MEANS ENOUGH THAT AN OFFICER OF THE NAVY SHOULD BE A CAPABLE MARINER. HE SHOULD BE AS WELL A GENTLEMAN OF LIBERAL EDUCATION, REFINED MANNERS, PUNCTILIOUS COURTESY, AND THE NICEST SENSE OF PERSONAL HONOR. *When a commander has by tact, patience, justice, and firmness, each exercised in its proper turn, produced such an impression upon those under his orders in a ship of war, he has only to await the appearance of his enemy's topsails upon the horizon. When this moment does come, he*

may be sure of victory over an equal or somewhat superior force, or honorable defeat by one greatly superior."

Read that letter again. It applies to Petty Officers as well as those of top rank, and if you're striking for a rating you can well remember it. Mark those words *liberal education, manners, courtesy, personal honor*. Those qualities of *tact, patience, justice, firmness*. Such characteristics were important for success in the eighteenth century, and they're important today. A gentleman and a leader—the country needed such a man in Jones' time, and still needs him in your Navy. Jones placed his emphasis on two levels—a man's honesty with himself and his honesty with his fellow men. The letter called for an all-round man, a man useful to himself and to his country. You can recollect it was written by John Paul Jones, a sailor who worked his way up the ladder from the bottom rung.

That letter got him to the top. It was read by Robert Morris, a Philadelphian recently appointed to the Marine Committee to handle its financial affairs. Robert Morris knew men as well as money. He immediately went to bat for John Paul Jones.

Hopkins, bitterly opposed to Jones, was dismissed as Commander-in-Chief.

A 74-gun battleship was being designed—the finest vessel ever built in America!—and Morris promised John Paul Jones command of the ship. But she would take two years to build. In the meantime would Jones take command of the new sloop, *Ranger*, making ready to sail at Portsmouth yard?

Would he?

Congress confirmed the appointment on June 14, 1777, with Jones' orders reading, *"We shall not limit you to any particular cruising station, but leave you at large to search for yourself where the greatest chance of success presents."*

On the same day Congress passed a resolution providing, *"that the flag of the United States be thirteen stripes, alternate red and white; that the union be thirteen stars, white on a blue field, representing a new constellation."*

This flag John Paul Jones raised aboard his brand new *U.S.S. Ranger.*

"*That flag and I,*" he wrote, "*are twins born in the same hour from the same womb of destiny. We cannot be parted in life or death. So long as we can float, we shall float together. If we must sink, we shall go down as one.*"

THAT FLAG AND I

The Revolutionary War (Part 2)

When John Paul Jones took command of *Ranger* in June, 1777, the warship was not yet completed. Jones, impatient to be off, had to comb Portsmouth for sail-cloth and sailors. Good recruits were hard to find, and canvas proved so scarce that the indomitable captain prevailed on the ladies of the town to aid him. So the story is that *Ranger's* sails were made of petticoat silks and satins, and that all sorts of lovely patchwork flew from her crosstrees. More probably the ladies provided the needlework, and Jones stripped some old ships of their canvas.

Leave him, then, for a moment among the local belles, and glance back at the grimmer war-picture.

Brooklyn, Manhattan, and White Plains fell to the enemy in the autumn of '76, and Washington withdrew across the Hudson to New Jersey. Howe followed with 20,000 men, outnumbering the Americans seven-to-one. Leading the Red Coats and the Hessian troops was Cornwallis. Washington, his artillery lost, his forces dwindling, retreated toward Philadelphia, halting at last on the Pennsylvania side of the Delaware River. With winter closing in, Howe held his forces on the opposite bank to wait for better weather and reinforcements.

December proved white and bitter, and Washington's army, in the snow, melted away. No pay. No supplies. No ammunition. By mid-December the camp numbered less than 3,000 men. Despite sickness and desertion, Washington hung on.

This was the winter when Congress muddled in Philadelphia, when Esek Hopkins let the warships gather barnacles in Newport. A lesser man than Washington might have thrown up the sponge in despair. But just when the situation seemed at lowest ebb, George Washingotn showed what he was made of. And he was made of plenty.

It was Christmas night, 1776, and a blizzard was blowing. Huddled in their ragged tents, the Americans shivered, listening to the wolfish wind and the crunching ice cakes in the freezing river. Then the order came to move. You've heard that Washington once threw a dollar across the Rappahannock—that's legendary. But this night he threw his army across the Delaware—this is history.

In the Hessian camp the bonfires were bright; there were puddings and beer steins and *"Ach, du Lieber Augustin."* The Americans caught the heinies playing bend-the-elbow, just as Washington had suspected, and knocked them for a row of Meerschaums.

Fighting through blinding sleet, Washington's men chased the Hessians eight miles to Trenton, then swung over to smash Cornwallis' best regiments at Princeton. Scared by this brilliant attack, Howe pulled his troops back to New York and New Jersey, for the time being.

That was plasma in the arm of every patriot—plasma for the spirit of Independence. And America needed that plasma. For in the spring of 1777 came the main invasion from Canada—8,000 fresh regulars under John Burgoyne.

The plan, dreamed up by His Majesty's War Office, was for Burgoyne to march south along Lake Champlain while Howe marched north from New York. The two armies would meet at Albany, and New York State would presumably be crushed in the nut-cracker.

The plan failed for several reasons. American marksmanship was one. Then General Howe—convinced Burgoyne could steamroller to Albany—diverted his troops over to Jersey for another try at George Washington.

This left John Burgoyne holding a one-handled nut-cracker, with a very tough nut to crack. And "Gentleman Johnny," although a former member of Parliament, a playwright, a personal friend of George III, and a great lover, was hardly the man to crack an American hickory nut.

Flags flying, Burgoyne came down the shore of Lake Champlain without opposition, reaching Ticonderoga early in July. For support, a Red Coat army under General St. Leger hooked down from Oswego into the Mohawk Valley, hoping to enter Albany from the west. Bang! St. Leger ran into tough old General Herkimer, and an army of fierce patriots, a detachment under Benedict Arnold. St. Leger's army was chased back into Canada.

Burgoyne faltered; then, pecked at by sharpshooters, he came on. It was August—where was Howe? Well, Howe had been skirmishing over in New Jersey. Giving up hope of trapping Washington, he'd decided to take an invasion fleet down Delaware way to capture Philadelphia from that direction. Washington met the invaders at Brandywine Creek, lost a savage battle, lost again at Germantown, and Philadelphia lay open to the enemy. But Burgoyne, up in northern New York, was out on a limb.

20,000 American squirrel-hunters under Schuyler, Gates, and Arnold closed in on "Gentleman Johnny" at a little town north of Albany and drove him west to Saratoga. There in the Adirondack foothills the Red Coat army was snafued. October 17, 1777, Burgoyne surrendered with 5,000 battered men.

This great victory cushioned the shock of defeat at Philadelphia, and made the Americans determined to fight harder than ever. Congress set up the nation's capital at Lancaster, then moved it to Trenton, protected by Washington's troops. Ben Franklin had gone to Paris to urge the French into the war as an ally, and Burgoyne's defeat would go far to encourage French aid.

Adventures of Ranger

Now go back to Portsmouth where John Paul Jones is out-fitting *Ranger*. Equipment is still lacking. So are sailors for his crew. But he takes anything he can buy or hire, for here come dispatches from Congress—Burgoyne has surrendered! He must sail at once, and race for France with this important news.

So *Ranger* set sail on November 1st, scudding out into the Atlantic. Captain Jones drove her bee-line, arriving at the French port of Nantes on December 2nd. Pretty good, considering *Ranger's* patched-up sails—and Captain Jones' delay in mid-Atlantic to capture two enemy vessels in the bargain!

But the cruise was not altogether to Paul Jones' liking. Another ship, starting earlier, had beaten him with the news. And *Ranger* had displayed several structural defects—in her hull and in her crew. The former would be corrected in drydock, but the crew was another matter.

Waterfront ragtag, the men had been the only ones available. But they could be trained. Chief difficulty, as usual, were the random-picked officers—three Down East codfish skippers commissioned as lieutenants. Mixing Puritanical bigotry with bargain-hunting avarice, they described John Paul Jones, on one hand, as a "godless South Carolina captain;" on the other, they wanted him to chase after prizes. When he rebuked them for not putting the Navy ahead of prize money, they turned sour, crabby, and insubordinate.

Now, leaving *Ranger* at Nantes to have her masts corrected, Captain Jones rushed to Paris to see about correcting the crew. A talk with Benjamin Franklin about the Navy might help. So Jones began an American naval campaign in the French capital.

Benjamin Franklin—there was a character for you! Maybe you've seen a statue of him—a quaint figure wearing kneepants and square-rimmed spectacles, like somebody's ancient grand-

father. Huh! There was more pep and ginger in Benjamin Franklin than you saw at your latest dance. He was the all-American thinker of his day, and one of the big inventors of the American Revolution. Besides that, he invented bifocal spectacles, the smokeless furnace, the laundry mangle, and a score of ingenious gadgets.

He also set up the first U. S. Weather Bureau, proposed daylight saving, organized the Post Office, ran the Philadelphia Fire Department, wrote popular songs, learned to play the harp, and became a champion swimmer. In his spare moments he edited a magazine, wrote a popular publication, *Poor Richard's Almanac*, and studied physics. Dabbling with electricity (in a day when all the world was afraid of it) was just a hobby, but to make it practical he invented the lightning rod, then devised an electric detonator for explosives. On the side he managed to get around town a good deal, and to fly his famous kite.

So he became America's No. 1 diplomat, heading the American Commission in Paris. To John Paul Jones he listened sympathetically, and he liked this fighting captain who demanded improvements in the naval service.

"But don't lose your temper, my boy," you can hear him soothing, "I'll see if I can't get you a better warship."

Better warship? Well, the French had made a loan, Franklin confided. And French engineers were just completing a big frigate, *Indien*, in a shipyard leased up in Holland.

"France is letting us have the ship, and if I can arrange it, you'll be her captain."

A frigate at last! John Paul Jones shook Franklin's hand in delight. But it was a chicken counted before it was hatched. For Franklin, like Jones, had to deal with wire-pulling and favoritism.

The other commissioners in Paris—Silas Deane, and the Virginian, Arthur Lee—didn't approve the arrangement. Lee in particular did not favor John Paul Jones, and neither did he get along with Franklin. A snob and a pecksniff, he had been criticizing Franklin's easy informality with the French Court, and criticizing Paris as a racy city. Furthermore, he talked so loudly about official secrets that the French Foreign Minister had refused to let him in on any confidential matter.

Now when Franklin proposed Jones as captain of *Indien*, this Arthur Lee talked so loudly around the drawing rooms that British spies picked up news of the frigate. That let the cat out of the bag. France was still neutral, and the French king had to cancel the whole deal. America had lost a warship before it was even launched.

So, John Paul Jones went back to *Ranger*. With her crew still balky, Jones took her up to Brest for another overhaul. Entering Brest, he discovered the French Atlantic fleet under Admiral

Picquet in the harbor. John Paul Jones hove to, and ran up the Stars and Stripes. Then he sent over a boat, requesting Picquet to salute his new flag.

The French admiral, who had never seen the Colors before, was dumbfounded. But the red, white, and blue flew proudly,

proclaiming the new nation across the seas. And at sundown the French battleships thundered military acknowledgement—nine guns for the United States of America. The Navy and John Paul Jones had won a formal salute to the flag in foreign waters.

The salute had repercussions. The English ambassador in Paris raged at the French for recognizing America as an independent republic. Great Britain, he said, would demand reparations or war. The French Foreign Minister shrugged. That salute had been made—France would not take it back. If Great Britain wanted to make something of it, why, "C'est la guerre."

So George III, asking more trouble, sent France an ultimatum. Whereupon France came into the war as America's ally.

Meantime, with *Ranger* refitted, Paul Jones put out into the English Channel, bucking rough seas and April weather. Three months ashore had put him in a fighting mood, and he had also devised an extraordinary plan. The first part of this plan was to raid the Scottish coast, and twist the lion's tail right under George III's nose. The second part—but wait until you see how *Ranger* accomplished the first.

Up on Solway Firth in northern Scotland lies the town of Whitehaven, not far from Paul Jones' birthplace. To repay the Red Coats for the burning of Falmouth, Jones determined to lay this big port in ashes. Right around England to Whitehaven he drove *Ranger*. Then—bad luck, again—storms prevented him from entering the harbor.

While he stood off-shore, waiting for clearing weather, he

caught a coastal schooner on his hook, and learned that the British warship *H.M.S. Drake* was taking on supplies at Carrickfergus Lough, over in Ireland. John Paul Jones decided to take on *H.M.S. Drake*.

It was a dare-devil exploit, for it meant entering an enemy harbor at night, scuttling *Drake* before she could turn and fight, then making a fast get-away. Every man had to be on his toes. So what happened? The crew snarled, the lieutenants scowled, the quartermaster broke into the liquor stores behind Jones' back. When *Ranger* raced into the harbor, the rummed-up helmsman steered wide off course, *Drake's* lookouts sighted the American and fired the alarm. Jones got *Ranger* out to sea just in time.

Without pausing to curse his foul luck, Jones drove back to Whitehaven, his original objective. The sea had flattened during his absence, and now he anchored off-shore, jammed two of *Ranger's* boats with men, and led them at night into Whitehaven harbor.

Some guards were yawning on the parapet of the fort at harbor entrance. Next thing they knew, their yawns were stifled by gags. Cutlasses flashed in the gloom. A fierce, cloaked sailor

with a Scotch accent was ordering men up the wall to spike the guns.

The fort silenced, Jones scouted into Whitehaven. But his men were out of incendiary candles. Tinder had to be rounded up. Dawn came swift-footed, and there was only time to set the main wharf ablaze, touch off a couple of cargo vessels, and haul away. But the attack raised a tremendous hue-and-cry in England. Before the week was out, an entire naval squadron was hunting *Ranger.*

With peril on all sides, Jones' unruly crew grew mutinous, and his lieutenants put up another demand for prize money. Damning the whole privateering system, Jones ordered his men to buckle up for another exploit. Wanted a prize, did they? How'd they like to catch a live one?

This was part two of his plan—a scheme that may seem fantastic today but had a lot to recommend it in 1778. In those days there was no regular means for exchanging prisoners of war. Men luckless enough to be captured in battle were left to rot in dungeons or drag their chains around work camps that rivalled in misery the prisons of Nazi Germany.

So he planned to capture a prominent nobleman, the Earl of Selkirk, and hold him hostage until prisoners were exchanged. Not far from Whitehaven, at St. Mary's Isle, lived this Earl. John Paul had seen the Earl's manor house as a boy, and he knew St. Mary's with his eyes shut.

On the night of April 23, 1778, Lady Selkirk was entertaining a lady relative and a neighbor with three charming daughters in her drawing room. There were tea and crumpets, and one of the maidens playing on a harpsichord. Then suddenly a scuffle at the door. A servant running in pop-eyed. Next minute the drawing room was full of sailors, barefoot tars who brandished pistol and cutlass.

Their leader, an erect figure in officer's greatcoat, swept off his cockade hat and bowed politely.

"Your pardon, ladies, if you will forgive the intrusion. We have come to call on the Earl of Selkirk."

Gasps of panic from the charming daughters. Servants running. Confusion. A wail from the butler, "They're Americans!

The house is surrounded." Lady Selkirk drawing herself up. "The Earl of Selkirk is in London."

It must have struck the officer in the blue greatcoat as a blow, but he did not alter expression. With utmost courtesy he inquired into Lady Selkirk's health, told her she had nothing to fear from his company, St. Mary's would not be harmed.

To do Lady Selkirk credit, she coolly poured him a glass of wine, offered another to his scowling junior officer, and invited the visiting company to dinner. The wine was politely accepted, the dinner invitation regretfully declined, and, having remained, all told, about ten minutes, the visitors left the house.

Everything had gone off as courteously as a social call, and in half an hour Paul Jones had his men back aboard *Ranger* and seaward. He was sick at the luck that had let him miss the Earl of Selkirk. But that was war, and the expedition would show the enemy that the American Navy was on the way. It would also show that American Navy men could be gentlemen as well as warriors.

Alas for this happy idea—*Ranger* was hardly out of the channel when Captain Jones discovered one of his lieutenants pawing over a bag of silver plate. While all had been courtesy within the manor house, one of Lady Selkirk's servants had ducked out of the back door with the family silver, and fallen into the arms of the crew outside.

There was hell to pay then aboard *Ranger!* You can imagine John Paul Jones exploding like a powder magazine, thundering at his dour lieutenants to know who the devil took Lady Selkirk's silver.

The lieutenants argued back. It was prize of war—the privateers did it—why should Jones scuttle every chance they had to make a little money from loot?

It took John Paul Jones just about three seconds to summon all hands and deliver a quarterdeck lecture that must have been a masterpiece in salty language. Then he sat down and wrote apologizing letters to the Earl and Lady Selkirk that would have done credit to Emily Post. To the Earl he explained the motive of the raid, the plan to hold him hostage until prisoners were exchanged. To Lady Selkirk he wrote, *"I wage no war with the fair."* While his crew snarled and growled and his lieutenants went ominously sullen, he sent the silver back.

The whole thing reads like romance, but the letters are on record, and if you ever make port in St. Mary's Isle you can see the self-same silver plate. The story is genuine naval history, as solid as the silver.

You might also make port in Belfast, northern Ireland. Well, there off Carrickfergus you can see some more solid naval history —the place where *Ranger* battled *Drake.* For John Paul Jones, with luck running against him three times straight, decided it was high time to win something for a change. The nearest thing at hand was the chance he'd previously missed. So he went back to Carrickfergus, hell-for-sailcloth.

This time he proposed to enter the harbor and attack the enemy warship in broad daylight, gun for gun. At once his lieutenants objected furiously, his crew snarled louder than ever. Expecting mutiny, Jones stood like iron on the quarterdeck, his belt braced with a half dozen pistols. Like an animal trainer in a circus cage, he bent the crew to his will, driving *Ranger* to Carrickfergus. And this time he caught *H.M.S. Drake* with her canvas down.

It was late afternoon when *Ranger* rounded the headland and slipped into Carrickfergus harbor. *Drake*, at anchor, was still taking on supplies. Innocent as any merchantman, *Ranger* hove to in the roadway, presenting her stern to the British warship. The Britons lowered a small boat and rowed over to examine Jones' ship.

Jones, waiting at the taffrail, noticed the smoke of signal fire rising from the hills around the harbor.

"What are those smoke signals?" he called down to the oncoming boat.

The visiting cox'n informed him they were alarm signals warning the countryside of an American pirate who was loose in the Irish Channel. One second later the stunned cox'n was staring down the throat of an uncovered chase gun and talking to the "pirate" in person.

When *Drake's* lookout saw the small boat tied up prisoner by the newcomer, he howled the alarm. *Drake's* captain Burdon beat to quarters, had the guns run out, and hoisted anchor to sail over and see what was cooking.

"What ship is that?" he thundered at Jones.

"The American Continental ship, Ranger!" Jones trumpeted back, while Stars and Stripes unfurled aloft from the halyards. *"And as the sun is only an hour from setting it is therefore time to begin."*

Drake began at once, firing a blast that hit nothing but water. Jones swung *Ranger* around—held fire until within pistol shot—then gave the enemy a salvo that shredded her rigging.

The English replied furiously, but Jones maneuvered *Ranger* so deftly that she glided about like a figure-skater, dodging each

enemy broadside. *Drake*, with her rigging badly damaged, was unable to do more than wallow. The Americans poured a hot fire into the British ship, hammering her with cannon balls, bullets, and grenades. Withing ten minutes *Drake* was reduced to a sitting duck.

The battle lasted half an hour; then *Drake* struck her mangled flag. Captain Burdon was dying, forty crewmen lay dead, the spar deck was blown to rubbish, and another broadside would have sunk her.

Ranger's casualties: two dead, six wounded.

Now in fire power both ships had been evenly matched, but the Britons had the advantage of forty more men and playing on their own "home field." When you add in the factor of *Ranger's* mutinous crew, this victory—the first major naval battle won by the Americans—seems incredible.

Put it down to the skilled seamanship of John Paul Jones and his insistence on gunnery practice. Put it down to the discipline he managed to maintain where a lesser leader might have lost control. TACT, PATIENCE, JUSTICE, FIRMNESS—John Paul Jones was a man who practiced what he preached. *Ranger's* astonishing victory over *Drake* was the pay-off.

Yet there are limits to such things as patience. One of the two men killed aboard *Ranger* had been Lieutenant Wallingford, the only junior officer Jones had felt he could trust. Now it fell to Lieutenant Simpson, one of the malcontents, to go aboard *Drake* as commander and take charge of the captured vessel.

Jones gave this underling explicit instructions. It would be ticklish business running the captive warship through English waters back to France. The whole Royal Navy would be out to stop them.

"The honor of our flag is much concerned with the preservation of this prize," Jones wrote out the orders. *"Therefore keep close by me and she shall not be given tamely up. You are to take your station on the Ranger's starboard quarter at or about the distance of a cable's length."*

With hasty repairs made on *Drake,* the two ships set out to run the gauntlet back to France. May 5th brought them almost within sight of the Normandy coast. Then *Ranger's* lookout sighted enemy patrols. Jones cleared for action, and at the same time Simpson let *Drake* fall behind and veer off. Jones signalled to the ship astern, and the signals were ignored. The distant enemy patrol went on its way, and Simpson went on his way. Before Jones could bring *Ranger* on a round-about tack, *Drake* was half way over the horizon.

This was mutiny at its worst, and John Paul Jones set his teeth like a beartrap, determined to recapture the prize. The race lasted throughout a night. Damaged *Drake* was as slow as Simpson's wits, however, and *Ranger* overhauled her the following morning.

John Paul Jones was out of patience now. Clapping Simpson in irons, he trained *Ranger's* guns on *Drake*, and drove her, double-captive, into Brest.

The French people went wild. An American, single-handed, had bearded the enemy lion in its den and come back with a prize warship to boot. When the news reached Paris, John Paul Jones was the toast of the hour.

He wasn't interested in toasts. Hot-foot he rushed to Paris to see about exchanging the English seamen he had captured aboard *Drake* for American prisoners held captive in England. In Paris, too, he dispatched by special messenger the letters he had written to the Earl and Lady Selkirk. And he lost no time in reporting the details of his cruise to Franklin and the American Commission.

Franklin gave the indomitable captain a big hand, and the exchange of prisoners was arranged. This alone was enough to make Jones' daring cruise worth while. Then the capture of a first-class enemy warship, snared at its home base, was a feat unequalled in the annals of naval warfare. Finally the raid of Whitehaven had thrown George III's Admiralty into a tremendous dither. The First Lords of George III's Admiralty were given to realize that the Revolutionary Navy could come across the Atlantic. This meant some of the Royal Navy would have to stay home to guard home waters. British coastal towns began to clamor for protection. The public raised an uproar. John Paul Jones really started something when he visited England with *Ranger*.

Now how was John Paul Jones rewarded for having dealt these blows to the enemy? Well, aside from Franklin, the American Commissioners in Paris received him as though he were peddling a case of measles. Word of the St. Mary's raid had reached France—the stolen silver business—the Earl of Selkirk was denouncing him to the world as a pirate. Furthermore, one of the people on St. Mary's had recognized him as the John Paul rumored to have killed a man at Tobago. Now the story was loose about his "changed name"—the Maxwell affair—all the rumors came back to haunt him.

So Mr. Arthur Lee, whose bumbling tongue had already cost America a warship, set out to cost America a great naval captain. His motives, of course, were political. His methods were red tape.

And he entangled John Paul Jones in the mesh. While Paris cheered Jones, this commissioner was undermining him.

Jones was demanding a court martial for mutinous Lieutenant Simpson. Arthur Lee demanded a long investigation. Seventy-seven members of Jones' rascally crew, calling themselves "The Jovial Tars," sent the Paris Commission a whining letter, claiming John Paul Jones had maltreated them. They declared they had originally enlisted in the Navy to serve under Simpson, *"who is now confined, innocently as we think, in a Lousey, Dirty, French Gaol."*

Overlooked was Jones' raid on the enemy homeland, his great victory over *Drake*, his effecting the release of American prisoners. The American Commissioners in Paris mulled over this mis-spelled scrap of paper from "The Jovial Tars" as if it were an authenticated legal document.

Simpson, summoned to testify, said he had fled off with *Drake* only to save her from the sighted enemy patrols. It was all a big mistake, and he'd never meant to desert Jones.

To Jones' utter amazement and against Franklin's urgent advice, Lieutenant Simpson was completely exonerated. On top of that, Simpson was made acting captain of *Ranger* and ordered to sail her back to America. Relieved of his command, John Paul Jones was left stranded in Paris.

There is only one answer to this staggering episode—backhall politics fighting for private patronage, plus the personal malice of a jealous conniver. But no conspirator could tread on John Paul Jones. Destiny and Ben Franklin went to work to help him obtain another ship. Result: the *Bonhomme Richard*.

Taps For Nicholas Biddle

It took Paul Jones nearly a year to get his new ship—you can leave him there in Paris fighting in a tangle of political red tape, and review the war in America.

Captain Jones was not the only victim of red tape. The little Revolutionary army and navy were snagged in the wrangly political stuff as though it were a field of barbed wire. Remember, each state wanted to run the war for its own benefit—meaning each one wanted special favors. Pressure groups campaigned around Congress harder than the British.

So military supplies were delayed, taxes went uncollected, the war effort bogged down, and George Washington had to replace good commanders like General Schuyler with mediocre ones like Horatio Gates. Similarly, the Marine Committee had been forced to wire-pull the list that had originally by-passed John Paul Jones.

Of these other Continental Navy captains, Nicholas Biddle was one who deserved his appointment without question.

Early in 1777, with the first of the new American frigates, *Randolph*, he put to sea. Ill luck caught him with a storm off Hatteras, and *Randolph*, carelessly built, snapped her masts. Some British prisoners being transported by the frigate staged a mutiny, but young Captain Biddle put it down neatly and brought *Randolph* into Charleston for repairs.

In this spring of 1777, you'll remember, Esek Hopkins was relieved of his command at Newport and Paul Jones was at Portsmouth struggling to equip *Ranger*. Now, while *Randolph* lay in Charleston being refitted, two more new American frigates put to sea.

These were *Hancock* and *Boston*—the former, a 32-gunner, rated as the finest American warship of her time, and under command of Captain John Manley; and the latter, a 24-gunner, under Captain Hector McNeil. Both of these captains were high above Jones on the Marine Committee's list, and much was expected of them.

Manley, you recall, was the one-time Royal Navy boatswain and Marblehead fisherman who had served well enough in Washington's mosquito fleet, but whom Jones had protested "*not fit to command a frigate.*" McNeil, a salty Celt, had been a good merchant captain, but knew little of naval warfare.

Sailing as a team, the two Yankee warships put out, leading a squadron of nine Massachusetts privateers. Late in June, off Newfoundland Banks, the squadron overhauled *H.M.S. Fox*, a brand new 28-gunner. A broadside from *Boston* and a raking blast from *Hancock*, and *Fox* was captured.

Manley decided the squadron should head toward Halifax, and McNeil protested. They ought to go to the West Indies—the enemy were thicker than fleas around Halifax. On this point both captains remained at loggerheads. Then Manley pulled rank; the squadron headed north.

Sloppy seas. Fog. Then on July 6, *Hancock* ran straight into *H.M.S. Rainbow*, battleship, with the brig *Viper* bringing up the rear. Sir George Collier, captain of the *Rainbow*, opened fire at once. Unwilling to risk fight with a two-decker, Manley crowded sail on *Hancock* to run. *Rainbow* gave chase like a thundercloud.

Manley signalled *Boston* for support. But McNeil had his own hands full, with *H.M.S. Flora* arriving over the horizon to cut him off. The chase lasted through one night, a foggy day, another night.

Flora, cutting in, recaptured *Fox*. *Boston* and *Hancock* became separated. *Rainbow* overhauled *Hancock* on the third day, and the battle was on.

Hancock's men fought desperately, giving the big Britisher broadside for broadside. But they couldn't stand off the two-decker. Down came *Hancock's* foremast in a crash of flaming canvas. One after another the Yankee gunners fell. *Viper* sailed in for the kill, and *Hancock* was lost. Down came her colors through the smoke. Marblehead Manley had lost his frigate.

McNeil escaped with *Boston* and took home news of the defeat. *Hancock* had been the pride of New England, and her loss was a stunning blow.

The public raged, blaming McNeil and demanding his court-martial. He was weighed, found wanting, and dismissed from the service. But today you can see that the fault was not so much McNeil's alone as lack of team-work. First, lack of team-work between the States. Then lack of team-work between the Marine Committee and the Navy. Finally, lack of team-work between the early American captains.

Meantime young Captain Biddle down in Charleston was doing a better job. *Randolph's* masts having been stepped in, Biddle headed her out for the Gulf Stream where he promptly caught a convoy of enemy merchantmen and captured four ships including one with 20 guns. But something was wrong with *Randolph*, and he had to put in for another overhaul.

A successful crossing to France with diplomatic messages followed, and he was again in Charleston where the Carolinians contributed four gunboats as a cruising squadron. Biddle headed straight for the West Indies to raid British traffic.

On March 7, 1778, *Randolph* was off the island of Barbadoes, slipping along through early morning mist. Suddenly, like a ghost-ship from nowhere, a huge battleship loomed dead a-beam in the fog. *Randolph's* lookout identified her as *H.M.S. Yarmouth,* 64 guns!

No chance to signal the gunboats for support. No chance to run. Captain Biddle could only open fire point blank. And with *Randolph's* guns outnumbered exactly two-to-one, he could only hope to wound this sea leviathan.

Boom! *Randolph* blazed a broadside. Boom! *Yarmouth's* guns returned fire. Began a fierce slugging match—frigate vs. battleship—on a par with CL fighting BB in this modern day. Or, in ringside parlance, it was comparable to middleweight against heavyweight, and Biddle knew his only chance was to dodge the enemy's haymakers, close in, and grapple.

He called for boarders and rushed forward to lead. A bullet struck his leg. Flashing his cutlass, he ordered his men to hoist him in a chair. And they were carrying him forward, cheering for the charge, when a shot struck *Randolph's* powder magazine.

The American frigate vanished in one, single thunderclap of fire. The little Carolina gunboats, barking in to join the fight, fell back stunned. *Randolph* was gone. Captain Biddle was gone.

Picked up five days later from a floating piece of driftwood, one solitary survivor lived to tell the tale.

Low Ebb

Loss of two brand new frigates, *Hancock* and *Randolph*, would have been enough to stagger the new-born American Navy. But that wasn't all. Throughout 1777, the Royal Navy had been coming across the Atlantic like a herd of whales to run down a school of little mackerel. Blow after blow they struck the American Continentals.

They captured the new frigate *Delaware* in the Delaware River before she ever put to sea. The new frigate *Congress* had to be destroyed at New York to save her from capture by Lord Howe. *Montgomery*, another of the new warships, was similarly scuttled in the Hudson River. Early in 1778, the frigate *Washington* was burned in Delaware Bay to save her from capture. The new frigate *Effingham* was destroyed at her berth in the same bay shortly afterward.

Five new warships lost before they started. Two more lost in action at sea. Why, the new navy was hardly launched, and —half its ships were gone! Now how about the rest?

Well, not long after *Randolph* was lost in the Caribbean, Captain Joseph Olney set out from Boston with the American brig, *Cabot*. Off Nova Scotia he was sighted by *H.M.S. Milford*, chased ashore, forced to run *Cabot* aground and leave her ignominiously on the beach.

About the same time, the new frigate *Virginia* put out from Annapolis. She was commanded by James Nicholson, another of those wire-pulled figures who was appointed over the head of John Paul Jones.

What happened? Well, Nicholson was short on navigation, and the first night out he ran *Virginia* slam on to a Maryland shoal. She lost her rudder, and Captain Nicholson lost his trousers. For when dawn came, it revealed a British warship on the horizon. And with *Virginia* stuck fast on the reef, Nicholson went overside into a smallboat so fast he forgot his pants.

While this character in under-drawers raced for shore and safety, a young lieutenant named Joshua Barney tried to save *Virginia* by running up sail and ordering all hands to man a jury rudder. The crew promptly mutinied, overpowered Barney, and broke into the liquor stores. When the British warship closed in, she found Virginia sitting with closed gun-ports, her crew carousing like a cheap clambake. The cheesy crew surrendered *Virginia* without firing a shot.

And to top off this burlesque performance, Captain Nicholson came clowning down the bay next day under a flag of truce to beg the British to return his trousers. Funny, you think? Well, the date was April, 1778, when John Paul Jones was fighting his head off overseas and capturing *Drake*.

Now Nicholson had been No. 1 in the long list of appointments which by-passed Jones. So the Marine Committee was in no temper to take shenanigans from Thomas Thompson, another high on the list.

Thompson commanded the new frigate *Raleigh*. He had officered a slaver in the old days, and he knew how to handle a ship—in peacetime.

Raleigh was a fine 32-gunner, and for partner she set sail with the old flagship *Alfred*. The two ships headed for the Caribbean, then over to France.

On the way, Thompson ducked out of a skirmish with *H.M.S. Druid*—chased away by a little corvette carrying 22 guns. *Alfred's* commander, Captain Hinman, openly criticised this tactic, and the two captains reached France with a ripening grudge.

They came back across the Atlantic, a bickering team. On March 9, two British ships were sighted. *Alfred*, nearest, sailed over to attack, discovering them to be two sloops. The sloops accepted the challenge, rushing at *Alfred* with flaming guns. Hinman, expecting Thompson to bring *Raleigh* into the battle, anticipated easy victory. Thompson didn't join battle. Instead, he sailed right on past the fighting ships, and made for the horizon.

Slow old *Alfred* was chopped to pieces, and after a desperate battle Hinman struck his flag. The two British sloops then set out to catch *Raleigh*. The new frigate had plenty of fire power, but Thompson, himself, didn't have a spark. Crowding on sail, he ran.

The little sloops chased him half way home to Portsmouth while he jettisoned gear and guns to lighten ship. He made

Portsmouth all right, but he never served in another naval vessel. Court martial for Thomas Thompson.

So the record goes in 1778 for the American Continental Navy. And as a final blow the Navy was to lose *Raleigh*.

With Thompson dismissed, the frigate was assigned to Captain John Barry, a two-fisted Irishman up from the merchant marine. Barry had been skipper of *Black Prince*, the freighter which was converted into *Alfred*. To repay Barry for the loss of his merchantman, the Marine Committee commissioned him a naval captain, and gave him the little 16-gun sloop, *Lexington*.

About the time Hopkins was cruising off the Bahamas, Barry took *Lexington* down Delaware Bay and handily captured the British 8-gun sloop *Edward*. The Marine Committee rewarded him by appointing him captain of *Effingham*, then building.

As previously mentioned, this ship had to be destroyed to keep her from falling to the enemy when the British blockaded the Delaware and closed in on Philadelphia. John Barry made a desperate effort to raise and repair *Effingham* right under the Red Coats' eyes. It was hopeless, and he applied for another ship. Under the circumstances reported, he got *Raleigh*.

Barry rushed to Boston where *Raleigh* was waiting. He was delighted with the frigate, and readied her to sail at once. She put out of Boston on September 25, 1778, and her first day out, at 1200, sighted two enemy warships.

These were *H.M.S. Experiment*, a big two-decker carrying 50 guns, and *H.M.S. Unicorn*, a 22-gun sloop-of-war. *Raleigh's* 32 guns were no match for this pair, so Barry had to light out.

He headed north for misty water, and the two Britons took off after him. For two days the chase went on. Then, just as Barry thought he'd got *Raleigh* away, he sighted islands dead ahead, and had to veer off on a wide tack seaward. The enemy made a tangent to bisect his course.

Unicorn, fast and vicious, came up first. *Raleigh* fought her off the quarter, blasting at the Briton with savage accuracy. But these English Jacks were good, and although hard hit, punched a salvo at *Raleigh* that wrecked her fore-topmast. This slowed Barry's ship in maneuver, and he swung in to make it a slugging match, hoping to wreck the sloop before the battleship arrived.

In twilight gloom the battle roared, but the sloop out-dodged the slower *Raleigh,* and fired signals for *Experiment* to snap into it. The big two-decker came up like Fate, and at 1700 was lobbing cannon balls at *Raleigh.* No chicken-hearted Thompson or Nicholson, Barry had his men fighting like wildcats, and for nine hours the action lasted hot and heavy. Then, his ship a shambles, his chances hopeless, Barry headed straight for the islands and rammed the frigate hard on the rocks.

While Barry and most of the crew escaped through the woods, the Britons sailed in and captured what was left of *Raleigh.*

Submarines! Torpedoes!

Low ebb. Very low. No wonder the Mother Country thought she'd won the war. On the land and on the sea the Americans had been badly beaten throughout 1778. Look at the Continental Navy—ships scuttled or captured—captains gone by the board. Look at the American Army—

Well, Burgoyne had been trounced the year before, but the enemy still held New York and Philadelphia, tightening the grip. Through the January blizzards of 1778, George Washington had been stymied in Pennsylvania, his troops barefoot, starving, huddled like a gypsy camp at Valley Forge. Food, clothing, weapons, munitions—the Americans lacked everything.

"These are the times that try men's souls," wrote Thomas Paine, while the Red Coat officers danced in Philadelphia, Washington's troopers died of pneumonia, and American money sank so low that all the mint could coin was the phrase, *"Not worth a Continental."* The Americans were in dire need, the Revolution at lowest ebb.

Now, you've heard that Necessity is the mother of Invention. Did you know that an American invented a SUBMARINE during the Revolutionary War? And TORPEDOES?

The record rivals anything from Jules Verne, and is one of the most fantastic stories in naval history.

The inventor's name was David Bushnell. A Connecticut Yankee, he was one of those idea men whose thoughts explore ahead of their time. He had gone to Yale College to study philosophy and come back with his head full of filberts—so his neighbors said.

Bushnell wanted to build a boat, but not an ordinary boat. For boats, as everyone knew, were built for the sole purpose of sailing on the water. But Bushnell's boat, he declared, was going to sail under the water.

Now who the devil ever heard of such a thing? Certainly not the hard-headed Yankees of Connecticut. They tapped their foreheads when they mentioned David Bushnell. But Bushnell, tapping his forehead, built the boat.

He called her the *Marine Turtle* or *The Maine Torpedo,* and she was the whackiest craft ever launched. The natives regarded

her with their mouths open. They didn't know that Leonardo da Vinci, three hundred years before, had drawn up plans for a similar submarine.

The *Marine Turtle* looked like a turtle. She was built of oak, her hull covered over in resemblance to a turtle's shell. Air inside, Bushnell said, made her buoyant. That was all right. But he proposed to dive her under water by a sort of fin-like contraption where her keel should be. Craziest of all, where a turtle had a tail, this *Marine Turtle* had a sort of screw which was turned by a handcrank inside. That was supposed to make her go! And to top it off, she had a big auger at her prow, which thrust out like a turtle's head. Could you beat it? Bushnell figured he could sneak along underwater and come alongside some vessel and bore a hole in her hull. Then he could stick a bomb in the hole and run.

That was in 1776. Bushnell made a trial run before Governor Trumbull of Connecticut, who was impressed enough to send him to New York. That winter the amazing thing happened. *Marine Turtle* waddled down New York Bay, dived, crept up to a British ship anchored on blockade, and tried to bore in. Unforseen obstacle—the ship had a copper bottom! *Turtle's* auger could not chew into the metal, and the bit broke off. But one of *Turtle's* underwater bombs exploded, and scared the enemy galley-west.

Late in 1777, with the British surrounding Philadelphia, Bushnell made another submarine run down the Delaware. As might be expected, poor *Turtle* submerging blindly, came a-cropper and cracked up. That the *Turtle* succeeded as well as she did was the amazing thing. Then, even more amazing, the Marine Committee refused to deal further with Bushnell's idea.

Cold water poured on his submarine, he now proposed another startling innovation—his torpedoes. These were simple devices, merely powder kegs with contact triggers attached, much like mines. But Bushnell's ingenious scheme was to launch them at the enemy, rather than have them moored where ships might run into them. Launch them? Well, they didn't have engines, but tide was to be the motive power. Let them sail down the Delaware on the racing current—dozens of these hair-trigger kegs—and they'd slam into the British blockaders at river-mouth and blow the enemy ships to blazes.

Late in December of that discouraging winter, about one hundred of Bushnell's torpedoes were launched at the enemy.

More Fate! That night the weather fell far below zero! The river, scummed with ice, went slow and sluggish. In the morning the torpedoes, caught in the freeze, went crawling downstream like flies in molasses. The British saw them inching along, and thought some American supply barge had capsized. Watchers were set to fend them off with boat hooks. Several were picked up by the English crews. And one enterprising boatswain, setting out to capture one from the ice, was blown to Kingdom Come.

The episode became known as the Battle of the Powder Kegs, and Bushnell was laughed at, kidded, and jeered. Wide publication was given a poem about the affair. Here's some of it:

> 'Twas early day as poets say,
> Just as the sun was rising,
> A soldier stood on a log of wood
> And saw a sight surprising.
>
> As in amaze he stood to gaze,
> The truth can't be denied, sir,
> He spied a score of kegs or more,
> Come floating down the tide, sir.
>
> Now up and down throughout the town
> Most frantic scenes were acted,
> And some ran here and some ran there
> Like men almost distracted.
>
> "Therefore prepare for bloody war
> These kegs must all be routed,
> Or surely we despised shall be,
> And British courage doubted!"
>
> The cannon roar from shore to shore,
> The small arms loud do rattle,
> Since time began, I'm sure no man,
> E'er saw so strange a battle.

Ridicule followed laughter. Bushnell could hardly appear on the street but what someone shouted verbal brickbats. The Marine Committee wouldn't see him. This patriot who had invented the first American submarine, the first contact torpedo, was laughed out of the war. He changed his name, retired to the backwoods of Georgia and became a country schoolteacher, embittered and forgotten.

Vive La France!

You begin to see the Revolutionary War was no walk-away for the Americans. Truth is, it was a long, hard, desperate struggle, and the Americans nearly lost. They might, indeed, have lost had not the French come in as an ally. As related, France joined sides with America in the spring of 1778. Franklin's genial diplomacy, Burgoyne's defeat, and Jones' victory over *Drake* were prime factors in winning France as an ally. Also, France had been at odds with Great Britain for years, especially since the loss of Canada.

But another, deeper motive brought France to America's aid. For all her royalist exterior, France was becoming democratic. In other words, the people were turning against the Old World system of monarchy, and hoping for a more liberal government. Writers like Voltaire were fighting for freedom of thought and speech. *"I may disgree with what you say,"* wrote Voltaire, *"but I will defend to the death your right to say it."* Many Frenchmen cheered the American Revolution from the starting gun, and volunteered valuable aid.

Every schoolboy knows about Lafayette who crossed over to offer his services to Washington. But there were two other Frenchmen who worked overtime for the American cause, and did even more than Lafayette.

One was Beaumarchais, a writer, musician, merchant, diplomat, and liberal thinker in the champion class. He raised money in France for the American cause. He contributed heavily from his own pocket. He ran a secret organization which sent supplies overseas to George Washington. Between 1776-77, he shipped 30,000 rifles, 200 cannons, munitions, tents, provisions which reached America just in time to save the patriot army.

Hats off to Beaumarchais! He gave his entire fortune to America, and when he died he was in actual poverty.

The other Frenchman was Vergennes, the Foreign Minister. From the first he urged the King of France to aid the American republic. He ran diplomatic interference for the Americans around Europe, and helped Franklin openly. Through Vergennes, Franklin was able to procure for John Paul Jones the *Bonhomme Richard*. This vessel was a venerable old hulk from the merchant service—a ship already condemned by the insurance companies, believe it or not—an old tramp named the *Duras*.

Her hull was barnacled, her decks were blistered, her sails were rotten, and her hold was a dark jungle of rats. But she was a 900-tonner, might be converted into a two-decker, and had room for guns. Jones, rushing to L'Orient to take her over was happy to accept anything that could sail. After a year ashore in Paris (snared in red tape) he was raring to get to sea.

He took command of *Duras* with bursting energy. During his lay-off in Paris, he'd studied naval architecture, and he set to work to make this hulk a battleship. It was tough going. But he ripped out wormy woodwork, tore up decks, installed gun mounts, applied paint. When she was done he christened her *Bonhomme Richard*, in honor of *Poor Richard's Almanac*.

Now his troubles began—first, the guns. The Ministry of Marine was low on ordnance; so they gave him a clutter of museum pieces that wouldn't have done credit to a Chinese junk. No matter—he got them cleaned, patched together, mounted. Liners were worn away and the cannon balls wouldn't fit? All right, the gunners would have to smear tar or putty on the round shot and make them fit.

Now for the crew—and what a crew! Sweepings of the French seaport towns. Malays. Portuguese. Lascars. A gang of British prisoners. It would take more than tar and putty to correct these misfits. But you could shape them into some resemblance of a crew—if you were John Paul Jones.

Among them (the crew numbered some 227 men) there were eighty Americans, former war prisoners released in the *Drake* exchange. These Jones used as the nucleus of his crew. One was Richard Dale, a young patriot who served under Barry and had been captured early in the war. He talked Paul Jones' language, so Jones made him his first officer.

Such was the *Bonhomme Richard* and of such stuff was her crew—a castaway ship full of castaways. Then, incongruously, the French government assigned to Jones a four-ship squadron to sail with *Richard*—French warships *Alliance*, *Pallas*, *Vengeance*, and *Cerf*.

Here was political idiocy. For *Alliance* was a brand new

American-built frigate—which the Continental Congress had donated to France. The French had put her under the command of Pierre Landais, an officer previously dismissed from the French Navy for insubordination! Now it wasn't enough that Paul Jones had to sail in ratty old *Richard* for his flagship. Landais at once wanted to be admiral. Strutting like a rooster, he tried to run the cruise; then he turned sour and sullen when Jones took command.

The other French captains, notably Denis Cottineau in command of *Pallas*, were anxious to cooperate with Jones. Not Landais. June 18th, the ships put out for a trial run. The second night out, Paul Jones signalled for a maneuver. Landais ignored the signal. *Richard* was crossing *Alliance's* bow. Landais refused to give way, and smashed straight into Jones' ship—a collision that wrecked *Richard's* jib and cracked *Alliance's* mizzenmast.

In white fury, Jones called Landais on the mat. Landais said he'd misread the signals. The ships had to limp into L'Orient for repairs. A lucky break, really, for it was then Jones picked up the Americans for his crew. Unlucky, too, for just before the squadron sailed again, Jones was directed by the French Ministery to share his authority with the four French captains. Landais had pulled some back-stage wires.

Imagine Paul Jones' feelings as the squadron once more set sail (August 14, 1779). Deprived of top rank—*Richard*, a wormy, old tub armed with castoff guns—a crew like the workmen of Babel—a cruise with every captain commodore, especially pompous Landais. Only the eighty Yankees, valiant young Lieutenant Dale, and honest French Captain Cottineau kept the thing from utter nightmare. Jaw set, thoughts dead ahead, Jones set the *Bonhomme Richard's* course for England.

Bonhomme Richard and Serapis

Everything went wrong. *Richard* proved slow and leaky. Landais bickered over the course and insulted Paul Jones to his face. The Frenchmen voted down a plan Jones devised for attacking enemy shipping off Scotland. In a fog, *Cerf* turned tail and made for home.

Doggedly Jones went on. Nothing could stop him now—and

early morning, September 23, *Richard's* lookout sighted a fleet of forty merchantmen skirting Flamborough Head, on the English coast. Jones sailed in to attack. The vessels were under convoy of British warships—*Countess of Scarborough,* a 20-gunner, and *Serapis,* a brand-new frigate carrying 50 guns. Jones signalled his squadron for battle formation, and headed *Richard* straight for *Serapis.*

But Pierre Landais held *Alliance* back, deliberately stalling. *Vengeance,* smallest of the French warships, dashed in to attack the English merchantmen—and sent them scattering for cover. Only Captain Cottineau followed Jones' signal, and brought *Pallas* in line to do battle.

Richard sailed right up to *Serapis* which was waiting as though astonished by the boldness of this approaching tramp.

"What ship is that?" Captain Pearson of *Serapis* challenged.

Jones didn't answer.

H.M.S. Serapis hailed again.

Still Jones refused reply. *Richard* was almost abreast of *Serapis* now—beam to beam. Then suddenly both ships fired simultaneously—a volcanic, double broadside. The roar clouded both ships with smoke.

As the thunder rolled aside, there were screams from *Richard's* main-deck, jets of flames bursting from below. Two of the

shabby main-battery cannon had exploded, slaying their American gun crews and firing the ship.

Now *Serapis* unleashed another broadside that struck Richard hard amidships. The old rag wagon reeled at the blast. There was hell below decks, guns blown from their mountings, splinters flying, pandemonium, flames, smoke. Young Dale, serving as gunnery officer, strove to keep the crews at their posts. The American gunners fought on, cheering. But the Portuguese and Lascars ran riot. *Serapis'* round shot came tearing through *Richard's* rotten hull as if it were cardboard. Another battery was shot away. Another. *Richard*, out-gunned from the start, lost every big gun she owned in the first few moments of battle. Dale rushed his gunners topside to man the secondary batteries.

Secondary batteries? The spar-deck was shot to hell'n-gone. *Serapis*, maneuvering swiftly, was raking *Poor Richard* at will, pouring a tornado of metal that swept the aged vessel from stern to stem. A great crater yawned in *Richard's* foredeck and sides where the exploding batteries below had burst her timbers. Men lay slaughtered from scupper to scupper, half buried under sprawls of rigging and burning canvas. Dale found only three cannon in action—three little 9-pounders—all that remained of *Richard's* rummage-sale artillery!

But those three little cannon were thumping. Paul Jones, a fierce, smoke-blackened figure, was serving as pointer for one of them on the quarterdeck. *Serapis* would thunder a broadside, and Jones' guns would crack like a horse-pistol, firing puny shots at *Serapis'* mainmast. Those shots were hitting, though. And the other two guns were smacking *Serapis* with rounds of grape and canister.

Meantime Jones was swinging *Richard* closer and closer to the Briton, trying to lock alongside and grapple. Once the ships collided for a moment, but the British Marines shot Jones' men away from the cat-heads, the great grappling irons tore loose, and the vessels drifted apart. But a moment later, Jones drove *Richard* squarely under the enemy's bow, and *Serapis'* jib boom rammed through the shrouds of *Richard's* mizzenmast.

Racing through a hail of bullets, Jones led a squad of sailors amidships, and with a heavy hawser succeeded in lashing the enemy's bowsprit to *Richard's* shrouds.

Serapis, her nose caught fast in *Richard's* rigging, was unable to break away, and Jones sent his riflemen aloft to pepper the Briton's spar-deck. Tied together like bulldog and mastiff, the two ships wrestled in a pall of smoke and flame. The mangey mastiff snarled and snapped. The British bulldog chawed and roared. One broadside after another ripped through *Richard's* hull until her main deck was shot completely out, her ribs were exposed, and only a miracle seemed to keep her whole upper deck from collapsing into her fiery interior. If there'd been a sea running, the old hulk would have swamped at first comber, but now she clung to *Serapis* like a burning sponge. The wild battle went on.

There were guns going off to northward where *Pallas* was fighting the *Countess of Scarborough*. But where was *Alliance?* Why didn't Landais come up?

No matter—Jones was too busy to worry about Landais. He was starboard, larboard, all over *Richard's* tottering deck, directing the gunners, shouting encouragement, running repair crews, aiming the 9-pounders.

In the midst of which, *Richard's* master-at-arms rushed up in sudden, mad panic, and tried to haul down the American flag, screaming, *"Surrender! Quarter! Quarter!"*

Paul Jones wheeled, snatched a pistol from his belt, and hurled it at the man, knocking him flat. But the cry echoed shrill and the English heard it. Captain Pearson hailed to know if Jones was surrendering.

"No!" John Paul Jones trumpeted back. "I HAVE NOT YET BEGUN TO FIGHT!"

The battle roared on—impossibly, incredibly, against all odds. *Richard* should have sunk long ago. She should have struck long ago. But the shattered vessel with the undaunted captain fought harder than ever, hitting *Serapis* with bullets, canister, grapeshot, grenades. The enemy staggered under this fusillade. Her mainmast was cracking. Her gun crews began to wilt. It was *Serapis*, now, who looked done in.

And suddenly a ship loomed through the smoke off *Richard's* beam. At last! *Alliance!* The Americans set up a wild cheer. Then the cheer was drowned by a tremendous roar from *Alliance's* guns—a terrific broadside that boomed like the thunder of cataclysm. THAT BROADSIDE WAS AIMED AT THE *BONHOMME RICHARD!* The blast lifted Jones' ship almost out of the sea. And when the riddled hulk settled back, only one thing alone seemed to keep her afloat. The unsinkable spirit of John Paul Jones!

Weeping in rage, the Americans saw treacherous Landais sail coolly off—no doubt that he had tried to sink Paul Jones. On top of this disaster, one of *Richard's* terrorized crew released the English prisoners in the forepeak, and they came pouring up out of a hatch like wildmen, convinced *Richard* was going down.

She was going down. Paul Jones sprang at the rioters with a brace of pistols, shouting, "*Man the pumps. It's your only chance to keep afloat. Serapis is sinking, too!*"

Richard Dale, at Jones' elbow drove the prisoners to the task— the ruse worked. To *Serapis'* captains it must have seemed a nightmare, for the ship he had reduced to wreckage went on fighting like a bloody spectre.

Discouragement took *Serapis'* crew. Clinging high in *Richard's* rigging, Yankee snipers kept up a deadly fire that drove the enemy tars from their guns. Sharpshooters began swinging over into *Serapis'* crosstrees. One of Jones' sailors, a lad named Hands (or Hamilton) crawled out on a yardarm with a bucket of grenades. "*On his own initiative*," as Jones described later, he clung to this hazardous perch .and began flinging his bombs at an open hatchway in *Serapis'* deck far below.

Down the hatch! A grenade struck home, and exploded a cartridge dump on *Serapis'* lower deck. Bam—Bam—Bam! There was a series of terrific blasts as the explosion jumped from gun to gun, setting off one powder box after another. As *Serapis'* gunners rushed topside to escape this holocaust, Jones' boarders swarmed over the rail, attacking with pike and cutlass.

Then while pitched battle raged hand to hand, the Americans were dumbfounded by the sight of *Alliance* circling in again. There could be no mistake. No chance for error. And once more Landais fired point blank at the *Bonhomme Richard*—two broadsides this time!—killing Jones' men right and left.

Unbelievable as was this treachery, its outcome remains one of history's most incredible episodes. For firing at Jones' ship was like shooting at a skeleton. *Alliance's* broadsides went clean through *Richard's* ribs, and some of those cannon balls struck *Serapis*. The English, unaware of Landais' doublecross, thought *Alliance* was shooting at them. Stunned at the prospect of fighting a fresh ship, Captain Pearson called, *"Surrender!"* and with his own hands hauled down *Serapis'* flag. The battle was over. The *Bonhomme Richard* had won.

Rather, it was the Americans who had won. For a ship is no more than the men aboard her, and poor old *Richard* was nothing—a tramp to begin with—a wreck to end with—and so beat up at the last that shortly after her crew was transferred to *Serapis*, she sank like a stone, carrying her flag down with her.

A stone? A monument. A monument to fighting American Navy men—to Seaman Hands (or was it Hamilton?)—to Lieutenant Richard Dale—to Captain John Paul Jones of the American Revolution.

Counter-Blockade

The *Richard-Serapis* battle was the last big sea engagement fought by the American Continental Navy. At the end of 1779 there was little of that navy left. Captains were lacking, crews preferred to sail on money-making privateers; there was no money for building new vessels, and such warships as remained were badly handled.

Bungling was inevitable. For the Continental Navy was a body without a head. No Commander-in-Chief had been appointed after the dismissal of old Esek Hopkins, and the Marine Committee was a political, not a military headquarters. Typical result was the fantastic beaching of John Paul Jones.

Colors flying, he headed captured *Serapis* for France, then was forced by a North Sea storm to make port in Holland. There, at the Texel, he rushed dispatches to Paris, describing the treachery of Captain Landais and demanding Landais' court-martial.

Alliance had meantime returned to L'Orient, and Landais' own junior officers had written to the American Commission, reporting their French captain a megalomanic unfit for a command. Benjamin Franklin promptly ordered Landais ashore and demanded Paul Jones be put in command of *Alliance*.

When Jones finally brought *Serapis* down-coast to France, he found himself an international hero. He was knighted by the King of France, who presented him a sword. Paris cheered him to its rooftops. And the Continental Congress in America awarded him a vote of thanks.

But when he took command of *Alliance*, it was to find Franklin's order countermanded. By whom? By Mr. Arthur Lee! Franklin had left Paris, and this Arthur Lee, this loud-talker, had been "got to" by Pierre Landais. Wherefore Commissioner Lee decided that since Landais had been made captain of *Alliance* by the Continental Congress in America, only that distant authority could remove Landais. So Landais was returned by Mr. Lee to *Alliance's* quarterdeck, with orders to sail her to America. And John Paul Jones was stranded.

He argued. Appealed. Wrote letters that almost burned up the dispatch bags. First he'd lost command of *Ranger* to a mutineer. Now he was beached in favor of a zany who had nearly blown *Richard* to pieces.

It was no consolation to learn that Landais, sailing *Alliance* to America, went raving insane and had to be confined by his officers. Yes, Landais reached Boston a blithering lunatic—which explains his ghastly conduct during the *Serapis* battle. But it didn't get Paul Jones his ship.

For months Jones waited around Paris, a celebrity to the French, a bane to the American Commission. But he finally obtained the little 20-gun sloop, *Ariel*, and raced for America. The Marine Committee had promised him command of the battleship *America* when she was finished, and he'd never forgotten that promise. He sailed into Philadelphia, his heart high.

Philadelphia roared welcome. The Continental Congress received him with honors. But he didn't get *America*. Just as she was ready to sail, Fate struck him a final blow. A French warship was lost off Boston. So the Continental Congress voted to give the new battleship to the King of France.

There was no other ship for John Paul Jones. He was stranded throughout the remainder of the war, and at its close he took sail for Europe where he volunteered in the Russian Navy.

Now a word on behalf of the French—don't confuse them with crazy Landais. With the American Continental Navy petering out, the French fleet was coming over to smash the Royal Navy's blockade just in the nick.

Merely the threat of French aid had forced the Red Coats to withdraw from Philadelphia in the spring of 1778. Washington had tried to trap the Red Coat army as it retreated overland across Jersey, falling on its flank at Monmouth. The Red Coats took a thrashing, but managed to escape the trap.

Monmouth was the last major land battle in the north, the enemy concentrating thereafter on Virginia and the Carolinas. There they met up with such hardy characters as Marion the Swamp Fox, Nathaniel Greene, and Lighthorse Harry Lee. These patriots and their men fought delaying actions, giving French aid a chance to arrive.

Meantime the American Continental Navy made a few more tries. In September 1779, Dudley Saltonstall took a fleet up the Penobscott in Maine to attack a British supply base. Against advice of his officers, he dropped anchor and delayed attack. Next day, a British squadron arrived to defend the base. Whereupon Saltonstall ran his ships aground and burned them without firing a shot. He was summarily court-martialled.

At Charleston the following year four American warships—*Providence, Boston, Queen of France, Ranger*—were trapped in the harbor, and surrendered helplessly.

Three large Federal ships remained to the Americans—*Saratoga, Trumbull,* and *Confederacy*. *Saratoga* foundered at sea in 1781. *Confederacy*, under Captain Seth Harding, ran into *H.M.S. Roebuck* and *H.M.S. Orpheus* down in the West Indies. Harding was compelled to surrender. And *Trumbull,* commanded by James Nicholson lost her canvas in a tremendous battle off the Delaware Capes with *H.M.S. Iris* and *H.M.S. General Monk*. This time Nicholson was captured—ship, pants, and all.

So the Revolutionary Navy faded out of the picture like ships drifting away in evening fog.

Four great sea captains deserve further mention. These were Wickes, Barry, Conyngham, and Barney. Although they served on and off in the Federal Navy, they won greatest fame as Revolutionary privateers.

Lambert Wickes was the captain who ran the blockade to take Benjamin Franklin to France. Later, as a raider, he took many a merchantman from England.

Barry, after losing *Raleigh*, went out on a privateer and harried British shipping all the way across the Atlantic. In the last days of the war he commanded *Alliance*, replacing Landais. Cruising as a raider, he captured a half dozen enemy vessels, including the sloops *Atlanta* and *Trepassy*.

Gustavus Conyngham, another Irish-born patriot, took his privateer, *Revenge*, on all kinds of excursions. Sailing in and out of French, Spanish, and Portuguese ports, Conyngham captured over sixty enemy merchantmen. These prizes paid the costs of the American diplomatic missions in Europe throughout the war.

As for Joshua Barney, his record reads like a magazine adventure serial. He, you remember, was the naval lieutenant who tried to save *Virginia* after Nicholson ran her aground in the Chesapeake. The British captured him, then released him in a prisoner exchange—to their regret.

At once Barney signed aboard a big privateer, *Pomona*. After she crossed to France and back, capturing two rich prizes, Barney reentered the Federal service as lieutenant on the new sloop, *Saratoga*. Down to the West Indies, and *Saratoga* captured a big, armed Indiaman, *Charming Molly*. Josh Barney was made captain of this vessel. Heading north, *Molly* ran into a tropical hurricane, the same storm that sank *Saratoga*. While Barney fought to keep his prize afloat, a British battleship took him captive.

He was sent to England on a convict ship, and, after a grim voyage, was jailed in Old Mill Prison at Plymouth. Barney tunneled out. Aided by the English underground (there were many Englishmen in sympathy with the American cause) he secured a British naval uniform and a fishing boat. With two other Yankees, he set out for France.

They were skimming on their way when—thunderation!—they were stopped by a big British privateer. Her skipper hailed to know Barney's business. "Nobody's business!" said Barney, standing bold in his British epaulets. "I sail on secret mission for the King!" But the privateer captain demanded papers, and insisted the fishing smack put back to Plymouth.

At Plymouth Barney escaped ashore, and lay hidden for three weeks in a garret. From there the underground sneaked him to London, and he obtained a passenger ship to the Netherlands. On the Channel crossing, he offered first aid to a seasick lady, who repaid him by inviting him to call on her in Brussels. Barney called, and found himself having tea with European royalty—including Emperor Joseph of Austria!

With this sort of luck, he was soon sailing for Spain where he caught a Yankee privateer, Boston-bound. So he reached America after two years absence. It sounds like Hollywood, but it's history.

These raiders did much to convince George III's War Office that the American Revolution was more than it could down. The supply lines to America were 3,000 miles long, and some 500 Yankee privateers were on the Atlantic by 1781, chopping at these lines. Upwards of 450 merchantmen were on Britain's missing list. With Barneys, Barrys, and Conynghams all over the sea, the Royal Navy had to loosen its blockade of the American coastline to obtain ships for convoy duty.

French sea power, then, was the telling blow. And as a cincher, French Foreign Minister Vergennes induced Spain and Holland to come in as America's allies. While Dutch and Spanish squadrons attacked in the West Indies, the French fleet sailed to Chesapeake Bay to blockade the Red Coats in Virginia.

It was too much for Lord Cornwallis, trying to hold the Yorktown peninsula. Baffled by George Washington, who'd fooled him with a brilliant feint in the direction of New York, Cornwallis found himself facing Washington and Lafayette landward, with the sea at his back. His lordship expected Red Coat reinforcements by sea. Instead, French Admiral de Grasse sailed over the horizon, plus Admiral Rochambeau with 6,000 French troops.

American land and French naval forces attacked with beautiful team-work, and with De Grasse sealing up the Chesapeake, the Red-Coat goose was cooked. George Washington did it to a turn. After a desperate, losing battle, Cornwallis surrendered.

It was October 19, 1781. The Americans had won their independence. Their new Ship of State was launched.

It took everything America could muster to keep the Ship of State afloat. During the ten years following the Revolution, the Americans did not have a Navy. The country was burdened with war debts, and there was no money to build warships as an escort for the Ship of State. Besides, many early Americans considered a navy a bid for colonial expansion, a means for undemocratic conquest. Others pointed to the poor showing of the Continental Navy, which had lost every one of its ships through mismanagement or disaster.

But President George Washington, captaining the new Ship of State, and John Adams, his executive officer, knew that a navy was vitally necessary. Wars might come, piratical attacks from overseas aiming to drive the new republic from its democratic course. The place to stop such attacks was on the sea. Never give the pirates a chance to board. America must have a navy escort.

It takes time to build such a navy, and there were those at the start who resisted the new plan. During the 1780's John Paul Jones wasn't there.

He had entered the Russian Navy to serve Catherine the Great. Three times the country of his choice had passed him over for the like of Thompson, Nicholson, mutinous Simpson, and crazy Landais. Now Empress Catherine offered to make him admiral —Catherine who posed as liberal defender of Holy Russia in a war against the invading Turk.

Crusader at heart, Jones headed for St. Petersburg, traveling through Scandinavia in arctic weather and making an incredible passage across the Gulf of Finland in an open boat. A story in itself, this wild voyage—Jones sitting in the stern sheets with pistol and compass on knee, ordering the terrified boatmen to row him through night and blizzard over a sea of tumbling water and plunging icebergs.

He arrived in Catherine's court to find her a tyrant worse than Cleopatra, for this was Czarist Russia, brutal and backward beyond imagination. True to contract, he took over a ratty fleet in the Black Sea, and by genius alone beat the Turks in the Battle of the Niemen.

By this feat he won the enmity of one-eyed Count Potemkin,

Catherine's Prime Minister and special favorite. This cancerous character, jealous of Jones from the start, conspired to undermine the victorious admiral. Promising Jones command of the Baltic fleet, he sent him to Petrograd, and had him smeared in a scandal —so obvious a frame-up that even the Russian magistrates dismissed the charge.

But to a man as sincere and square-cut as Paul Jones, this trickery was the last straw. There was no honor in Catherine's service, and he was glad to return to France.

He reached Paris in 1790. The French Revolution was on. Franklin had returned to America, old friends were scattered, others dead. In Russia, Jones had corresponded with Thomas Jefferson, who had encouraged him to hope for another commission in the American Navy. But the navy was now disbanded.

There was no job for a sailor. Jones felt himself a shadow on the sidelines. Gouverneur Morris, the new American Minister,

snubbed him. Paul Jones was tired, low in spirit, ill—he had never quite recovered from that desperate trip across the Gulf of Finland.

On July 18th, 1792, he was found lying across his bed with his feet braced on the floor. John Paul Jones died with his boots on.

The French Revolution stormed in Paris, and the lonely naval captain was buried—and forgotten?

Not quite.

Little by little his story became known. As the years went by his genius became acknowledged. His ideas were incorporated in the American Navy's structure. His principles of leadership became fundamentals—standards to be met by every American naval officer.

Still, outside the Navy, he remained in strange obscurity. A century after his death he was only a vague legend in schoolbooks, a vague name to the general public. Fate seemed determined to bury him. Other Continental captains were publicly glorified. As late as 1900 Congress was urged to erect a monument to "The Father of the American Navy." The name proposed was not Jones.

Militarily he stood head and shoulders above the other Continental captains, the only one who never lost a battle or a ship. And one of the few who never sailed a privateer for profit, never faced a naval court of inquiry.

So at last he emerged from obscurity to take his rightful place in the Navy's history.

In 1905, at the instigation of President Theodore Roosevelt, a search was made for Jones' grave by the American Ambassador in Paris, General Porter. Historians provided valuable clues, and after careful investigation, the grave was located in the old Protestant Cemetery of St. Louis. Excavations were made, and there, in a forgotten corner of Paris, the body was found in a lead coffin.

In July, 1905, a squadron of American warships brought the captain home to the United States. Today he lies in the Chapel of the Naval Academy of Annapolis. Fitting resting place for John Paul Jones, who who answered the hail to surrender with—

"I HAVE NOT YET BEGUN TO FIGHT!"

Pirates!

The old 'Frisco waterfront used to be called the Barbary Coast. It was a rugged neighborhood where a sailor could get himself shanghaied for the price of a dime, and it was worth your weight in blackjacks to walk down an unlighted alley. The rookeries swarmed with rats and racketeers ready to slug the unwary seaman and deprive him of his pay. Honest mariners steered clear of the place, and greenhorns learned of it too late as the home of Mickey Finns and huggermuggery.

But this 'Frisco tenderloin didn't hold a candle to the original after which it was named. Long before 'Frisco was ever heard of, the original Barbary Coast was going full blast, doing a holiday business in murder and piracy along the shores of the Mediterranean.

The Barbary Coast

Look at your map of the Mediterranean and you'll see Morocco, Algiers, Tunis, and Tripoli lying on the North African coast. Your Navy was in there making headlines in 1942, you may recall. But that isn' the first time those ports were put in headlines by the U. S. Navy.

Allied together, Tripoli, Tunis, Algiers, and Morocco were known as the Barbary States, each under command of a pirate chief. Of course, they didn't call themselves pirate chiefs—big

racketeers always prefer some high-sounding name. So, translated into the Arabic lingo, there was the Bashaw of Tripoli, the Sultan of Morocco, and that "exalted personage," the Dey of Algiers. And these Barbary pirates became the terror of the Mediterranean.

They owned large fleets of fast ships manned by fierce-whiskered, turbanned corsairs who knew every hide-away along the shore and would rather fight than eat. They would lie in wait for some square-rigged merchantman and pounce on the prize like wolves on a lamb. Millions of dollars in rich cargo fell to these voracious highjackers. Captured sailors who failed to produce ransom were sold into slavery or put to death by torture.

Then the pirates cooked up a new idea—make the maritime nations pay yearly tribute, in which case their ships could go unharmed. This was nothing more or less than the "protection" racket as practiced by the modern gangster—pay up, or else! The maritime nations groaned at the squeeze, but they paid.

England paid, and Spain paid. Italy, Portugal, Holland, and Sweden paid. It became a sort of tradition, this paying the pirates for safe passage through the Mediterranean, and the Europeans forked over as a matter of course.

But when it came America's turn, the payments weren't made quite so gracefully. Uncle Sam was trying to break away from European traditions and set up some new democratic ideas of his own. This traditional tribute to the Barbary pirates struck the Yankees as a hard pill to swallow, and the first American Congress protested long and loud.

Nevertheless, Uncle Sam had to take the pill. It may surprise you to hear about it today, but the fact is that Uncle Sam swallowed large doses of this Barbary blackmail for quite a time, coughing up a lot of tribute and ransom money to these grinning racketeers.

Good American dollars collected from hard-working American people were paid through the nose so American ships could sail the Mediterranean unmolested. It was a swell racket while it lasted, and it lasted until it was cleaned up. In the case of 'Frisco's Barbary Coast, there were the Vigilantes. In the case of North Africa's pirates, there was your Navy—

But here's the story.

The Protection Racket

When the first ransom notes came along, America was just recovering from the Revolutionary War. The nation was struggling to get started on its feet, and (mark this) the "Navy of the United Colonies" was disbanded. Most of the Revolutionary captains were retired. The two remaining warships were sold. And John Paul Jones had gone over to fight for Russia.

This left the United States WITHOUT ANY NAVY AT ALL! Between 1785 and 1793 American sea-power was at its lowest ebb. It couldn't go any lower. It was zero.

In 1785 Spain signed a treaty with the Algerians permitting them to operate in the Straits of Gibraltar. The ink was hardly dry before they'd captured two American merchantmen and sold the luckless crews into slavery. In due time the American Government received the ransom note. Then, instead of despatching some G-men warships to  deal with the kidnappers, all it could do was send an envoy.

This sort of thing went on for the next eight years. And

President George Washington couldn't do anything about it. Burdened with war debts and stewing with home politics, the nation didn't feel it could afford a Navy. The poor showing of the Revoluntionary Navy didn't sit well in memory, either. Besides, many Americans thought the best thing to do was ignore international relations. So the Government tried to buy off the extortionists.

The trouble in dealing with blackmailers is that they always jack up the ante. When they saw Algiers collecting from Uncle Sam, Tunis, Morocco, and Tripoli climbed on the bandwagon. Tripoli, for instance, demanded—and got—a treaty guaranteeing upwards of $20,000 yearly tribute and an annual donation to the Bashaw of a few extra grand. Immediately the other Barbary States demanded more.

In 1793 the corsairs had a banner year. That year Portugal framed a treaty allowing the pirates to extend their activities into the North Atlantic. Within a month eleven Yankee sailing ships were highjacked, their crews enslaved and up for ransom.

In 1794 Uncle Sam paid $800,000 tribute to the Barbary States. That was enough for the American people. In particular it was enough for Vice President John Adams, who'd been hitting the ceiling every time a ransom note arrived. The nation needed some warships to handle this piratical situation. John Adams, who'd done it once, set out to do it again.

Pretty soon six frigates were a-building in the American yards, and the builder of those frigates was one of the greatest ship-designers of all time—a Philadelphia Quaker named Joshua Humphreys. Did he build good ships? Well, one of those warships is still afloat. Her name, *Constitution*. You can see her in Boston Navy Yard to this day.

She was 175 feet long, 180 feet tall in the mainmast, with cleaner lines, thicker sides, and stouter spars than the conventional frigate. Armed with 44 guns she slid down the ways at Boston on September 20, 1797.

Her sister ships *United States* (44 guns) and *Constellation* (36) had been launched at Philadelphia and Baltimore some weeks before.

Word of this American naval program made the Barbary Pirates laugh. Only the year previous, Algiers had hooked the

United States on a pledge to pay $22,000 annual tribute and a large cash ransom for kidnapped seamen in the bargain. That year the Algerians tapped the American cash-box for over one million dollars.

Spent on warships instead of blackmail, this money could have armed a squadron to blow Barbary off the map. Now the three frigates were enough for John Adams. Elected President the year they were launched, he decided that good ships must have good men. And while they were at it, they might as well build a good, sound Navy.

Trouble with the old Revolution Navy had been lack of a head—poor leadership—every captain for himself—hang-dog crews, undisciplined, underpaid, and underfed. Beginning at the top, Adams campaigned for a Navy Department and a Secretary who should sit in the President's cabinet. On April 30, 1798, the Navy Department was organized, and Benjamin Stoddert, a patriotic business man, became the first Secretary of the Navy.

At the other end Adams set out to enlist sturdy recruits and trained seamen. The merchant service offered $10 a month, so Adams urged the Navy to offer $15. Prospective recruits were allowed to go aboard ship and look the situation over. Shanghai-ing was out, and a good ration list was assured. The American Navy would have the best-paid, best-fed sailors on the sea.

As for officers, John Paul Jones had outlined the requirements. There would be no more "politicking" and squabbling over prizes. From here on out the Navy would be a national arm serving the people of America, and the officers would serve accordingly.

John Barry, the Revolutionary veteran. Samuel Nicholson (brother of James who lost his pants). Silas Talbot. James Sever. Richard Dale. Thomas Truxtun. These were chosen to command the six new frigates.

However, much of this was on paper, only three of the frigates were completed, and the Barbary Coast was still going strong when Uncle Sam had trouble with some other international relations. The argument grew heated in the Caribbean, and the relations in this case were French.

Shortly after the American Revolution, the French people staged their own revolution. Unfortunately the nation became involved in a war with England, the government became a dictatorial Directory and the French Foreign Secretary was a foxy character named Talleyrand. In 1797 the Directory issued a proclamation classing all Americans found aboard British vessels as pirates. It also announced that any American ship which refused to hand over a list of the crew would be seized.

President Adams sent envoys to Paris to discuss the matter. Talleyrand refused to see them unless they agreed to a little private cash exchange plus a sizeable American "loan" to the French Directory. Whereupon the American envoys said, "Nothing doing," and took the next ship home to America. In Paris the French go-betweens were referred to as X, Y, and Z. So the episode became known as the XYZ Affair.

The Americans wanted no part of this alphabet soup cooked up by Monsieur Talleyrand. The "loan" involved smelled too much like a shakedown. Rallying 'round the cry, *"Millions for defense, but not one cent for tribute,"* angered Yankees went all out for the Navy program.

President (44), *Congress* (38), and *Chesapeake* (38) were rushed along in the shipyards. Seaports were a-shout with sailors crowding in to volunteer. Shippers donated all sorts of craft to the Government. Overnight the new Navy grew from infant to stripling, almost bursting out of its jeans.

War with the reactionary French Directory looked close. But Americans still remembered Lafayette. American sympathy had been with the French people during their revolution. So Congress refused to declare war when French privateers began to chase Yankee merchantmen through the West Indies. However, the new U. S. Navy was sent out to police the area, and the first new warship on the job was *Constellation* under Captain Thomas Truxtun.

A Jamaica, Long Islander, this gray old sea-dog had served a long apprenticeship on the briny. Ran away to sea at twelve—refused a mid's berth in the Royal Navy—shipped all over the globe on merchant vessels—captained two privateers in the Revolution. This was his first command on a naval vessel, but he was as nautical as a sextant, and the Navy couldn't have commissioned a better man.

Bowling down to the Leeward Islands, he ran a taut ship. There was some trouble over the water ration, and the crew began to mutter. Several men loafed around. Truxtun cut the ration further, and some sea-lawyer muttered mutiny. So the Old Man lined Marines along the quarter-deck, piped all hands, read the Rules for the Regulation of the Navy (as set down by John Adams). Those, Truxtun said, were the rules aboard *Constellation*. Thus far no man aboard had been up for punishment, but every man would get it if those rules weren't obeyed. That was that.

The rules were obeyed, and a few days later the men received full rations. Every seaman in the foc'sle agreed the Old Man was fair, and there were no more mutters of mutiny under Truxtun. Perhaps it was because he dealt the same discipline to his junior officers. Impatient at the rules, a number of these determined to resign in the first port. Go head, said Truxtun, the new Navy doesn't want you. But he held one sulky mid, young David Porter, and bawled the daylights out of him. Didn't he want to stay in the Navy and become a real officer? Porter did.

Tough discipline, but square. No favors for officer or man. That was Truxtun's way. And by the time *Constellation* reached the Leewards her crew was as full of spirit as a shaker full of salt. *"With these officers and men,"* a lieutenant wrote home, *"I should feel happy to go alongside the best 50-gun ship of the conquering French."*

It wasn't a 50-gunner, but it was 36-gun *Insurgente* who came sailing over the horizon one morning off Nevis. February 9,

1799, on the calendar, 1500 on the clock when *Constellation* overhauled her.

For answer to Truxtun's hail, the other frigate ran up the French flag. For answer to that, Truxtun gave her a thundering broadside. At once the two ships were at it hammer and tongs, the French gunners aiming at *Constellation's* rigging. One shot shattered *Constellation's* top-foremast. A ton of canvas threatened to rip loose and carry the mast overside. It was David Porter who climbed aloft through a rattle of enemy sniper-fire to cut away the halyards, secure the plunging sail, and save the mast.

Hit hard by the Yankee gunners, *Insurgente* lost her mizzen-topmast and head-sail. Her guns were blown from their mountings, her decks raked into rubbish. Seventy Frenchmen lay dead or wounded and Truxtun had lost only three when *Insurgente's* captain surrendered. Lieutenant John Rodgers and Midshipman David Porter were sent to board the French captive and take her into St. Kitts.

Capture of *Insurgente* was a great victory for the new Navy, and the fame of *Constellation* and her crew went high as the stars. But in Paris Monsieur Talleyrand learned nothing from the lesson-book. The French privateers continued their raids. So the young U. S. Navy did some more policing.

Down the Gulf Stream John Barry took a lively squadron: frigates *United States* and *Constitution*, four corvettes, and a couple of revenue cutters. In a year's cruise the squadron captured a dozen small French privateers.

Down the Gulf Stream also sailed a little schooner-rigged cruiser named *Enterprise*, under Lieutenant John Shaw. In the skirmish with French sea power she proved so enterprising that she captured eighteen privateers and rescued eleven merchantmen before the trouble was over.

Other American naval vessels also gave a good account of themselves. And finally *Constellation* and Truxtun did it again. Evening of February 1, 1800. Not far from the spot where they'd taken *Insurgente*. Lookout reported, "Sail ho!" Truxtun crowded on the canvas. The stranger was overhauled, and the wish for a 50-gunner came true. She was French—named *Vengeance*—52 guns!

A lot tougher than *Insurgente*, she didn't wait for a hail, but opened fire with stern guns roaring. Truxtun held his fire until the range was point blank. Then he gave the Frenchman a broadside that staggered her in the water.

Beam to beam the ships raced along, hitting each other with everything they had. Truxtun ordered his gunners to take good aim and fire with precision, and before long *Vengeance* should have changed her name to *Regret*. But *Constellation* was hard hit, too. In the thick of it she lost the shrouds to her mainmast. High in the crosstrees, young James Jarvis, a midshipman, refused to come down when a sailor warned him of the danger. *"My post is here. I can't leave it until ordered."* The mainmast crashed overside. Jarvis went with it. With that sort of spirit aboard her, *Constellation* couldn't lose.

In fact, *Vengeance* had already struck her colors. But in the dark and battle-smoke the Americans failed to see it. So when *Constellation's* mainmast crashed, the beaten French frigate veered off in the night and escaped. Days later she staggered into Curacao and ran up on the beach, a shattered wreck, reporting 160 battle casualties. No

Constellation hobbled into Jamaica with 39 casualties. No casualty to her fighting spirit, however. *"Why,"* one of her jubilant officers wrote, *"we would put a man to death for looking pale aboard this ship."* A bit of swashbuckling, of course, but typical of the spunk inspired by Thomas Truxtun.

So Truxtun inspired the new Navy—set it a standard of leadership and discipline on the foundation laid by John Paul Jones. And incidentally ended the argument with France. Talleyrand had lost enough of it. And Napoleon Bonaparte, coming into power just then, decided he'd rather try to conquer all of Europe than take on the little Republic overseas.

And now Uncle Sam, his sleeves rolled up, was ready for those Barbary pirates.

The Tripolitan War

"A huge, shabby beast, sitting on his rump upon a low bench with his hind legs gathered up like a tailor or a bear, who extended his forepaw as if to receive something to eat." So Captain William Bainbridge, USN, sent to North Africa

115

with the yearly installment, described the Dey of Algiers. The Dey's name was Ali Baba, and he couldn't have been better named. For in 1800 (at the close of the French trouble) this zoo-like specimen was extending his forepaw for a bigger yearly tribute and a bonus of something like $200,000.

What's more, he got it. Uncle Sam hadn't quite settled up accounts with the French, and it wasn't yet time to send a bill-adjustor to Ali Baba.

But then the rest of the Forty Thieves became dissatisfied. Especially the Bashaw of Tripoli. Noting the increased payment to Algiers, the Bashaw stuck out his own bear-paw, demanding a flat $20,000 per year, a bonus of $250,000, and an American-made frigate as a Christmas gift.

The American consul in Tripoli said, "No!" So the American flag was torn down, the flagpole was chopped down to make it permanent, and the consul given 24 hours to pack his bag. Whereupon Uncle Sam decided it was high time to bash down the Bashaw of Tripoli.

Thomas Jefferson, newly elected President, was all for it. He was probably the most un-warlike man in America—a great scholar and great gentleman in the finest sense of the word. Because he disapproved of military imperialism and hoped America could stay home and mind its own business, he was mistaken in some quarters for a pacifist. He feared a large standing army might prove the basis for a military dictatorship, and shortly after taking office he reduced the size of the Navy. This displeased some of the Navy men—particularly some of the older officers who had to swallow the anchor. They failed to notice that only the aged ships were sold, that the new fast frigates were kept along with the new up and coming men. They also forgot that Jefferson had written, *"Naval force can never undermine our liberties."* Along with that he'd declared: *"Tribute or war is the usual alternative of these Barbary pirates. Why not build a navy and decide on war? We cannot begin in a better cause or against a better foe."*

It was May 1801, when the Bashaw chopped down the American consul's flagpole. The Bashaw didn't know it, but the Stars and Stripes were already on the way. They were flown by

frigates *President* and *Philadelphia*, war-sloop *Essex*, and schooner
Enterprise—squadron under command of Richard Dale.

Scouting ahead down the Mediterranean, little *Enterprise* ran
into the corsair warship *Tripoli*. The two vessels were evenly
matched, but the pirates were no match for the American gunners.
After a fierce three-hour battle, the corsairs threw up the sponge
with 51 casualties. Aboard *Enterprise* not a single man was
killed or wounded!

Unfortunately Tripoli, itself, was not as soft a customer. Pushing forward to lay seige. Dale found his squadron up against
a city of stone walls and ugly fortifications, the harbor bristling
with land batteries and fleets of armed Arab feluccas. Out-
gunned and held at distance, the American squadron sat down

on blockade. The Tripolitans also sat. For a year the stalemate went on, then Dale had to take the squadron home as the seamen had ended their year's enlistment.

Meanwhile Congress (on February 6, 1802) had declared war on Tripoli. Determined to push it, the Navy Department gave the Mediterranean squadron to Captain Richard Morris with sailors on two-year enlistment.

Constellation, Chesapeake, New York, John Adams, Enterprise, and *Boston* headed for Tripoli, but the cruise became a bungle. *New York's* powder magazine exploded. Maintenance and repair were neglected aboard the other frigates. *Enterprise* and *John Adams* demolished one corsair vessel, but Tripoli remained on the map, so Morris was sternly recalled. The Bashaw needed a thrashing, and the Navy needed a man who could dish it out. Truxtun had resigned and retired. Where to find a man like Truxtun?

He was there on the Navy Department's list—a man named Preble.

Meet Captain Preble

He was born in Maine where there's a salt tang to the breeze. At 14, he was at sea as a midshipman on a letter-of-marque. After the Revolution, he entered the merchant service. He was a captain, a master mariner at the age of 23, when he accepted the offer of a Naval commission as a lieutenant aboard *Constitution.*

That gives you some clue to the man's character—it's not easy to be master of your own ship and then sign up to serve as lieutenant on another. And in those days merchant captains were founding fortunes in the shipping trade. A Naval lieutenant earned something like $30 a month, while a captain, the highest rank commissioned, was paid around $60 a month—less than a seaman 1/c draws today. True, money stretched farther in those days, but it didn't stretch that far. When Preble reported for duty aboard *Constitution* he must have been thinking of just two things—serving his country and the Navy.

There were no easy berths aboard *Constitution.* Sam Nicholson, first captain, was a moody man, and there was trouble aboard. nant Preble stayed out of it, keeping his mind fixed on

French privateers. He'd heard of Truxtun's record, of course, and he determined to set his own course "according to Truxtun."

It was hard training, self imposed—and there you have Edward Preble. He learned to rule himself. He learned to be ruled. And he learned how to rule other men.

He was given to storms of temper which he had to fight—he was high-strung, over-quick. You never know the private struggles that go on within a man, but from Preble's record you can judge that he must have had to grip himself with an iron hand.

You see the portrait of a hatchet-faced man with frosty eyes. You read of him as a "driver" who introduced "iron discipline" in the Navy. But if he was strict with his men he was no more easy on himself. He never expected his men to do what he couldn't do himself, which is one of the first precepts of great leadership. And here's another mark of greatness. On occasion when he, himself, was wrong (as you'll see), he was fair enough to admit it, which is an indication of a pretty big man.

When you can discipline yourself to that extent you're in a position to ask discipline of others.

Navy Regs

"Vinegar face!"

"Ramrod up his back, that's what he's got."

"Cut out our grog ration yesterday. A slave driver on the quarterdeck. He ain't human!"

Preble's sailors complained. So did the junior officers in the wardroom, youngsters resentful of the iron hand.

"Drill, drill, drill. Gunnery practice and more drill. All we get aboard this ship is discipline!"

Well, it's a sailor's privilege to gripe, and you can suspect that Preble's boys made the most of it. Just as today, they weren't head over heels in love with discipline.

You hear a lot about discipline before, when, and after you enter the naval service. Today you get it in indoctrination lectures, pamphlets, private advice, and Navy Regs. You think of rules and orders and penalties—paragraphs listed "1a, 2a, 3a." Sometimes it's sugar coated, and sometimes it lands on you with both feet. It brings up thoughts of punishments and restrictions. DISCIPLINE—a ten-letter word meaning pain in the neck.

But wait a minute. Take a little time out, as Preble did, and examine this business of discipline. It's not as painful in the neck as shark teeth—or an enemy bullet—or a pirate's scimitar. Good discipline could save a sailor from such things.

You can't do anything in life without learning how to do it first, and the effort to learn anything at all takes discipline. A baby gets it learning to walk—from bumps. Those bumps are Nature's way of teaching it to stand on its own feet. That's discipline. A kid gets it in school. He either learns his ABC's, or he doesn't acquire the "know-how" and gets disciplined later by ending up without a job. Education and skill pay dividends. Ignorance and inability invite poverty—the toughest kind of discipline.

Discipline runs all the way through the pattern of life—whether you like it or not, there it is. Eat too much, and you get sick (discipline). Drink too much, and you'll get sicker (more discipline). You can't beat Nature's laws and get away with it, any more than you can beat such axioms as "Practice makes perfect." And "Crime doesn't pay."

The cop on the corner represents another form of discipline. But if you didn't have him there you'd have pickpockets and traffic jams. This brings up the point that discipline is reciprocal —it's for your own benefit as well as the other man's. The traffic signal that holds you up at one corner makes it safe for you to gallop through the next. Agreed?

Discipline in Nature—discipline in civilian life—it's nothing new or extraordinary when you enter the Navy. But the rules and regulations are somewhat stiffer in the Navy than in civilian life because the natural laws of the sea are somewhat stiffer than those on land. You can't beat a storm without "know-how." You can't argue with wind and tide.

The ship has to obey the laws of the sea, or it's a goner. And the men have to obey the rules of seamanship to make the ship obey. Seamanship means team-work—for on shipboard, more than anywhere else, you're all in the same boat. Add the hazard of warfare, and team-work is doubly necessary. It

can't be "every man for himself" when it takes ten to serve
a gun. You must row in unison, sailor, or your oar will catch
a crab. You know what a losing stroke can mean if there's a
batch of Barbary pirates after you in a felucca. You don't regret

that boat drill when you're in a race with Old Skull and Crossbones. You're mighty glad you're in a well-trained crew with
a cox'n who knows his stuff.

Discipline—obedience—team-work—that was Truxtun's winning
formula. And Preble had good reason to copy it. During the
Revolutionary War he'd seen sailors jump ship, swim ashore,
and go home to plant their farms in the spring, leaving the ship
short-handed. He'd seen men imperilled by others, who'd deserted
their posts in battle. He'd seen gunners slain in serious accidents
because they lacked training. Many men, lions at heart, were
incapable of team-work in a pinch.

The officers, too, had been of various character and conduct.
Some were sloven, some lackadaisical, others were high-handed
sundowners. Acting independently, often jealous of individual
authority, the old captains had frequently sailed the brink of
disaster. Truxtun had shown the way. If the Navy wanted to
avoid defeat and chaos, it must follow the square discipline of
Truxtun.

So Preble took up where Truxtun left off. Appointed captain
of *Constitution* and commodore of the Mediterranean squadron,
he ran a taut ship. Gunnery practice. Seamanship. Put up sail.
Lower sail. Not a day went by without its quota of rigid exercises and drills.

As he himself toed the mark, so his junior officers and men
toed it too. The squadron got a thorough indoctrination in Navy

RULES

FOR THE

REGULATION

OF THE

NAVY

OF THE

UNITED COLONIES

OF

NORTH-AMERICA;

Eſtabliſhed for Preſerving their RIGHTS
and Defending their LIBERTIES, and
for Encouraging all thoſe who Feel
for their COUNTRY, to enter into its
Service in that way in which they
can be moſt Uſeful.

PHILADELPHIA:

Printed by WILLIAM and THOMAS BRADFORD, 1775.

Regs, and you may think they were pretty severe when you read some of the rules and regulations of that day's Navy.

At the start of the Revolutionary War, back in 1775, these rules and regulations had been sponsored by John Adams and adopted by the Continental Congress. Written by Adams, they were based on the rules at that time governing the British Navy. They were in force when Preble came to command, and here are some of them.

Art. 1. *The Commanders of all ships and vessels (of the U. S. Navy) are strictly required to show in themselves a good example of honor and virtue to their officers and men, and to be very vigilant in inspecting the behavior of all such as are under them, and to discountenance and suppress all dissolute, immoral, and disorderly practices; and also, such as are contrary to the rules of discipline and obedience, and to correct those who are guilty of the same according to the sea.*

Preble, in holding his own conduct to account, was obeying this law as rigidly as when he was *"vigilant in inspecting the behavior"* of his men.

Art. 2. *The Commanders of the ships are to take care that divine service be performed twice a day on board, and a sermon preached on Sundays unless bad weather or other extraordinary accidents prevent it.*

Art. 3. *If any shall be heard to swear, curse, or blaspheme the name of God, the Captain is briefly enjoined to punish them for every offense, by causing them to wear a wooden collar or some other shameful badge of distinction. If he be a commissioned officer he shall forfeit one shilling for each offense, and a warrant or inferior officer, six-pence. He who is guilty of drunkenness (if a seaman) shall be put in irons until he is sober, but an officer shall forfeit two days pay.*

You can imagine the old ships' carpenters were kept pretty busy making wooden collars, and there were probably a lot of pay-forfeits, **too.**

Art. 4. *No Commander shall inflict any punishment beyond twelve lashes upon his back with a cat-o-nine-tails. If the fault shall deserve a greater punishment he is to apply to the Commander-in-Chief of the Navy in order to the trying of him by court-martial, and in the meantime he may put him under confinement.*

Stiff discipline, the "cat." And when the lashes were "well laid on," a dozen could be a tough penalty. But many old tars were as striped as zebras—and proud of it!

Art. 7. *The Captain is to cause the articles of war to be hung up in some public place of the ship, and read to the ship's company once a month.*

So Preble's squadron became well acquainted with the articles.

Art. 26. *When in sight of the ship or ships of the enemy, and at such other times as may appear to make it necessary to prepare for engagement, the Captain shall order all things in his ship in a proper posture for fight, and shall in his own person and according to his duty, hearten and encourage the inferior officers and men to fight courageously, and not to behave faintly or cry for quarter on pain of such punishment as the offense shall appear to deserve.*

Another principle of good leadership, the above—the officer must set his men a good example.

Art. 27. *Any Captain or any officer or mariner or others who shall basely desert their duty or station in the ship and run away while the enemy is in fight, or in time of action, or entice others to do so, shall suffer death or such other punishment as a court-martial shall inflict.*

Preble, reading that law to his men, could remind them of John Paul Jones cracking a craven's head aboard *Richard*, or tell them how young Jarvis of *Constellation* stuck to his post.

Art. 29. *Any officer, seaman or marine who shall begin to excite, or join in any mutiny or sedition in the ship to which he belongs, on any pretence whatsoever, shall suffer death or such other punishment as a court-martial shall order to be inflicted.*

A law as old as the sea—as old as plots and mutineers. As it applied to merchantmen in the beginning, so it must apply to naval vessels—with this difference. Aboard a merchantman, mutineers would be shot by their officers on sight. Aboard a naval vessel, court-martial would inflict death *"or such other punishment"* as might be fairly adjudged.

Art. 30. *None shall presume to quarrel with, or strike his superior officer, on pain of such punishment as a court-martial shall order to be inflicted.*

But—

Art. 31. *If any person shall apprehend he has just cause of complaint, he shall quietly and decently make the cause known to his superior officer, or to the Captain, as the case may require, who will take care that justice be done him.*

Fair enough, those early Americans!

Art. 33. *If any person shall sleep upon his watch, or negligently perform the duty which shall be enjoined him to do, or forsake his station, he shall suffer such punishment as a court-martial shall think proper to inflict.*

For a sleeper endangered the lives of his shipmates—and so did a man who left his station. The law must be stern, accordingly. In the early days of the British Navy the guilty man was hung in a basket off the bowsprit, "with a can of beer, a loaf of bread and a sharp knife, and choose to hang there until he starved or cut himself into the sea."

Art. 34. *All murder shall be punished with death.*

Against the law anywhere.

Art. 35. *All robbery and theft shall be punished at the discretion of a court-martial.*

With special punishment for stealing the ship's equipment.

So the *Rules for the Regulation of the Navy* went on—44 Articles in all. There were some quaint regulations regarding "fishing," "pudding bags," "beef" and other rations. Rules pro-

vided for the care of the sick and wounded, a cooper being instructed to make them wooden buckets. Other regulations concerned living quarters and uniforms.

Have some of these "Navy Regs" of 1800 sounded familiar? Today there are no floggings, wooden collars, and irons, such stern punishments having been ruled out in the 1850's. Other of the old regulations have gone the way of sailing ships and jack tars. But the *Articles for the Government of the Navy* in force today are based on those early laws. Your modern "Navy Regs" include many of them which have come down through the years almost word for word. They are the foundation stones of today's Navy discipline, the articles which you hear called "Rocks and Shoals."

Commodore Preble, entering the Mediterranean, read these laws to his men. Enforcing them, he was considered a hard disciplinarian. But the discipline paid off.

Here's how it paid off.

What Ship Is That?

A moonless night off Gibraltar, the weather going thick, and *Constitution*, wallowing in choppy seas, felt her way through mist.

Suddenly a shadow loomed off the bow. The Yankee lookout had scarcely time to call the warning when a hail came from the stranger out of the dark.

"Ahoy! What ship is that?"

"Ahoy, yourself!" Preble returned. "What ship are you?" Corsairs had hailed in English before, and this might be a ruse.

"You will find out who we are," was the reply, "when you disclose your own identity!"

"You will learn that," Preble retorted, "when you disclose yours." The stranger was drawing abeam, and Preble raised his voice through the speaking trumpet. *"I now hail for the last time. If you do not answer, I'll fire a shot!"*

"If you do I'll answer with a broadside!" came the threat.

"I shall like to see you try that!" Preble challenged. *"I now hail for an answer. What ship is that?"*

A moment's silence tense with the creak of straining cordage and timber, tight as men's nerves. Then—

"This is His Britannic Majesty's 84-gun ship, Donegal. Sir Richard Strachan. Send a boat aboard!"

"This is the United States frigate, Constitution, 44, Captain Edward Preble, and I'll be damned if I'll send a boat aboard any ship! Blow up your matches, boys!"

The boys blew up their matches. It wasn't necessary to fire. A shout informed them *Donegal* was sending over a boat, and she proved to be only a 32-gunner with a very polite captain and crew.

There was talk in *Constitution's* foc's'le after that. Chuckles, grins, and backslapping.

"Say, the Old Man's all right, eh, lads?"

"Wouldn't knuckle under to 84 guns even if the other ship had owned 'em."

"Glory, he ain't afraid of hell or high water!"

The wardroom was equally impressed.

"That wasn't a bluff. He called theirs! Old Preb was ready for a fight!"

The glow of this incident shows Preble in another light—a man unafraid to risk battle. Neither reckless nor trigger-happy, he was rock-firm when it came to a showdown.

He was carrying heavy responsibility lightly when he stood *Constitution's* quarterdeck in command of the Mediterranean squadron. Commodore at the age of 42, appointed over the heads of three senior captains, he had to prove his mettle. For two years the war with the pirates had gone badly. Now not only Preble's reputation was at stake, but the Navy's. The little bi-play at Gibraltar showed the world as well as the wardroom the cut of Preble's jib.

Aboard *Constitution* there was a ring to the yo-heave-ho! Preble had always run a smart ship and a taut ship; now he had a willing ship.

In the squadron besides *Constitution* were the frigates *Philadelphia* and *John Adams*, two 16-gun brigs, two schooners, and famous *Enterprise*. Preble ordered *Philadelphia*, under Captain Bainbridge, on to Tripoli while he stopped in at Tangiers, Morocco, to talk things over with the Sultan.

Surprising how polite these pirates were when you had a well-armed squadron (with decks cleared for action) in the harbor. Preble was wined and dined. For two weeks compliments were exchanged, while the Sultan, one eye on the harbor, assured the American Navy he wanted no difficulty with the U. S. A. When the squadron sailed, loaded down with parrots and Morrish rugs, everything was hunky dory with Morocco.

Over to Gilbraltar for a refit, and Preble sent the frigate *John Adams* back to the States. Then he headed for Tripoli, hoping to join *Philadelphia* at a prearranged rendezvous. But in passing Sardinia, he learned from a British vessel some bad news. To the ears of all Americans, terrible news!

Philadelphia had run afoul in Tripoli harbor. Bainbridge and his Yankee sailors had been captured by the Tripolitan pirates!

Stephen Decatur

There were two brothers, James and Stephen Decatur. The Navy was in their blood. Their father had captained a privateer during the Revolution, and later had been commander of the *Delaware*. Naturally, the boys couldn't wait to "get in."

In 1798 Stephen was a midshipman, and he had his first lieutenant's sword by 1802. He was given command of *Enterprise* in Preble's squadron. In the same squadron, James, a midshipman, commanded one of the gunboats.

Stephen had been in the Mediterranean two years before. He was tall, dark, and handsome, as the girls would have it; and when angered there was a flash like flint on steel in his eye. At Barcelona, while in charge of a shore party, he'd been fired on without warning by a pepper-headed Spanish official attempting to stop his landing boat for a show of papers. Stephen Decatur showed something more than a few flimsy documents when he boarded the harbor vessel next day and demanded to see the captain. When told the captain was ashore, Decatur left his card.

"Inform him that Lieutenant Decatur pronounces him a cowardly scoundrel, and if we meet ashore I will cut his ears off!"

It is on record that the Spaniard preferred to save his ears.

Then at Malta, not many months later, there occurred a more serious encounter. While a company of American sailors was being entertained at a Malta opera, a naval officer was deliberately jostled by the Governor's secretary. When the young midshipman protested, he was jostled again by the comment, *"You Americans will never stand the smell of powder."*

Why is there always some wiseacre in every party who has three beers and tries to start an argument? The offender in this case, obviously in his cups, asked for, and was flattened by, a fist. But the following day he challenged the young midshipman to a duel.

Decatur, a friend of the challenged, volunteered to stand as second. Then, making inquiries, he learned that the Malta secretary was a champion dueller with a long string of kills to his record. Immediately Decatur offered to fight in the midshipman's place. No need. The professional, shaken by Decatur's insistance that the duel be shot out at four paces, lost his aim and missed. A moment later he was a dead man.

For this outcome Decatur was held responsible and officially reprimanded. But as duelling was the code of the day, it was admitted he had seconded the affair with honor.

There were to be no similar affairs under Preble's command. Duelling he counted as a wasteful risk of life. No use training a good man to have him go ashore and be shot down in some futile squabble with a popinjay. No waterfront scrimmages for Preble's sailors, either. The boys should keep their energy in reserve for bigger battles. Be keyed up for serious emergency should one arise.

Such as emergency they were faced with now in 1803—the loss of *Philadephia.*

Philadelphia and Intrepid

Captain Bainbridge was a good officer, worthy of better luck. He had sighted a Tripolitan corsair not far offshore from the pirate city, and had run up sail in hot pursuit. The corsair turned tail for Tripoli harbor, and the American frigate was gaining when she got into a tide rip in uncharted water. No time for soundings—a grinding snarl under her bottom-boards, and *Philadelphia* was on a reef.

Bainbridge tried every trick to get her off, even cut away her foremast to reduce her weight, but she was snagged. Nightfall brought a horde of pirates in small boats howling alongside, circling like Indians around a mired buffalo. Worse luck, the tide went out, leaving Philadelphia listed over on a beam end, her broadside batteries out of action. The small guns could hold out for a while, but they were outnumbered a thousand to one, and help couldn't come for weeks. Bainbridge could only burn the code books and sadly run down the flag.

It was a bitter blow for the Navy, and worse was to come. *Philadelphia* was hardly surrendered when a gale struck the Tripolitan coast and lifted her clear and practically undamaged from the reef. This gave the jubilant pirates a first class frigate to add to their already sizeable fleet. They tied her up in their harbor under guard of a long line of forts, and the Bashaw rubbed his hands in delight. Now let the Americans visit Tripoli!

Preble was on the way. From Sardinia he led his little squadron as fast as canvas could go, bucking the worst winter storms the Mediterranean had known in a century. Green seas combing her decks, her yards frozen, her poles and shrouds made of ice, *Constitution* forged grimly ahead to show the world a little weather couldn't tie up the American Navy.

It was touch and go in the zero gales with men's hands raw on the ropes and a climb to a yardarm worth any sailor's life. How did these Navy men find time to run down and capture a pirate ship in the bargain? Preble chased her down through high water and hell, refusing to let his gunners sink her at a distance. She was a little ketch, and didn't seem worth the effort. So the gunners must have grumbled. But Preble had his own ideas. One of them was to make this rakish craft a tender and christen her *Intrepid*.

Presently Preble signalled Decatur to come aboard his flagship, and the squadron soon knew why the pirate craft had been named *Intrepid*. Carrying her Arab sail, she could enter Tripoli harbor unsuspected. Stephen Decatur was to lead a raiding party to board *Philadelphia*. The frigate was to be blown up where she lay. Preble was calling for volunteers.

The crew of *Constitution* volunteered as one man. So did the crew of Decatur's *Enterprise*. Decatur handpicked eighty-four, and gave them their instructions.

"You'll leave your guns behind you, lads. This is to be a cutlass fight."

February 14, on a night of stillness and moonlight, the *Intrepid* crept into Tripoli harbor, quiet as a cat. Eighty-four Yankee tars, their cutlasses honed like razors, crouched like coiled springs on the raider's deck. At the helm, a Sicilian pilot who knew Tripoli like a book. On the bow, Stephen Decatur with a gleam of battle in his eyes.

"Quiet now, lads. There she is."

Philadelphia, a black silhouette of spars under the moon. Pirate craft moored all around. Pirate shore batteries waiting.

The raider advanced casually, tacking in on the frigate's quarter. The pirate watch aboard *Philadelphia* hailed. *Intrepid's* Sicilian pilot answered boldly, shouting in the Moslem tongue.

"Allah yeseemliq! We are a blockade-runner, my brother, coming in with provisions."

"Allah be praised. Come alongside."

Intrepid sidled in, and the pirates tossed a line. Too late the corsairs leaning over the frigate's taffrail sighted the gleam of steel, the tarred queues of Yankee Navy men.

"Rouni!"

"Board!" Decatur shouted, leading his men in a storm up the frigate's side.

Pikes jabbing, cutlasses a-swing, the Americans poured across *Philadelphia's* quarterdeck, driving two hundred screaming pirates

ahead of them toward the forecastle. Guns flared in the dark. New England blades clashed on scimitars, showering sparks and blood. In a trice, it seemed, the wild battle was over.

While the boarders pinned the frantic Tripolitans against the frigate's bows, a demolition party raced astern with powder kegs and coals. Down to the second deck. Down to the magazine. Fast, now, boys! Touch the fuzes! We're off!

Without the loss of one man, Decatur and his tars were overside and away. Shore batteries opened up on the racing ketch, but she was out of the harbor and down to the sea before the Bashaw of Tripoli could rub the astonishment out of his eyes.

Looking back, the men in the stern sheets cheered. A roar of flame seemed to rise to the moon, and *Philadelphia's* silhouette scattered under the stars.

Hearing about it later, British Admiral Lord Nelson called it, *"the most bold and daring act of the age."*

Decatur and Preble

But the destruction of *Philadelphia* did not release her captain and crew sitting ironed in the Bashaw's dungeons. Through weeks of bad weather in that spring of 1804, Preble and his squadron were on blockade off the coast of Tripoli, immovable as rocks.

Yet the Tripolitan shore batteries were equally immovable. Preble sent his ships in to bombard them, and they did some damage, but his broadside guns could hardly reduce a mile of land batteries, nor could he storm them with sailors outnumbered a hundred to one.

Early summer, with the bombardment continuing as a stalemate, Preble held conference with Decatur. It was planned that *Constitution* would lay down a barrage while a flotilla of gunboats ran in under her fire and engaged the corsair fleet moored under the pirate fortifications.

Action took place on August 3, Decatur leading the gunboat flotilla. The corsairs swarmed out to meet the attack, closing around the Americans so the frigate could not shoot, outnumbering Decatur three to one. Tripolitans and Yankees grappled together in a savage combat as brief as it was bloody. In this fierce pitched battle Decatur's brother, James, commanded one of the smaller gunboats. Feigning surrender, one of the corsair captains came alongside James Decatur's boat, then whipped a pistol from his sash and shot the young midshipman between the eyes.

Decatur, hearing that his brother had been killed, went wild with fury. Ordering his crew to overtake the guilty corsair at all cost, he caught the Tripolitan assassin before the pirate could gain the harbor. Leaping aboard the pirate craft, Decatur was confronted by the corsair leader, huge and crimson-bearded. Decatur hurled himself at this ogre like a madman, dealing such a blow at the corsair's pike that his own cutlass snapped at the hilt. Locked together, the two rolled on the deck, the giant striving to split Decatur's skull with his scimitar. The deadly blow never fell, for a Marine named Frazier wrote his name in history by throwing himself forward to fend the blow with his shoulder. The act undoubtedly saved Decatur's life, giving him a moment to grip the pistol in his pocket and send a bullet crashing into his adversary's gigantic midriff. When Decatur climbed to his feet this dead Goliath, it was to see the Tripolitan gunboats fleeing in panic back to their lair. On the deck around him lay thirty-five pirates, dead.

Grim-jawed, his uniform tattered and scarlet-smeared, Decatur reported to Commodore Preble.

"*I have brought you three of the enemy's gunboats, sir.*"

Preble stood frosty-eyed. Then suddenly stepping forward, he caught and shook Decatur by the collar.

"*Aye, Sir!*" he roared. "*And why did you not bring me more!*" Pivoting on heel, he left Decatur standing white-faced, and marched into his cabin.

Junior officers stared thunderstruck, and crewmen gaped in astonishment even as many historians have been astonished by this incident since. Some like to believe that Preble's outburst was a trick by which he hoped to rouse Decatur from the shock of his brother's death. But a survey of Preble's temperament indicates otherwise. Highstrung, worn with months of strain, it seems likely that for the moment he lost his self control. Within him reared a sudden, irrepressible jealousy—envy of his junior officer, his dash, his youth, the brilliant name he was making.

For a moment Preble had been mastered by the commonest of human failings. But Preble was never a common man. Hardly had he slammed into his cabin when a summons was sent to Decatur.

"*The commodore wishes to see Captain Decatur.*"

Lieutenants and midshipmen gathered near the hatchway, exchanging glances. No sound issued from the commodore's quarters below. Finally someone, uneasy at the silence, knocked at Preble's door and opened it wide. Seated on the cabin bench, arm in arm, were Preble and Decatur. The cheeks of both men were wet with tears.

Preble, who had made a mistake, was a big enough man to apologize for it. In history he remains one of the American Navy's great leaders.

End of Intrepid

Not every victory was easy in the Tripolitan War. Preble kept his squadron firing through most of August, and *Constitution's* practiced gunnery began to score. Some of the harbor fortifications came loose, the city caught some round shot, the minaret over the mosque was brought down, and a cannon ball bounced into the castle and almost knocked out the Bashaw's teeth.

With things growing warm, the Bashaw sent out a message offering to reduce the price on captured American sailors from $1,000 to $500. Preble scorned the offer.

He was backed up now by *John Adams*, newly returned from America with fresh munitions and word that four more battleships were on the way. But the pirates were threatening to slay Bainbridge and his men, and Preble could not wait for these reinforcements.

A new plan of attack was devised, again featuring *Intrepid*. Loaded to the gunwalls with powder, the ketch was to be run into the harbor under cover of night and fog. The pirate ships were moored together like a clutter of sleeping crocodiles. *Intrepid* was to plow in among them, her fuzes sputtering, and blow the entire batch to kingdom come.

Ten volunteers were called for—unmarried men. It was risky business, for the raider would be a floating powder keg demanding a fast get-away. But again the entire squadron volunteered.

Lieutenants Wadsworth and Richard Somers, and Midshipman Israel stepped forward to lead. On the night of September 4, under cover of dark mist, the powder-ship went in. She was gone some time in the gloom when the listening squadron heard a volley of shots, wild shouts. *Intrepid* had not quite entered the harbor when she vanished in a blast of flame. Every American aboard vanished with her.

Reinforcements arrived a week later, and that autumn a land campaign to enter Tripoli by way of Egypt was decided upon. A soldier-of-fortune army was recruited around Cairo, and eventually there was some skirmishing on the Tripolitan border. With his coast blockaded and his border threatened, the Bashaw reduced the price on *Philadelphia's* crew to $300. The Navy did not want to pay this ransom. Not a dime of it. But back home in America, diplomacy seemed the better part of valor —the squadron was needed in the Atlantic, for another storm was brewing. So Captain Bainbridge and his men were finally freed.

In the meantime Preble had been ordered home. The voyage was a naval holiday. In every port *Constitution* was saluted, cheered, and welcomed. In America Preble was presented by Congress with a sword, and President Jefferson offered him a place in his Cabinet. But Preble preferred to remain quietly in the Navy, and of all these recognitions he is said to have cherished most the one presented him in the Mediterraneaen by Decatur.

Picture the scene. Preble is on the quarterdeck of *Constitution.* The other officers and crew crowd around. Decatur steps forward to face Preble.

There they stand—two great naval figures, each knowing the other's capabilities, the other's faults. There is understanding in their eyes.

And then, without a word, Decatur hands over the scroll. In complete silence, Preble reads—

We, the undersigned officers of the squadron late under your command, cannot, in justice, suffer you to depart without giving you some small testimony of the very high estimation in which we hold you as an officer and commander.

For years afterward those officers and men liked to call themselves "Preble's Boys."

And it wasn't long before Preble's Boys were again in action.

For back home, America was finding itself in need of a navy, and in need of fighting men to man it. There was trouble piling up, danger at sea. Only **too soon** would Preble's Boys be in the thick of it again.

THE MOST DARING ACT OF THE AGE

The War of 1812 (Part 1)

When James Madison became Commander-in-Chief of the American Navy—that is to say, President of the United States—the storm clouds over the Atlantic were darkening. Madison was a small figure rolling up his sleeves there in the White House. As a matter of fact, standing only a little over five feet, even on tiptoe, he was the smallest man ever elected to the Presidency. All the same, James Madison was a mighty big American.

For instance, while a student at Princeton he had been sent home to die. Instead of dying, he lived to be eighty-five.

Turned down as a volunteer in the Revolution, he volunteered for the Government and took all the notes of the Continental Congress single-handed, inventing a system of shorthand to accomplish the job. Refusing pay for his services, he labored long and hard, helping to frame the nation's Constitution. He will always be remembered for establishing Freedom of Religion in America by his insistence on the separation of Church and State.

But mainly he is recalled as President during the War of 1812—the war in which your Navy established Freedom of the Seas.

For Great Britain had embarked on a policy of impressing American seaman. Which means her warships were stopping American cargo vessels and taking off Yankee sailors on the claim that they were deserters from the British Navy. No doubt a few of these claims were genuine, but by far the great majority were trumped up out of salt air.

Some 2,000 American mariners were shanghaied between 1800 and 1809, and hot notes were exchanged between Uncle Sam and his cousin, John Bull. Uncle Sam wanted the sailors back, and Cousin John pointed out that they were already serving in the British Navy, were Englishmen to begin with, and Britannia ruled the waves.

American lawyers hemmed and British lawyers hawed, but proof of citizenship was hard to confirm in those days when birth certificates were unknown and documents were sketchy. *"There is no difference in language between Englishmen and Americans, and but little difference in appearance,"* decided a British court. And while Congress wrangled with the First Lords of the Admiralty, things remained all at sea.

But wait a minute before you square off for an argument with a modern British Jack. Remember all this happened over a hundred years ago, and in those days the impressment of seamen was something of a European tradition. If the French or the Dutch or the other maritime nations wanted to build up their navies, it was customary for press gangs to go out and round up the necessary men. The British Admirals were accustomed to this tradition.

And there were other causes behind the War of 1812. After the Revolutionary War the diplomats on both sides had failed to make certain treaties clear. The Canadian border, for example, had neven been satisfactorily surveyed and the settlers were given to arguing the matter with squirrel rifles. American isolationists were refusing to buy British goods, at the same time competing with British commerce in the Caribbean. There was trouble on the unmapped western frontier over who should control the Indians. So there was considerable bickering and bad temper all around, and this business of the shanghaied seamen brought these troubles to a head.

In 1798 a British naval squadron stopped the American warship *Baltimore* off Cuba, and took off fifty-five men as British deserters. The Americans, who didn't give a toot for Old World customs and traditions, declared the British had kidnapped fifty-five American Navy men. Captain Phillips, in command of *Baltimore*, was dismissed from the service for not fighting.

In 1807 the United States frigate, *Chesapeake*, was refitting at Washington Navy Yard. Came a note from the British minister that three British deserters were in *Chesapeake's* crew. The commandant of the Navy Yard questioned the men named, and decided they were about as English as Boston baked beans, although one might possibly have been born on the Canadian border. That didn't make anyone exactly a Cockney, so when *Chesapeake* sailed, the three sailed with her.

Off the Maryland capes lurked His Majesty's Ship, *Leopard*, prowling with unsheathed guns. Forty miles out she overhauled and stopped the *Chesapeake*, demanding the three "British deserters."

Captain Barron, USN, denied the British Vice-Admiral in command of *Leopard* the right of search. Accordingly *Leopard* opened fire before Barron could uncover a gun, sending broadside after broadside crashing into *Chesapeake's* hull. In fifteen minutes the American's deck was a bloody shambles, three men dead and a score wounded. Barron could fire only a single shot for the honor of the flag, and haul his colors down to stop further

slaughter. *Leopard* took off the three men, who were shipped to Halifax, two of them to be flogged through the fleet, the third hanged.

The United States protested furiously, and Barron, for not having his ship ready for action, was suspended from the service. The British Government expressed regret, but reminded the States that English deserters could not serve in American naval vessels.

Thomas Jefferson, President at the time, put an embargo on

British goods, shut American ports against foreign shipping, and tried a policy of complete isolation. Fishing boats gathered barnacles, cargo ships sat empty at docks, and prices rose to all-time highs in Boston and New York.

> *"America needs no wooden walls,*
> *No ships where billows swell.*
> *Her march is like the terrapin's*
> *Her home is in her shell."*

So sang embittered tradesmen along the seaboard. Impossible to have the ocean at your door and stay at home. Americans were always travelers, going places. How long could Uncle Sam remain in isolation like Robinson Crusoe?

So the ships went out again. So the British impressed more seamen. So when James Madison became President more than six thousand American sailors had been kidnapped. So President James Madison sent bitter protests over to London. So London in return sent a new minister to America—Mr. Copenhagen Jackson.

As a diplomat this character was a pinch of snuff. He sneered at Americans as "homespun rabble." He sneered at James Madison as an "uncouth little man." And he couldn't forget that he'd won his name as a commander in a successful war against Denmark.

But Denmark was somewhat smaller than America, just as Copenhagen Jackson was somewhat smaller than James Madison. While Copenhagen Jackson sneered around Washington, the United States warship *Spitfire* was cruising off the coast of Maine. She was overhauled and stopped by *H.M.S. Guerriere*, a big frigate which made the mistake of grabbing one of *Spitfire's* seamen.

When Madison heard of this, he ordered *U.S.S. President* out of Norfolk Navy Yard to find *Guerriere* and bring the Yankee sailor back. John Rodgers in command of *President* was a veteran who had served under Truxtun. Enough said. *President* was away within the hour, every inch of canvas spread, and in the middle of May she sighted a British man-o'-war off the

Jersey coast. The stranger resembled *Guerriere*, and Rodgers gave immediate chase, overtaking the Britisher after nightfall.

"Ahoy!" Rodgers hailed. *"What ship is that?"*

For an answer the British vessel opened fire, rocking the American warship with a thundering broadside. But this time the Yankees were ready. Before the stranger could fire again, *President's* main battery unleashed a broadside that almost lifted the British vessel out of the water. Another broadside and another roared from the American guns, bringing the Britisher's spars crashing, and punching great holes in her side. A hail of surrender stopped the gunfire, and Rodgers discovered he had blown to pieces *H.M.S. Little Belt*, with many of her crew dead and her hull sinking.

Great Britain demanded immediate reparation, and Copenhagen Jackson in a sputter of fury told Madison it might mean war. Madison reminded the minister that *Little Belt* had fired first, and *President* had fired last. Snuffing and sneezing out a splutter of threats, the sneery diplomat retired to write a batch of special delivery letters to secret agents in New England and Louisiana. The letters proposed an uprising in Louisiana, and urged New England to break away from the United States.

Little Madison, suspecting such skullduggery, was already watching the mails, and when American agents brought in these decidedly undiplomatic documents, he ordered Copenhagen Jackson to pack up his snuffbox and his sneers and get the devil out of Washington. While Mr. Jackson fled the city in a varnished barouche, Madison handed the secret papers over to Congress. Congress voted, and the war was on.

Mr. Madison's War

They called it "Mr. Madison's War." That is, when it was going badly. When it was going well, they called it, "The Second War for American Independence."

But most of the time it was going badly; and looking back, you can see the War of 1812 as one of the strangest wars ever engaged in by the United States, or, for that matter, any country.

To begin with, it was bound to be a sea war, but from the first the Government in Washington (over Madison's head) decided it should be fought on land. "We can't beat the world's biggest Navy, but our pioneers are the world's greatest marksmen, so let the enemy come over here."

You heard talk like that at the beginning of World War II, and in 1812 the enemy did come over, and to everybody's surprise gave the American land army a great pasting.

Madison called for thirty-six thousand regulars and eighty thousand militia, the War Department being convinced an invasion of Canada would be a walk-away. New England refused to recruit any men at all, the militia of many States declared themselves "home guard" only, and the New York militia marched as far as Niagara Falls, then refused to cross the state line.

In command of the American Army, General Wilkinson waddled around, going to tea parties in New England while the British captured all of what is now Michigan, Wisconsin, and Illinois.

In 1814 New England, which had the most to gain in a war for Freedom of the Seas, held a convention at Hartford, threatening to secede from the Union and trade with the British enemy.

The British, on the verge of conquering northern New York, were soundly beaten at Sackett's Harbor by a corps of militia under the generalship of a Quaker.

In Tennessee, Andy Jackson, one of the greatest fighting generals in America, was refused leadership of the Army as a "crude frontiersman."

Half way through the war, the British captured Washington by the use of weapons that weren't intended as weapons at all, as you'll presently see. Then, instead of holding the capitol, they didn't know what to do with it, and marched out.

Finally the greatest land battle of the war was fought two weeks after peace was signed.

Some Seamanship

You can read the above heading as "some seamanship." Or you can read it this way—SOME seamanship! Whichever way you read it, you are reading about that 1812 American Navy.

Imagine the situation. When the war broke out the only American warships ready for any kind of action were *United States, President, Congress, Essex, Hornet,* and *Argus,* all in

New York Harbor. Count 'em. Six warships—one little squadron —under command of Commodore John Rodgers.

Constitution was tied up down in Chesapeake Bay, some other ships were a-building, and the Government had voted for a new fleet of gunboats. But six warships at New York were the only ones immediately available against a navy that numbered her men-o'-war by the dozens, and owned fleet upon fleet of gunboats. Talk about Jack and the Giant!

Rodgers' first order was one commanding him to dismast his ships and moor them along the coast as floating batteries! Clip the wings of the American eagle and leave her moored like a sitting duck!

Fortunately before the stunned commander had time to obey, the fantastic order was countermanded, and he was ordered to put to sea to protect the merchant fleet coming home across the Atlantic. He had his hooks up on the double, the squadron away before anyone else could change his mind. *Essex*, needing repair, had to be left behind.

Five ships sailing out into the teeth of the whole British Navy! Bent on an offensive, too, for Rodgers had in mind to capture a great train of British merchantmen due north that June from Kingston, Jamaica, with a cargo of silver.

Rodgers just missed this fabulous prize, managing to sight the silver ships far out in the Gulf Stream under convoy of a lone British frigate. The American squadron was off in hot pursuit, *President* racing along in the lead. She drew close enough to pepper the frigate with round shot, and the Americans were cheering their heads off when suddenly one of *President's* big chase guns exploded, killing sixteen men, wrecking the foredeck and felling Rodgers with a broken leg. *H.M.S. Belvidere* got away, and in night and fog the British merchantmen escaped.

Lamed and swallowing bitter luck, Rodgers made a futile cruise south, and a month later, needing supplies, headed back to Boston. But this cruise was not the failure it seemed. For the British had a strong naval squadron readying at Halifax to raid American shipping. In rushed *Belvidere* with words that an American naval squadron was at sea on the offensive. The alarmed British admiral decided he must keep his frigates together for protection. So instead of scattering to capture American merchantmen, which would have been easy prey, the Halifax warships came down from the north in a pack.

While all this was going on, *Constitution* had refitted and sailed out of Chesapeake Bay. On her quarterdeck stood Captain Isaac Hull, and the great ship never had a better commander. For Hull was a sailorman from jib to jackstaff, and a fighter to his tops'ls. Isaac Hull was one of Preble's Boys.

A sailor and a fighter—there you've got a Navy Man! Sailing hell for canvas, Hull took *Constitution* up toward New York and then, mid-July off the Jersey coast, not far from the place where *President* had sunk *Little Belt,* he ran smack into the British squadron from Halifax.

In this day and age of binoculars, not to mention high-powered radar, such a thing could never happen. But *Constitution* was on top of these British frigates, thinking them ships of Rodgers' squadron, before the lookouts could see that Hull's signals were not being recognized. When the truth became apparent, Hull was all but surrounded like Daniel in the lion's den.

Not quite. A light breeze was blowing. While the enemy frigates closed in under clouds of sailcloth, Hull cleared decks for action, ran up every inch of canvas aboard and headed straight for mid-Atlantic. The British frigates, flying their kites, pursued.

At dusk the breeze gave out, leaving *Constitution* and her foes bunched together, becalmed. Not quite as calm as the

weather, Hull ordered out the lead line, found his anchor could reach bottom, and tried kedging. Kedging calls for deepwatermen who know their seamanship, and Hull's sailors were such men. You take out an anchor in a small boat, drop it overside some distance ahead of the ship, then the crew on the foredeck sings a chanty around the capstan, and the ship moves forward while the anchor-cable is wound in.

Hard work, my hearties! Desperate, sweaty work taking up the hook, boating it out once more, winding the big frigate forward another lap. When it's a life and death matter with enemy warships crowding your stern, that's kedging!

Isaac Hull moved *Constitution* forward half a mile before the enemy got wise. Then the becalmed Britishers began to kedge. The entire squadron was put to moving the flagship *Shannon*, and by morning they were almost within gunshot of *Constitution*.

Just as it seemed *Constitution* must be overhauled, a wind came up and the American frigate went racing, picking up her smallboats lickety-split. No delay with the davits or throwing lines. No missing the mark with boathooks, or faulty steering. Hull was a sailor, and his quartermasters, bos'n's mates, and cox'n's knew their work. One slip, and a smallboat would be lost. Delay, and the American frigate would be caught by the British.

Constitution got away, and the chase went on. Then the wind gave out again, and the smallboats were overside, kedging the rest of the day. Men's hands went raw at the oars, back-muscles ached at the capstan. The British tars, joining hands between ships, were able to spell each other off, but there was no relief for the Americans. Hour after hour the gruelling race went on, the anchor was carried ahead and dropped, the sailors labored at the groaning capstan. *Constitution* creaked forward, an inch at a time, it seemed, while *Shannon* came on doggedly astern, and the other enemy frigates including the 64-gun battleship *Africa*, closed in slowly on either beam.

The sun burned down to blister straining backs, the air lay motionless on the sea, and the water was as dead and sluggish as liquid lead, but *Constitution* forged on, yard after yard. Let her men falter now, let the anchor become fouled, the links tangle in the chain locker, the smallboats fumble, and the ship lose way, and she would be caught by the enemy squadron astern and chopped to pieces. Hold on lads! Hard at it! Keep going! Your lives and *Constitution's* are at stake. Go on, boys, go on! Anchors aweigh!

Panting at the oars, stumbling with fatigue around the capstan, *Constitution's* sailors kept on going. No Super-man comic or

Hollywood thriller could equal the drama of that endurance contest off the Jersey coast.

The salt stung like fury when they split open the palms of their hands. The sun scorched their crusted eyelids, their lips dried with thirst, just as yours dry when you're thirsty today. They were tired to the breaking point, they shouted, they swore, they were scared. Human nature was the same a hundred years ago, just as the sea off the Jersey coast was the same. And three days in 1812 were just as long as they are today. That's how long those sleepless sailors aboard *Constitution* kept going without relief. Three days!

Shannon came so close at times her cannon balls splashed *Constitution's* afterdeck. *Africa's* 64 guns and round shot drew nearer and nearer. You can't outrace fresh men with weary men. You can't outfight a five-ship squadron with one ship. But you can out-smart the overpowering squadron—with seamanship. And when it came to seamanship, Isaac Hull was one of the world's past masters.

There was a moment during the third day when it seemed as if the Americans could go on no longer. Human endurance has its limits, and the bos'n's mates, the cox'n's, and the men who manned the oars, the heaving lines, and the capstan were staggering with exhaustion.

Captain Hull went up the shroud lines this noon to scan the sky ahead with his glass. Ha! A small, dark cloud hovered low on the horizon, a feather of rain no bigger than the feather in Yankee Doodle's hat.

Instantly Hull had his boys aloft, reefing the tops'ls and stripping the yards of canvas, readying *Constitution* for a hurricane. On deck the men battened hatches and ran to lash everything fast.

Quarter mile or so behind, *Shannon* and *Belvidere* spied their quarry frantically trimming sail, and guessing that Hull had sighted a tempest over the horizon, sent their own men into the tops to reef in canvas. The other British warships caught the signal and followed suit, anxious eyes watching the storm cloud now visible.

The cloud grew and darkened, ominously advancing toward *Constitution*, bringing a rush of choppy water and a squall of

rain. Bare poles to the sky, the American warship rode straight into the squall, and then, while his ship was screened in the foaming downpour, Captain Hull rushed his men like monkeys into the tops to spread all canvas at top speed and send *Constitution* racing and plunging through the smother. Expert mariner that he was, Hull judged the ominous cloud was no more than a squall, tricked the enemy into reefing canvas in the belief a hurricane was coming, and had his sails ready for the wind gusts when they came.

They were there on the other side of the cloud as Hull had forecast, and *Constitution* blew out into the clear and raced on out into the Atlantic at a speed no British squadron could attain. When the enemy came out through the rainstorm it was to see *Constitution* far out on the horizon no bigger than a gull.

THAT'S SEAMANSHIP!

Guerriere and Constitution

Guerriere is a French word meaning "warrior," and Captain Dacres of the British frigate with the French name liked to boast that he commanded the best fighting ship on the sea. He could handle a sword like a Spanish *conquistador*, he was as suave as a Duke, and he wore the uniform of a peacock. He probably looked on the American Navy captains like Isaac Hull, with their shiny-seated britches and homespun names, as rustic mossbacks'.

Dacres' *Guerriere* was the ship which had overhauled *Spitfire* and impressed one of her seamen. *Guerriere* was also in the squadron which had chased *Constitution* off the Jersey coast (the Americans were bloody lucky, Dacres doubtless assumed.) So Dacres didn't think much of the American Navy. In fact, before the war broke out, he was visiting along the American seaboard, making a lot of bets. One of these bets was pretty reckless. While anchored in Chesapeake Bay, Dacres once declared that his *Guerriere* would beat any American warship in fifteen minutes of fighting, and offered to bet a hat.

Dacres' poor opinion of the Yankees became a finger-snap after the *Constitution* chase. Apparently. A few weeks later, with his ship in need of supplies, he dropped out of the southbound squadron and started contemptuously back to Halifax, alone. The Yankees? Fiddlesticks! Their handful of pinetree frigates had run for cover. Singly or by the dozen they'd never dare test the powder of *Guerriere*.

Consider, then, Dacres' surprise when on the afternoon of August 19th at 1530 the lookout called, "Sail ho!" and the masts of an American frigate came over the horizon. Dacres, squinting through his spyglass, couldn't believe it; this vessel coming straight at him must be a Dutchman.

She wasn't a Dutchman, she was *U.S.S. Constitution*, of all ships the one Captain Dacres had wanted to meet, of all ships, the one that had wanted to meet up with *Guerriere*. And if Dacres' voice rose shrill with pleasure, Isaac Hull on *Constitution's* quarterdeck rubbed his hands with delight, his drums beating to quarters and clearing the decks for action.

Now the guns were run out, ammunition rushed up through the hatches, powder monkeys racing, gun crews waiting tensely at their batteries. The distance closed between the warships, neither one giving way. Boom! *Guerriere* opened fire first, trying to get in a broadside as Hull swung *Constitution* on a tack so that the enemy shots fell short. Boom! Another enemy broadside missing. The ships closed again, and a third broadside from *Guerriere* dug some splinters out of *Constitution's* deck and sent iron fragments whistling through the canvas.

Hull's gunnery officer was dancing with excitement, shouting to ask if he could open fire. Hull's voice echoed harshly through the speaking trumpet, *"Not yet, sir, not yet!"*

A fourth broadside roared from *Guerriere.* The frigates were running beam to beam, almost within distance of musket shot. A cannon ball ploughed *Constitution's* afterdeck. Marines in the Britisher's rigging began to snipe, and a Yankee seaman went down. The gunners looked nervously at Hull.

"Not yet! Hold your fire! Not yet!"

Sweat broke on the jaws of the gunners. Was the Old Man going to wait till they could see the whites of their eyes? They could hear *Guerriere's* men cheering; see the British tars loading their cannon, the officers running to and fro, flashing their swords, the Marines high in the rigging. Another musket volley

raked *Constitution's* deck. Good Godfrey! Was old Hull going to let them stand there and be murdered?

Then a swinging wave drove *Constitution* even closer, and as the frigates lined up almost within pistol shot, Hull's trumpet bellowed the order.

"Fire! Pour it into them, boys!"

Every gun aboard seemed to let go at once, a terrific blast that shook the frigate from stem to stern, lit the sea with a volcanic burst of fire, and filled the air with a thunderhead of smoke. When the smoke surged away, the Americans saw *Guerriere* half listing on her beam, the deck a shambles of wreckage, littered with wounded and dead.

"*Fire!*" Hull bellowed again.

Again *Constitution* shook with the thunder of a broadside. This time *Guerriere's* mizzenmast came down in a tumble of splinters, canvas and cordage, flames broke from the forecastle, and the ship staggered as though she'd struck a reef.

Hull shouted at his gunners to direct their fire at the enemy's waterline. Don't bother with her rigging. Shoot low. The order rang from his speaking trumpet. "*Hull her, boys!*"

The crew took it up as a jubilant chant, "*Hull her! Hull her!*" with pumping ramrods and running ammunition handlers pouring round after round into the wounded vessel. Gaping holes appeared in *Guerriere's* waterline, holes her men below decks strove desperately to patch. Flames burst from her forward hatches as cannon balls smashed through her bow and whirling chainshot swept men and gear from her foredeck.

Coming up under *Guerriere's* bowsprit, Hull loosed another broadside that brought the Britisher's foremast crashing and set her afire in forty places. As the frigates locked bows for a moment, Dacres screamed at his boarders to rush the Yankee, but the marksmen in *Constitution's* rigging wiped out the boarding party to a man. *Guerriere* was on fire. *Guerriere* was sinking. Crash! Another broadside had chopped down her mainmast, smothering her decks in burning canvas and tangled cordage. As the two ships separated, the Americans fired still another broadside into the Briton's hulk that left her rolling, dismasted and down at the head like an abandoned derelict. *Guerriere* would never reach Halifax now. She was blown to Halifax!

With seventy-nine of his men dying or dead, his ship shot to pieces, Captain Dacres hauled down his flag. American casualties counted seven dead and seven wounded.

Presently Dacres was standing, his face like a skull, on *Constitution's* quarterdeck, offering homespun Isaac Hull his sword. Hull, who disliked that sort of thing, declined the offer.

"But if you don't mind, Captain, I'll trouble you for that hat."

Constitution's great victory over *Guerriere* did for the Americans of 1812 what the great naval victory at Midway did for your morale in 1942. Uncle Sam threw his hat in the air and cheered. From Bangor to Savannah the Navy was welcomed and toasted; the sailors were the talk of every town. *Constitution* soon was known throughout the nation as "Old Ironsides."

It was a victory that came just in time. The territories of Michigan, Illinois, and Wisconsin had fallen to the British that summer of 1812, and the Minnesota area was invaded. There was ominous news from the St. Lawrence, army deserters were roaming the back woods in swarms, and New England had threatened to leave the Union. Now with *Constitution* sailing victorious into the Boston harbor, all that was changed. Farmers stood in line at the recruiting stalls, and Congress voted big appropriations for the Navy.

John Rodgers, his leg healed, was sent out of Boston with *President* and another frigate to take another crack at the enemy. Stephen Decatur with a small squadron was sent toward the Azores to raid British shipping. And *Constitution* with the warships *Essex* and *Hornet* was dispatched to the South Atlantic.

Then the cheering over *Guerriere* had hardly died down when the news came in that Rodgers had captured the British frigate *Swallow* with $80,000 in gold for the governor of Canada aboard. And the country was still applauding that feat when it heard about—

Wasp and Frolic

Wasp was an American sloop which had slipped out of Chesapeake Bay, fast as a leaf in the autumn wind. She was commanded by sharp-nosed Jacob Jones, an elderly Naval officer from Delaware who, like Hull, was one of Preble's Boys.

By mid October he was in the North Atlantic with two captured British merchantmen in tow. On the night of October 16th *Wasp* was struck by a tempest which smashed her jib, and the following morning, bucking high seas, she sighted a merchant convoy guarded by His Majesty's brig, *Frolic*.

Wasp and *Frolic*—the warships were aptly named. *Frolic* came frolicking across the waves, her guns out and decks stripped for action, spoiling for the fight, and Jacob Jones rolled the sleeves back on his batteries and gave it to her.

Beam to beam, the vessels started shooting, both ploughing through tall seas that combed their bows and almost swept the gunners from their stations. *Frolic* let go a tremendous broadside that brought a patch of *Wasp's* rigging down a-heap and gave the Britishers the idea the Yankee was foundering.

Jacob Jones' ship wasn't foundering, but he was bringing her around in the trough of the seas so that she rolled her beam ends under.

"Fire on the down-wave!" he roared through his trumpet, *"Give her a broadside!"*

Now naval guns in those days weren't the hydraulically driven guns of today. Mounted on wheeled platforms that rolled backwards in recoil, they were returned to battery by hand, their muzzles thrust through the gun ports.

Then the guns were fired from a fixed position, elevation or depression being decided by the vessel's roll. It was the generally

accepted practice to fire on the up-wave in an attempt to rake the enemy's deck and superstructure. Jacob Jones, firing on the "down-dip" was following the tactic of Isaac Hull.

In this way, he was sending cannon balls smashing into *Frolic's* waterline where the sea could rush into her holds and the hot shot explode her magazines. Before this last could happen, however, the ships collided, and the American crew stormed over *Frolic's* bow and rushed her with pistol and cutlass.

They found no one to fight. Those who could run had fled below to stop the holes in *Frolic's* waterline. Only one helmsman stood at the wheel, and three wounded British officers limped forward to surrender their swords. With ninety casualties in a crew of one hundred and seven, *Frolic* surrendered, stung to death by *Wasp*.

United States and Macedonian

Stephen Decatur, whom you read of as Preble's best-known boy in the Mediterranean, came back from the Barbary Wars to find himself the best-known officer in the Navy. It didn't go to his head, and he was liked all the better for his quiet manners and modest way.

When war broke out in 1812, he was made captain of the frigate *United States*, and commodore of the squadron heading out toward the Azores. Like Hull, Jacob Jones, and the rest of Preble's Boys, he believed in drilling his men daily in seamanship and gunnery.

Captain Samuel Carden of His Britannic Majesty's Navy was a gentleman of another sort. Although he thought gunnery drills were a useless waste of powder, he believed in cat-o'-nine-tail drills as good discipline for the men, something to keep them in line for the King—a monarch often confused in his mind with a mental picture of Captain Carden.

Carden was in command of the brand new frigate *Macedonian*, sent out from His Majesty's realm to hand these Americans a real thrashing. He was to find out that thrashing his own men was one thing and thrashing the Americans was another.

For the American he ran into was Stephen Decatur, commanding the frigate *United States*, not quite the man or ship to take a flogging from any Captain Carden. The warships sighted each other on October 25, not far from the Canary Islands off the coast of Africa. Decatur was alone, having dispatched the rest of his squadron down to raid the Caribbean. But he accepted

Macedonian's challenging gunshot as quickly as he'd once scared the ears off a Spaniard.

The ships jockeyed into range, and the battle was on, Carden opening fire with his main batteries at long distance, and peering complacently through his spyglass at some tattered sailcloth in the America's tops. On target at first shot! That would teach the Yankees a lesson!

Then as smoke-puffs floated from the distant Yankee guns, Carden was horrified to hear the rip of canvas above his own head. A man came thudding down from a broken yardarm, and a moment later a storm of roundshot came crash! crash! crash! down on *Macedonian's* deck, a rain of death that fell on the frigate from foc's'le to afterhouse, killing men all over the ship.

Carden, realizing his guns were out-ranged, screamed at his men to put on sail and close with the enemy. But *United States* tacked off, continuing to fire at long range. While the British spotters saw their broadsides falling short, Decatur's gunners fired steadily, swiftly, and with lethal accuracy, sending salvo after salvo smashing into *Macedonian*.

The Briton was a faster ship, and Carden, raging, managed to drive her closer to the American. This proved a fatal maneuver. Although the British got a few hits, the American gunners were

murder at close range. Aboard Carden's ship all hell broke loose —rigging and canvas came plunging down, the mizzenmast toppled, splintered spars flew like kindling over a chopping block. One of the British sailors described it later as like a tremendous, deafening thunderstorm.

For half an hour Decatur's men pounded *Macedonian* with devastation, shooting her decks to bloody ruin, and again firing on the "down-dip" to stave in the enemy's hull below the gun ports. Down came *Macedonian's* colors, with the ship a floating scrap-heap on the water.

Decatur sent a tender and a young lieutenant to escort Captain Carden over. Aboard the beaten ship, the young American lieutenant encountered the British surgeon.

"How do you do, Doctor?"

"I have enough to do," the surgeon showed crimson hands. *"You have made wretched work for us with your guns."*

The young lieutenant suggested that *United States* might send a surgeon or two over to help, and the Englishman wanted to know how the Americans could spare any help with so many wounded in their own cockpit.

"But we had only seven," the young lieutenant smiled cheerfully. Seven! And the enemy's casualties totalled one hundred and five!

"What will become of me?" Carden mourned. *"The first British naval officer who has struck his flag to an American!"*

But he was wrong—he had not yet heard about *Guerriere* and *Frolic*.

Constitution and Java

William Bainbridge had almost broken his neck to reach America in time for the war. The veteran captain was in Russia when he heard war between England and the States was brewing. Shipping in the Baltic was ice-bound, so Bainbridge went rushing across Finland in a stagecoach, determined to reach Sweden and open water. During this dash, the stagecoach skidded over an embankment, nearly finishing Bainbridge's naval career then and there.

But a wilderness snowbank couldn't finish Bainbridge any

more than could a Tripoli dungeon. He crawled out of the wreck badly lamed, and went on by oxcart to reach Sweden. Presently he was rolling across the North Atlantic in a sailing vessel, and he hobbled into Washington in March 1812, three months before war was declared.

In Washington he urged President Madison to let the Navy go out and fight, and when Isaac Hull brought *Constitution* in that June with *Guerriere's* battle flag, Bainbridge had already been given command of "Old Ironsides." Why? Well, it was a matter of poor communications again. Hull, it seemed, had missed an order originally intended to hold him at Boston. The Navy Department thought he had taken *Constitution* to sea without authority, and so appointed Bainbridge to take over. Never mind. When word of Hull's great victory at last came home, the paper work could have been straightened out, but Bainbridge was a rugged officer and Hull wanted the man who'd had such bad luck with *Philadelphia* to have a crack at the British Lion.

October 26th, the day after Decatur's great victory off Africa (and of course with no news of it) Bainbridge took *Constitution* out of Boston.

By late November he was cruising down off Central America, and December 29th found *Constitution* riding the equator, off the coast of South America, rolling down to Rio. You could see a distant shoreline of jungle away west where the Amazon lay, and then the American lookouts saw something else—and *Java*, thinking the American in flight, gave speedy chase.

Shortly after noon the ships were in range, and with his decks stripped and gun crews ready, Bainbridge began firing. *Java* returned the broadside, and under the broiling equatorial sun a violent gun duel broke loose.

The faster ship, *Java* managed to make it a battle at close quarters, running in swiftly to rake *Constitution* with everything from cannon to pistols. The Yankees returned as good as they got, but in this fusillade Bainbridge was struck in the hip and sent stumbling by a musket ball. A surgeon tended the wound, and the captain limped around the quarterdeck, trumpeting at his men to heat up their fire and keep *Constitution* abreast of *Java's* beam.

Crash! crash! crash! the American heavy guns thundered, splintering the enemy vessel along her waterline, while the secondary batteries swept *Java's* deck with chain and canister, and Marine sharpshooters in *Constitution's* shrouds riddled the enemy's rigging. Now the two ships became vague in clouds of boiling smoke jabbed by spouts of flame. Thunderclaps echoed far across the blue tropic water to frighten flocks of seabirds along the distant shore. *Java's* Captain Lambert, a capable and courageous officer, directed his fire shrewdly, and almost dealt *Constitution* a fatal blow. A cannon ball ripped across *Constitution's* quarterdeck, smashed into the helmsman, carried away the wheel in a

shower of splinters, and exploded almost at Bainbridge's feet. Bainbridge crumpled, a bolt driven by the blast into his leg.

Cruel luck for the former captain of *Philadelphia*. Savage luck! His health undermined from those months in a pirate's dungeon, his back lamed from that accident in Finland, and now he was wounded twice within a quarter hour. Worse than that, his ship was wounded, her steering appartus shattered by a hit that wouldn't happen once in ten thousand tries. Writhing on the deck, William Bainbridge must have thought of Napoleon's famous remarks that he didn't want any officers who were unlucky.

But Bainbridge wasn't the man to sit around complaining about tough breaks. He was on his feet in a trice. Face contorted, teeth bared with pain from his smashed hip and bleeding leg, he clung to the rail, trumpeting orders at the quartermasters to steer by jury rig, by the rudder-chains, by the post if they had to turn it with raw hands.

Sensing *Constitution* was hurt, Lambert tacked in to grapple, and was surprised when the American steered away, fending off with a blasting volley that swept *Java's* decks like a tornado. The Briton, badly damaged, swung aside and then veered back on a long swell to ram her bowsprit over the American frigate's stern.

The collision shook "Old Ironsides" to her figurehead. Britishers seemed to leap up everywhere from *Java's* deck, pouring up out of her hatches by the hundred, men and more men rushing over the bows in attack. Bainbridge, in consternation, realized the enemy was a troopship—in hand-battle *Constitution's* crew would be massacred.

Rallying his marksmen aft, he directed a fusillade at the enemy's bow. In the after rigging, the Marine sharpshooters poured a hailstorm of lead at the charging Britons. Lambert, leading the charge, fell dead as a bullet broke his back. And while the assault troops withered under this blasting, *Constitution's* steersmen labored like giants at the rudder post, the ship got free of *Java's* bowsprit and broke away.

This gave *Constitution's* stern guns a chance to rake, and their roaring salvo turned *Java's* foredeck into an inferno. The Briton's foremast fell with an earthquake crash. Her canvas caught fire, yards fluttered in wild tangles, spars came down like twigs in a forest gale. One after another her batteries went silent.

Bainbridge maneuvered around and raked again. Down came *Java's* mizzenmast. Down came *Java's* mainmast. Then dismasted, powerless, her decks heaped with hills of dead, the very picture of *Guerriere*, down came *Java's* colors.

Casualties: *Java*, one hundred and sixty-one. *Constitution*, thirty-four.

Napoleon put his faith in "lucky" officers. America put its faith in officers like William Bainbridge.

Navy Score

Constitution beats *Guerriere*.
Wasp beats *Frolic*.
United States beats *Macedonian*.
Constitution beats *Java*.

The Americans tallying this box-score almost went out of

their heads with joy. Four engagements the first year of the war, and the U. S. Navy the victor in every one.

True, the Navy suffered two minor losses—*Vixen* and *Nautilus*, a pair of small gunboats captured by the enemy. And *Wasp*, after destroying *Frolic*, had come to grief and capture at the hands of a huge 74-gun British battleship which ran down Jacob Jones before he could get his sloop into safe harbor. But that didn't count as an even contest, and when the odds had been fairly matched the American Navy had won hands down.

John Bull stung to agony by the Wasp and Hornet.

Score, too, John Rodgers' capture of the Canadian governor's pay-ship. And some twenty odd British merchantmen taken prize by the American Navy. Add the fact that *U.S.S. Hornet* had forced a British warship to interne herself in San Salvador. And then, just before the great year ended, there was *U.S.S. Essex* fighting and capturing *H.M.S. Alert*. Five straight victories in the first five engagements. No wonder the home folks shook hands with every Navy man they met, while across the sea the wounded Lion roared.

And what reason lay behind this amazing exhibition, this bantam Navy winning five straight rounds from the former heavyweight champ? "Luck!" observed some of the astounded neutrals, forgetting Bainbridge. "Miracles!" forgetting that the British could have forecast the same weather which saved Hull.

Nor was it—as the punch-drunk Lords of Admiralty declared—battleships disguised as frigates with overwhelming fire power and heavier guns.

No, the factors of victory were something else—factors you can plainly see, even from the distance of today.

SEAMANSHIP—there you have one answer. Superior seamanship by sailors who knew their ropes, their block and tackle. Oarsmen like Isaac Hull's who could have a smallboat out of the davits and away in less time than it takes to tell. Quartermasters like those under Bainbridge, who could steer a frigate when its helm was shot to kindling. Bosun's mates and cox'n's who did their jobs on the double. Men who were experts with compass, log, and lead. Sailors who were seamen to their fingertips.

GUNNERY—there's another answer. Gunners who drilled every day when the enemy gunners did not. Marksmen who could put a shot through a sailing ship's mast at 1,000 yards. Crews trained to work together as teams until a battery became a unit of iron, brawn, and brain. Hits per gun per minute—that's the formula that wins in naval warfare. And you can see how it won back in 1812 exactly as it wins today.

For Decatur and the others, following the principles of Preble, had believed in TRAINING. Daily drill, constant practice, and strict discipline. But not the flogging, cat-o'-nine-tail discipline that sent men whipped and sullen to their posts. No, the kind of discipline that was fair for all, share and share alike, each man expected to carry his portion of responsibility, but always rewarded with a word or prize for work well done.

So you have MORALE, another factor in these smashing American victories. Men who pitched in because they wanted to pitch in. Who weren't driven by threats and fear of punishment, but took their orders realizing that a disciplined ship meant a taut, a safe, and a winning ship. Inspired by the example of officers like Decatur and Bainbridge, they also knew what they were fighting for. You don't have to explain to such sailors the meaning of Freedom of the Seas.

And here among these 1812 Navy men you can see a final winning factor—one having its roots in democracy, in a New World breaking away from the Old. For these early Americans were pioneers, never fearful of attempting something new, whether it was a new method of government or a new method of gunnery. They didn't cling to the "old" as though a method were a cherished antique. They were great believers in room for improvement. Maybe the new wouldn't work, but at least you could give it a try.

And just as democratic government was new at the time (and considered by Europeans a dangerous novelty) so was firing on the "down wave" a new method of naval gunnery—a break with long-established custom—and one that threatened to sink the enemy fleet. Call it "being ahead of the game," if you like. Call it "inventiveness" or "ingenuity." Or call it PROGRESSIVE THINKING. The Navy of 1812 wasn't the Navy that turned down David Bushnell's submarine.

Superior seamanship—superior gunnery—superior morale—progressive thinking. In a nutshell: BRAINS, DISCIPLINE, TARGET PRACTICE—the formula that will always mean naval victories.

Don't Give Up the Ship!

But the Navy couldn't do everything. And the Army of 1812 was doing next to nothing. While General-in-Chief Wilkinson sat, the enemy massed along the Great Lakes and the Indians rose in Ohio. Meantime His Majesty's Admirals woke up to the fact that the Yankee Navy was handing them Hail Columbia, and in February 1813 they sent an immense battle fleet to blockade our Atlantic coast.

Now the Giant was after Jack in earnest. Decatur with his squadron was locked up in New York Harbor. At Boston, Rodgers' squadron was hemmed in. *Constellation*, which had been refitted, was sealed into her Norfolk anchorage, like a ship in a glass bottle. *Chesapeake*, which had come home for repairs, was blockaded, and "Old Ironsides," too, was fastened up at her berth.

At every port, outnumbered ten to one, the American warships were held trapped by squadrons of enemy frigates which patrolled the mouth of each harbor like hungry sharks. Would the little Navy gather barnacles and the coastline slowly starve while the British landslide swept in from the North and West? Any attempt to run the blockade would amount to suicide.

So Rodgers ran it, taking *President* and *Congress* out of Boston Bay and through the enemy fleet under cover of a booming nor'easter. And a few weeks later he captured *H.M.S. Highflyer* off the coast of Ireland.

Lieutenant Burrows, commanding *Enterprise*, ran it several months later, skipping out of Portsmouth, New Hampshire, to capture *H.M.S. Boxer* in a terrific fight in which the fiery lieutenant was killed.

Lieutenant William H. Allen ran the blockade with *Argus*, taking a new ambassador over to France. He had been Decatur's gunnery officer when *United States* riddled *Macedonian*, and before that he was in *Chesapeake's* crew when that frigate was set upon by *Leopard*. It was said young Allen fired the only shot at *Leopard*, carrying a blazing coal in his fingers to touch off the gun. He was that kind of man, for on leaving France he sailed his little brig straight into the British Lion's mouth to raid shipping in the Irish Sea.

Before the Lion could snap, this Yankee dare-devil had snared twenty merchantmen costing the enemy two and a half million dollars—not a bad run for a modern raider. The Lords of Admiralty tore at their wigs and gathered an entire squadron of frigates to hunt down *Argus*.

She was overhauled by His Majesty's brig *Pelican* just as she was scuttling a British wine ship she had captured, and in the desperate battle that followed young Allen had his leg shot off. A few minutes later, the second officer in command was killed, then the third officer. Their brig afire, their commanders dead, the sailors of *Argus* could only surrender. But they'd already accomplished their mission. Some set-backs were inevitable.

Every Navy man has heard of Captain Lawrence. Another of Preble's Boys, James Lawrence had commanded *Hornet* when she bottled up an enemy warship in San Salvador. In February, 1813, Lawrence had abandoned this miniature blockade to raid shipping in the Caribbean.

Result: the sinking of *H.M.S. Peacock* with gunfire of such murderous accuracy that *Peacock* was holed along the waterline as if a giant auger had made evenly spaced drill-holes from stem to stern. American cartoonists had a field day picturing John Bull stung in the britches by a wasp and a hornet, and Lawrence was promoted to the command of *Chesapeake*.

The warship lay in Boston Harbor at this time, and Lawrence was ordered to run the blockade immediately and get out into the Atlantic. The British were waiting, Lawrence knew, but he was never the man to dodge a battle. Over six feet tall, with shoulders that had to go sideways through a hatch, Lawrence stood like a monument on his frigate's quarterdeck while she slipped down the bay with her colors flying. Beyond the headlands where everyone could see her on patrol, was His Majesty's frigate *Shannon*.

The two warships rushed at each other like bulldogs in a pit, and in almost the first exchange of shots James Lawrence was hit in the thigh. Then a broadside from *Shannon* tore *Chesapeake's* forestays away, crippling the American frigate's ability to tack. This gave the Briton a chance to rake with a murderous broadside that poured shot and shell the length of *Chesapeake's* deck. Three junior officers and the boatswain were killed.

The Yankee gunners gave *Shannon* broadside for broadside, but the Briton closed in on the wounded ship, rammed *Chesapeake's* stern, and threw out grappling hooks to make it a cutlass-fight. Lawrence rallied his men aft, and they were fighting like tigers when they caught a blast of gunfire from Marines perched in *Shannon's* tops. A sniper's bullet pierced Lawrence's body, and he plunged to the deck, mortally wounded.

He was carried below while the battle went on, the British tars storming across *Chesapeake's* deck with their commander, Captain Philip Broke, in the lead. Below decks, Lawrence was dying. He could hear the yells, the thud and crash of conflict, the enemy bugles and cheers.

"*Don't give up the ship!*" he panted to the men around him. "*Sink her first! Don't give up the ship!*"

Too late—the crew had been driven to the foc's'le head, trapped. Word came up that Lawrence was dead and half the crew was down. In a desperate effort to rush the enemy and carry out

Lawrence's command, Second Lieutenant Budd charged forward, collided straight into British Captain Broke, and split his skull with a single slash of the cutlass. An instant later Budd was riddled, and one of the bloodiest sea battles of the war was over.

Historians have called it a "glorious episode in American history"—and in case words like "glory" don't mean anything to you, you can still remember that *Chesapeake's* crew fought like hellions, you can still take off your hat to Lawrence and his men. And you can remember something else—*Shannon's* commander, Captain Broke, was ONE OF THE FEW OFFICERS AT THAT TIME IN THE BRITISH NAVY WHO BELIEVED IN DAILY GUNNERY PRACTICE!

If you're a Navy gunner today (and maybe a little fed up with feeding dummy projectiles to a loading machine) that bit of history may mean something. You might remember it as the Navy has always remembered the brave last words of Lawrence —DON'T GIVE UP THE SHIP!

DON'T GIVE UP THE SHIP

The War of 1812 (Part 2)

No, the Navy couldn't do everything. But look at what it did.

In the autumn of 1813 the American situation was desperate. Having proposed a great scheme to invade Canada, General Wilkinson had allowed the Army along the Canadian border to go to grass. Supplies were bogged down, recruits wouldn't drill, whole companies straggled off, and in some instances the regulars refused to fight. Instead of invading Canada, Wilkinson had left the door wide open for invasion by the enemy.

Only General William Henry Harrison was on the ball in the West, holding the Indians off with the left hand and the British off with his right. Veteran Indian fighter, endeared to his men as "Old Tippecanoe," Harrison had his thin fringe of frontier riflemen strung across Ohio in a line that began somewhere down near Kentucky and ended up at Sandusky on Lake Erie.

He was facing hordes of Indian tribesmen, and a British army under General Proctor was threatening to come across Lake Erie and crumple up his northern flank. General Harrison's canoe was tippy for a fact. Scouts brought in word that Proctor was gathering the invasion fleet. At all odds, this enemy must never cross Lake Erie!

And what was to prevent it? In those days the American shore of Lake Erie was just woods and wilderness. Harrison couldn't pull in his line from the south; the Indians would break through to Pennsylvania. Even if he massed at Sandusky, Proctor's invasion fleet would land somewhere else. And there was no use calling for reinforcements from Tanglefoot Wilkinson. In desperation, Harrison appealed to President Madison.

An invasion fleet? Great thunder! It would have to be stopped by the Navy. Send the Navy to a howling wilderness? Impossible!

But the Navy had been doing the impossible. So Madison sent Oliver Hazard Perry.

The Navy Crosses New York

"Hazard" was a good middle name for this lanky, young Rhode Islander embarking for frontier desolation to build a fleet. Son of a former Navy commander, he'd been fretting around Newport in charge of a blockaded gunboat flotilla. Itching for action (another of Preble's Boys), he had written the government a letter appealing for a busier post. Now he had it and a tough job with it.

Yes, he had some Navy shipfitters and a handful of carpenter's mates and the crews from his eight gunboats. And up on Lake Erie at Presqu'Ile there was a schooner captain named Dobbins, a rickity boathouse, and a couple of shipwrights. But Perry and his men were in Newport. Lake Erie was a wilderness away. Presqu'Ile consisted of four log cabins. Dobbins and his shipwrights were completely out of supplies—no canvas, no cordage, no anchors, nothing. And Oliver Hazard Perry had to get up there on the double (and in wartime), and organize a naval base and build a fleet of fighting warships.

Today you see a statue of Perry in a park. In March 1813, when Perry set out for Lake Erie, he didn't look any more like a statue than you do, and he wasn't standing stationary. Neither was the Navy. Picture a train of supply carts, Conestoga wagons, horses, and men moving through the forest trails and over the blizzard-swept hills of northern New York. A mighty strange wagon-train, with sailors on horseback, the carts loaded with ship's gear, anchors, cannons, chain, and cordage, while seamen brought up the rear, dragging long lines of hawsers and hempen cables. Did you know an American naval fleet once crossed New York State on foot?

Impossible! Of course it was impossible! Whoever heard of navigators dragging an anchor through a forest? Of quartermasters boxing the compass on horseback? Of bosun's driving mule teams? Of sailors cutting down trees to make their own yardarms and masts?

At Presqu'Ile things seemed hopeless. The shipwrights had fled. The ice was melting, leaving the land a sea of mud and the lake accessible to the enemy. The British were coming! Intelligence brought in word that five enemy warships under a Commander Barclay were preparing to set sail from the Canadian side.

This Commander Barclay, by the way, was a veteran who had served under Nelson at Trafalgar. It looked as though the next of kin were soon to be advised about Oliver Hazard Perry.

One faint hope glimmered in this gloomy picture. Guarding Buffalo, not far away, were five small lake-schooners under Commander Elliott. And in the rickety Presqu'Ile shipyard Perry found the frameworks of two half-built sloops. If Elliott could bring his armed schooners over from Buffalo with some supplies, and if these sloops could be finished in time—if!

Perry and his tired men set to work. Day and night they worked, chopping, sawing, pounding, hammering, like beavers at a dam. No sitdown strikes. No overtime. No extra rations. No Ship's Service. When they ran out of tobacco, the hell with tobacco. When they ran out of nails, they made wooden pegs.

All through the spring rains they worked; desperately through May. Some Pennsylvania militia arrived at the base to help a little. Barclay sent spies to see what was going on, then delayed attack to add a heavy corvette to his own flotilla.

Now the two 20-gun sloops were finished and launched. Perry christened them *Lawrence* and *Niagara*.

But the supplies and ammo hadn't arrived from Buffalo. Although stricken with chills and fever, Perry got out of bed and galloped down the lake to Fort Erie. He found the fort in British hands and Elliott's schooners blockaded. Fort George

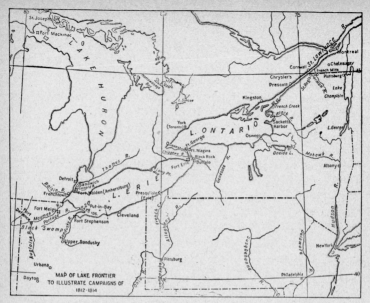

MAP OF LAKE FRONTIER
TO ILLUSTRATE CAMPAIGNS OF
1812-1814

on the Niagara River was the bottleneck, so Perry led a company of Marines to smash the neck from the bottle. After which, the enemy cleared out of Fort Erie, and Perry got Elliott's schooners into the lake.

They were almost trapped by Barclay's ships, but they managed to reach Presqu'Ile to find a call for help from General Harrison at Sandusky—could they come at once, before the British broke his line?

Perry hadn't enough men to man his sloops. A desperate appeal for four hundred sailors was answered by a detachment of seventy—green recruits who'd never seen water deeper than a pond. Before Perry could train them, came another urgent message from Harrison. The British were on him. If the Navy didn't stop them on the lake, he was lost.

Perry put out at once, his flagship, *Lawrence*, flying a patch of blue bunting which carried the words, "Don't Give Up the Ship!" Terrible luck almost stopped him at the start, for the squadron wasn't out of the harbor before *Lawrence* ran aground on a sand bar.

For two days the crew worked frantically to float the vessel, and by that time the enemy knew Perry was sailing. Down from Canada came Barclay's warships in a pack to chase Perry's squadron to Sandusky. It was a close shave for Uncle Sam with the American ships short-handed, two schooners left behind for lack of crews, and Perry ill with fever. But they made Sandusky.

"Old Tippecanoe" shook Perry's hand and told him he had saved the day. If Perry could now sink the Britons out in the lake, Harrison declared, the invasion of the West would collapse.

Perry asked for men, and got one hundred Kentucky sharpshooters, buck-skinned pioneers who'd spent half their lives with a rifle in hand. On the 10th of September, Perry's flagship was again on the lake with frontiersmen in her crosstrees, farmers in her bows, Navy gunners at the batteries, and lake sailors at the helm. Behind *Lawrence* came *Niagara* with an equally odd crew. Trailing the two sloops there were a 4-gun and a 3-gun schooner followed by five leaky little 1-gun lake-boats, ragtag and bobtail of the waterfront.

Barclay, wearing his Trafalgar medals, must have laughed when his glass spied this jerrybuilt fleet. Did the Americans expect to beat him with flotsam and jetsam? Aboard his 20-gun flagship *Detroit*, he led in line of battle *Queen Charlotte* (17 guns), *Lady Prevost* (13), and *Hunter* (10)—sixty heavy guns against Perry's forty, to start with. A 3-gun schooner and a 1-gun lakeboat concluded Barclay's squadron. More than a match, he figured.

The Americans fired the first shot, getting on target at long range. *Detroit* answered with a prompt broadside, and the two squadrons in parallel line went stringing down the lake, firing hammer and tongs. With the advantage in minor caliber guns, Perry struck out boldly to engage *Detroit*, but the Yankee gunboats failed to come up. *Niagara*, too, fell behind, winded. The next thing Perry knew, his flagship was caught in a box, *Queen Charlotte*, *Lady Prevost*, *Detroit*, and *Hunter* pouring fire at *Lawrence* from all sides.

On either beam, off the bows and astern, the shots came crashing, sweeping *Lawrence*'s deck line like an iron hurricane. Perry's Marine lieutenant was shot down. Riflemen fell from the crosstrees. Cannon balls, crashing into the sloop's hull, wrecked her lower deck. The gunnery officer raced aft from the foredeck, his gun crew blown to pieces. Vainly Perry signalled for help. *Niagara* was far in the distance. Where were the gunboats?

Where? The Buffalo flotilla, you'll recall, had been under Commander Elliott. Elliott was now in command of *Niagara*. Afterwards, he claimed his ship was becalmed. But there was evidence that Elliott had wanted to command the whole squadron, had resented Perry's appointment as commodore, and deliberately held back to "come to the rescue" with a grandstand play. If so he delayed too long, and his shirking almost cost the battle and the American West.

For *Lawrence* was shot to a hulk. Two long hours the battle raged—one ship holding off four. The surgeon came topside to man a gun. Powder monkeys rammed and pointed and fired like veterans. Bearded frontiersmen sprang to replace sailors at the ropes, and wounded men crawled aloft to load muskets for the snipers in the rigging.

Her canvas in tatters, decks blasted and fire-blackened, hull shrouded in a welter of smoke, *Lawrence* was ready to sink like a sponge. Not ten men remained unwounded, and not a single battery could be fired when Perry finally put a boat overside,

shouted at the few unwounded to man the oars, and hauled down *Lawrence's* battleflag.

Barclay thought the American had surrendered, and the British ceased firing to cheer. Surrender? They couldn't see the legend on that blue battleflag! What they did see, to their astonishment, was Perry's smallboat racing out of the smoke-pall and heading full speed for *Niagara*. In the lifeboat's bow stood Oliver Hazard Perry, a blue flag clutched in his hands, and on the thwarts labored a handful of ragged seamen.

Maybe you've seen it as a painting—the tall officer in heroic pose—the fiery background—the flag. But Perry and his men weren't posing for any oil painting. They were battle-scorched, smudged with grime and sweat, and pulling for dear life. The enemy gunners woke up and tried to stop them. A storm of shots whistled over the lifeboat, near hits sending up fountains of spray. Canister splashed the water all around. Bullets chipped the lifeboat's gunwale. One shot splintered an oar. But the lifeboat ran the gauntlet and got away.

Aboard *Niagara* Perry took over, ordering Elliott off the ship to fetch the dillydallying gunboats. Up went *Niagara's* canvas. Up went the blue battleflag. Heading straight for the enemy squadron, Perry drove *Niagara* full-sail between the British ships, firing broadsides to port and starboard.

Unknown to Perry, Barclay's men were all exhausted from their two-hour battle with *Lawrence*. *Niagara's* flaming assault now threw the Britons into confusion. *Lady Prevost* and *Queen Charlotte* fouled their lines like frantic dowagers at a dance. *Hunter's* captain was killed when his ship caught a broadside that almost blew her out of the water. A blast swept *Detroit*. Perry slewed *Niagara* around, his coonskin riflemen firing volley after volley, batteries roaring, the ship going through the British line like a shooting gallery.

Barclay was hit three times, and *Detroit* surrendered. *Queen Charlotte* had already given up. *Hunter* and *Lady Prevost* struck their flags, and one naval flag remained flying above the smoke and blood on Lake Erie.

You can see that flag today at the United States Naval Academy at Annapolis. Its blue is pale, like the waters of the Great Lakes; its hem is torn like the rocky shores of Lake Erie. The

173

lettering is crude, but the message for over a century has echoed the words of Captain Lawrence and the courage of Master-Commandant Perry—

"Don't Give Up the Ship"

Then Oliver Hazard Perry left some memorable words of his own when he wrote his despatch of victory to General Harrison. You may read these words carved on the base of some monument to Perry, and they may seem cold and formal, just some more words carved in stone.

Forget that you're looking at a statue. You're looking at the Navy doing it again. You're looking at sailors carrying their guns overland to stop an invading colossus. You're watching the flash of gunfire in a lake—a little squadron of warships fighting to clear the way for Old Tippecanoe so his army, a few weeks later, could sweep the enemy from America's West.

Perry's message?

"WE HAVE MET THE ENEMY AND THEY ARE OURS."

Treachery!

Freedom of the Great Lakes, secured by Perry and his men, was the headline victory of 1813. Stop to think what might have happened had the invasion forces held their grip on the lands of Minnesota, Wisconsin, Illinois, and Michigan, and broken through Ohio to Pennsylvania! But your Navy and Harrison's frontiersmen cured that headache.

You can remember some other names along the Great Lakes, too. Captain Isaac Chauncey who built a fleet at Sackett's Harbor and held an enemy fleet stalemated on Lake Ontario. Lieutenant Melancthon Woolsey who took his sailors across the lake to storm Toronto.

And doff your hat in passing to that strange militia commander, Jacob Brown. This character acted on his own initiative to defend Sackett's Harbor when Chauncey's fleet was out and Sir George Prevost came raiding down from Canada to slaughter the base. Quaker and man of peace that he was, the amateur general gave professional Sir George a lesson in something

174

besides Brotherly Love. Bellowing "thee's" and "thou's" at the panicky militia, Brown rallied four hundred retreating troops to beat Sir George's regulars to a fare-thee-well. The feat should be noted at this point. Because they were faced with this kind of opposition—whirlwind Navy and fighting Quaker!—the enemy decided to bypass the Great Lakes entirely.

But they didn't give up the invasion plan. Not a bit of it. Swinging back east, they concentrated on Lake Champlain, the last big lake on the American-Canadian border.

But as the storm-clouds gather over Lake Champlain, look at the situation elsewhere. Bad weather? The ground hog saw more than his shadow that February 1814—he saw the shadow of the entire British fleet, five hundred warships holding the Atlantic seaboard in iron blockade. And black clouds overcast the Gulf of Mexico where British warships held a stranglehold on the Mississippi delta.

Over Washington the sky was like ink, and cold gloom hovered in the War Department where news that Napoleon had fallen in Europe meant the release of thousands of British veterans to come across the Atlantic.

Cold gloom in the White House where the truth was coming home to Madison—the truth that General-in-Chief James Wilkinson was a scoundrel and a turncoat, a spy in Spanish pay, a traitor who'd deliberately misled the Army, and altogether the most treacherous coyote ever to wear an American uniform.

Even the Navy Department was engloomed, hearing that *U.S.S. Essex* (Captain David Porter) had been lost in a bloody battle off the coast of Chile. On board was a salty, nine-year-old midshipman named David Farragut. How do you like that—a midshipman nine years old! You'll hear more of "Mister" Farragut, who was lucky to live through that adventure aboard *Essex*. Not many of his comrades survived it.

Who knows the depths of treachery achieved when one like Wilkinson starts undermining his country? Had he sold the American battle plans to the British? Had he betrayed government codes to Spain? Madison never knew, and to this day the man's conspiracies remain obscured, too far underground to be traceable.

But his record stands unequalled, a monument of double-crosses and scurvy lies. Greedy, conniving, he had early amassed a fortune by cornering the tobacco market and profiteering. During the Revolution he'd become involved in some dubious Spanish deal. His governmental post he had won by betraying the dictator-schemes of Aaron Burr, a former friend, and his ambitions were as notorious as his boudoir scandals. Finally dismissed in disgrace, he was allowed to slip down to Mexico and away, for Madison hardly knew how to handle so greasy a character.

Why is this crapulous scoundrel mentioned here? To show you the odds the American forces had been up against with this traitor undermining the whole war effort. You can also see how integrity is a "must" when it comes to leadership in the armed forces.

Personal honor has been a Navy standard since the day of John Paul Jones. Good character was established as a No. 1 requirement for naval officers and men.

This doesn't mean the Navy is a floating Sunday School. It never will be, and it never was. Boys will be boys, whether they're modern boys or Preble Boys, and a little hell-raising now and then is relished by the best of men.

But there's big difference between a square player and a cheat, just as there's a difference between hard, salty language and calculated, ratty obscenity. It's the difference that lies between the man who fights with his fists and the sort who sneaks out a knife. Your Navy recognizes such character differences, and judges its men accordingly.

The Rockets Red Glare

How would you like to have been an American in the summer of 1814 and seen headlines like these?

ENEMY MASSING ON LAKE CHAMPLAIN. GREAT BATTLE BREWING. OUR TROOPS OUTNUMBERED TWO TO ONE.

BLOCKADE TIGHTENS ON ATLANTIC COAST. OUR WARSHIPS UNABLE TO BREAK OUT. FOOD RIOTS IN COASTAL CITIES.

SITUATION GRAVE IN FLORIDA. EVIDENCE OF SPANISH PLOT TO SEIZE GEORGIA. GENERAL WILKINSON INDICTED FOR TREASON.

LOUISIANA THREATENED. DUKE OF WELLINGTON, HUGE ARMY, EXPECTED TO ATTACK NEW ORLEANS BY AUTUMN.

MISSISSIPPI RIVER CHOKED OFF. GUERILLA WARFARE FLAMES. INDIANS SIDE WITH ENEMY.

NEW ENGLAND THREATENS TO SECEDE FROM UNION. APPEASERS CALL FOR NEGOTIATED PEACE. DECLARE WAR LOST.

ENEMY LANDING ON ATLANTIC SEABOARD. MARYLAND INVADED. NATION'S CAPITAL THREATENED!

These news reports appalled the Americans of 1814, and lowered the temperature in men's hearts. But not in the hearts of the Navy's men.

On August 18th a British fleet entered the Chesapeake and effected a surprise landing—about 5,000 veterans seizing a Maryland beachhead. This army, under British Admiral Cockburn, struck boldly inland on a drive for Washington.

Hair rose in the nation's capital while government war bonds dropped to the value of wallpaper, and government workers dug trenches in the city's outskirts.

Madison called on General Winder to defend the city. Winder, with some 5,000 odd militia, proposed to make a stand along the main turnpike at Bladensburg.

Also with Winder were 400 sailors and Marines from Washington Navy Yard. These deployed smartly, taking their position on a small hill overlooking the threatened village.

The British marched into Bladensburg behind a brass band, then gave off a blast of bugles at sight of the American pickets. Cockburn's forces maneuvered into ranks like chessmen, and marched toward the Americans with flying colors.

Bullets began to fly as the opposing riflemen let go and the U. S. Navy gunners on the slope opened up. Then something else began to fly—something that soared up from the British line and sailed across the sky like a fiery comet.

Fizz-pop! Up went a streak of sparks. Whiz-bang! Another. Winder's militiamen stared bug-eyed. What kind of secret weapon was this? One of the comets landed in a pasture near the American line and went smoking and zigzagging through the grass, dragging a long tail of fire.

"Run!" some dough-head in the militia probably wailed. "It's a dragon!"

A dozen recruits threw down their rifles, and before you could say Jack Robinson all the American troops at Bladensburg were running like Jack Rabbits, throwing down weapons and equipment, pellmell on the turnpike back to Washington.

No, not all the Americans at Bladensburg. On that knoll above the field, the Navy sailors and Marines stood like rock. Staggered by the flight of the militia, stunned at finding themselves abandoned, they held their ground, firing desperately until the enemy charge crashed over them, and their little company was overwhelmed.

But that small knot of sailors who stuck it out undoubtedly

178

saved the day for President Madison. For he'd driven in his carriage to Bladensburg to be at the front with his troops, and he was almost there when the whole kiboodling militia came in stampede down on top of him. Unrecognized in the uproar, he was nearly capsized by the rush. If the British troops had not been delayed by those Navy men, the President would certainly have been captured, and a terrible blow dealt the nation.

As it was, the nonsensical panic cost the loss of the City of Washington—as crazy a military set-back as any in the nation's history. President Madison and his wife escaped from Washington just in time. British Admiral Cockburn walked into the White House, sat down and finished the President's dinner, then ordered the capital burned. The White House was set afire, the Navy Yard was burned, the Treasury Building and a few houses were burned. And it seemed as if American hopes must end in ashes, too. But the enemy quit the capital and moved north to capture Baltimore.

The British didn't capture Baltimore. As their ships approached the harbor entrance they ran into a storm of fire from a line of harbor forts. Chief of these was Fort McHenry, manned by Navy gunners.

All night long the British warships cannonaded Fort McHenry, and all night long Fort McHenry held the British warships at bay. There was an American civilian detained aboard one of the British vessels. His name? Francis Scott Key.

You know the song. Key scribbled the words on the back of a stray envelope, fitting them to the tune of an old folksong as he watched the raging bombardment.

Up from the British fleet and over the American battlements soared flaming comets that streaked the night with colored fire. Bright stars burst, painting the channel with blue-green light. More comets arching skyward exploding.

Key knew what they were, just as the sailors and Marines at Bladensburg had known what they were while the militia fled away from them in panic. Pyrotechnic signals! Star shells! The militia at Bladensburg had been routed by a handful of fireworks!

Francis Scott Key retrieved the blunder by writing the great lines of America's national anthem.

"AND THE ROCKET'S RED GLARE—THE BOMBS BURSTING IN AIR--"

In the morning the flag was still there, and the British, defeated, pulled away from Baltimore.

The Battle of Lake Champlain

As you may have suspected, the thrust at Washington and Baltimore was only a diversion. The main attack was set to hit New York State by way of Lake Champlain.

Here was the situation. At the head of the lake there's the American Army at Plattsburg under General Wade Hampton. But during the spring and summer of 1814 the army has melted considerably from desertion, sickness, and lack of replacement until it totals only some 4,000 men. Opposing this force you have a British Army of 11,000 seasoned regulars, and more on the way. At the Canadian end of the lake, there's a flotilla of British warships which has been playing hide and seek around Isle aux Noix, a sizable naval force under Captain George Downie. Now look down at the lake's southern end—the little American flotilla under Master-Commander Thomas MacDonough.

What odds will you take on the Battle of Lake Champlain? Even money on the Americans? Don't be a chump! The British will give you five to one. How can they lose—11,000 against 4,000 on land; on water *H.M.S. Confiance* alone mounting 37 heavy guns, able single-handed to blow MacDonough's entire force off the lake.

Here are some other odds MacDonough's flotilla was up against. He had to draw his naval stores from Troy, New York, miles away, and it took eighty teams of horses to haul a single consignment. He couldn't trust the natives of the countryside, for his supplies were liable to be stolen. The woods were full of appeasers, isolationists, malcontents, and spies. Smugglers went sneaking up the lake, carrying supplies to the enemy.

It isn't pleasant to remember, but the fact remains that two thirds of the fresh beef consumed by the British Army in 1814 was smuggled over the line by American farmers. On the home front around MacDonough, the breakdown was critical. Madison ordered the Vermont militia to MacDonough's aid, and the Governor of Vermont refused to let them march.

You will agree that those were pretty stiff odds with the United States of America at stake. Do you wonder the British flagship was named *Confiance*—French for "confidence"—and that the British commanders sent teasing letters through the American line, inviting the Americans to come out and fight?

"Captain Fisher begs the honor of presenting his compliments to Commodore MacDonough. He is extremely sorry that he gave him the trouble of sending all his flotilla after him this morning, but as the gunboats of the squadrons are about equal there can be no difficulty in trying their strength on any morning between Point au Fer and Wind Mill Point—"

This and a dozen similar invitations arrived at MacDonough's headquarters, and MacDonough answered politely, but refused to rise to the bait. His only chance on Lake Champlain was to build a couple of little ships in secret and try to approximate the enemy's fire power. He had to take taunts for time while his sailors endured the hardest strain of all—waiting.

Waiting. You know how it is. The uncertainty. The scuttlebut. "This is it!" Then it turns out to be only another drill. Then the flotilla starts out again. This time you're going! No, it's only another confounded practice maneuver. It takes a lot of discipline—waiting.

Would they ever get out and fight? Well, sometimes you also serve while you only stand and wait, and here's the kind of service those Navy men were doing. Along with drill and guard duty and all the rest of it, they were building ships. Early in 1814 MacDonough got hold of a New York shipbuilder named Browne. This was a stroke of luck. He told MacDonough he could build a 26-gun corvette in sixty days if the men pitched in.

The men pitched in under MacDonough's driving influence, and *Saratoga* was built from keel to topmast in forty days!

Then MacDonough appropriated a half-finished schooner, and in three or four more weeks there was *Ticonderoga* carrying the American flag and 16 guns. Shortly afterwards the brig *Eagle* (20 guns) was in the water, followed by the 7-gun sloop *Preble*. Where they'd begun with a few oar galleys and a pine forest, MacDonough and his men had built their fleet.

Just in time! The British, building her in secret, had put the finishing touches on *Confiance*, and Prevost was ready to launch the invasion. Along with *Confiance* (37 guns) the enemy squadron included the brig *Linnet* (16 guns), sloops *Chubb* and *Finch* (11 guns each), and twelve galleys (which would correspond to your PT boats of today), five of them carrying heavy caliber guns.

Look at the line-up in terms of fire power, and give the enemy 80 heavy guns against MacDonough's 69. But the guns on *Confiance* far out-ranged the American heavies, and she should have been able to out-shoot the whole American flotilla.

In crew-power, too, the Americans were outnumbered. The British squadron was manned by a fresh contingent of crack sailors from Montreal. The Americans were dog-tired, ragged, and discouraged by months of bad news. But they didn't let down, those American Navy men. And they had a great leader in Thomas MacDonough.

He was another Preble Boy. More than that, he'd been with Decatur on the night *Intrepid* burned *Philadelphia* in Tripoli harbor. In fact, he was the mid who led the charge against the pirates in the forecastle while demolition squads worked below.

He came from Delaware where the salt air blows, and he was adventurous, devoutly religious, full of strange pranks—he once sent a sick friend a coffin for a Christmas present—and a driving worker all in one. Like Preble, he could train. Like Hull, he was a seaman. Like Decatur, he could attack. Like Perry, he was a fighter. But perhaps MacDonough's outstanding quality was his inventiveness, his ingenuity, that imagination which gives a man the jump on the other fellow.

And MacDonough thought up something new. This was an anchor cable which worked on a spring arrangement rigged to a hawser running fore and aft under the ship. By tensioning a bow cable, the ship could be turned about-face from a standstill. Similarly, while at anchor, its stern could be slewed around. The device gave a ship, otherwise dependent on wind-power, a great increase in maneuverability.

His vessels rigged with this novel contrivance, MacDonough raced his squadron north up Lake Champlain to meet the enemy attack developing around Plattsburg. Luckily the Plattsburg Army had been put under the command of American General Macomb. Good earthworks had been dug, and the militia lines were holding against the British.

Prevost was keeping the main body of his invasion force on the border, the plan being for the British naval squadron under Downie to sail in first, smash the Plattsburg water defenses, and gain control of the lake. MacDonough's squadron reached Plattsburg Bay in time, and braced for the enemy attack. It wasn't long in coming.

Early morning, September 11, 1814, the British warships came down from the northeast. As the enemy hove in sight, big *Confiance* leading the battleline, MacDonough sounded GQ aboard

Saratoga, read the Episcopal prayer service, then rushed to fire the opening gun.

Soon an iron thunderstorm was rolling across Plattsburg Bay. Downie brought his squadron around the headland in great style, but ran into an uncertain wind which carried the sloop *Finch* off course and straight into MacDonough's line of fire.

The whole American squadron let go, and *Finch* was a clay pigeon.

But in return the Americans received a devastating blow. Her guns outranging anything on the lake, *Confiance* delivered a broadside that struck *Saratoga* full on the beam, setting her afire in two places and felling forty men on the spot. With a fifth of his flagship's crew out of action, MacDonough, himself, aimed a gun at *Confiance* and fired a shot that crippled the Briton's steering wheel.

Downie was forced to drop anchor within a quarter mile of *Saratoga* where MacDonough's batteries easily found range. The American gunners, skilled from long months of training, got to work. Toe to toe, *Saratoga* and *Confiance* began to slug it out, exchanging broadside for broadside.

Meantime *H.M.S. Linnet* and the sloop *Chubb* swung in to attack the brig *Eagle*. While *Eagle* was trading broadsides with these two adversaries, *Ticonderoga* was putting the finish to *Finch*. *Preble*, tail-end-Charley in MacDonough's squadron, was holding off the British galleys.

The battle mounted to hurricane pitch. *Ticonderoga* drove *Finch* ashore, a burning wreck, but little *Preble* had a time of it. The British galleys and armed craft surrounded the American sloop with a ring of fire, while MacDonough's armed craft were scattered. In a short time, *Preble* was out of it like *Finch*, shot to wreckage.

Now the galleys swerved in force to attack *Ticonderoga*. *Chubb* swung over to join this attack, and the American schooner was hard pressed, for her ordnance had not been completely assembled; firing locks had failed to arrive for her guns and they had to be fired by pistol-flashes. This dangerous job was done by a young mid, Hiram Paulding, while *Ticonderoga's* captain, Stephen Cassin, served as pointer with the main battery. Three times the enemy force attacked, and three times Cassin and his men drove them back.

At the northern end of the line *Eagle* and *H.M.S. Linnet* were engaged in a furious gun duel. *Chubb* came around to give her sister ship a hand with the American brig, but *Eagle's* fire was too savage for both enemies. One blast sent *Chubb* reeling, killing and wounding half her crew and driving her in a helpless drift toward *Saratoga.*

Things were hot aboard *Saratoga.* MacDonough's flagship, giving *Confiance* a pounding, was getting one from the Briton's heavy guns in return. A number of *Saratoga's* broadside guns had been blown from their mounts, her decks were fire-blackened, her rigging mangled.

In exchange, the American gunners had smashed in the Briton's bow. One raking salvo swept the length of *Confiance's* deck, struck a gun in front of Captain Downie. The explosion killed the British commander instantly. Lieutenant Robertson, his second in command, took over and signalled *Linnet* for help.

Linnet came down the bay, chased by *Eagle.* The Britisher gained a good position in the maneuver, and began to flay *Saratoga* with broadsides. If it had been hot for MacDonough's ship before, *Saratoga,* now caught between two fires, was in a furnace.

Spars and rigging came down in flaming tangles. One gun after another was silenced. The men fought on desperately. MacDonough, himself, was three times wounded—twice when flying splinters knocked him down, and again when a hurtling dead man sent him spinning across the deck to fall unconscious.

Cheers resounded from *Confiance* as she saw *Saratoga* falling to pieces in the cross-fire. *Eagle* was sending shots into the British flagship, but she was no match for *Confiance's* heavy batteries. And when a salvo from *Linnett* silenced *Saratoga's* last starboard battery, the battle seemed all but won.

You can hold your breath at this point—MacDonough must have been holding his. It was now or never. Now or never for the *Saratoga,* her crew beat up, her deck a shambles, half paralyzed with her starboard guns out of action.

It was the situation MacDonough had foreseen, the emergency he had prepared for. You recall the spring arrangement on his anchor cables?

"All hands forward to man the capstan!"

Orderly despite the deadly fire, *Saratoga's* sailors went forward, sweated it out around the capstan, and slowly swung the ship clear around to face *Confiance* with portside batteries.

This astonishing maneuver was too much for the enemy frigate. Unable to follow the operation, her bow anchors fouled. *Confiance* had to take broadside after broadside on her already damaged beam. Hot guns began to explode. She went into a starboard list that tilted her batteries beyond their normal angle of fire. In a few minutes she was hurt beyond repair. Down came her flag.

Chubb had long since struck. MacDonough worked his "Springs" once more, to round on *Linnet*. A broadside and *Linnet's* gun-deck sank under water. The oar-galleys fled, and the remaining British squadron surrendered.

Losing hope of effecting a break-through in northern New York, Prevost withdrew his armies into Canada. The Navy had done it again. MacDonough's "springs" had won a lake, and a great crew of fighting Navy men had stopped an invasion.

Turn of the Tide

The Champlain victory marked the tidal turn in the War of 1812, ending the enemy's invasion plans and convincing the King he could not even bite off Uncle Sam's head, much less chew it. Parliament was fed up with the war which many Englishmen had voted against in the first place. The war was proving a rank extravagance.

Commercially it was a disaster. British merchantmen were setting out with fine cargoes all right, but somehow or other they weren't delivering the goods. What was happening to these British merchantmen? In 1813 and 1814 over eight hundred of them were on the "missing" list. Eight hundred ships with valuable cargoes! True, a war was on, but the Yankee Navy was held land-locked by blockade. What accounted for this amazing phenomenon? American privateers!

Now you've come to one of the most dramatic stories of the War of 1812!—or any war. For you can think of privateering as the "silent service" of those days, despite the fact that it was all on the surface. Sailing on her own, her guns concealed behind trick ports and camouflage, the American privateer was a ship of mystery—blockade runner, destroyer, scout, and sea-raider combined.

As during the Revolution, these privateers were commissioned by the government, their officers and men corresponding somewhat to those of the modern Merchant Marine Reserve. Of Baltimore

clipper design, built like streamlined racing yachts with the tallest masts and widest spreads of canvas yet seen, many of these privateers were the fastest things afloat. All heavy timbering (the armor plate of those days) was sacrificed for speed. In the main their guns were of minor caliber, but they usually carried one "long tom" which was mounted amidships on a swivel.

America, Chasseur, General Armstrong, Globe, Neufchatel, Rambler—a score of these daredevil raiders rampaged across the ocean, making the trade routes unlivable for enemy traffic, and leaving great records and great names.

By late 1814 these raiders numbered close to five hundred. Typical of them was *Chasseur*, two-masted and two-fisted, breezing down into the Caribbean to tackle the island of St. Vincent single-handed. When the British sent a frigate to chase her away, she raced across the ocean to raid the English Channel. Over twenty merchantmen fell prey to *Chasseur's* fighting crew before she was run down by a 20-gun cruiser. Run down? *Chasseur* turned on the cruiser like a sea-going wildcat, rammed her bow over the enemy's figurehead, caught her with grappling-hook claws, and after a wild hand-to-hand fight captured the enemy warship!

Other privateers skimmed along in the Irish Sea. Still others were off the coast of Scotland. Outsailing, outshooting, outsmarting their opponents, the raiders accomplished an incredible feat —they counter-blockaded the British lion!

No one knows how many enemy ships were sunk by those

swivel-mounted "long toms." No one knows the exact total of captured merchantmen. But millions of dollars worth of shipping was destroyed; over nine million dollars worth of cargo was taken prize. To announce the loss of a ship, they used to ring a great bell at Lloyd's of London. It must have seemed to the Londoners as if that bell were tolling all the time.

You can take your hat off to those early American raiders who rang the bell with their racing yachts, their racing crews, and their ingenious "swivel-mounted" guns. And there it was again. Seamanship—gunnery—morale—brains—that winning combination!

The Second War for Independence

No longer was it "Mr. Madison's War." Now it was "The Second War for American Independence." MacDonough's victory on Champlain following Perry's on Lake Erie, and now the victories of these Yankee raiders—well, news that the Navy had gone places finally traveled through America despite slow communications.

The news reached the English King, too, in angry communiques from an Admiralty sick of having its ships caught with their pennants down. Grudgingly he conceded the war was hopeless, and sent his envoys to deal with American statesmen waiting to discuss peace terms at Ghent, Belgium.

The British envoys were inclined to bicker, as there was yet a chance an expeditionary force might successfully invade Louisiana. Such a force had set sail for America early in September, 1814, and the British envoys, late in December, were still stalling for good news.

They stalled too long.

For the British invasion fleet bound for New Orleans had stopped at the Azores to stock up. Instead of stocking up, it was shot up—by a Yankee privateer! She was *General Armstrong*, commanded by Captain Sam Reid, a blow-me-down sailor as full of fight as a stick of dynamite. He, too, had stopped in the Azores to stock up, and he wasn't going to be pushed around, even by an enemy invasion fleet led by a brig, a 38-gun frigate, and a 74-gun battleship!

Get that picture—that little Yankee raider in the harbor, and those three big warships crowding in like huge sea hawks around one Mother Carey's chicken.

"Surrender!" thundered British Commodore Lloyd.

"Surrender, hell," replied Captain Sam Reid, ordering the tompion out of his Long Tom.

Lloyd didn't want trouble in a neutral port, so he sent four tenders under cover of midnight to quietly scuttle the sassy raider. Reid's men heard them coming, and opened fire, smashing the four tenders into driftwood.

Lloyd ordered out more barges and loaded them to the gunwales with four hundred men. *General Armstrong's* crew numbered only ninety, and the four hundred boarders were primed to do a job. Sweeping in with muffled oars, they succeeded in coming alongside in the dark and fastening a grapple to the privateer's side. But Captain Sam Reid had been waiting for them, and so had his ninety Yanks. Hell broke loose in the harbor as defenders struck at boarders with cutlass, pike, and knife. For an hour the battle raged hand to hand, blade against blade, pistol against pistol. When the boarder finally retreated, the water was strewn with their floating dead, and they had killed but two of Sam Reid's men.

The enemy realized they'd caught a Tartar. Lloyd, hopping mad, sent the 18-gun brig *Carnation* special delivery instructions

to move up and blow this Yankee hell-ship to Kingdom Come. There was no pussyfooting about this attack. Morning was coming as *Carnation* began to bloom broadsides, letting go at the privateer with all her might. It wasn't enough. The British gunners missed and set the harbor town on fire. Swivelling their Long Tom as if it were a sniper's rifle, the American gunners didn't miss, and set *Carnation* on fire. By mid morning *Carnation* was out of it, a battered hulk with her mainmast uprooted, her decks a-sprawl and bloody. The bay was jammed with capsized tenders, wrecked barges, and bodies. Commodore Lloyd was tearing his hair and little *General Armstrong*, firing shot after shot, was holding off the frigate *Rota* and the battleship *Plantagenet*—fourteen guns against one hundred and twelve!

Only when two more of His Majesty's warships entered the harbor to see what the shooting was all about—only then did Captain Sam Reid give up. He didn't strike his colors, though. Not on your tintype! He simply aimed that swivel-gun down a hatch and blew a hole through the *General's* bottom. Then he rowed ashore through the smoke and wreckage with his boys, and interned himself in an Azores castle to become a legend in naval warfare and the man who rearranged the stars in your modern American flag.

And he also rearranged the New Orleans invasion time table by delaying the enemy fleet in a battle that cost them three hundred and fifty casualties against an American loss of nine! More. That delay cost the enemy Louisiana!

For the British, forced to wait for replacements, were weeks late in reaching New Orleans. And a general named Andy Jackson got there ahead of them. On January 8, 1815, this frontier fighter with an army of buckskin riflemen turned New Orleans into an enemy cemetery. 10,000 British veterans came ashore to charge American trenches containing 4,000 pioneer sharpshooters. General Sir Edward Pakenham died with a bullet in his head. It was that harbor in the Azores all over again. When the smoke blew away over 2,000 Britons lay dead in the Mississippi mud. American losses: 13.

The enemy had one last victory at sea, but it was a thin one. On January 15, 1815, His Majesty's warships, *Majestic*, *Endymion*, *Pomone*, and *Tenedos* caught an American frigate running the blockade off Long Island in a storm. She was *U.S.S. President;* her commander, Stephen Decatur.

Or, rather, she was caught on a sandbar when the enemy sighted her. Decatur's boys pumped like fury, and got her off. *H.M.S. Endymion* ran in to sink her. Four broadsides, and *Endymion* almost ended in Davey Jones' locker, retreating from the accuracy of Decatur's gunners with her canvas blown down like laundry in a hurricane. But *Majestic* and the other two Britons closed in; *President* got it from three sides, and Decatur took a bad slash from a flying splinter. He kept his batteries pounding, but his ship had started her seams on the bar and was leaking as badly as his chest-wound. In the thick of this precarious situation he was struck down by a smashing blow on the head. Then, unwilling to see his men die in hopeless slaughter, he surrendered.

Oddly enough, peace had already been signed, and the war was over. But the news had not yet reached America.

So it remained for the U. S. Navy, which had fired the first shot of the war, to fire its last. And dramatically enough it was *Constitution*—*"Old Ironsides"*—who fired that last shot.

She had been blockaded throughout 1814. On Christmas Day she broke loose and went down the Atlantic, seeking battle. An entire British squadron set out in chase, but they never sighted her topsails. For her captain this time was Charles Stewart, a Preble Boy, the last of that great Navy team.

Stewart took the famous warship on a bee-line for the Portuguese Islands, hunting enemy warriors on the sea lane to Madeira. He didn't have to look long. On the 20th of February, 1815, he sighted two warships, *Cyane* and *Levant*, with fifty-two guns between them to match "Old Ironsides'" forty-five.

No word of peace had reached these ships, of course, and soon the shots were crashing in a seascape of foggy moonlight.

Cyane went first, her deck whipped to shambles by a thunder-clap from *Constitution's* guns. Seeing her companion mortally hurt, *Levant* tacked around to the rescue with great bravery, but her smaller guns couldn't stand "Old Ironsides'" fire.

Afterwards, in Stewart's cabin, the losing captains argued bitterly, each blaming the other for faulty tactics. Stewart offered to return them to their captured vessels to fight the battle over again. The offer was cordially declined.

No doubt about it, now. The United States Navy had finished the War of 1812.

WE HAVE MET THE ENEMY

Over the Bounding Main

Shortly after the close of the War of 1812 there arrived in the mail of the President of the United States one of the strangest letters ever written to anybody. If you don't believe it you can see this letter today in the archives in Washington.

Its opening salutation remains a masterpiece of magnificent word-slinging.

"With the aid and assistance of Divinity," it begins, *"and in the reign of our sovereign, the Asylum of the World, powerful and great monarch, transactor of all good actions, the best of men, the shadow of God, director of the good order, King of Kings, Emperor of the Earth, Emulator of Alexander the Great, possessor of great forces, son of the Emperor and Conqueror Mohammed Khan (may Allah and his life be prosperous, and his reign be everlasting and glorious) his humble and obedient servant, actual sovereign governor and Chief of Algiers, submitted forever to the order of His Imperial Majesty's noble throne—Omar Pasha (may his government be happy and prosperous). Greetings!*

"To his Majesty, the Emperor of America, its adjacent dependent provinces and coasts, and wherever his government may extend, our noble friend, the pillar of all Christian sovereigns, the most glorious among the princes, elected among many lords and nobles, the happy, the great, the amiable James Madison,

193

Emperor of America (may his reign be happy and glorious), wishing him long possession of the seal of his blessed throne, and long life and health, Amen. Hoping that your health is in good state, I inform you that mine is excellent, thanks to the Supreme Being, constantly addressing my humble prayers to Allah for your felicity."

There were several pages of this sort of thing, and then the letter got down to business. Would the Emperor of America, James Madison, etc., kindly remove the "shadow of Stephen Decatur" from the otherwise sunny shore of Algiers? As an American consul, Stephen Decatur was very amiable, etc., but he had demanded a treaty from Algiers which was wholly impractical from the Algerian point of view. Amiable Captain Decatur had not been very diplomatic about this matter, and the Dey of Algiers, the best of men, the shadow, etc., regretted that he could not stand by the transaction.

"I inform you, therefore, that a treaty of peace having been signed between America and us during the reign of Hassan Pasha, twenty years past, I propose to renew said treaty on the same basis stipulated in it, and if you agree, our friendship will be solid and lasting. We hope that with the assistance of God you will answer this our letter immediately after you have carefully perused its contents. Requesting only that you will have the goodness to remove your consul as soon as possible, assuring you that it will be very agreeable to us. These are our last words to you, and we pray Allah to keep you in his holy guard.

"Written in the Year of Hegira 1231, on the 20th day of the moon Dge Mazirl Covel, corresponding to April 24, 1815. Signed in our well-beloved city of Algiers.

"Omar, Son of Mohammed,
Conqueror and Great."

Enclosed with the letter was a neat little price list.

Captains	$6,000
Mates	4,000
Passengers	4,000
Seamen	1,400

A footnote politely reminded "Emperor Madison" that the Algerians still held the American brig, *Edwin*, in captivity. Brig and eleven crew members, captured in 1811, would be returned at bargain rates. But the Americans had better buy soon (it was hinted) or *Edwin* and her crew might end up in a fire sale. Last price from Omar, Son of Mohammed.

As an example of polished diplomacy this epistle has never been equalled, even by the pious ultimatums of Adolph Hitler and the written works of Al Capone. But the flowery phrases smelled like stinkweed to James Madison.

To begin with he was about as far from an Emperor as anybody you could imagine. He was a good staunch Virginia democrat who'd been duly elected President of the American Republic. He had no use for Emperors, and he didn't feel like one, especially after the British had chased him out of the White House and he'd just managed to get his coattails out in time with the Declaration of Independence hidden under them, while his wife, Dolly, followed with George Washington's portrait tucked under her skirt.

No he didn't care for noble titles, particularly since the War of 1812, and he cared less for this perfumed ransom note from a pirate on the mud-flats of Africa.

It may surprise you to learn that throughout the War of 1812 the United States had continued making blackmail payments to Algiers. But you recall how the Tripolitan War, against Preble's wishes, had been settled by a negotiated peace. Then the war in the Atlantic came along as a full-time job, and the Barbary clean-up had to wait. So Uncle Sam had paid his yearly tributes although the installments had been considerably reduced by Preble and his boys. That was the "shadow of Decatur" referred to in the letter—a treaty which had cut the Algerian slice to $25,000 a year. And now Omar the Dey, regretting he had signed such a treaty, was demanding a revised treaty based on the one awarded Hassan Pasha in the good old days.

Omar's timing was unfortunate. Doubtless he'd heard America was at war, but he'd probably been reading the London newspapers which published a somewhat colored version. Or perhaps his court astrologer had put Mars too far away from the moon of Dge Mazirl Covel. At any rate, he doesn't seem to have known the War of 1812 was over. And he certainly didn't know that Stephen Decatur had just been released from British internment in Bermuda.

James Madison was in no mood for monkey-business. He sent Omar's poetic note to Congress with the recommendation that something be done about the pirate, and Congress agreed it was high time to chastize the old son of Mohammed. On March 3, 1815, the United States declared war on Algiers.

War With Algiers

Decatur and Bainbridge, having been on the binnacle list, were given a few weeks to recuperate, and then were assigned this new Mediterranean mission. Itching for a chance to repay the Barbary pirates for the death of his brother, Decatur was away on the 19th of May. His squadron included *Constellation*, *Epervier*, *Macedonian*, and *Ontario*, and his flagship bore the name won from the British—*Guerriere*. Bainbridge, with his usual bad luck, was delayed at the takeoff, and by the time he reached the Mediterranean it was all over.

Decatur was off Gibraltar by mid June, and he had hardly sighted the Rock before his glass picked up the pirate ship

Mashuda, a 46-gun frigate flying the flag of Rais Hammida, old Omar's number one admiral.

Instantly he had his top men aloft, *Guerriere* blossoming white sail, signals flying up the halyards, and gunners racing to their batteries.

One glimpse of Decatur's squadron bearing down, and Admiral Hammida must have muttered, "Kismet!" Fate had certainly caught up with him, and *Guerriere* overhauled him, too, booming down on *Mashuda's* stern like a fleecy cloud that turned into a cyclone.

The wormy old pirate vessel was no match for the American warship, just as wormy old Hammida was no match for Stephen Decatur. The Yankee gunners had a field day, and in ten minutes *Mashuda* was smashed to matchwood. Hammida lost his head, literally, when a cannon shot removed it from his shoulders. The corsairs fought on a few minutes longer, then down came the Algerian flag.

Decatur took the pirate ship in tow, and the following day, scouring the African coast, his scout craft sighted the Algerian corsair, *Esteido*. Tacking in on her quarter, they drove her ashore and blew her up. Then Decatur headed straight for the "well-beloved city of Algiers."

Omar, son of Mohammed, transactor of all good actions, best of men, the shadow, etc., was doubtless in the midst of his harem when word came that the American Navy was in his harbor. Omar, not wishing to be bothered, sent his High Commissioner to receive the expected tribute. Surprise! Instead of tribute, the commissioner came back with word that the Algerian Navy was at sea-bottom, the admiral was dead, and the corsair racket was ruined.

"By the Beard of the Prophet!" bellowed Omar. "This cannot be true!"

The commissioner assured him that it was direful fact. The Americans were holding captive Rais Hammida's second officer, who told the story as a personal experience. Not only that, the *Roumi* leader was Stephen Decatur, the very shadow which Omar had wished removed from his shores.

Omar sent out the Swedish consul to verify this depressing news, and when the Swede returned with a cheerful nod, bringing further information that Decatur demanded the safe return of all American captives, reparations for past piracy, and assurance there would be no future piracy, Omar went into a super tantrum.

Then, being an Arab, he tried to barter, asking time to think it over. No time, said Decatur flatly. Sign now, or the American naval squadron would blow Algiers into a dust-heap.

Weeping in his beard, Omar signed. The brig, *Edwin,* and her sailors were handed over unharmed. Out came a felucca loaded with bags of gold for indemnity. The Algerian War was over, and the whole peace arrangement had been settled in three hours. Which may lead you to note that there is just one way to deal with piratical racketeers, no matter how poetic their approach.

Meantime, since arriving in the Mediterranean, Decatur had learned that Tunis and Tripoli weren't living up to the treaties previously made. He had no time to send a ship overseas to advise Washington, so he decided to strike while the iron was hot. Leaving Algiers under the horizon, he was presently in Tunis, demanding $46,000 reparation for damaged American rights. Negotiations were made through the American consul whose name was Mr. Noah, but who quickly convinced the Bashaw that the ship ready to take him out of the harbor was not the Ark.

Recalling Decatur's name with vivid clarity, the Bashaw signed the new treaty on the double.

Tripoli also signed on the dotted line with alacrity. The date was August 7, 1815. Within the brief space of seventy-one days, the American Navy had established freedom of the Mediterranean.

A dying snake always tries a final wiggle, and in 1816 old Omar made a last attempt at ransom (from the Europeans).

Holland, encouraged by Uncle Sam, refused to pay. And England sent a fleet which bombarded Omar's strong-hold into a rubbish-pile. So the sun finally set on the Dey of Algiers.

You might note something at this point—an aspect of your Navy which perhaps you haven't previously considered. That aspect has to do with DIPLOMACY.

Diplomacy and Naval Power

From the first your Navy was something more than just a combat organization.

When Thomas Jefferson came to realize that isolation was impossible, he did an about-face and recommended a strong American Navy. This was a surprise to people who had named him a pacifist, and recalled that he once said America was "running navigation mad." They accused Jefferson of changing his mind.

But Jefferson had not turned into a militarist or war-monger. He was an honest thinker, that was all—one of the most intelligent men America ever had. He sincerely hated war as ruinous and bloody. But he saw that aggressors couldn't be stopped by appeals for peace. A strong Navy might prevent war. And if war came despite it, a strong Navy could beat down the aggressor.

He saw that America was bound to grow, that Americans were "going places." They had long been shipping cotton and tobacco, lumber, corn, and molasses to Europe, and importing dress goods and manufactured articles and wines and spices in return. This was honest commerce and brought prosperity to the nation. A strong Navy would serve to protect honest commerce. And the Navy could lead the way, not in conquest, but as guide, charting strange waters, visiting the foreign ports, arranging reciprocal trade treaties, establishing friendly relations.

The Navy set out early on diplomatic missions. Preble, as you know, was assigned diplomatic authority. Then you saw Captain Bainbridge on his "mission to Moscow." In 1817, Captain Biddle, aboard *Ontario*, was doing the rounds in the South Pacific where David Porter had broken the ice. In 1820 Captain Henley sailed *Congress* out to China to open a treaty port. Not long after that John Rodgers was sent to Turkey to

ange a commercial treaty with the Sultan, and seven years
Melancthon Woolsey was negotiating a treaty in the far-off
Faulkland Islands. The American Way was carrying out the
basic function of diplomacy—winning friends.

Sometimes this took a whole cargo of tact and skill, especially
among the island primitives and Oriental people where everything was a matter of "face" de-

manding elaborate ceremony. But
the early American Naval officers
weren't fazed by that. Courtesy
was a part of their military code,
while the relief to much monotony
at sea was ceremony.

Similarly flag salutes, dipping
the ensign, and saluting the quarterdeck had long acquainted
American Navy men with formal
honors. Dipping the flag, for ex-
ample, goes far back in naval history. Originally, a merchantman, on meeting a warship, was supposed to haul in her canvas
to show herself a peaceful vessel on honest voyage. As this often
caused a long delay, the rule of dipping the ensign was substituted.
Today it is done as a compliment, and United States Naval vessels
return dip for dip. (Note that your Navy ship never dips her
ensign except to acknowledge a compliment.)

Have you ever wondered about the honors paid a ship's quarterdeck? The ceremony goes far back into the centuries. In the
ancient days of Greece and Rome, ships carried a shrine which
was usually located aft. In the shrines of the Roman ships were
placed the little doll-sized images called *pupi* (which gives you
the origin of the term "poop deck"). Sailors coming aboard
would bow to these shrines in obeisance. Then in medieval
times the pagan shrine became the shrine of a Christian saint,
similarly revered. This was later replaced by the "king's colors"
as symbolic of authority and demanding a salute from those
who came board. And today the quarterdeck is still saluted as
the honored part of the ship.

Thus with many ceremonies and customs of their own, the
early American Navy men were understanding of foreign cus-

toms and ceremony. They knew how to enter a foreign port with colors flying, how to honor another's traditions, how to act as guest, or to play host and entertain.

Piping over the side was a formality inherited from the British Navy, and it began when commanders visited one another at sea. Often the weather would be too rough for the gangway, and the visiting officer would be hoisted up the ship's side in a net or basket. The O.O.D. would summon several members of the crew to assist the visitor in making a happy landing. If the officer were young, a lieutenant, say, he would be nimble enough to get along with only two helpers. If older, a commander, or a captain, he was doubtless heavier amidships, and needed four. It could be assumed that an admiral, weighted with responsibility and years, would need six or eight.

In departing, especially after a full dress banquet, the visitor was liable to be even more in need of assistance, and the helping hands would be mustered to his aid again. So the regulation custom of "side boys" became established to attend the visitor at arrival and departure. Today, piping an officer or official visitor alongside and over the gangway is traditional Naval courtesy.

As a Navy man, you will be practicing diplomacy when you visit in neutral or allied ports. Should you stand as side boy or turn out on review, you'll be doing your part in the Navy's ceremony. And if you go ashore on liberty you can do even more. A liberty party of decently behaved American sailors can be a big advertisement for Uncle Sam. You can carry your end of making a good impression in your country's behalf, and you can show you know how to act as a guest. Winning friends, remember, is part of diplomacy—and diplomacy, remember, is part of your Navy's job.

Then there's that other aspect of diplomacy—influencing people. The American Navy has always been good at that, too. For honesty is sometimes left out of the diplomatic game. Then the only diplomacy Uncle Sam can resort to is slamming his hand down and calling the bluff. Omar's deal is a typical episode, calling for naval influence as exerted by Stephen Decatur.

Presently you'll see some other examples of the Navy's "diplomatic influence." Meantime a new situation needed handling by the Navy as a combat organization. Another sea was becoming troubled—the Caribbean. Another brand of pirate had reared its ugly Death's Head—the buccaneer.

Buccaneers

"Buccan" is a Caribbean creole word meaning a small bonfire over which a chunk of meat is barbecued. As the Caribbean pirates had a great taste for barbecues, they were nicknamed "buccaneers."

These rapacious sea rovers began operating in the Caribbean not long after the first Spanish conquest, raiding the sea lanes and attacking honest commerce. If you look at a map of the West Indies you will see that the Caribbean Islands were a natural for high piracy. From Cuba and Haiti all the way down to Trinidad, the Windwards, and Leewards provided the buccaneers with hundreds of inlets, outlets, hidden harbors, and secret coves.

Throughout the 1700's and 1800's the maritime nations conducted an endless war against these sea-wolves. They succeeded in capturing such famous cutthroats as Black Bartlemy and Captain Kidd, and managed to keep buccaneering at a minimum. But shortly after 1800 it broke out again like a strawberry rash, and by 1815 the pirate's bonfires were twinkling on half the islands in the Caribbean.

The reason, of course, was that the American and British navies were busy elsewhere. Napoleon's fleet had also been otherwise occupied. Spain had never been able to control Hispaniola and Cuba, and it was hard to distinguish between a Spanish warship and a pirate galleon in the first place. The buccaneers were as thick as fleas around Haiti, where the Negro slaves had just won a great war of independence, freeing themselves from France, but leaving them without a single warship.

So it was, "Yo, ho, ho, and a bottle of rum!" and the Black Flag rode a high crime wave on the Spanish Main. All of which may sound delightfully romantic in the light of pirate stories and pirate movies, but the fact is that these freebooters were a plague on the face of the earth. Mutton was not the only flesh to be barbecued over their buccan fires, and their treatment of captive women reached an historic high in atrocity. As men they were as close to scum as any who were ever hanged, and their pirate lairs were cesspools of treachery, disease, and cruelty.

Uncle Sam rolled up his sleeves and decided that since he'd been cleaning house he might as well go after these local pests. Freedom of the Caribbean was another job assigned to your Navy.

Operations began in the Gulf of Mexico under Commodore Daniel Patterson. Patterson was a fighting Navy officer who had cooperated with Andy Jackson at New Orleans, holding the flank against the British invasion fleet on the delta.

The situation at New Orleans was difficult. The near-by island of Barataria was a stronghold for the pirate, Jean Lafitte, who had offered aid to "Old Hickory" in the battle against the British. Now the War of 1812 was over. New Orleans was a booming seaport flooded with all the shipping which had been pent-up in the Mississippi. This rich tide of commerce was too much for Lafitte, who forgot his former allegiance to the cause of freedom and began a series of savage raids on American traffic. Patterson, with a small flotilla of armed schooners, was ordered to put Lafitte out of business. It seems there were some bribes being passed around, but the Navy remained immune. Briskly and efficiently Patterson's force descended on Barataria and blasted the pirate stronghold off the map.

Meantime Naval patrols were probing into the West Indies where the crime wave had mounted to a tidal wave. Things had become so bad that buccaneer attacks on merchant ships were a weekly occurrence. Every port in the Caribbean was telling its story of horror—liftboats coming ashore with murdered seamen on the thwarts—scuttled ships drifting in with sailors hanging from every yardarm—in several instances the bodies mutilated, the rigging fiendishly decorated with arms, legs, and heads.

The Navy uncovered a midden of skullduggery. A number of the buccaneers turned out to be renegade Britons, American desperadoes, Navy deserters, ex-mutineers, the usual criminal backwash that takes advantage of the unsettled conditions which follow a long war. But the majority were sailing under the guise of privateers, camouflaging the Jolly Roger behind counterfeit flags and flying the colors of "The Republic of Puerto Rico" or "The Carthaginian Junta," or whatever fabulous nation they might invent. Upon being overhauled, many produced papers claiming Venezuelan registry. As Venezuela was at that time revolting from Spain, these pirates declared themselves lawful forces, and claimed the Caribbean a "war zone."

Of course this claim of "legality" was a farce, and in 1819 Captain Oliver Hazard Perry was dispatched to Venezuela to see about it. He was authorized to arrange a treaty with the Venezuelans which would stop their issuing papers to any crew of ruffians that came along. Once more you see the Navy assigned to an important diplomatic mission.

Renowned as "the Hero of Erie," Perry would have been a good man to send had his health not been failing. But the Great Lakes campaign had worn him down. He could have gone on the binnacle list, but in 1816 he was off for the Mediterranean as captain of captured *Java*, a hard cruise during which Perry became involved in an acrid quarrel with an insubordinate Marine Corps captain. When the Marine officer came off second best with a black eye, he filed charges. Perry filed countercharges. There was official investigation, and Perry was absolved with a reprimand, whereas today he would doubtless have been absolved as a victim of battle fatigue.

To add to the strain of this affair, Commander Elliott, who had failed to support Perry on Lake Erie, took occasion to publish some vitriolic comment about the Erie victory, stating that he, Elliott, had won the battle by his "delaying" strategy, and that Perry had actually surrendered when he lowered the battleflag on *Lawrence*. On the heels of this insult, Perry was challenged to a duel by the Marine captain he had corrected aboard *Java*.

Immediately Stephen Decatur volunteered to serve as Perry's second. The contestants met as the code demanded. Perry stood at ease throughout the count. His opponent, unnerved, fired and missed. Then Perry aimed his own pistol in the air, fired, wheeled about-face, and walked from the field. When you realize that he had previously apologized to his adversary, you can appreciate the character of Oliver Hazard Perry.

But Elliott's public slurs were another matter, and Perry demanded a court-martial and official investigation of Elliott's conduct on Lake Erie. These incidents are set down here because they bear on later developments in the Navy. They also show you Perry's caliber as a man. For he could have "pulled rank" on Elliott, challenged him and shot him down, or retired from the service and rested on his laurels. Instead, he preferred to fight the official way and let the Navy stand as judge. The case was pending when Perry was assigned to the mission to Venezuela.

He was worn with strain, tired, in ill health, and could have requested replacement. But the mission was important, and he accepted. He succeeded in negotiating the treaty—the first between the United States and Venezuela. But the effort cost him his life. In Venezuela he contracted yellow fever, and died in the West Indies on his way home.

The buccaneers remained out of hand, and on December 20, 1822, Congress authorized a full naval squadron to suppress piracy in the Caribbean Sea. The squadron was commanded by Captain Biddle, who had served as lieutenant aboard *Wasp* during her fight with *Frolic*. With two frigates, two corvettes, and several smaller vessels, Biddle cruised through the West Indies, driving the picaroons to cover. Off Puerto Rico a minor sea battle was fought when the gunboat *Grampus* was attacked by a square-rigged buccaneer. The Navy gunners wasted little time on this freebooter. Within five minutes the pirate was a sinking wreck.

Most of the pirates fled for their secret coves, where they remained in hiding like grinning crocodiles. Biddle was then without the men or small boats to flush them out, but in 1823 the Navy sent David Porter. Captain Porter took with him a small fleet of shallow-draft schooners and armed craft. He also took along a young lieutenant named David Farragut and a crew of sailors trained in amphibious operations—just the men to go after crocodiles.

It was dangerous work, coasting into a fever-infested lagoon, establishing a beach-head, and then combing unknown jungle for some murderous Blackbeard. More than one good American bluejacket died in a West Indies ambush.

More dangerous than the pirates was Yellow Jack. Porter, himself, contracted this deadly fever. A score of officers and men were buried at sea, and Captain Porter had to lead the squadron back north to break up the epidemic. But crew morale remained at fighting pitch, and Porter was not the man to be swerved from his course. Doggedly he returned through the Windward Passage and went "island hopping" down the Indies, smashing one pirate cove after another.

By the end of 1824 not a single Jolly Roger remained in the Caribbean. Buccaneering came to a dead end. And from that day to this the only skull and crossbones flag seen in the Western Hemisphere was one a few years ago around New York—flying from an undertaker's pleasure yacht.

While the Navy can take a bow for this salubrious clean-up, credit must also be given to the forthright mind of James Monroe. A neighbor of Washington, Jefferson, and Madison, he followed Madison into the White House as the last of the "Virginia Dynasty"—the name given those Virginia-born founding fathers who were elected to the Presidency.

Don't let that title, "founding father," fool you. Major Monroe was no elderly patriarch with a beard. He was six feet tall in his Virginia boots, and a patriot. He'd won his brevets in the Revolutionary Army, and he carried a bullet buried in his shoulder which pained him like the devil when the weather changed. In other words, he was a soldier's soldier.

As a soldier he is generally not associated in the popular mind with the Navy. But James Monroe played a big part in shaping American naval policy as you'll see.

He was President—and Commander-in-Chief—when the Caribbean pirates were put down, and he had no use for piracy in any form. Mark that phrase, "in any form."

For pirates do not always wear brass earrings and floppy-top boots and come lurching at you with a dagger in clenched teeth. Like old Omar, a pirate can dress up like a Sultan or a king. And piracy, garbed as diplomacy, can sometimes be subtle as silk.

It was this silky type of picaroon—a new and subtle form of high piracy—that Major Monroe was confronted with toward the end of his administration. Fortunately it failed to deceive his penetrating eye, and he was a rugged American who didn't care for silk.

The thing opened up in England when, early in August 1823, George Canning, the British Minister of Foreign Affairs, summoned Richard Rush, the American envoy, to his office. Canning gave Rush some important information. From the American point of view, mighty important information!

He told the American envoy that the Holy Alliance had just met in great secrecy and determined on a plan to subjugate the Central and South American republics. Former colonies of Spain, these countries had revolted against Spain's misrule and declared their independence at about the same time as the American

Revolution. Inspired by Simon Bolivar (the George Washington of South America) they were trying to establish themselves as democracies on the American plan. But now the Holy Alliance had decided to put an end to them and reconquer them as outlaw territory.

Who were the Holy Alliance? Well, as a historian once described the Holy Roman Empire—as neither holy, Roman, nor an empire—the Holy Alliance, a somewhat similar European set-up, was neither holy nor exactly an alliance.

Briefly, it was the brain-child of Prince Metternich, the Foreign Minister of Austria. And it was a cunning brain-child, hatched by one of the craftiest brains in Europe. The Holy Alliance consisted of the Emperor of Austria, the King of Prussia, and the Czar of Russia, as despotic a trio as ever joined hands. These three rulers were pledged to reestablish in the world the "divine right of kings" which had lately been losing a lot of ground to democracy. In short, this sanctimonious alliance proposed to set the clock back about five hundred years and put an end to all this talk about liberal governments and people's rights and November elections.

They began in secret by smashing a democratic movement in Italy. Then they loaned troops to the King of Spain and stamped out a republican movement in Spain much as Hitler and Mussolini recently conspired to aid Franco. With these successes to encourage them, they invited the King of England to join the party. England sent the Duke of Wellington to sit in on a secret meeting at Verona. And when the Duke saw what was cooking, he walked out.

What was cooking was this proposal to stamp out democracy in Central and South America. Liberal government was also to be ended in Europe. In effect, the Holy Alliance meant to end all governments "of the people, by the people, and for the people" everywhere, and run the world by absolute monarchy instead.

Does that sound unbelievable? Well, the Holy Alliance adopted a series of Articles at Verona, and here is Article I:

"The high contracting powers, being convinced that the system of representative government is equally as incompatible with monarchial principles as the maxim of the sovereignty of the

people is incompatible with the divine right of kings, engage
mutually in the most solemn manner to put an end to the system
of representative governments in whatever country it may exist
in Europe, and to prevent its being introduced in those countries
where it is not yet known."

Read that last line again. *"To prevent its being introduced in those countries where it is not yet known."* That meant the countries of South America, and Central America, and Mexico! That meant the whole southern half of the Western Hemisphere! The Holy Alliance planned to step into those countries, sentence them to Old World rule, and set up a continent of kings and emperors right under Uncle Sam's republican nose. In other words, the invasion fleets of Austria, Prussia, and perhaps Russia would soon be visiting Mexico, Brazil, and the Argentine. That was the cat let out of the bag by the British Foreign Minister for the benefit of Richard Rush!

Now the English not only washed their hands of the Holy Alliance, but tipped the Americans off. And here you see the beginning of a friendly relationship, later strengthened by a number of similar incidents, which resulted in America and Britain standing side by side as allies. These historic incentives are sometimes forgotten. Just as the reasons behind the Monroe Doctrine are forgotten—why it was devised, what it prevented, and what it stands for.

The Monroe Doctrine

Any good American Navy man ought to know about the Monroe Doctrine. You already know the main reason behind it—the Holy Alliance conspiracy. Well, when Richard Rush got a whiff of that stew, he sent the recipe back home in a hurry.

That was a pretty kettle of fish to serve President Monroe! He took one look at Rush's notes, and he knew the U. S. A. was up against a brand of pirate diplomacy that made Omar the Shadow's look amateurish in comparison. And kicking the buccaneers out of the Caribbean would be a polka compared to throwing out the combined powers of Spain, Austria, Prussia, and Russia.

For the impoverished peasants and peons of Central and South ica would never have a chance against those great European ers. Monroe's republican sympathies were naturally for opsed peoples in revolt. He didn't want to see Spanish tyranny another foothold on his nation's doorstep, with the Prussian Guard in Mexico or the Austrian cavalry in the Andes. And he saw something else. If those powers became rooted in South America, Imperial Russia would become similarly rooted at North America's back door, for the Czar shared discovery claims in Oregon Territory as far south as Spanish California. The United States was threatened with a gigantic squeeze by powers pledged to stamp out democracy! The whole scheme burned Major Monroe worse than the Revolutionary bullet in his shoulder.

Meantime, the British Foreign Minister had proposed that England and the United States make a joint announcement. *"We conceive the recovery of the colonies by Spain to be hopeless— we could not see any portion of them transferred to any other power with indifference."*

Monroe wrote to the wisest man he knew for advice. Old Thomas Jefferson roused himself from retirement to denounce the Holy Alliance as a grave threat to American democracy. He advised the cultivation of Great Britain's friendship. *"With her on our side we need not fear the whole world."*

But John Quincy Adams, Monroe's Secretary of State, suggested that it was an American problem, and the United States of America could best handle it alone.

Adams, himself, outlined the declaration which President Monroe, on December 2, 1823, announced in his annual message to Congress. Monroe advised the powers of Europe that:

"THE AMERICAN CONTINENTS, BY THE FREE AND INDEPENDENT CONDITION WHICH THEY HAVE ASSUMED, ARE HENCEFORTH NOT TO BE CONSIDERED AS SUBJECT FOR FUTURE COLONIZATION BY ANY EUROPEAN POWER."

President Monroe further announced to the European powers that: *"we should consider any attempt on their part to extend their system to any portion of this hemisphere as dangerous to our peace and safety."*

He added that the United States had no intention of interfering with any present colonies existing in the Americas, but would back up those colonies which had established their independence.

He concluded that the United States did not intend to interfere with the existing governments of Europe, but intended, *"to cultivate friendly relations with it, but submitting to injuries from none."*

And here's where the Navy comes in. Where? Well the United States could hardly have announced such a policy without the means to back it up. As a matter of fact, when Monroe did announce it, a good many Europeans and almost as many Americans wondered if the United States could make it stick.

For between their alliance and the continents of America lay the Atlantic Ocean. And on the Atlantic Ocean was the U. S. Navy. A fox like Metternich was no fool. He had heard of Preble, Bainbridge, and Decatur. The conniving King of Spain could tell him about those big men-o'-war with the long guns and tall masts and Stars and Stripes fluttering atop. Anyone could tell him about the War of 1812. So the plan to stamp out democracy in Central and South America went fizz-pop! The countries of Latin America retained their independence. And today you have the Good Neighbor Policy.

TO CULTIVATE FRIENDLY RELATIONS

Navy Gets Up Steam

From 1830 to 1860 the U. S. Navy didn't have much to do, unless you want to call this a job—developing new ordnance, charting the seven seas, engaging in polar exploration, patrolling the China Coast, carrying on diplomacy, convoying troops in the Mexican War of 1845, launching the Academy at Annapolis, and opening up the Orient to American trade. But it was a "quiet" period—or it would have been if the Navy hadn't gone through another revolution.

Not a revolution in the ordinary sense of pitched battles, torn flags, and armed revolt; it was what you might call a "silent revolution." But it was as violent as any overthrow in history. It raised a ruction in the country, caused hard fighting in Congress, created a storm at sea, turned the Navy topsy-turvy, and finally obliterated every sloop, frigate, and ship-of-the-line in the American fleet. Within a few years it wrought more changes in the maritime world than had been wrought in fifty centuries.

But like the War of the Revolution, it had been simmering quite a time before the explosion. It began over in Europe around 1750—in the cottage of a poor Scotchman.

Tea Kettle Tempest

Like John Paul Jones, James Watt was a Scotch lad with an inquiring turn of mind. But whereas Jones became interested in sea water, young Watt became interested in hot water.

One day, according to the story, the lad found himself watching a tea kettle on the kitchen hearth, and wondering what made the kettle tick. It was bubbling and singing with hot vapor pouring from the spout and the copper lid dancing a jig. Why? Wasn't it because the steam pushed up against the underside of the lid? And if a little steam could lift a little lid on a little kettle, couldn't a lot of steam lift a big lid on a big kettle?

Sure, mon! And if a lot of steam can lift a big lid, why, it means that in steam there's driving force—power. That's what James Watt was thinking about, watching that kettle. STEAM POWER!

For if steam had the power to lift a lid, it could shove a plank or turn a wheel. How about forcing it into a shaft to shove a movable arm? He went to work on the idea and right off he had a disappointment. Somebody else had thought of it first—an Englishman named Thomas Newcomen, away back in 1705, had patented a steam-driven piston to pump water out of coal mines. It was a slow, expensive contraption, full of breakdowns. Even so, it accomplished the work of fifty men.

So Watt turned to studying science, and a few years later he was on another tack, making astronomical instruments for the University of Glasgow. But when someone walked in one day with one of Newcomen's steam pumps to repair, Watt jumped at the job.

The trouble with Newcomen's pump was that the steam which drove the piston was released from the chamber and allowed to blow away while the piston made its return stroke. Watt saw a way to save this wastage and get up more steam. Feed the steam from the piston into a separate box, and drive it back into the piston again. Better—use the same steam to drive the piston on its return stroke! And better yet, apply this back-and-forth movement of the piston to operate a crank and turn a wheel!

In 1769 James Watt gave the world his great invention—the condensing steam engine which could turn a wheel.

Whistling up all sorts of accompanying mechanical devices, steam engines introduced the Machine Age. By 1800 world-wide

Industrial Revolution was on the way. Hand-work gave way to steam-driven machines in factories. The old mill became a steam-driven mill. In particular, the revolution (this steam engine which could turn a wheel) affected transportation. On land, horse and ox-power would soon give way to snorting iron horses which would haul amazing loads on wheels. While at sea—

Of Interest to You Engineers

Here enters an American inventor named Fitch. While pioneers were exploring the frontier west of the Appalachians, John Fitch was pioneering with the idea of a steam-driven boat.

Such an idea had occurred to one Johnathan Hulls of England

fifty years before, but Hulls never did anything about it. John Fitch did. In 1785 he launched the world's first steamboat on the Delaware.

Fitch's steamboat was a marvelous craft. Twelve vertical oars were rotated by gears and a sprocket wheel driven by a steam engine. With smoke pouring from the flue, steam whistling from the boiler, and the vertical oars churning water, Fitch's steamboat waddled like a fantastic monster on the river. Old sailors hooted like the steam coming out of the boiler valve, and Fitch received much the same treatment awarded David Bushnell for his submarine. But he went right on to invent the first screw-type propeller and made his mark in history as the "Father of Steam Navigation."

Then in 1802 Colonel John Stevens came along with an Archimedes-type screw to drive a steam vessel. This screw, as you know, is not unlike the auger you use in a brace-and-bit. Stevens figured such a screw would bore in the water and force the ship ahead. Unfortunately on first trial his ship ran in circles—as would any single-screw ship today if it had no rudder.

Then the Colonel tried twin screws which revolved in opposite directions. Success! The steamship went forward.

The Colonel used Watt engines which developed a steam pressure of 50 psi. Don't laugh, you modern Water Tenders, Machinist's Mates, Motor Macs and Firemen. Standing around one of those early firetube boilers with the steam pushing 50 psi was like leaning on the heavenly box office requesting a ticket to the Hereafter. To minimize danger of explosion, Stevens constructed a boiler with the water inside the tubes instead of around the outside. That design is in water-tube boilers today.

While Stevens was tinkering over his boilers, Robert Fulton, another American steamboat pioneer, was demonstrating his stuff in France. The sensation of Paris in 1803, Fulton launched his first steamboat on the Seine. At the same time he tried to sell Napoleon Bonaparte a submarine. But the cautious French rejected both inventions. Packing back to New York, Fulton retired to his machine shop on the Hudson and set to work on a bigger and better steamboat. In 1807 he launched the famous *Claremont* which paddle-wheeled from New York to Albany— 150 miles in 32 hours, a new record!

216

Spurred by *Claremont's* success, Fulton went on to build the world's first steam-powered warship. This was in 1814. War with England was going on and the nation was Navy-minded. Congress approved Fulton's design and contracts were given to the Adams and Noah Brown shipyard on New York's East River. In May, 1815, the vessel was launched and christened *Demologos,* meaning "Voice of the People."

Demologos was a novel warship, no mistake. Her length was 165 feet, she was 50 feet in the beam, she displaced 2475 tons —gigantic for those days. Her engine, a one-cylinder job with a 48-inch bore and a five-foot stroke, drove a paddle-wheel 16-feet in diameter. Fulton's big feature was mounting the paddle-wheel in a trough inside the ship to protect it from gunfire.

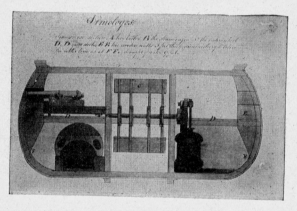

This vessel, known as *"Fulton's Steam Battery,"* had some other remarkable features. She carried 44 guns including four monster 100-pounders. Linked up with her machinery was a mechanism which operated 300 cutlasses and iron pikes, jabbing them out of ports along either beam so that she could go into action bristling like a mechanical porcupine. These spurs were intended to prevent an enemy's boarding. And British spies reported that as a further defensive measure *Demologos* could discharge 100 gallons of boiling water a minute at an oncoming enemy. The U. S. Navy's first steam warship was something to be reckoned with.

Unfortunately Fulton died before *Demologos* got into action. She performed so nicely on her trial run that a news commentator of the time described her as a "novel and sublime spectacle." Her sea-keeping qualities proved much better than expected when she made an average speed of 5½ knots, top speed 8½. Yet David Porter, her commander, had little faith in the "Voice of the People." Along with that he installed a pair of useless masts on the vessel. Then the war ended. She was re-christened *Fulton*, and tied up to a Brooklyn dock to gather barnacles. But in spite of rugged opposition from old sailing captains, steam navigation went straight ahead.

Following Fulton's *Claremont*, Henry Bell launched the steamer *Comet*. By 1819 the United States could count 100 steam vessels on the water. England had 43. The next fifteen years saw steamers puffing on rivers all up and down America—200,000 tons of steamships by 1839, and 4,000 tons out on the Atlantic.

You can furl up your sails now, Jackie, there's a new type of naval officer coming aboard. Instead of fighting against this revolution, he's going to lead it. His name? Matthew Calbraith Perry.

Steam on the Sea

Matthew Calbraith Perry was the brother of Oliver Hazard Perry. Although he never achieved the fame of the "Hero of Erie," his work in the Navy was every bit as important. In leading the fight for steam, he became "Father of the Steam Navy." Later on you'll hear of him out in the Orient with an even bigger title.

Around 1835 young Calbraith Perry was ordered to the New York Navy Yard to superintend the building of a new warship. There he probably acquired a few fatherly gray hairs. The ship he superintended was the Navy's second steam vessel, another *Fulton*. Fantastic *Demologos* (Fulton No. 1) had accidentally blown up in 1829. Now someone with a brain thought the service ought to have another steamship.

As soon as he got to work on *Fulton II*, Calbraith Perry was all for it. Her design was more conventional than the original, but her engines were more powerful, and she was armed with the new Paixhans guns. This big-caliber artillery threw shells instead of solid shot, the shell being a hollow cannon ball capable of bursting. Delighted with this fancy ordnance, Calbraith Perry was even more interested in the vessel's steam power. When *Fulton II* was launched, he immediately applied for her command, although as a captain he was slated for a big, wind-jamming ship-of-the-line.

On her trials *Fulton II* did better than 12 knots. Perry sent her steaming up the Potomac River to Washington. President Andrew (Old Hickory) Jackson and his cabinet were more than impressed by this warship that sailed by steam instead of wind. Still many Navy old-timers thought her a freak, and vowed they'd never serve aboard such an ungodly vessel.

Perry set up a school aboard *Fulton II* to train Paixhans gunners and steam engineers. He also established a proving ground at Sandy Hook where his steamer could be severely tested. The new shell-guns got on target with deadly effect. And the new steam engines proved so good that Perry went completely overboard for the idea.

Chief difficulty—personnel. Steam engines demanded engineers, and the old-line sailors weren't mechanically-minded.

Besides that, they were suspicious and superstitious, and considered steam engines beneath their dignity. Shovel coal? Grease wheels? Not by the Great Horn Spoon! They even got together on a strike, refusing to hoist the cinder buckets out of the vessel's fireroom. There was nothing in Navy Regs about handling ashes, they said.

Perry steadied the safety valve on his temper, and sent ashore to recruit civilian mechanics and steam men. He got the Navy Department to commission them as a specialist corps, and he put them in full charge of *Fulton's* machinery.

This didn't work, either. The sailors looked down on the engineers as "coal heavers," and the engineers regarded the seamen as rope-pulling block-heads. Fights broke out between deck and fireroom crews, arguing seamanship versus steam-power. The answer, Perry saw, lay in training cruises to develop teamwork among all hands.

These were minor troubles compared to the second difficulty—selling steam navigation to the old-line captains and Congress. By 1839 Calbraith Perry was up to his chin in a campaign for bigger and better steam warships. *Fulton II* had been resigned as a harbor battery. The Navy ought to have seagoing steam vessels to get out into the Atlantic.

At last, backed up by a few other steam enthusiasts, Perry somehow persuaded the government to vote for two ocean-going steam warships for the USN. Result: the paddle-frigate, *Mississippi*, a great battleship bigger than the *Constitution*, and the steam-powered *U.S.S. Missouri*. The silent revolution was not yet won, but it was well begun. *Congress*, laid down that same year, was the last sailing ship of any major size to be built for the U. S. Navy.

Something For You Gunners

While Calbraith Perry was leading the fight for steam power, another revolution was on—this time, it was fire-power.

Naval guns didn't change much in design and operation between the days of Queen Elizabeth and the period which introduced steam. They were made of brass or cast iron, and were rated by the weight of shot they could throw (viz: a 24-pounder threw a solid iron ball weighing 24 pounds).

Examine one of those old 24-pounders as typical. Mounted on a wheeled platform, it had a barrel nine feet long and weighed over two tons. It was trained by paying out or hauling in on side tackles which were attached to the gun carriage and the side of the ship. Maximum train angle on most guns was 30°, meaning 15° to right or left. The gun was elevated by prizing up on the breech with a hand-spike. Then a wooden wedge called a quoin was fitted under the breech to hold the gun in proper angle of elevation.

There was, of course, no hydro-pneumatic recoil system to take the shock of recoil and return the gun to battery. The breech of the gun ended in a huge pad-eye through which a hawser was rove. As the gun had a kick like a Missouri mule, the hawser for a 24-pounder was seven inches in diameter. The two hawser-ends were secured to ring-bolts in the deck at either side of the gun muzzle. As the gun rolled back in recoil it brought up against the rope, kerwham!

Another rope, called a "preventer," was secured to the tail of the gun carriage to prevent the gun from rolling to the rail if the ship rolled while the charge was being loaded. Two men would take up slack to hold the gun at loading position. Then after it had been sponged and the charge rammed home, they would pay out on the "preventer," allowing the gun to roll to battery position. If the ship were in flat water, the gun was shoved to battery position (muzzle at gun-port) by hand.

The charge for a 24-pounder consisted of three powder bags, each colored for identification. Six pounds of powder was good for close range, seven pounds for middle range, and the eight-pound bag was used for long range—somewhere around 1,000 yards.

The powder charge at the breech was fired by the gunner at the instant when the roll of the ship was right. A match (called a "quick match") did the trick. Actually it was a slow-burning, punk-like match on an iron-pointed stick which could be stuck into the wooden deck beside the gun when not in use. It must have made a first-class fire hazard, despite the tub of water placed near at hand for emergency. This "match tub" caught the sparks from the glowing match, and also served as a scuttlebutt for the gun crew!

The 24-pounder fired round shot (cannon balls), chain shot, bar shot, and grape. Bar shot consisted of cast iron bars tied together in a bundle and rammed into the gun barrel. When fired, the cord holding the assorted sash-weights burned away, and the bars went flying like a flock of crows through the enemy's rigging. Grape shot was even more murderous. The "grapes" were miniature cannon balls. A whole bag-full would be rammed into the 24-pounder. When that magnified shotgun went off it was curtains for anyone in the way.

There were twelve men in the gun crew of a 24-pounder.

What with hauling the gun around and operating the ramrod, they were a hardy bunch of Gunner's Mates. Perhaps you think a modern gun is complex. But there's quite a contrast between today's simple gun commands and the following *words of command for the exercise of the great guns,* listed in Navy Regs for 1818. How would you like to hear these orders come over your telephones while an enemy dive-bomber roars at you?

Silence.
Cast loose your guns.
Level your guns.
Middle your breechings.
Take out your tompions.
Take off your aprons.
Prick and prime.
Lay on your aprons.
Handle crows and hand spikes.
Point your guns at the object.
Level your guns at the object.
Blow your matches.
Take off your aprons.
Fire.

No, there weren't dive bombers in 1818. But with an enemy ship coming suddenly out of fog, her guns primed, maybe, and ready to go, those were a heap of orders. Yet these gun-orders, and the guns themselves, had remained basically unchanged for several hundred years. Ordnance was considered beyond improvement, and gun-orders, like mail boxes, were not to be tampered with.

Now steam-power, adding so many knots to a warship's speed, demanded a rapid speed-up in gunnery. There was no longer time for a long routine of rope-hauling, crowbar-handling, match-lighting, and fiddling with aprons. Yet the old-timers were yawning, and ordnance men dozed. Someone had to wake up the Navy in a hurry. That someone was John Adolphus Dahlgren.

Dahlgren, born in Philadelphia, came of Swedish ancestry—meaning he had a Norse strain in his blood. The Norsemen, you'll remember, were sea-followers from way back. Dahlgren was applying for a midshipman's warrant in the Navy when he was only fifteen.

His application was turned down, but that didn't discourage young Dahlgren. He sailed before the mast on the brig *Mary Becket;* then returning from the Caribbean, he again applied for naval service. This time he was accepted, and in 1826 he was cruising the South Atlantic aboard *U.S.S. Macedonian.*

He saw action against slavers and buccaneers, and then served in the Coast Survey. In 1837 he suffered one of those hard-luck breaks that can change a man's whole career—for the better, if he's a fighter like Dahlgren. He began to go blind!

The Navy gave him a leave, and he went to France for treatment. No relief. But careful attention to his eyes, and an iron jaw to beat misfortune, got him back into the service despite poor vision. Poor eye-vision, that is.

For although Dahlgren's eyes had blurred, he had seen that something must be done about naval gunnery. Out on a three-year Mediterranean cruise aboard *Cumberland,* he tried out the new Paixhans shell-guns. There was a lot of prejudice against shell ammunition in the Navy. It was the first ordnance improvement in a long time, and officers and gun crews looked on the shells with distrust. Dahlgren at once saw their shattering advantage. As a gunnery officer, he began drilling his Gunner's Mates morning, noon, and night. Meantime, he developed a means for correcting the gun-level—laying the dispart by the horizon—which was the forerunner of the modern directorscope.

Still, rate of fire remained hog-tied by the old, slow methods. Dahlgren set to work to speed up the clumsy routine. He thought up and wrote down an ordnance system based on two principles which were to have an immense effect on naval gunnery.

"Speed," he wrote, *"is an essential requisite for a first class ship of war."* And he added with dry humor, *"But essential only to go into action, not out of it."*

His second principle was one which eventually brought about the salvo.

"The greatest strength will be found in the simplicity and concentration of guns of one caliber, if this caliber is the largest which it is practical for ships to carry."

Necessity being the mother of invention, Dahlgren determined to become a busy father. The powder explosion escaping from the gun's vent had always destroyed the firing lock, causing expensive replacement. One of Dahlgren's first inventions was a spring percussion lock which would not be broken.

Presently he was in the Washington Navy Yard, assigned to make improvements on signal rockets. He was not there three months before he was handing plans to BuOrd—plans for the naval gun factory which you can see at Anacostia today. In 1847 he was instructing gunnery classes at Annapolis, and three years later he was inventing guns of a novel design.

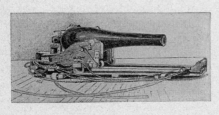

Weighing 9,000 pounds, these were 9-inch shell guns, built on unheard of lines. Cast-iron mono-block and smoothbore, their originality lay in their enormous caliber, and what Dahlgren called their "curve of pressure." From his studies, Dahlgren reasoned that the explosive force was greater at the breech than at any point in the gun. Therefore strength must be concentrated at the breech around the powder chamber, rather than along the chase or at the muzzle. So Dahlgren's guns were built with a great bulge of metal at the breech—a design which won them the nickname of "soda bottles." Look at any big gun today and you'll see the same general design.

Dahlgren's 9-inch "soda bottle" brought him world-wide fame, and began a new era of gun construction. He went on to turn out 11-inch and 15-inch naval guns, and even experimented with a 20-incher. These big-caliber guns were made possible only by his reinforced gun-breech.

Dahlgren didn't stop there. Now he made a study of rifling— the cutting of spiral grooves in a gun-bore to give the projectile a spin and improve its accuracy. It had been tried (and discarded) years before. Dahlgren recommended it. The Bureau of Ordnance couldn't see it. But he did succeed in introducing small arms rifles into the service—the first of their kind in America.

He also experimented with breech-loaders, urging Navy ordnance men to develop some such device. Finally he invented the first practical gunsights for naval guns, and worked out scientific computations to be used with gunsights.

If Calbraith Perry was the father of the new steam navy, John Adolphus Dahlgren fathered modern gunnery. Quite a project for a man who had found himself going blind and fought to keep all kinds of vision.

Up In the Chart Room

The "room for improvement" is probably the biggest room in the world. Architects are working on it all the time. So steam power, speeding up the warship, called for an increase in fire power. And at the same time navigation needed an overhaul to keep the pace. With steam vessels puffing all over the ocean, logging unheard of knots, improved navigational methods were essential. For steam power didn't banish winds and tides. Instead, it bucked them harder than ever. Rocks and shoals became a double menace to a fast moving ship-load of machinery. Something had to be done to keep the harbors and coastlines clear of expensive wreckage.

Today every naval vessel and merchantman puts to sea with a full set of pilot charts published monthly by the Hydrographic Office of the Navy Department. Prevailing winds, currents, weather information, sea lanes, and a lot of navigational data are shown on these charts. No ship would leave port without them. Any QM2c can tell you that each chart bears the legend: *"Founded upon the researches made and the data collected by Lieut. M. F. Maury, U. S. Navy."*

Matthew F. Maury is third of the three big names which made history in your Navy during the "silent revolution." Maury was from frontier Tennessee, and he had a lot of the same hickory which hardened the jaw of Andrew (Old Hickory) Jackson. He wanted to join the U. S. Navy and go to sea. His father, wanting him to do something else, said, "No!" However, in 1825 young Maury was an acting midshipman in the U. S. Navy, having horse-backed into Washington, D. C. to enlist.

Aboard ship, Maury determined to earn his salt. He studied Spanish, trigonometry, and navigation, working hard during off-duty hours. On duty, he would chalk problems in "spherical trig" on the round shot in the gun racks, and study the equations while he walked the deck.

He read Bowditch on navigation, and pretty soon he was writing his own book on the subject. To his surprise he found a publisher. His work was applauded in England. Not long after that it became a standard text in the American Navy.

Encouraged, Maury proposed a school ship with a staff of first-class instructors to teach all kinds of subjects. This idea of a naval school finally came to the attention of Navy Secretary Bancroft, and started him thinking. Later on, you'll see the result.

But Maury's main interest remained in navigation. After a time, he was placed in charge of the Depot of Charts and Instruments then at Washington. No doubt his game leg, which healed badly after being broken in a stagecoach accident, had to do with this appointment. A lesser man might have accepted it dourly, willing to take the office for a dull Snug Harbor. There was no Snug Harbor for Matthew Maury.

He was too well aware that harbors were full of treacherous channels and shifting shoals. The ocean was equally unsafe—a bounding mystery of currents, winds, and tides. To date, no one had made a careful, scientific study of all this water, wind, and weather. In those days there were no accurate pilot charts bearing the name of Lieut. M. F. Maury, USN.

So Maury determined to devise some. When a mid, he'd been made navigator of the sloop *Falmouth*, Rio bound. Before sailing from New York, he'd tried to round up information on the winds and currents to be encountered on the cruise. Nowhere had he been able to obtain such information. Rumors there were a-plenty. And old sea legends. But Matthew Maury had no use for rumors and legends.

He listened skeptically to stories of the Sargasso Sea—a vast area of seaweed somewhere "off the Caribbean," its grassy surface littered with the skeletal hulls of sailing ships trapped in its morass. He was just as skeptical of that old-time tale which described the northeast coast of Brazil as circled by deadly currents which would grab the unwary vessel and whisk it toward a "magnetic" shore. To avoid these supposed dangers, sailing captains had for years steered a course far out in the

Atlantic, then come swinging back to South America on a European sea lane. Young Maury had been surprised to find naval captains following this traditional route. Now, working in the Depot of Charts and Instruments, he set out to smash this foolish, time-wasting tradition. How? By accurate data. By assembling all the authentic information he could find, and developing a set of North Atlantic "Track Charts" which any mariner could follow.

This meant combing through a ton of old log books and records, but work never bothered Matthew Maury. So he began the famous Wind and Current Charts which were soon to take navigators by storm. Meantime he reorganized the old depot, turning it into the Naval Observatory, and establishing the Hydrographic Office.

Maury's first charts didn't satisfy him. There were too many blanks and empty spaces. To fill in these oceanic blanks, he launched a campaign in the maritime world. He urged captains and navigators to make daily observations and send him the records of every voyage. In return, he promised to furnish them free charts with sailing directions based on their observations.

Naval and merchant captains were enthusiastic. Soon the observations were swarming in. Temperatures at a certain latitude and longitude. Compass variations. The set of a current—wind direction—weather condition—soundings. As usual, old-timers looked askance on this new project. But when navigators, following the charts, began to cut days and weeks off former runs, the world woke up to the work of Lieutenant Maury.

In 1844 he published a lengthy report on the Gulf Stream. Up to then little had been known about this mighty ocean current. And it was Maury who recommended sailing on a great circle whenever possible. Any Quartermaster today can tell you why, but it was a new idea to the mariners of those days.

By 1850 navigators everywhere were clamoring for Maury's charts. Without cooperation from many seafarers, these charts wouldn't have been possible. Now Maury proposed an international conference—all the great maritime nations to get together and set up a standard method for charting the World Ocean. Great Britain, France, Holland, Belgium, Portugal, Spain, the

Scandinavian countries, and Russia sent delegates to the conference in Brussels. Representing the U. S. A., Maury steered the affair. And he was able to announce that the U. S. Navy would forward charts to any foreign merchant captain who would furnish the required nautical observations.

From there on, the conference was a winner. Delegates were of differing nationality—and some of those Europeans hadn't spoken to each other for years—but all were sailors at heart. Over maps, compasses, chronometers, and logs they shook hands like Rotarians at an Atlantic City convention.

"Rarely has there been such a spectacle," Maury wrote. *"All agreeing to unite and cooperate in carrying out one system of research in regard to the sea. Though they may be enemies in all else, here they are friends."*

Not long after the conference, nineteen nations joined in the common effort to chart the Seven Seas. Maury, the man behind it all, was wearing medals and honors from every corner of the globe.

As head of the Naval Observatory, he also furnished the soundings and other marine data used in laying the first Atlantic cable. This remarkable trans-Atlantic, underwater telegraph-line was completed in 1858. Cyrus Field, the engineer, said that he did the work, but *"Maury furnished the brains."*

"Navies are not all for war," Maury said. *"Peace has its conquests, science its glories. And no Navy can boast of brighter chaplets than those which have gathered in the fields of geographical exploration and physical research."*

The Atlantic Cable—the Naval Observatory and Hydrographic Office—the pilot charts used aboard your ship today—these were the accomplishments of Lieut. M. F. Maury, USN. Unfortunately, for all his research in water, wind, and weather, he failed to forecast the hurricane gathering over America. And when it came later, he was swept up as in a fatal tidal wave.

But when the storm receded, his great work remained—to pilot the world's navigators over the World Ocean.

The Mutineers

One gray morning in 1820 two American Naval officers paced a misty field near Bladensburg. One was Commodore James

Barron who had commanded *Chesapeake* in the War of 1812. The other was Stephen Decatur.

There was a gleam of pistol-barrels in the early light as the two men halted, wheeled, and faced each other. Silence, as a second stepped forward to give the count. Barron's face was grim, mouth tense. Decatur stood at ease, waiting.

He had answered a savage letter from Barron with the words, *"Between you and myself there has never been a personal difference."* But the thing had gone too far. As President of the court-martial which had suspended Barron after the *Chesapeake-Leopard* fiasco in 1812, Decatur had won Barron's emnity. Besides, one of Barron's best friends in the service was Elliott, the squabbler who criticized Oliver Perry's conduct in the Battle of Lake Erie. Decatur, appointed an investigator in this case, had given Perry clean credit for the victory, pointing out that Elliott's own conduct had been sour.

Sea-lawyer Elliott had run to friend Barron, and the pair had launched verbal salvos at Decatur. Decatur finally replied with spirit, and Barron invited him to choose his own weapons. Code demanded prompt answer—Decatur chose pistols.

"Gentlemen!" Commodore Bainbridge, Decatur's second, gave instructions. "The count will be three. You will ready and aim at one, and fire as you may on two or three thereafter. Can you possibly speak at this time to defray this unhappy affair?"

Rejecting sensible settlement, Barron spoke bluntly to Decatur. *"I hope, sir, that in another world we may be better friends than we've been in this."*

Decatur answered quietly, *"I have never been your enemy, sir."*

They raised their guns at the count of, *"One!"*

At, *"Two!"* both officers opened fire.

And so fell Stephen Decatur, blood spurting from a mortal wound—to end one of the Navy's finest careers.

It was all according to code and tradition, but it raised a storm in the service, and sank Barron's career with Decatur's.

A great Navy leader dead —a veteran officer ruined —such was the outcome of this shooting match. More, it divided the Navy into two rival camps— pro-Decatur and pro-Barron—creating bitter arguments in wardrooms all over the sea. So duelling in the American Navy was banned.

Some other codes and traditions might have been banished at the time. For example, the traditional distrust of education which Maury found time to criticize. Molasses in January was greased lightning compared to a Navy man's chances for advancement under this system. It was all a matter of waiting for the man at the top of the ladder to retire, then everyone might go up one rung. As the Old Man at ladder-top clung to the rung until his beard grew like Spanish moss, nobody got anywhere for the next thirty years. Around 1840 the quarterdecks in the American Navy began to look like homes for the aged.

While this gave the service a lot of Father Time captains, it also established a list of juniors who resembled Ancient Mariners. It was nothing for a lieutenant to be sixty-three, and there was a mid on record with the ripe old age of fifty. Far below these veterans capered the newly appointed midshipmen, fresh as monkeys. And 'way at the bottom of the ladder were the enlisted men with no chance of getting anywhere at all.

Old men are often "Sot in their ways," and some of the moss-backed officers had the outlook of granite bulls. Witness the uproar against steam and shell-guns. Anything new was a red flag to be attacked at once, and they didn't like youth, either; they were all for holding it down with an iron hand.

Such a veteran was Captain Alexander Mackenzie in charge of the training ship *Somers*, with a crew of 130 new midshipmen and apprentice seamen aboard. An officer of the "old school," and a sundowner, Mackenzie was not quite the sort to be in command of a young and lively crew, even in the year 1842.

Oldest lad aboard was twenty-two, and the youngest around fourteen. Straight off they got in Mackenzie's hair. Straight off, he unlimbered the cat-o'-nine-tails. The brig cruised over to Africa with misery aboard, and when it started the home voyage many of the boys were striped like zebras.

Mackenzie dealt out more lashings, and the ship became a powder keg. All it needed was a spark—the spark that came from the zaney wits of a young midshipman named Philip Spencer.

If this youth wasn't mentally off, he certainly was a scatter-brained fool. Dismissed from college for bad conduct, he had entered the Navy as a lark, and had promptly been ousted. But his father, Secretary of War Spencer, pulled wires to have the boy reinstated. Apparently young Spencer figured he could "get away with anything." He should have known better than to keep up his capers aboard *Somers*.

Two weeks out from Africa. Midnight. Purser's Mate Wales, walking the deck, was stopped by a furtive figure—Philip Spencer.

"Look, Wales. Do you fear the sight of a dead man?"

"Eh? What's that?"

Spencer rolled his eyes and made high-signs. Told him a group of mutineers were plotting to seize the ship. They would soon be on their way to the Caribbean as pirates.

Such was the tale Wales babbled at one bell to Captain Alexander Mackenzie. Mackenzie, his mind aflame, had Spencer watched all next day. Yes, Spencer was seen whispering privately to Bosun's Mate Cromwell and Seaman Small. The whole crew was whispering. Mackenzie pounced like a lion, and had the three boys put in irons.

Then, searching Spencer's seabag, Mackenzie and his officers found a paper scrawled with mysterious Greek letters, also a rusty knife and a couple of paper-back pirate novels. The writing in Greek turned out to be names of the crew, one list under the ominous heading, "to be killed." That was enough for Captain Mackenzie.

Summoning a drumhead court, he had the three lads grilled to a turn.

Cromwell denied any knowledge of a mutiny.

Seaman Small said he'd heard Spencer talk a lot about pirates, but so far as he knew there was no mutinous conspiracy.

Spencer, himself, declared it had been only a prank. He liked to read pirate stories. He'd written the lists in Greek just to practice the Greek alphabet. He talked of dead men to Wales just to tease him. With upraised hand he swore he'd never meant to start a mutiny.

Mackenzie had the boys returned to irons and bagged— meaning a canvas sack was tied over each lad's head (a punishment reserved for the most desperate criminals).

Then he wrote out a long list of Spencer's offenses, and recommended to the court that the three conspirators *"should be put to death in a manner best calculated to make a beneficial impression upon the disaffected."* The disaffected being the other young members of *Somer's* crew who had gone sullen after Spencer's arrest.

So the hanging took place next morning, with the whole ship's company summoned to watch, and Mackenzie reading the Articles for the Government of the Navy.

Philip Spencer went to the yardarm praying. Seaman Small was too terror-stricken to speak. And to the last, with the noose being slipped over his head, Bosun's Mate Cromwell shouted that he was an innocent man being slain without reason.

The drum rolled its death-knell, and the bodies dangled in the wind. It was a grim, bitter ship that sailed a few weeks later into harbor at Brooklyn.

Mackenzie marched the boys ashore to church service and then ordered them back aboard while he shut himself in his cabin to write his report to the Navy Department. But a newspaper correspondent on hand for a story of the cruise got word of the tragedy. Next day the whole ugly business came out in the press.

Didn't that raise a thundering uproar! The son of the former War Secretary hanged from a yardarm! Although without "family influence," Seaman Small and Bosun's Mate Cromwell were equally featured in demands for investigation. Newspapers all over America carried the headlines. The tumult echoed in Washington. Reverberations shook the whole Navy structure.

Reading Mackenzie's report today, you might wonder if justice was done. He says he didn't like the "look" in Spencer's eye. He notes that Spencer had a queer way of making music by squeezing his hands—as if that were an indication of criminal character! Certainly Spencer was up to some antic. But the idea of one lad, or even a few lads, seizing a warship seems absurd. The officers, forewarned by Wales, could have easily held the boys in the brig. Also, if Spencer really plotted mutiny, would he have left plans lying around, and confided in the unfriendly Purser's Mate? Finally, Small's guilt as a conspirator was doubtful and there was no proof at all of Cromwell's. From this distance it seems that Mackenzie let imagination and temper override his judgment, and it looks as if young Spencer was just a brainless playboy. Result: three burials at sea.

After long investigation Captain Mackenzie was officially exonerated—on the ground that a captain's judgment must be law at sea and he'd acted in what he considered the security of his ship.

But, as the press pointed out, if a man is to have that much authority he must be a well-trained, capable officer. The midshipmen, too, must be lads of high caliber—no hoodlums like young Spencer. The fault lay in a system which developed mossbacks at the top and permitted unschooled ne'er-do-wells at the bottom. To keep pace with advancements in steam, gunnery, and navigation, the Articles for the Government of the Navy and the Navy's personnel system needed overhauling.

So the queer *Somers* mutiny had its beneficial side. Navy Regs were improved, and today there could be no such drumhead court as passed death sentence aboard *Somers*.

Mutiny, of course, remains a crime punishable by death. However, no death sentence in the Navy can be carried out without the approval of the Commander-in-Chief, the President of the United States.

Meantime, to keep such cracked characters out of the Navy, new enlistment methods were devised. And in 1845 the Navy set up an officers' school.

The Secretary of the Navy was George Bancroft. An historian, he was well up on naval history and the theories of John Paul Jones. He was also the kind of man who wouldn't let politics interfere with principles.

He'd accepted his appointment from President Polk on the assurance that he could start such a naval school as Matthew Maury had recommended. Congress, however, was deaf to the idea. In 1844 another naval disaster had given Congress a jaundiced eye concerning the service.

One of the first steam warships was *U.S.S. Princeton*. She was built for deep water, and propelled by a new-type screw designed by the Swedish inventor, John Ericsson. Her captain, Robert Stockton, was himself an inventor, and he installed aboard *Princeton* a huge 12-inch shell gun of his own design.

Princeton made a trial run down the Potomac with the President and his cabinet aboard as observers. Everything was gala until Stockton's monster gun blew up, killing the Secretary of State, the then Secretary of the Navy, and several Congressmen. There was another stormy investigation, and Congress soured on any new program for the Navy.

But the *Princeton* blast, following the *Somers* tragedy, solidified Bancroft's conviction that the Navy needed a good naval school. His first move was to fire all the old sea-going professors. Next, he arranged to take over an old Army post at Annapolis. Finally he put Franklin Buchanan, a sharp, salty officer, at head of the school.

The school opened on October 10, 1845. It had four academic instructors and a lieutenant to teach engineering and gunnery. Three midshipmen made up the student body. Classes were held in a wooden shed.

Franklin Buchanan ran a taut school. As more midshipmen were admitted, teachers were added. Some of the mids went rowdy, thinking they could get away with it because they were "Congressional appointments." Despite political uproar, Buchanan and Bancroft threw them out.

The school continued to expand as it trained young officers who could keep pace with the new steam-power, fire-power, and methods of navigation.

Today, as an educational institution, it equals the finest. It is equipped to graduate over a thousand midshipmen yearly. Now as yesterday, the students are Congressional appointees. They must be of top-flight caliber to win appointment, and must be able to pass the stiffest kind of competitive exams. Enlisted men who have made exceptional records in the fleet are also eligible.

Ordinarily the midshipmen go through a four-year course, studying their heads off. They take a little time out to play football—ask West Point. But the entire course is aimed at turning each man into a naval officer capable of leadership, sea duty, the exacting life demanded of one in the service of the nation, and the sacrifice of life he may be called on to make in war time.

Such men are trained at Annapolis—the school that opened one hundred years ago in a dingy wooden shed and is today the famous United States Naval Academy.

The Mexican War

While the Navy was busy reorganizing to keep pace with new inventions, trouble was brewing in a distant area of the American continent.

The thing began deep in the heart of Texas. Eastern Texas had long been settled by pioneers from the United States. The territory of Texas belonged to Mexico, and these American settlers supported the Mexican government. But the Mexican Government at that time was a tough one to support.

In 1835 a general named Santa Ana announced himself dictator of Mexico. The settlers of Texas proclaimed their allegiance to the former constitutional government. The following year Santa Ana and his cavalry swept across the Rio Grande and massacred 183 American Texans isolated at Alamo Mission. At near-by Goliad, 280 more settlers were slaughtered.

With the cry, "Remember the Alamo!" the pioneer Texans rose under fighting Sam Houston. Houston and his sharpshooters caught Santa Ana's army at San Jacinto and smashed it into human kindling. Santa Ana himself was captured.

Under Houston's leadership, Texas declared itself an independent republic and raised its famous Lone Star flag. Mexico refused to recognize the territory's independence, but could do nothing about it except threaten.

For nine years the Texas Republic flew its independent flag. Meantime the American Texans wanted annexation with the United States. When James K. Polk became President in 1845, his administration agreed to admit Texas to the Union. Mexico advised that such a move would mean war. Polk ordered General Zachary (Old Rough and Ready) Taylor with 4,000 regulars to the Rio Grande frontier. A larger Mexican force attacked, and the war was on.

After a stiff battle at Palo Alto, Old Rough and Ready drove the Mexican Army back to Monterrey. There the war became stalemated throughout the autumn of 1845.

At sea the U. S. Navy had gone into prompt action, sailed down the Gulf and handily captured the Mexican seaport of Tampico. As Mexico had no navy to speak of, the American sea force held all the cards.

Fighting over mountain and desert, forging its way down to Mexico City, the U. S. Army had much tougher going. Another American Army, under Colonel S. W. Kearny, headed west across New Mexico to invade California, advancing through enemy

MEXICO
Showing
PRESENT & OLD FRONTIER

territory all the way. After an incredible year's march, Kearny with 100 survivors reached San Pasquale on the California coast. A large force of Mexican lancers attacked the weary Americans. Kearny's position would have been desperate, but a Navy flotilla under Commodore Sloat sailed into the picture, and fighting sailors landed to save the day.

Like the Texans, American settlers in California had demanded independence from Mexico. Their banner a white flag with a bear painted on it, the Californians now rose to support Kearny. When Commodore Sloat pushed an American fleet into San Francisco Bay, the "Bear Flag Revolt" turned into war under the Stars and Stripes. The poorly organized Mexicans were soon defeated by American riflemen and well-trained Navy brigades, and California was won. .

Down in Old Mexico the battle was harder. Santa Ana had been released to return to Mexico on the promise that he would organize a new government and negotiate a peace. But a leopard isn't likely to change its spots, and the same goes for a dictator. Once back in Mexico, wily old Santa recruited a new army pledged to wipe out the Americans on Mexican soil. In February 1847, this force attacked Taylor's army at Buena Vista. Artillery manned by West Pointers threw back the fierce-fighting Mexicans with heavy loss. But the Americans also suffered heavily, and the war again bogged down.

President Polk had hoped for a peaceful settlement with Santa Ana. The war was unpopular at home, and several northern states had refused to send recruits. Many Congressmen feared that Texas would upset the political picture—you'll see why later. Others, like Abe Lincoln from Illinois, questioned the sending of an army into Mexico. Polk wanted a quick decision. Accordingly Winfield Scott, in top Army command, decided to attack Mexico City by way of Vera Cruz.

Here the Navy played its biggest part, convoying Scott's 10,000 men down the Gulf, and joining in the bombardment of Vera Cruz fortress, one of the strongest in the world. Matthew Calbraith Perry replaced Commodore Connor as head of the naval force, and Vera Cruz fell in March 1847, after five days' action

The Army had a hard fight to reach the Mexican capital, but by September it was pounding at the gates. The war was over when Santa Ana surrendered.

Peace was signed in 1848. Mexico acknowledged Texas as part of the Union and ceded New Mexico and the bulk of California above the peninsula to the U. S. A. In return, the U. S. paid Mexico a $15,000,000 consolation fee.

Look at the map and you'll see that your country had acquired an immense area of land. Of more interest to Navy men, it had also gained a Pacific coast.

Meet the Japs

You can blame it on the whales that Japan was ever opened up in the first place. If the best oil whales hadn't set up house-keeping right off the islands of Japan, the whalers from the U. S. A. and other countries wouldn't have visited that area of the Pacific Ocean. Then the Japs wouldn't have tossed them into prison when their whaling ships ran aground on the isolated shores of Honshu, Shikoku, and other islands of the "Closed Empire."

Closed empire? Correct. For years the Mikado and his boys had refused to deal with the outer world, or even recognize there was such a world. The Nipponese thought themselves the only people in creation, and their Emperor the lord of creation. Ships bound for China were frequently wrecked in the uncharted Japanese waters. And with sailors and whalers from L. A. and 'Frisco being kicked into dungeons on Hokkaido, Uncle Sam decided to investigate. The investigator assigned to the job was Matthew Calbraith Perry.

Perry's abilities weren't limited to steam-power. He was a sea-going officer who'd proved his braid in the Mexican War, also a diplomat who could handle a bow in a drawing room. Early in his career he'd managed several ticklish diplomatic plays in African and Mediterranean waters. He knew his way around in European court circles. The Czar of Russia once offered him an admiral's commission in the Russian Navy.

Accordingly, the State Department gave Perry a free hand in a diplomatic poker game that had baffled Europe's experts for a century. Perry took two years to study the hand. In Washington he examined all the reports on Japan he could find. He listened to the tales of travelers from the Orient, and pored over the records on imprisoned seamen. Of the maritime nations, only the Dutch had been able to dent Japanese isolationism by establishing an outpost at Nagasaki. Even the neighboring Chinese were barred.

Perry decided the reason the big maritime powers had failed to get anywhere with Japan was because they'd dealt with the Japs on a reasonable Western basis. But Japan was Oriental. The Nips loved ceremony, formality, and pomp. They were embalmed in an ancient caste system. They looked down on their supposed inferiors, and would only heed anyone they believed superior. In other words, the Closed Empire was all bluff. Perry determined to out-bluff the Closed Empire.

His primary mission was to make Japan safe for American mariners in Jap waters. However, he decided to make a bid for the whole jackpot and arranged commercial treaties with Japan. So he took all the aces he could draw to play against the Mikado's royal flush. These included the two steam frigates, *U.S.S. Mississippi* and *U.S.S. Susquehanna,* and the war-sloops *Saratoga* and *Plymouth.*

Aboard were stowed all kinds of modern novelties to impress the Japs with the wonders of civilization. With these Perry carried an imposing letter from President Millard Fillmore. The expedition left Norfolk in the autumn of 1852, and arrived in Yedo Bay in July, 1853.

Didn't that create a sensation in Japan! Hardly had the fleet dropped anchor when a swarm of picket boats came out from shore to circle around the American warships like gaudy beetles. Buzzing excitedly, they meant to tell Perry he couldn't come ashore, couldn't anchor where he was, and, please, would he depart. Japan was closed to foreigners.

But Commodore Perry didn't hear the brush-off. Aboard his flagship, *Susquehanna,* he kept to his cabin, ignoring all the hullabaloo outside. His plan was to play superior to the Japs, and he remained as aloof as the Grand Llama of Thibet to the uproar.

In fact, he took for himself the title of "Lord of the Forbidden

Interior"—the only U. S. naval officer ever to hold such exalted rank! And he sent a warrant officer out to inform the Jap boatmen that, "The Lord of the Forbidden Interior is so high and mighty that he doesn't even think about boatmen, much less see and speak to them."

"But we have the Vice-Governor of Uraga aboard," the Japs proclaimed. "Will the Lord of the Forbidden Interior designate an officer of rank low enough to speak with the vice-governor?"

Perry would. He allowed that a Lieutenant (jg.) was about low enough to speak to a Jap vice-governor. So, presently a "Jig George" appeared on deck to look down a haughty nose at the Vice-Governor of Uraga.

"The Lord of the Forbidden Interior has a letter from the Mikado of the United States of America to the Mikado of Japan." trumpeted the jg. "This letter is too precious to be seen by any eyes but those of the Japanese Mikado."

Wearing a fancy-dress costume which had already won him the nickname of "Jack of Trumps" from the irreverent American seamen, the Vice-Governor of Uraga was quite a card. But not enough of a card to stay on the table in a game with Mikados showing. Blinking his eyes, he dealt himself out of the play, and retired to the shore to hold a conference.

Next day out from shore came a fancy gilt barge with the Governor of Uraga, himself, in the stern sheets. The Governor was a higher card than the jack of trumps. Still, he wasn't high enough to take a hand with the "Lord of the Forbidden Interior."

However, as a great concession, and contrary to Hoyle, the Governor was at length received by two Under Lords of the Forbidden Interior—Captains Franklin Buchanan and H. A. Adams. The hand was getting hot, now, and the Japs were upping the kitty.

After a lot of Japanese ceremony and double-talk, the Governor of Uraga suggested that the letter from the Mikado of America be handed to the Dutch at Nagasaki for delivery to the Japanese Mikado. Nothing doing, said the American Under-Lords of the F. I. The letter must be delivered to the Japanese Mikado by the Lord of the Forbidden Interior in person.

"No can do," said the Governor blandly. "How do I know in the first place there is such an honorable letter?"

Captain Buchanan showed it to him—a fine scroll in a rosewood box elaborately carved and inlaid with gold. Carved boxes inlaid with gold were something the Governor of Uraga could appreciate. He was also impressed by the poker-faced formality of the two under-lords. He begged time out for another conference.

Perry gave him three days. Back came the Governor of Uraga with a commission authorizing relay of the letter to Prince Toda of Izdu for delivery to the holy Mikado. First Conselor to the throne, and third ranking big shot in Japan, Prince Toda was a top card. The Lord of the Forbidden Interior consented to this deal.

So Jap carpenters and decorators were set to work on a special ceremonial pagoda on the shore. The whole shoreline around the pagoda was blocked off with hundreds of paper and wood screens. The crowds of common people couldn't look on the mighty Lord of the Forbidden Interior as he came ashore from the *U.S.S. Susquehanna*. Prince Toda also was too sacred for the public eye.

After several days of feasting, ceremony, pomp, and red tape, the letter in the rosewood box was handed over. Then Perry broke out his traveling salesman's kit, and set up a fair-ground exhibit that had the Japs bug-eyed. He'd brought along all sorts

of American-made gimcracks and inventions, including a telescope, a plow, a telegraph set, and a midget railroad complete with train and tracks.

Those were the chips that won the show-down. The telegraph astounded the Japanese ministers. Excited, they chased alongside the telegraph wire trying to see where the evil spirits entered the wire to carry the clicking messages. Then they were as delighted as children with the train. Nothing for it but they must perch aboard the cars as the Tom Thumb engine went steaming around the little amusement-park track.

The Jap ministers also got themselves highly involved with Yankee brandy and Kentucky corn which the Americans had brought along to aid the festivities. Commodore Perry sailed off on a six-month cruise to give the Japs time to sober up and think it over. When he returned, the Japs were waiting with a glad hand, willing to promise hospitality toward American sailors, and anxious to sign a trade treaty with the United States.

So the Closed Empire was opened up at last to enjoy the benefits of civilization. Trouble was, the Japs got the benefits without the civilizing. The Mikado still sat on the throne, pretending to be a god. A few lordly families continued to run the empire. And the Japanese people went on believing themselves the only pebbles on the beach.

It was just under a hundred years ago that Commodore Matthew Calbraith Perry, USN, opened the Japanese Empire. (December 7, 1941, your Navy set out to bottle it up again.)

To Make Men Free

While the Navy was converting from sail to steam, and improving the gunnery, navigation, and personnel—and while Perry was opening up Japan—things were happening in the United States of America. Grim things. Stern things. Things that were to rock the nation (and the Navy) and threaten the very existence of the American Republic.

Look back over your country's history at this point, and you'll see one phrase running through the story all the way— THE RIGHTS OF MAN. Other phrases stand out brightly among the pages. Freedom of Thought—Freedom of Worship—Freedom

242

of Speech—Freedom of the Seas. But these are only chapter titles under the larger headings. The story of America has been the struggle for human rights—equal rights for all.

You have all these rights as a citizen of America today, but the citizens of America one hundred years ago came mighty close to losing them. They almost lost them because of another phrase that got tangled into the workings of Democracy— STATES' RIGHTS.

What is a state and what are states' rights? The citizens of America asked, and argued. The American Republic was a nation made up of states united under a Federal Government. It was also a Democracy, pledged to support the rights of man. The Federal Government was designed to rule the Republic and enforce the national laws.

Ah, said the spokesman for states' rights. If those laws *should* conflict, the Federal Government cannot enforce Federal Law, for the state has the right of SECESSION—the right to quit the Union whenever it feels like it.

No, said the Federal authorities. The Federal Government does not permit secession. For if any state could leave the Union whenever it felt like it, there soon would be no Union, no American Republic. Thus James Madison planned Federal intervention when New England threatened to secede during the War of 1812. And Andy (Old Hickory) Jackson, elected President in 1829, thundered the toast: *"Our Federal Union! It must and shall be preserved."*

But then John C. Calhoun, of South Carolina, replied: *"The Union, next to our liberty, most dear. May we all remember that it can only be preserved by respecting the rights of the States."*

State governments or Federal Government? Which was the supreme authority?

In 1832, South Carolina, clashed with the Federal Government over a tax law, and moved to secede from the Union. *U.S.S. Constitution,* a Federal warship, sailed into Charleston harbor with loaded guns. South Carolina backed down. So the U. S. Navy won the first round in the War Between the States.

Old Hickory's (and the Navy's) action might have settled the states' rights argument in 1832, but for one fact. The fact that it masked an even deeper issue. It was this deeper issue that was developing a two-sided America—undermining the foundations of the Republic. Between 1830 and 1859, the real issue behind the states' rights wrangle was the business of SLAVERY.

For in this "Land of the Free," over 3,000,000 human beings were held in bondage. The slave owners (a minority) said it was a matter of states' rights. The abolitionists said it was a matter of human rights. The Republic (A Democracy of majority rule) voted to stop the extension of slavery. So the states which wanted to extend human slavery seceded from the Union. Whereupon the Federal Government stepped in, determined to maintain the Union.

The result was the greatest war America had yet seen.

NAVIES ARE NOT ALL FOR WAR

The Civil War (First Half)

In the summer of 1828 a gaunt, young Kentuckian went flat-boating down the big river to New Orleans. In that gaudy, booming town there were plenty of attractions. Luxurious mansions and fancy buildings created a background for Mardi Gras, while dance halls and gambling joints worked overtime to keep up the town's reputation as the "wide-openest" port on the continent.

But the hard muscled, young flatboatman wasn't much impressed by the tinsel of this creole metropolis. What impressed him most was the market down by the old Cabildo—the market where Negro slaves were auctioned off to the highest bidder. This pool of misery in the midst of hilarity was a scene the Kentuckian never forgot.

That young flatboatman's name was Abraham Lincoln. And he wasn't the first American to see the injustice in slavery.

After the Revolutionary War, George Washington and Thomas Jefferson hoped slavery would be abolished, and both willed freedom to their slaves. Throughout the country many anti-slavery societies were organized. Laws were passed to better the slave's lot, and a strong movement was afoot to free the slaves and return them to Africa.

"We must exterminate slavery root and branch," said the Abolitionists. "Human bondage is a crime."

"We must stop the *extension* of slavery," said the more conservative. "Eventually it will die of its own accord, for slave labor cannot compete with free enterprise."

"Let us alone," protested the slave owners. "Free your own slaves if you wish, but this is our own business."

There you have the argument that was to shake the American Republic. But how did it become an earthquake? How did it split the country into North and South and explode a terrible war in 1861?

The Powder Train

In 1787 the New England States, New York, and Pennsylvania voted to end slavery. It was also excluded by ordinance from the North-West Territory (which encompassed Ohio, Indiana, Illinois, Michigan, Wisconsin). New Jersey abolished slavery in 1804. Notice this line-up and you'll see that these so-called "Free States" made up a solid block in the North. The nation, right at the start, was divided about half-slave, half-free.

In 1808 Congress passed a law prohibiting the importation of slaves in America. This move was aimed to stop the slave trade right at the source. Financially it was a blow to many New England ship owners who'd made huge profits carrying black cargo across the Atlantic. But the majority were glad to wash their hands of the enterprise and employ their ships in a better field of commerce.

As usual a few racketeers tried to beat the game, and went in for slave-smuggling—"black-birding." To smash this racket, the U. S. Navy went to action. Patrols were set up in 1819 to cruise off Africa and hunt the smugglers down. It was a game of gunfire and murder, for the black-birders had a trick of throwing the chained slaves overboard to lighten ship and escape. A good many human cargoes were mercilessly drowned in mid-Atlantic by the slave runners. But hard-hitting American Navy men led by such officers as Matthew Calbraith Perry soon broke up the murderous racket. Great Britain had abolished slavery, and the Royal Navy cooperated in this campaign. So black-birding went to the bottom of the sea along with piracy.

Meantime, Louisiana's admission to the Union as a "Slave State" had brought in still more slaves. Here was another angle to the problem. As the nation expanded westward and new states joined the Union, should they come in "slave or free?"

This question gave Congress a terrific headache. Politically it divided the nation right across the middle. The Northern states, as previously noted, had abolished slavery shortly after the nation was founded. In general their leaders wanted to see the new states come in free. But the slave-holding states of the South wanted just the opposite.

There were many Southerners who had hoped to see slavery abolished. At the time of Louisiana's entry to the Union there were more anti-slave societies in the South than in the North. But abolition failed utterly. Reason: the boom in Southern cotton.

Eli Whitney's cotton gin did it. Invented in 1793, this cotton-cleaning machine put cotton on a big paying basis. Almost simultaneously, spinning and weaving machines were invented, first in England, then in New England. This created a tremendous market for cotton.

How did this affect the slave business? Well, the majority of slaves were field hands, and the boom created a rush demand for slaves to plant and pick the cotton. The value of slaves went up. The profits from cotton went up. The planters became the most influential men in the South. Money talks, and the planters talked louder than the abolitionists. To protect their profits, they wanted to see slavery protected as an institution. And this meant increasing the number of slave states.

Congress tried to compromise. In 1820 when Missouri entered the Union as a slave state, a line was drawn which halved America more or less across the middle. "Hereafter," said Congress in effect, "the states coming in north of the line shall come in free. Those south of the line shall have slavery if they wish."

The Missouri Compromise was seen by many as a fatal blunder. It launched a rush of settlers into such territories as Kansas— abolitionists and slave-owners each fighting the other to take over. Most tragic perhaps—it did nothing about the human-rights aspect of slavery.

By 1840, when the nation had a total population of 17,000,000, one person out of every seven was a slave. Drama there was a-plenty as Texas came in as another slave state, then Iowa came in free, and the balance see-sawed on the fatal line. Tragedy there was, too, in "bloody Kansas" where the settlers tried to settle it with gunfire, and fierce old John Brown, fanatical abolitionist, thinking he heard the voice of God, set out to exterminate the slave owners.

Bitterness increased as the see-saw went faster. The crash almost came in 1849 when California, although south of the line, voted to join the Union as a free state. Oregon upset the balance further by coming in free. During the next ten years the North-South division widened until the two sections faced each other like two opposed nations.

Running for Congress in 1858, Abe Lincoln of Illinois summed up the situation. In debate against his famous rival, Stephen (the Little Giant) Douglas, tall Abe declared, *"A house divided against itself cannot stand. I believe this government cannot permanently endure half slave and half free."*

Yes, the American Republic had become a divided house. In the South, over 3,500,000 slaves worked in bondage. To the slave owners they represented a tremendous money investment, for by 1859 the value of a good field hand had risen to $1600. They also represented the labor supply for the great cotton plantations. These vast plantations occupied a major part of the agricultural Southland and supported an almost regal aristocracy of planters who had a saying: "Cotton is King!" Although these wealthy planters were a minority, they (and King Cotton) ruled the land.

In the North the picture was totally different. Cities growing. Factories mushrooming everywhere. Like the Navy, the North had "gotten up steam." A thousand new inventions were industrializing and modernizing the land. In 1844 Goodyear had discovered the process for vulcanizing rubber. Morse's telegraph was marketed the same year. The sewing machine, the rotary press, Bessemer steel, and the locomotive had set Northern factory whistles blowing. These whistles were attracting foreign immigrants by the thousands—Germans, Scandinavians, Irish— to work in New England, New York, Pennsylvania, the North-West.

Then a tragic drama occurred which shook America like the thunder of a coming storm. Old John Brown came out of the West in 1859, determined to liberate all the slaves in Virginia.

John Brown's Fort, Harpers Ferry, W. Va.

A madman (if you were a Southern slave owner)—a crusader (if you were a Northern Abolitionist)—Old John and a small band of followers seized the Federal arsenal at Harper's Ferry.

Doing their duty, Col. Robert E. Lee and a company of Marines shot it out with Old John. He was captured, tried, convicted as a public enemy, and hanged. And while John Brown's body lay a-moulderin' in the grave, the storm-clouds went marching on. And now the old question of states' rights flickered like incendiary lighting across the sky.

"If the North gains further control of the government," Southern leaders were threatening, "the Southern states shall stand on states' rights and secede from the Union."

To which many Northern leaders were replying, "The Federal Government is above states' rights. The Union, as set up by the Federal Constitution, cannot be broken."

Secession!

Lincoln had come a long way since that day he'd stood watching the slave market in New Orleans. Up by his own bootstraps, he'd studied law, served a term in Congress, become a big figure in Illinois—an independent thinker with a mind as keen as a woodman's axe. Like John Paul Jones, Abe Lincoln climbed the ladder from the bottom. Taking the helm of the Ship of State, he was strictly a mustang.

He didn't particularly hanker to be President. When the Republican Party nominated him, Southern leaders threatened secession louder than ever. Many uneasy Northerners feared to vote for him, and it looked as if Breckinridge, a Southern Democrat, might win the election. Only a split in the opposition made possible Abe Lincoln's election in November 1860.

On December 20 the leaders of South Carolina signed a declaration announcing that, *"the Union now subsisting between South Carolina and the other States under the name of the 'United States of America' is hereby dissolved."*

Lincoln wasn't due in the White House until the following March; James Buchanan, the retiring President, didn't know what to do. So he sat on the fence. While he was sitting there, 1861 came around. By February 1st, Georgia, Florida, Alabama, Mississippi, Louisiana, and Texas had quit the Union. Delegates from the seceded states met at Montgomery, Alabama. The CONFEDERATE STATES OF AMERICA was formed. Jefferson Davis of Mississippi was chosen President of the Confederacy. America woke up with a shock to find that the Union was broken—a new nation had raised its flag in the South.

The Confederacy began to arm itself against possible intervention. Federal arsenals were seized and supplies commandeered. In general the Federal officers in the South offered no resistance. But Major Robert Anderson, in command of Fort Sumter guarding Charleston harbor, refused to surrender Federal property.

On March 4, unhappy Buchanan climbed down off the fence, and turned the worst situation in American history over to Abraham Lincoln.

Now what would President Lincoln do about Fort Sumter? Forlorn March was melting into April. A pall hung over the country. In Washington, D. C., Southern officials and Congressmen were resigning to join the Confederacy. Appointing replacements for the officials, President Lincoln said dryly that he *"sat there like a man letting lodgings at one end of his house, while the other end was on fire."*

He told his Cabinet that he would send reinforcements to Sumter. This decision was conveyed to the Confederacy, and on April 12, 1861, the Confederate batteries of General P. G. T. Beauregard began the attack.

For 32 hours Major Anderson and his 128 men held out against over 5,000 Confederates. It was a queer battle—not a man killed or wounded on either side. But on April 14, aflame and in red ruin, Fort Sumter surrendered. Down came the Stars and Stripes. Up went a strange new flag—the Stars and Bars.

The next day Lincoln called for 75,000 volunteers.

The dark and bloody war had begun.

Blue vs. Gray

It was called the Civil War—the War Between the States—the War of the Rebellion—the War of the Secession—the Brothers' War. Each of those names gives you a fragment of the picture. And perhaps the last suggests the most tragic feature of the conflict—American against American—cousin fighting cousin, and in some instances brother locked in death-grip with brother.

For no sharp geographical Mason-Dixon line severed North and South. After the fall of Fort Sumter, Virginia, North Carolina, Tennessee, and Arkansas joined the Confederacy. But, Delaware, Maryland, and Missouri, although they were slave-holding states, did not quit the Union. And for all her Southern accent, neither did Kentucky.

As state sentiments were confused, so was public sentiment. Many Northerners thought the seceding states should be permitted to leave the Union. While Northern patriots volunteered, anti-Lincoln riots broke out. The mayor of New York proposed that in event of war the city remain neutral. At the same time there were Southerners who refused to accept the Confederacy. There was strong Union sentiment in Tennessee, for example. In some of the other states, including Georgia, the Confederate leaders were afraid to trust secession to a public vote, and the matter was left solely to the state legislature. The people in the mountainous western part of Virginia determined to secede from Virginia, set up the State of West Virginia, and join the Union.

So it wasn't all "Dixie" or all "The Union Forever." A civil war can even break up your home. Such well-known families as the Breckinridges, Clays, and Crittendens had men on both sides. That great acting family, the Booths—the Barrymores of their day—became divided. Lincoln's wife had relatives who fought for the Confederacy.

To most of the Southern-born Americans, Lincoln's call for volunteers seemed to mean an invasion of their homeland. So old Army officers like the Johnston brothers, Longstreet, T. J. Jackson, and Jeb Stuart said good-bye to their pro-Union service comrades and signed up to fight for their States. Altogether a good third of the Army's officer personnel "went South."

Colonel Robert E. Lee must have found it a mind-racking decision. He had freed his own slaves long before the war. He had many friends in the Army. But his home-State, Virginia, had seceded. She was the most powerful state in the Confederacy, and Richmond had been made the Confederate capitol. Now Virginia was seizing Federal arsenals and arming. He, himself, had led the Law against Old John Brown for seizing a Federal arsenal. As sure as shooting, Federal forces would now enter Virginia. Yet this prospect of invasion was unbearable. Lee's home at Arlington overlooked the Union capital. Blue troops were at his very gate. To Lee, it seemed that the states which had joined the original Union voluntarily should have the right to leave it voluntarily. Sadly he resigned his commission in the U. S. Army, and offered his services to the Confederacy.

Comrades similarly parted company in the Navy. Two great officers, Franklin Buchanan and Matthew Fontaine Maury, resigned to serve under the Confederate flag. One fifth of the Navy's officers eventually joined the Confederacy—those who commanded warships in foreign waters returning their ships to the Federal Government, as honor bound, before resigning.

But there was divided sentiment too, in the service forces. One of the greatest Union soldiers, General George H. Thomas, left the South to serve under Lincoln. Mr. J. Toucey, Secretary of the Navy under President Buchanan, was a Connecticut Yankee but strongly for secession. Before retiring from office he'd done his best to scatter the Federal warships all over the globe in order to give a Confederate Navy time to organize. On the other hand, Franklin Buchanan's favorite brother "went North" to fight for the Union. And the Navy's greatest leader was a Tennesseean who stood staunchly by the Stars and Stripes— David Glasgow Farragut.

The North—the Union—numbered 23 states with a population of 22,000,000. The South—the Confederacy—numbered 11 states

with a population of 9,000,000 of whom over 3,500,000 were slaves.

The heavily industrialized North controlled two-thirds of America's bank account and most of the manufacturing; she had good highways and numerous rail lines. The South, largely agricultural, had practically no heavy industry. Its bank account was mainly in the hands of wealthy planters and cotton brokers. Its railroads were sparse; its highways poor.

On the surface it would seem the odds were all against the Confederacy. But there were factors on its side. Although 75% of the Southerners owned neither plantations nor slaves, by and large they all gave enthusiastic support to the war. Many of the best Army officers were Southern men, ready to provide trained leadership for the boys in gray. Cavalry was an important military arm, and Southern horsemanship needed no training. Manufacturing lack was somewhat balanced by the fact that large military supplies stored in the South were immediately available. Confederate leaders counted on striking *"fustest with the mostest."* Failing a knockout, they'd have the big advantage of fighting a defensive war, in which case poor roads and rail lines would help more than hinder. And finally there seemed a good chance of European aid for the Confederacy.

Cotton, the Southern leaders declared, would win the war. Without it, a Confederate Senator cried, *"England would topple and carry the whole civilized world with her, save the South. No, you dare not make war on cotton. No power on earth dares to make war upon it. Cotton is King!"*

The North surely had the advantage in money, materials, and men. But too often the boys in blue were officered by rule-book old-timers, or by amateurs who thought war a matter of uniforms and flags. While Richmond armed to the teeth and grimly planned to "give 'em hell," Washington enjoyed reviews and parades.

Diplomatically the North was unpopular. France and England were showing official sympathy for the Confederacy, and it looked as if they might furnish the South with supplies. Most of the crowned heads favored King Cotton. In all Europe, the North had but one supporter—Russia. But the huge Slavic nation, which proved friendly to the Union throughout the war, was too far away to offer appreciable aid.

In one great respect the North started out with a big advantage. That was on the sea. When the war began, the American Merchant Marine was second in the world, and the majority of its ships were New Englanders. The U. S. Navy, with 42 warships, including four modern steam frigates and fifteen screw-driven cruiser sloops, could be a powerful striking arm—when it was ready. At the opening gun it wasn't ready, as you'll see. But for Secretary of the Navy, Lincoln picked Gideon Welles, who quickly proved that he knew the score.

Lincoln saw at once that the Confederacy's main chance of survival lay in maintaining its connections with Europe. The U. S. Navy could win the war by cutting those connections.

Two weeks after the war began, Lincoln announced the great blockade.

Blockade

In Washington that April, Secretary of Navy Welles looked at the map and perspired.

The Confederate coastline ran from the Chesapeake Bay down to Florida and over to Brownsville, Texas—3,549 miles long! There were the seaboards of the Carolinas and Georgia—a coastal puzzle of inlets, coves, and island-hidden bays. The long Florida peninsula with its Ten Thousand Islands and the Keys. The Gulf Coast of lonely lagoons and deep Louisiana bayous. Hundreds of places where light, fast ships could dodge in and out at moon-dark, and get away. Hundreds of places where the raiders commissioned by Jeff Davis the day after Sumter fell could dart out at unwary traffic, or moor and hide.

In this coastline, too, the great Southern seaports were imbedded—Charleston, Wilmington, Port Royal, Savannah, Fernandia, St. Augustine, Mobile, New Orleans. Not to mention the Virginia ports on the Chesapeake, and Confederate control of the whole vast Mississippi delta.

Blockade? It would be the most gigantic naval operation the world had ever seen. And to undertake this stupendous project, the U. S. Navy—you can imagine Welles staring at his reports—the U. S. Navy had four available warships!

Four ships in home waters, flying the Stars and Stripes. Oh, yes, there was the U. S. fleet of some thirty-odd steam vessels and a score of older canvas-backs. But these were scattered all the way from Japan to Turkey.

Resignations had been coming into Welles' office with every mail. Captain Josiah Tatnall—one of the Navy's best—had "gone South." An order to Captain H. A. Adams of *Brooklyn*, stationed at Pensacola, had been answered by a weird letter which stated that this officer, on his own hook, had tried to arrange an armistice with Confederate General Bragg. Other orders from Welles' office had been mysteriously countermanded. Dispatches were being tampered with. The telegraph to Baltimore Navy Yard had been cut. In the Washington Navy Yard, where Commodore Buchanan had been in command, shells and powder bags were discovered filled with sawdust. Welles found the Navy and the Navy Department falling apart around him.

On April 20 had come the worst news yet. The Confederates had seized the big naval base at Norfolk, Virginia. Commodore McCauley, in charge of Norfolk Navy Yard, had done too little, and that too late. Failing to get the Norfolk squadron out in time, he had scuttled it in haste and panic. Nine Federal warships had been lost to the USN, including the brand new steam frigate, *Merrimac*, one of the finest battleships built. Capture of the

yard had also given the Confederates a great store of supplies
and 3,000 cannon.

Blockade? Why, the four warships on hand weren't enough
to blockade a single major port, much less patrol 3,549 miles
of enemy coast. Furthermore, not one of those four was ready.
Roanoke, Wabash, Colorado, Minnesota—all were tied up in dock,
their firerooms as cold as igloos, their forecastles without crews.

Gideon Welles made no delay. He called in his Yankee friend,
Captain Silas Stringham, and made him a "Flag Officer" (the
rank of Admiral didn't appear in the service until later). Stringham was to work out the blockade details.

He called in Gustavus Fox, a smart business man and ex-Navy
officer. As Assistant Secretary, Fox was to work on strategy.

He moved the Navy Academy to Newport, Rhode Island.

He wired Mr. George D. Morgan of New York, another smart
executive, and told him to buy up every ship, schooner, tug,
and ferryboat he could lay his hands on.

He contacted Ericsson, the inventor, and told him the Navy
Department had an open pocketbook and an open mind. He
called in Ben Isherwood, chief engineer of the Washington Yard,
and told him to install engines on everything afloat. He crammed
the Northern shipyards with rush orders for gunboats. He put
the heat on mills, foundries, and munition works for everything
from buttons to bombs. And by the end of June, the U. S. Navy,
ruptured by the nation's explosion, was coming back into form.

Still the vast blockade was only on paper, and the international
experts were sure that the North was done for. Across the sea,

England's Tory leaders were openly hostile and derisive. Hostile because a blockade would stop the cotton shipping which fed England's textile industry. And derisive because not even the Royal Navy would attempt to plug up a ragged, harbor-laced, 3,549-mile coastline. "A naval impossibility!"

The Conderates were even more scornful. To them it was "*Abe Lincoln's Soapbox Navy.*"

Old Man River

In World War II the U. S. Navy had a "two-ocean" job. You know what a job that was. In the Civil War, back in '61, the Navy found itself up against an "ocean-and-river" job. That was a whale of a job. For that river, considering the day and time, looked as big as the ocean.

In length, the Mississippi almost equalled the Confederate coastline. Much of its 2,466-mile channel had not been charted, and the sections that had been were unreliable, what with shifting bottoms and wandering bars. Its tide and floods were as unpredictable as rain. The Confederate coastline was problem No. 1; and just as certainly, the MISSISSIPPI RIVER with its ox-bows, channel islands, swamps, tributaries, catfish towns, and fortified ports was No. 2 on the puzzle parade. To understand this Mississippi naval problem, review the situation on dry land.

The first sharp fighting was in western Virginia where a Confederate army of 8,000 was rushed from Richmond to bring those pro-Union counties back into line. Queer situation—Virginia seceding from the Union, then refusing to let those western counties secede from Virginia. Must have given leaders like Lee their first shadowy doubts. For if states had the right to secede from the Union, what law was there to keep them from quitting the Confederacy?

Too late for logic—the bullets had begun to fly. Down from Ohio came General George B. McClellan, retired Army Officer dispatched by the Governor of Ohio with a volunteer army to aid the West Virginians. On June 3rd the Union troops struck the Confederates at Philippi under Rich Mountain, capturing the base and driving the enemy over the mountain. And West Virginia was saved for the Union.

Now, in July, the fighting switched to the District of Columbia

—the hottest spot on the Union front. Already the Navy had secured the upper Chesapeake and had strong forces in the Potomac River, but all was not quiet on the Potomac.

In fact, Washington was close to bedlam. For weeks the troops had been pouring in—men from New England, Pennsylvania, Michigan, everywhere. Some had rifles. Many were without. Some, like the New York Fire Zouaves, came in gorgeous uniforms as fancy drill teams. Others were raw country boys in overalls. The War Department wasn't ready. While baggage wagons jammed Pennsylvania Avenue, recruits tented on the White House lawn. There was no fodder for the horses, no provisions for the men, no military organization, no discipline. The city was honey-combed with Confederate agents, and a large Confederate force was reported massing a few miles west; no one knew what would happen next.

What might happen was a Confederate smash at Washington. In Richmond there'd been no such floundering as in Washington. Jeff Davis, former West Pointer, had been quick to install a military set-up. To Joseph E. Johnston he gave command of the Army of Virginia, and Johnston was rated the best officer in America. Around him he gathered Lee and Jeb Stuart and that genius from V.M.I., Thomas Jonathan Jackson—field commanders second to none. Although Davis underestimated the West Virginia set-back as picayune, he had a shrewd eye for strategy. A hard punch at the Union capital might floor the North in the first round.

Northward, therefore, came General Beauregard, CSA, with an army of some 15,000 boys in gray. Meeting no opposition, he seized the railroad junction at Manassas, Virginia, a short distance from the capital. Northward too came General Johnston with 15,000 more men in gray—up the Shenandoah Valley to swing over and reinforce Beauregard.

Meantime the Northern public had been shouting, "On to Richmond!" Lincoln was against it, but his political advisers urged action. Reluctantly, he ordered General Irvin McDowell to move against Beauregard and Johnston. McDowell crossed the Potomac at Arlington with 28,000 boys in blue who were green as grass. Another blue-green Union force of 22,000 under

General Patterson swung out and around, hoping to outflank Johnston in the Shenandoah.

On July 21, 1861, the Yanks ran into the Confederates at Bull Run—a little creek which wandered cross-lots at Manassas —and it was one of those battles which generals don't like to talk about. Down the road with McDowell had trailed crowds of picnickers, Congressmen and their ladies, hawkers selling flags and popcorn—all out to see a field day. The day, July 21, 1861, was a scorcher. Dust and heat hung over the pasture land. You can imagine what happened to all the jaywalkers when the bullets started to fly.

All morning the battle swirled along Bull Run creek. The Union troops charged valiantly, and there was a moment when it seemed McDowell might win. But on the field was the Confederate General T. J. Jackson. "Look!" a Confederate officer shouted as the gray line fell back along the ridge. *There stands Jackson like a stone wall.* And "Stonewall" Jackson turned the tide. By the afternoon, McDowell's men were out of ammunition, supply lines were tangled, all organization was gone. General Patterson never showed up. Johnston came charging over from the Shenandoah to aid Beauregard, and the Union line broke to pieces. McDowell's whole army raced back to Washington, leaving guns and equipment strewn behind.

That was the Battle of Bull Run. A Union fiasco, it was also a Confederate bungle. Instead of charging on to Washington, the Confederates sat down to celebrate, thus giving McDowell time to reorganize. When the boys in gray recovered, it was too late. The Potomac was lined with cannon, and Washington was too tough to take.

So the Virginia front became stalemated. West Virginia was a solid sector. Kentucky, next door, whose governor issued a proclamation of neutrality, was on the fence. The front-line, extending westward, then crossed the Mississippi River just below Cairo, Illinois, and followed the Missouri-Arkansas line over to Kansas.

Some hard fighting occurred along the Missouri front in August. Confederate sympathy threatened to divide Missouri, and a gray army came up from Arkansas to attack. On August 10, in a savage battle at Wilson's Creek, the Union troops were

259

thrown back. But the Confederates couldn't follow up the blow, the fighting bogged down, and Missouri was secured for the Union.

Now you've got both armies stalled while their leaders grope for a place to break through. Mountain passes are guarded—roads are blocked—where will the break come? Well, there's one big highway running north-to-south—a big, yellow road that goes right down into Southern territory—the Mississippi River.

Union General Halleck, in command of the western line, sees it, too. And Gideon Welles has studied every mile. It's a waterway, and that means Navy.

Since early summer plans have been on "Uncle Gideon's" desk—plans for a joint Army and Navy drive—a big amphibious operation to enter the Confederacy by way of Old Man River.

And where were the ships to come from? The guns? The sailors? Why, even if a fleet were on hand, the whole thing would have to be moved a thousand miles inland. Meantime, the Confederates were aware of the river's strategic value. From Columbus, Missouri, down to New Orleans they were fortifying the banks, planting obstructions, mining the channel with torpedoes.

The Navy must do the job. Clear away the mines. Beat up the Confederate forts. Convoy the Army supply ships and transports. Spearhead the attack while the Union Army advanced by land.

The Navy was underway. Early as May, "Uncle Gideon" had detailed John Rodgers II, USN, to go to St. Louis and organize a naval base. With Rodgers went naval constructor Samuel Pook to design river-going warships.

In St. Louis Rodgers ran into a mess of profiteers and claims of priority by the Army. Rodgers stubbornly bucked forward and by the end of July had rounded up some honest river pilots and three sidewheelers for the Navy. But braid and red tape were getting him down. So "Uncle Gideon" gave him a sea command, and sent Flag Officer Andrew Foote to replace him.

Foote set up his headquarters at the Cairo, Illinois, naval base, and got things done. Sam Pook designed eight river gunboats, blunt at bow and stern, with big guns aboard. Built for action, these gunboats were heavily armored at the forward end, their engines protected by slabs of iron. These were the first iron-clads built by the Navy, although on August 3, 1861, "Uncle Gideon" had authorized the construction of a sea-going ironclad to be called the *Monitor*.

The Mississippi gunboats, which became famous as "Pook's Turtles," marked the end of wooden ships and iron men—began the era of iron ships and iron men. They were built by James B. Eads. With no use for graft, he promised to build the ships in two months, and delivered the first one to Flag Officer Foote in forty-five days.

In Cairo, Foote was training enlisted men, drilling gunners, moulding a flotilla into shape. He was also making friends with an unassuming Army general—a man who hadn't done too well at West Point; a man who had served in the Mexican War, but resigned his commission afterwards, protesting the rowdy conduct of troops at Vera Cruz. Now he volunteered at once for the Union, whipped a tough Illinois regiment into shape, and was appointed General in command of Western Kentucky. Apples were the last things he polished, and Foote liked his plainspoken honesty. His name was Ulysses S. Grant.

In autumn Grant proposed action. A Confederate army was massing down river at Belmont. With Foote's gunboats in support, Grant devised an attack to test the enemy. The boys in blue struck the gray camp on the river bank November 7th. Confederate reinforcements drove Grant back, inflicting stiff losses. The gunboats *Lexington* and *Tyler* covered his retreat up stream, and the first big battle on the Mississippi was counted a Union defeat.

The big Union amphib was merely trying its legs. At HQ, Grant and Foote put their heads together. Soon the biggest amphibious operation the world had yet seen was to be launched. The Union was out to capture Old Man River.

Thunder at Sea

Now go back to the Navy's No. 1 problem—the blockade. To be effective, a blockade must be something more than an official announcement. All the legal documents in creation weren't going to stop Confederate ships from trans-Atlantic runs, or to stop foreign ships from entering Confederate ports.

Bull Run had left the North with a gloomy hang-over. The news from Wilson's Creek was no pick-me-up. For the benefit of national morale, a victory was called for. A sea victory which could enforce the blockade was doubly in order. It was up to "Abe Lincoln's Soapbox Navy."

Late in August '61 a squadron gathered at Fortress Monroe. This task force, under Flag Officer Stringham, wasn't quite so rickety as its deriders liked to think. Armed and manned were *Minnesota* and *Wabash*, steam frigates the equal of any afloat. With sloops *Cumberland* and *Susquehanna*, with the gunboat *Pawnee* and transports carrying 800 men under General Ben Butler, it carried considerable weight.

The plan was for an attack on Hatteras Inlet, a fortified Confederate strong-point on the North Carolina coast. Sandbars narrowed the approach, and twin forts guarded the inlet; but Stringham was confident he could capture the works.

The squadron got up steam. Down the Cape it ran into a Hatteras storm. Then, trying to land in surfboats, about half of Butler's men became snafued on a sand bar. It was the Navy's job; and despite high water, Stringham moved in.

Navy gunners opened up against land artillery, and the Union sailors won. The first fort fell on August 28, and its twin caved in the next day. The surrender was made by Confederate Captain Barron, a former officer of the USN.

So the Navy won the Union's first major victory, and the giant blockade was begun. Next project was to hit the big South Carolina shipping base, Port Royal. Loss of this fine seaport would be a hard blow to the Confederacy. But it would mean a rugged battle; the harbor approaches were tricky and the headlands thicketed with big naval guns transplanted from Norfolk.

In command was Union Flag Officer Samuel DuPont. "Uncle Gideon" saw to it that he had a good task force—eight gunboats (four brand new), six armed steamers, sloop *Susquehanna*, and big *Wabash* for his flagship, plus transports carrying 13,000 Union troops.

October came before this force was mustered, and in the

meantime Confederate espionage was working. Despite secret orders and great precaution, the plan leaked to Richmond, and Jeff Davis rushed reinforcements, under Captain J. Tatnall and General Robert E. Lee, to Port Royal.

Gray weather also sided with the Confederates. Setting out in late October, DuPont's fleet ran south into a heavy gale. Two transports were damaged off Hatteras, and their men had to be rescued. The gunboat *Isaac Smith* had to jettison her batteries to keep afloat. Storm-thrashed and battened down, the squadron arrived off Port Royal on November 4th.

The Confederates had removed lights and buoys, and DuPont's ships had to feel their way in. Out rushed eight armed steamers under Tatnall to delay the advance; but when the Union Dahlgrens boomed, they scurried for cover. DuPont dropped anchor to hold a Captain's conference and explain his battle-plan. Forts Walker and Beauregard covered the harbor entrance to Port Royal. DuPont proposed to copy Stringham's maneuver at Hatteras Inlet—keep the ships moving in mid-channel between the two forts—hold them to a single-file orbit—make the land artillery shoot at moving targets. The troops would be out of it, for all the landing boats on the transports had been storm-smashed. Again it was an all-Navy job.

DuPont's flagship took the lead. On the morning of November 7 the squadron steamed in. In single file ten warships paraded past Fort Beauregard, hammering the fort with broadsides, while a small force of five Union gunboats drove ahead to chase Tatnall's Confederate pickets up a creek. Then, deep within the harbor, the main column executed a perfect corpen, and steamed back in line past Fort Walker.

Completing the orbit, the Union warships went around again, this time altering the course so the Confederate batteries would have to rediscover range. Smoke and fire stormed across the harbor as the Confederate gunners returned shot for shot. But the gray artillerymen were no match for the Navy gun crews— couldn't hit those ships clanking by like moving targets in a shooting gallery. On the other hand, the Confederate forts were as stationary as two gravestones, and the Navy gunners were hitting them with everything. When the Union ships came around for a third go on the circuit there were no Confederate guns to answer DuPont's fire. Port Royal was won for the Union.

This was a tremendous Union victory. DuPont's losses—eight killed and twenty-three wounded, and no ship seriously damaged —were far below the Confederate toll. Although Lee had declared Fort Walker the strongest on the Confederate seaboard, the fort and its twin had been shot to rubble. It was obvious that land fortifications couldn't take it from Navy gunners and Navy guns.

Lee advised Jefferson Davis that fixed coastal forts were tombs. The Confederacy must move its defenses inland, out of naval range—keep them mobile and elastic, able to snap into action up and down the coast rather than stationary on some headland.

With a single blow, DuPont's squadron drove the Confederate defenses back from the Atlantic shore line. It forced the abandonment of many small harbors, inlets, and coastal islands. It captured a great port in the heart of the Confederacy. And it gave the Union Navy a strategic base of operations for the blockade.

From Fort Royal the Union gunboats could patrol southward to Florida, northward to Virginia, fencing Confederate shipping in. King Cotton would feel the first numbing stroke of paralysis. But it would take a lot to kill him. There were still the great Atlantic seaports of Norfolk, Charleston, Wilmington, and Savannah. There were still the open ports on the Gulf.

And out on the broad Atlantic—

International Relations

On the Atlantic the Union Navy came up against problem No. 3. This concerned Confederate merchantmen on foreign trade runs. It also concerned Confederate sea raiders out to strike at the Union merchant fleet. Confederate warships were being built in foreign ports. Finally, there was the business of warning Europe that the war was an American matter and that the North would uphold the Monroe Doctrine.

Because of the international angles, this Atlantic problem was knotty, and it gave the Union some of the closest calls of the war. The North's foreign relations were shaky in '61. Land military reverses had given Europe a poor idea of Union chances for victory. The French said, "Sacre bleu!"—annoyed because

Lincoln's blockaders threatened to stop French wines from reaching the South and Southern cotton from reaching the French mills on the Seine. British mill owners were also peeved. And so were English liberals who'd expected Lincoln to free all the slaves at one stroke.

Ruler of France in '61 was Napoleon III. Hoping to copy the original Napoleon, he'd been looking for territory to conquer. Now his eye lit on Mexico.

The Mexican Government owed France some money. Trying to throw off another dictatorship, the Mexican people were staging a revolution. So Napoleon III stepped in. First, to collect the money; then to pose as "Defender of the Faith." But these disguises didn't fool Abe Lincoln. He knew that what the French Emperor really wanted was to establish French rule in Mexico. And with America rocked by Civil War, what could be done about it?

The Union could do nothing. Neither could the Confederacy. French warships steamed into Vera Cruz and 30,000 French troops marched into Mexico City. Napoleon III appointed his royal relative, Archduke Maximilian of Austria, puppet Emperor of Mexico. Uncle Sam found a European power at his doorstep, waiting for his divided house to fall.

Lincoln reminded Napoleon III about the Monroe Doctrine. The French Emperor played deaf, and throughout the Civil War the Austrian Max ruled Mexico. As a friendly gesture to Lincoln Russia dispatched a warship squadron which visited New York and Alexandria, Virginia. The expected attack on the dis-united states never came.

Confederate Navy

The Union Navy's job was only started in '61. At sea as on land the Confederacy was a tough opponent, and its battle leaders didn't take anything lying down. From the opening gun they realized that sea power could settle the issue, and they got to work in Richmond on plans to launch a naval counter-attack on the Union.

In warships, ordnance, and material the Confederate Navy began practically from zero. But not in men. Franklin Buchanan was a topnotch leader, and Matthew Maury one of the world's foremost scientists. The officers and men who signed up under the Stars and Bars were as full of fight as they were convinced of the rightness of the Confederate cause. Necessity encouraged invention, and to the office of Confederate Navy Secretary, S. R. Mallory, came G. J. Rains and H. L. Hunley—men with ideas. John L. Porter, Chief Confederate Naval Constructor, was another idea man with a punch. Meanwhile, Norfolk had hardly fallen into the Confederacy's lap when Lieutenant J. M. Brooke presented the scheme of plating a ship with iron and sending it out to defy the shot and shell of the Union blockaders.

The idea of an armored ship was not originally American. The French Navy featured ironclads in 1855, and demonstrated their value in action. Mossbacks scoffed, of course, but the alert Confederate heads weren't sitting around idle. Mallory gave Porter and Brooke the green light. The Norfolk Navy Yard furnished the mechanics, the metal, and the *Merrimac*.

Merrimac, you'll remember, was the big new steam frigate which panicky Federal officers had scuttled before abandoning the Norfolk base. The Confederates raised her, found the hull sound, and put her into dry dock. Then, working under a shroud of secrecy, they removed her masts, stripped her down, and set to work building a barn-like casemate over her deck. The sloping sides of the casemate were timber, 22 inches thick, covered with 4-inch iron plates. Ports were fashioned for eight broadside guns and for fore and after pivot guns. Topside of the casemate was decked over with an iron grating.

Design called for a heavy iron fantail to shield the ship's rudder and propeller. As a further novelty, a great cast iron beak something like a mammoth plowshare was attached to the ship's bow as a ram. As the work went forward on *Merrimac*, the Confederates were satisfied they "had something." Mechanics rushed the job. Secret agents reported an armored vessel under

construction in Philadelphia. The men at Norfolk knew they were engaged in a grim, ironclad race.

Metalwork took time in those under-the-gaslight-days, and while the *Merrimac* job was pushing slowly ahead, the attack at sea was being handled by a few dashing Confederate raiders.

Outstanding among these "lone wolves" was Captain Raphael Semmes. Semmes answered Jeff Davis' call for privateers, and the second month of the war saw his ship ready at New Orleans —a fast 5-gun steamer christened *Sumter*.

Privateering had been recently outlawed by international law, so the Confederates hurriedly changed the status of their raiders to full-fledged war vessels. *C.S.S. Sumter* slipped down the delta, dodged past *U.S.S. Brooklyn*, and steamed out into the Gulf, stripped for action.

Semmes headed for the West Indies and north-bound traffic. July 3rd he snapped up the clipper *Golden Rocket* off Cuba, and set her afire. Another half dozen Yankee merchantmen fell into *Sumter's* bag before the Union Navy sent a squadron down to the Indies to snare the raider.

Semmes got wind of the hunters on his tail, and went dodging down through the islands, leaving loud talk and false clues in every port to mislead the pursuit. But the smoke of burning merchantmen marked his wake, and *U.S.S. Powhatan* followed it. Captain of *Powhatan* was David Dixon Porter. Lincoln had rushed him down to Florida to save Pensacola for the Union. But shillyshallying Federal officers had handed the base to the Confederates on a platter. Now, joining the chase after the audacious Semmes, David Porter was fighting mad.

Ducking around the hump of Brazil, Semmes learned that Porter was dogging him, so he tied down *Sumter's* boiler valves and doubled back to the French island of Martinique for coal. While *Sumter* was coaling, *U.S.S. Iroquois*, another of the Union squadron, happen-chanced into the harbor. *Sumter* sat, while *Iroquois* waited with aimed guns.

Neutral authorities ordered *Iroquois* to leave the harbor. The Union captain bowed to international law, but rigged a little scheme with the skipper of a schooner lying in port. Undoubtedly the Confederate raider would try to slip out at night, and the schooner was to signal the Union warship with her masthead lights—one if *Sumter* headed north, two if she went south. Apparently the Union captain had read about "Paul Revere."

Captain Semmes had a wary ear, however. Somebody talked on the waterfront, and Semmes got wind of the plan. On the night of October 23, he moved out of the harbor, heading south. When two lights appeared on the schooner's masthead, he swung hard around and raced northward under forced draught. Hours later, *Iroquois* was still chasing in the direction of the Southern Cross, while *Sumter*, out in the Atlantic, was sighting Polaris.

Sumter reached Europe without adventure, and in January 1862 put in at Gibraltar with empty bunkers and a lame engine. Three big Union warships came out of nowhere to patrol off the Rock, and the neutral British ordered Semmes to leave. The Confederate ship was trapped, and Semmes knew it. So he sold her on the spot, and journeyed cross-country with his crew to catch a Channel boat for England. In England he met up with Confederate agents who ordered him to stand by for a secret warship—"No. 290"—being built for the Confederacy by Lairds at Liverpool.

Now while Semmes stands by, impatiently smoking up a supply of cheroots, the story shifts to Norfolk Navy Yard where the Confederates are putting the finishing touches on *Merrimac*.

The ironclad, rechristened *Virginia*, was ready to sail. And on March 8, 1862, she steamed out to fight one of the greatest battles in naval history.

Monitor vs. Merrimac

You've heard of the famous sea fight, of course—the battle between the *Monitor* and the *Merrimac*. Historians generally give the Confederate ironclad her original name, and thus the battle's title. But she went into action under the Stars and Bars as *Virginia*, and you can recognize her by that name as the No. 1 ship of the Confederate Navy.

To understand the significance of this naval battle, take another glance at the over-all war situation. Until 1862, the land front had been pretty well stalemated. Then the Union forces in the West gathered for an amphibious push down the Mississippi. General Grant with 15,000 men and Flag Admiral Foote with a small fleet of gunboats (including four ironclads) joined in a smash at Fort Henry on the Tennessee River. The Navy got there first and shelled the Fort to ruins before Grant's forces arrived.

Pushing on to Fort Donelson on the Cumberland, Foote's gunboats and Grant's men ran into a hornet's nest of shell fire. The gunboats were quickly disabled, and the Navy was out of the fight. But Grant hung on, and a few days later Fort Donelson surrendered unconditionally. The fall of Forts Henry and Donelson doomed Columbus, Kentucky, and the Confederate forces had to pull their northern Mississippi anchor down stream.

In the East, Richmond was beginning to feel the pinch of the blockade, now finally taking effect. And shortly after the Mississippi victories of Foote and Grant, Lincoln ordered General McClellan to start driving on Richmond.

Here's where your great sea battle comes in. To stall the drive on Richmond—to hearten the Southern populace after the setbacks on the Mississippi—to loosen the grip of the blockade—the Confederacy had to act fast.

Spies reported the Union ships gathering at Fort Monroe. And Richmond headquarters knew all about McClellan's coming campaign, for Confederate agents had only to read the Northern newspapers, which openly discussed the Union's battle plans. Obviously a punch should be delivered in the direction of Fort Monroe. A punch? A stunning haymaker by the Confederate Navy's secret weapon—the *Merrimac* converted into the invincible ironclad *Virginia*.

March 8, 1862. She was ready. So was her captain, Franklin Buchanan, the leading line officer of the Confederate Navy. About noon that day he took her out of Norfolk on what cheering crowds thought was a trial run. However, two small gunboats joined her, and she kept on going.

On the opposite shore of Hampton Roads, off Newport News, a Union squadron was lying on blockade. *Congress*, an elderly 50-gun sail frigate—*Cumberland*, 24-gun sail sloop—*St. Lawrence*, another old windjamming frigate—and two heavy steam frigates, *Roanoke* and *Minnesota*, hard by. Imagine the astonishment of the Union sailors when they saw chugging toward them what looked like an iron barn under clouds of coal smoke and the Confederate flag.

Virginia's advance was slow, for her original *Merrimac* engines were in poor condition. But *Congress, Cumberland,* and *St. Lawrence* couldn't move at all. Hardly a breeze was stirring, and the old canvas-backs sat as though paralyzed. The iron barn came on. Out rushed *Zouave,* a Union picket boat, to fire her one gun at the monster. No damage—the iron mammoth plowed steadily forward.

Straight at *Congress* the ironclad drove. The Union bluejackets opened fire at three quarters of a mile, then stared aghast. Their shots bounced off the advancing vessel. Swinging past *Congress,* the incredible *Virginia* roared a broadside that chopped the old frigate's spar-deck to splinters. *Cumberland,* heavily armed with Dahlgren batteries, was next in line. But even the Dahlgrens could only dent *Virginia's* casemate, while the ironclad's fire raked the sloop with death and destruction.

In fifteen minutes *Cumberland* was a shattered wreck. Then *Virginia* backed away, gathered steam, and charged like an armored rhino, ramming her great bull-horn into the injured vessel's side. Crash! The horn broke off from the impact, but left a mortal wound in *Cumberland's* hull. As the snorting ironclad backed off, the Union warship began to sink. Although her captain was ashore at the time, her crew stuck desperately to the guns, and she went down with batteries firing—a wooden ship with iron men.

The iron ship with iron men now wheeled around to finish *Congress.* Trying to make sail, the big frigate had run aground close in on Newport News. She was hay for the Confederate ironclad. And as *Virginia's* broadsides began to eat into the helpless frigate, Captain Buchanan must have set an iron jaw, For his own brother was aboard the Union ship, and *Virginia's* fire was turning *Congress* into an inferno.

With sails flapping, *St. Lawrence* had gone on a bar. Steam frigate *Roanoke,* in port for repairs, couldn't start her engines. In the outer channel *Minnesota* was hard aground, her engines unable to budge her. Waiting at their battle stations, the crews of these stranded warships could only watch the destruction of *Congress* in powerless dismay, knowing their turn would come.

In evening twilight, *Congress* was setting like the sun. With her captain dead she struck her colors, but when Buchanan sent a smallboat alongside to take off prisoners, one of the shore batteries opened fire, chasing the smallboat off. Believing the shots came from *Congress*, Buchanan in a rage grabbed up a rifle and climbed topside on the casemate to shoot at the burning wreck. A sniper on the beach promptly fired, and Buchanan fell back with a broken thigh.

Command of the ironclad passed to Lieutenant Catesby A. R. Jones. As *Virginia* was leaking badly where her ram had broken off, and an ebb tide threatened to strand her, the Confederate officers decided to run her back to the Norfolk side of the Roads for the night. Plenty of time to finish off the other Union ships in the morning. After riddling *Congress* with a final blast of hot shot, the ironclad steamed away through the dusk. Some hours later—a red volcano in the dark—the Union frigate blew up.

The blast echoed all the way to Washington. Echoed along the north-bound telegraph wires in frantic messages to Lincoln. On the dawn of March 9th there was panic in the Union capital, and the President was holding one of the gravest Cabinet meetings in the nation's history. The U. S. Navy had suffered its worst defeat to date.

Lincoln crossed his long legs and remained thoughtful in a roomful of uproar. Someone suggested that underwater bombs and nets might stop the Confederate ironclad. Secretary-of-War Stanton cried that no power on earth could stop her. *"Why, it isn't unlikely that we shall have from one of her guns a cannonball in this very room before we leave it."*

Lincoln listened and let them talk. Was he listening for the sound of engines bucking a gale off the Chesapeake Capes? For the clank and heave of a flush, flat deck forging slowly southward through rough waters? Lincoln didn't know—Navy Secretary Welles didn't know—even the men aboard that south-bound vessel didn't know on that gray dawn if they were going to make it.

Storm had smothered them throughout the previous night— held them off the Cape in a blackout of wind and water. No man had slept while the helmsmen had fought to hold the wheel, the engineers fought to resuscitate the engines, the captain fought to keep life in the vessel. Half-drowned and awash, this strange

Union vessel moved in, and gained the lee of stranded *Minnesota*.

Dawn, Sunday morning—out came *Virginia* to deal the finishing knockout to Union hopes. With her came flag-decorated steam tugs and gala excursion boats packed with newsmen. The Confederate ironclad moved on ahead of the pretty escort and steamed grimly across Hampton Roads to deliver the death-blow to *U.S.S. Minnesota*.

Then, on lookout station, the Confederate seamen sent back a cry. *Virginia's* commander, Catesby A. R. Jones, put a glass to his eye and stared. What he saw in the telescope's glass was a strange, dark object that came gliding around the Union frigate's hull like a floating plank—a big plank of driftwood upon which some beachcomber had set an iron pot!

"Cheesebox on a raft!" That's how one of the distant news observers described it. But the baffled Confederate commander soon saw that the strange craft was made of iron, and as it grew in focus he thought it was some kind of floating water tank.

Then as *Virginia's* crew glared in astonishment, the "water tank" ran up the Stars and Stripes. Smoke bloomed from a funnel, and the iron pot revolved on its base—the thing housed two big naval guns! Bearing down on *Virginia* was the only ship of her kind on any ocean, the first warship in the world to feature a gun-turret—*U.S.S. Monitor.*

Of all new designs submitted to "Uncle Gideon's" Navy Department at the start of the war, Ericsson's *Monitor*, or "Floating Battery," had seemed the craziest. Fed up with brass hats and red tape, the Swedish inventor had been reluctant to submit it in the first place. As usual, the conservatives were against it, saying it couldn't be done. But Gideon Welles liked the idea of a revolving pot that shielded two big guns which could train in any direction. Also the idea of an iron raft whose low freeboard presented a thin target to the enemy.

Given the go-ahead by Lincoln, Ericsson rushed the job. The Monitor was built at Greenpoint, Long Island. Designed for shallow water, she drew only $10\frac{1}{2}$ feet, her iron-plated deck only 2 feet above the waterline. Her turret was 9 feet high, 20 feet in diameter, 8 inches thick. Two 11-inch guns composed her battery.

From the shipyard she emerged, full of bugs: her fires wouldn't draw, her turret choked up with gas fumes, her big guns couldn't be loaded in the confined space. So, working his brains non-stop, Ericsson invented blowers to force the draft, flues to ventilate the turret, and ammunition hoists for the guns.

Her trial nearly ended in disaster when the turret stuck, her rudder jammed, and the green seas poured over her deck, flooding the ventilators. But at last she was manned and ready. Her captain, Lieutenant J. L. Worden, ran up her flag and started her down to Hampton Roads through the storm.

His men were worn ragged, and Worden himself was ready to hit the sack, when *Minnesota* sent over an officer with the alarming news. Turn in? Not the men on *Monitor*. Every one was at his station when Sunday morning came and the Confederate ironclad puffed into view.

So the cheese-box on a raft steamed out to meet the iron barn. *Virginia* fired first, her forward gun crashing. The projectile struck *Monitor's* turret—only to burst in a shower of ricochetting sparks.

Then Worden gave his gunners the order. *"Fire both guns as they bear!"*

Monitor's twin 11-inchers thundered a salvo that struck the Confederate ironclad a tremendous blow, denting her casemate and felling some of the crew with the stunning concussion.

So began one of the strangest combats in all naval history as the iron ships passed, came about, and again passed each other, blazing away pointblank. The Confederates used shells, the Union gunners fired solid shot. And while *Virginia's* projectiles burst on *Monitor's* turret in explosions of iron confetti, *Monitor's* round shot carommed off *Virginia's* casemate like billiard balls.

Again and again the vessels passed, exchanging broadsides. Once *Monitor* tried to ram, and just missed her foe. Then *Virginia* swung to ram, but she could deal the iron raft little more than a glancing blow, and the impact opened the leak in her bow where her metal beak had sheared. Veering off, the two warships continued the savage bombardment.

Both vessels suffered engine trouble. In the turret of the Union ship the gas fumes were stifling. With every shot there was danger of a flashback. Instead of jamming, the turret's drive gave trouble on the "stop," and the gunners had to fire "on the fly."

For two hours the slugging match continued, neither champion giving an inch. Then the Union gunners discovered they were running low on ammunition. At the same time a shell hit *Monitor's* little pilot house and blinded Lieutenant Worden, who was peering through the sight-hole. Fearing the steering gear had been injured, Worden ordered *Monitor* back to shallow water for a brief overhaul. Simultaneously *Virginia* swerved away.

Monitor was heading back to fight, and little harmed. *Virginia* on the other hand was showing cracks in her armor, great dents where another cannon-ball might bash through. Leaking dangerously, her engines limping, she needed time out for repairs. Catesby A. R. Jones could only give the order.

"Right full rudder. Set course for Norfolk. Steer 176."

Monitor, short on ammunition, did not follow. It was Sunday noon—the battle was over. Union Commander Worden with bandages over his eyes, did not see it. But his cheering bluejackets told him of the Stars and Stripes aloft, and the Stars and Bars fading over the horizon.

All Noisy on the American Front

Abraham Lincoln shook Worden's hand and told the blinded naval officer that *Monitor* had saved the day. Had the Confederate ironclad not been stopped, she might have gone on to smash the whole blockade—might have chased the Union Navy up to Boston, and won powerful trans-Atlantic allies. Now with *Monitor* on guard, the blockade could be held until the Union Navy secured control of the seas. Also the dauntless "cheese-box on a raft" had cleared the path for McClellan's transports on the Richmond drive.

And while Northern papers cheered the Hampton Roads battle as a victory, Southern headlines set up the same cheer. Although *Virginia* hadn't delivered a knock-out, she'd struck the Union a mighty hard blow. She'd sunk two enemy warships and thrown a scare into every wooden vessel in the North. She was spring tonic for Confederate morale. And she slowed McClellan's advance, gaining time for the reinforcement of Richmond.

With McClellan delayed at Fort Monroe, Confederate General Joe Johnston was able to mass the Army of Northern Virginia along the Richmond front. When McClellan finally moved in April, marching his men up the James River Peninsula, Johnston was ready. Instead of catching the Confederates off guard, the Federal troops caught hell. April showers thawed the ground, and McClellan's wagons and cannon stuck in the mud. Johnston let the blue columns crawl forward until they crossed the Chickahominy River and stood within sight of Richmond. Then, the last day of May, he threw his troops against McClellan's at Seven Pines, trapping the Union vanguards on the bank of the rain-flooded river.

Only superior artillery saved the Union line. In the midst of battle Johnston was wounded, and Robert E. Lee took command of the Army of Northern Virginia. That was the end of the Union push.

Lee outplayed McClellan's every move. He drove the Union Army foot by foot down the muddy peninsula. After a month of desperate fighting, McClellan was back where he'd started—at the end of the peninsula and almost at the end of his rope.

Still, McClellan had retreated with much skill, and the Union Army remained intact. With Navy transports waiting, there was a chance he could get his men across the water to Northern territory. So Lee arranged a trap near White Oaks Swamp—a deadly snare intended to bag McClellan's whole army. The "string" of this trap was left up to Stonewall Jackson.

Now Jackson was one of the world's greatest combat generals any six days of the week—but the seventh day was Sunday. Intensely religious, he was known to his friends as "Old Blue Light." Having smashed McClellan's diversionary wing in the Shenandoah Valley, Stonewall made an amazing forced march to join Lee on the James peninsula—only to receive orders to attack on Sunday morning. Nothing doing. Instead of charging, Jackson ordered an all-day prayer meeting. And while his men sang hymns, and he told the Almighty what was going on, the enemy pulled out of the White Oaks trap.

McClellan's forces gained Malvern Hill, a high point protecting their transport base at Harrison's Landing. Here Lee devised another trap, and gray and blue fought it out in what became known as the Seven Days' Battle. The Union boys held out for a full week. This time poor communications and bad weather conspired against Jackson, and McClellan escaped the snare.

McClellan's army reached the transports, the Union Navy covered the withdrawal, and in July the boys in blue were safe on the Potomac-side in Washington. The bloody Peninsula Campaign was over. The Confederacy has won a spectacular victory. Richmond was saved. Now the Northern troops would have to start all over again.

But what the Confederates forgot was that the North could start all over again. The Union Army had lost, but not the Union Navy. The Atlantic blockade was tightening like a tourniquet. Three weeks after it was launched, McClellan's drive had washed up against Norfolk, and the Confederates were forced to burn *Virginia* to save her from capture. On May 25, Norfolk Navy Yard was won for the Union by the United States Marines.

These reverses, like Stonewall Jackson's quirks, were overlooked by the jubilant Confederacy. Lee had won a great battle. To the South that seemed enough. The Southern leaders ignored the Union Navy, and, not liking to think about it, they tried not to notice what had happened out in the West.

Pair of Shears

In the West the Union forces were carrying out their amphibious operation—that major operation designed to cut the Mississippi River out of the South. As Flag Officer Foote described it, the Army and Navy were working together, *"like the two blades of a pair of shears."*

Their objective in 1862 was the Confederate stronghold, Island No. 10. This island, you'll remember, now anchored the northern end of the long chain of Confederate river forts which guarded the waterway down to New Orleans. More immediately, it blocked the river approach to Memphis, Tennessee. Because of its importance the Confederates had made it as strong as concrete.

To make it tougher, the river made a big loop back north, so the Union transports would have to go all the way around, after passing Island Number 10. The island itself lay in mid-channel at the bottom of the loop. Dense swamps protected it from overland attack, and a long line of shore batteries backed it up on the river-bend. Against this island Gibraltar, the Union forces began to move in February '62.

Army operations were under General John Pope, who conceived the plan of digging a canal across the north end of the big river-loop so small transports could by-pass Island No. 10 entirely. This was all right, but it would put the army around the bend without naval support, for Foote's gunboats couldn't navigate a shallow canal. Island No. 10 had to be wiped out sooner or later, so Foote sent his gunboat squadron to do it sooner.

On March 15—five days after the *Monitor-Merrimac* battle—the Union gunboats advanced on Island No. 10. For two weeks the naval gunners hammered at the fort while the Army sweated it out farther up-river with pick shovel. The canal proved an easier job than Island No. 10. Pope got his men across the northern end of the loop while the Navy bluejackets were still slugging it out with the island and its heavy shore batteries.

Now Pope found himself out in front, his troops dangerously exposed. Flag Officer Foote had to send help somehow—would anyone volunteer to run the gantlet past Island No. 10? Commander Henry Walke and the crew of gunboat *Carondelet* volunteered. They would take a murderous fire from the Confederate batteries, but they piled bales of hay along the gunboat's sides, determined to chance it.

A "hay-clad!" Fellow sailors told them it was suicide. Walke and his bluejackets set their jaws. Night of April 4, the river at flood, *Carondelet* steamed down-channel in a pouring thunderstorm. The current swung them slewing. On the bow, silhouetted in flashes of blue lighting, a sailor swung the lead.

"Mark one! Mark twain—!"

Somehow they missed the shoals. Now they were seen by the Confederate shore batteries, which opened up, adding flame and explosions to the night's lightning and thunder. Past one battery after another—past the big guns of Island No. 10—somehow, without a scratch, *Carondelet* got through.

Seeing it could be done, another little gunboat ran the gantlet two nights later. Foote's squadron, standing by, continued to bombard the island. Then Pope, reinforced by the two gunboats, moved down on the Confederate stronghold's other flank. On April 7, Island No. 10 surrendered. Pope took the surrender, and a few weeks later was rewarded with command of McClellan's army in the east. Maybe—just maybe—credit for the victory should have gone to the Navy men on that "hay-clad" fire hazard—the sailors who ran the gantlet, the leadsman who swung the lead.

Loss of Island No. 10 was a serious defeat for the Confederacy. The river defenses had to pull back to Memphis. And in the meantime Grant had moved down into Tennessee to threaten the Confederate position at Corinth by occupying Pittsburg Landing on the Tennessee River. Corinth guarded the flank of Memphis. With the Union Navy coming down the Mississippi toward Memphis, the Confederates determined to stop Grant at any odds.

The effort to stop Grant at Pittsburg Landing exploded the Battle of Shiloh—one of the bloodiest of the Civil War. Against Grant came General Albert Sidney Johnston. With 45,000 men, he struck Grant's 30,000 like a Southern tornado. Fighting raged around Shiloh Church, and the Union troops at one crisis were almost routed.

But Grant got off a hurry-call to Flag Officer Foote. And Foote sent naval help—gunboats *Lexington* and *Tyler* rushing at forced draught along the Tennessee. The bluejackets arrived just in time to bombard the Confederate line and knock out some gray batteries on the river bank. The Confederate attack was broken up. Leading a charge, Albert Sidney Johnston was mortally wounded. It was a close shave for Grant: 10,000 casualties—but the Confederates were thrown back with equal loss. Corinth was done for, and so was Memphis on the Mississippi.

The shears were really cutting now. With Grant controlling one blade and Foote controlling the other, Memphis might have been scissored immediately. Unfortunately, a wound Foote had received three months before at Donelson had failed to heal. On May 9 he was invalided home and replaced by Captain C. H. Davis, USN. Davis promptly took up where Foote left off. In teamwork with Grant, who was attacking Corinth, he aimed an attack at Fort Pillow, the Mississippi stronghold which defended the approach to Memphis.

On a high river bluff, Fort Pillow was another Gibraltar. And it was supported by a Confederate squadron of eight river steamers armed with cast iron rams. On top of this, Davis discovered that his gunboats would have to make the attack on their own. Reason? General Halleck.

Halleck, you'll recall, was supreme commander of Union forces in the west. Having ordered Pope's army back east, he now worried about the losses at Shiloh. Accordingly he put the brakes on Grant, and he himself took over the drive on Corinth. As a result the drive moved slowly. Although Corinth fell at the end of May, the Confederate Western Army had time to reorganize under General Braxton Bragg. Meantime the Union Navy at Fort Pillow had to do the job alone.

Davis hit the fort on May 10, and this time the Union squadron included floating batteries and mortar boats capable of high-angle fire. Arching shells screamed up the bluff, and Pillow was hammered like an anvil. In the thick of this bombardment, the Confederate rams came charging around the river-bend, and the Union squadron was caught at anchor. Gunboat *Cincinnati* was rammed and sunk. Another small Union vessel was gored. A wild free-for-all followed, Union gunboats and rams tangling and firing point-blank. Then the Confederate rams ran back down-river, practically unhurt.

Doggedly, the Union gunboats continued to pound the fort with mortar fire. Pillow crumbled on June 4, and surrendered. Memphis, protected by the fierce Confederate rams, was another matter. Davis stubbornly pressed on. On June 6 the Union gunboats were before the city. Everybody in Memphis was out to see them defeated by the rams.

Led by Captain J. E. Montgomery, CSN, the rams charged out to repeat the Fort Pillow play. But Davis was on to the game. Four Union gunboats, steaming abreast, ran in to meet the Confederate wedge. Just as the rams came up, the gunboats separated, and through the opening came two Union rams like flying tackles. While the gunboats ran perfect interference, the Union rams charged the enemy. One Confederate ship was cut in half. Another went down. Three were demobilized by gunfire. The remainder fled down river, and Memphis fell to the Union Navy.

Loss of this big river port was a hard blow to the Confederacy.

But it was nothing compared to the stunning punch landed by the Union Navy on New Orleans—the South's largest city, biggest seaport, and outlet of the Mississippi River.

The Confederates said the great city could never be taken. On the Gulf side it was guarded by two powerful forts—St. Philip and Jackson. A Confederate squadron, spearheaded by the iron-clad ram *Manassas*, guarded the levee. Two more big ironclads were being built in the city's shipyards. A great litter of under-water obstructions, mines, cables, logs, and sunken hulks, blocked the outer channel. Far to the north the giant fortress of Vicksburg guarded the river in that direction. No Union warship would ever reach New Orleans.

Flag Officer David Dixon Porter thought differently. Early in the war he had suggested a naval attack from the Gulf. When the Union recaptured Pensacola late in 1861, giving the Navy a base in Florida, the plan was revived. Command of the oper-ation was given to Flag Officer David Glasgow Farragut

Remember the little nine-year-old midshipman who served in *Essex* when she was shot up in the War of 1812? The youngster lieutenant who'd hunted Caribbean pirates? The officer who nearly died of yellow fever in the Mexican War? Fifty years of service in the U. S. Navy and Farragut was still going strong. On April 17, 1862, aboard his flagship *U.S.S. Hartford*, Farragut led a Union fleet up the river to attack New Orleans.

The Confederates knew he was coming. Yet with plenty of time to prepare, they weren't ready. Urgent calls to Richmond for reinforcements were met by indifference. Louisiana officials said no power on earth could break Forts Jackson and St. Philip. Trouble developed between slothful local militia and Confederate naval officers like young Lieutenant Beverly Kennon, who saw the danger. Leaders squabbled over who should command the defenses, and as Farragut approached the city, one of the fort garrisons staged a mutiny.

But New Orleans was not a push-over. For a week Union mortar boats commanded by Porter bombarded the two forts. Those mortar boats were something. Small rafts, not much bigger than an LCVP, they had to be tugged, poled, and jackassed into position, for they had no power plant. Each boat carried an 11-inch mortar. About two feet long with walls 18 inches

thick, it was mounted on a trunnion so the range could be adjusted. It could lob a 200-pound shell about 4,000 yards.

Farragut had a saying, *"The best protection against an enemy's fire is a well sustained fire from your own guns."* Porter's mortars believed it and threw a shell at St. Philip and Jackson every half minute by the clock. But the forts held out. The mortars ran low on ammunition. Farragut, impatient, decided to run the gantlet.

He spent ten days preparing his wooden warships. Masts were taken down, pilot houses were wrapped in cocoons of rope, bags of coal and sand were piled around the boilers. Cables were draped overside to protect each vessel's beam, and each ship was camouflaged with Mississippi mud.

Then the little gunboat *Itasca* was sent up-river to cut a monster chain the Confederates had strung across the channel. Working at night, and under fire, the boys drove *Itasca* against the submerged links. After considerable pushing, the big chain finally gave way.

Night of April 24, at 0200, two red lights from *Hartford* signalled the advance. Slowly the fleet steamed forward, groping through the breach in the underwater barricade cut by *Itasca*.

The fleet moved in three divisions—gunboat *Cayuga* and sloops *Mississippi* and *Pensacola* with two smaller vessels leading. *Hartford* and two sister ships followed. A squadron of gunboats brought up the rear. Erupting like volcanoes, the two forts opened fire at *Cayuga* as she cleared the barricade and was spotted.

But by hugging the bank closest to the screaming guns of the fort, the fleet was able to sail under the deadly archway of Confederate shells and in turn discharge its cannon almost in the faces of the fort's defenders. Scorched and dying, the shore gunners broke.

But the fight was only beginning! Out charged the Confederate river squadron. Out charged the iron ram *Manassas*. Out charged a flock of fire rafts, cut adrift on the swift current to blaze down on the Union fleet. *Manassas* got in the first heavy blow, smashing into the big sloop *Brooklyn*. *Brooklyn* staggered, but the ram, glancing off, skated under the bow of *Mississippi*. Hot shot from the latter plunged into the iron clad ram. The ram's plates caved in, and a few minutes later, like a giant bomb, *Manassas* blew up.

An incendiary raft jammed into *Hartford*. Leaping flames boarded Farragut's flagship and raced along the spar deck, driving several gun crews from their stations. Farragut got off another saying. *"Don't flinch from that fire, boys. There's a hotter fire than that for those who don't do their duty."* Trained up to the mark, the boys stood on the burning deck, and the fire party managed to douse the flames.

Farther up river, Union and Confederate gunboats were in a wild dog-fight. Leading the Confederate flotilla was *Governor Moore*, "a cotton-clad." Lacking iron, the Confederates had armored a number of river steamers with bales of cotton. Hard stuff for a cannon-ball to penetrate, but a lovely fire hazard for hot shot. It took nerve to run a cotton-clad the way Confederate Lieutenant Beverly Kennon ran *Governor Moore* down to attack U. S. gunboat *Varuna*.

Moore got her iron ram into *Varuna's* side, then couldn't back off, and couldn't bring her forward gun to bear on her enemy. Broadsides from the Union vessel were tearing little *Moore's* cotton-clad prow into fragments. Through a storm of lead, Lieutenant Kennon sprang to the bow-gun and fired through his own deck and bow to slam a shot into *Varuna*. The Union gunboat went down as *Moore* tore free. Then broadsides from the sloops drove the Confederate cotton-clad shoreward; with *Moore* disabled, Kennon surrendered.

No, cotton couldn't save New Orleans—King Cotton's days were numbered. Guns slugging at Fort Jackson and Fort St. Philip, Farragut's fleet got through. Losses were heavy, but in the morning thirteen Federal ships accepted the surrender of the South's biggest port.

So New Orleans was lost to the Confederacy. The Mississippi River—save for the big inland fortress of Vicksburg—was lost to the Confederacy. Vicksburg was bound to fall, and then Texas, Arkansas, and Louisiana would be cut off from the South. Union troops could now advance down the great waterways and strike inland to the Confederacy's heart. And cotton could no longer go to Europe to buy French support and warships made in Liverpool.

"The occupation of New Orleans," wrote the Confederate Ambassador to England, *"has struck our cause a fatal blow."*

Credit your U. S. Navy. Flag Admiral Andrew Foote, whose gunboats started the amphibious operation. David Glasgow Farragut, who captured New Orleans. And all those bluejackets who did the job on Old Man River.

THE BEST DEFENSE IS A WELL DIRECTED FIRE

The Civil War (Second Half)

It was a long war and a tough war—you can tell that by the songs. The South enlisted to "Dixie." The Northern boys marched off to "Rally 'Round the Flag." But as the months of fighting wore on, the gray camps sang the homesick ballads of Stephen Foster. And the boys in blue sang "Tenting Tonight"—"Just before the Battle, Mother"—"Tramp, Tramp, Tramp"—and that greatest of all battle hymns, "Mine Eyes Have Seen the Glory of the Coming of the Lord."

It was a bloody war. In both North and South the casualty lists were endless, and life was grim for the common folk. Fire power had increased tremendously, but medicine hadn't kept pace. If you were wounded aboard ship there were no skilled Corpsmen to tend you—no anaesthetics—no such healing drug as sulfa. On a battlefield you might lie dying for a week. Deep flesh wounds, meaning gangrene, were almost always fatal. One Northern surgeon reported a new technique of amputating with a red hot wire that cauterized as it cut—the only trouble being that none of his patients survived. Flag Officer Foote died shortly after he was invalided because the wound he received at Donelson lacked proper dressing.

It was a desperate war. Caught in a vise between the Atlantic Ocean and the Mississippi, the Confederacy set its teeth and strove with might and main to break the bonds. Its might was an array of battle leaders whose names remain brilliant in military history—Lee and his generals. Its main was an army of lean, gray boys who fought like gladiators, on and on and on.

See-Saw Battles

They couldn't break the iron blockade which held the eastern seacoast. They couldn't shake the iron manacle fastened on the Mississippi. But there was still a chance they could rig up a navy and ship out of Mobile on the Gulf. Still a chance their armies could break the northern handgrip on the vise—the Union front from West Virginia to Washington. In 1862 the Confederacy called up the first American draft to build its armed forces to peak strength. Following McClellan's defeat, Lee drove straight north, and in the summer of '62 his army was once more massed at Manassas.

Against this formidable force stood the Union Army of the Potomac, now under General Pope. General Pope was the sort who made speeches. So he made one assuring the world that the war would soon be won now that he was in command. On August 29 he charged into a trap laid by Lee, Stonewall Jackson, and Longstreet. He lost 8,000 men and the Second Battle of Manassas.

To the North's alarm, Lee now drove into Northern territory, fighting through Maryland to encircle Washington. Lincoln tried McClellan again. Little Mac threw the Union forces against Lee's at Antietam. The boys in blue won the field after savage battle. But McClellan, slow as always, failed to pursue Lee's tired battalions. Instead, he requested reinforcements. *"Sending reinforcements to McClellan,"* Lincoln commented, *"is like shoveling flies across a room."* So McClellan was replaced by General Ambrose Burnside.

Burnside took his Union troops down into Virginia after Lee. Late autumn he stood with 113,000 men facing Lee's 80,000 at Fredericksburg. Union odds looked good. Fredericksburg was close to Richmond. And Lincoln had reinforced the Union offensive with a tremendous diplomatic move.

This was the Emancipation Proclamation. Briefly it was a Presidential order designed as a step toward freeing the slaves. Ever since the war began, Lincoln had pondered such action. Originally he'd hoped the Federal Government might free the slaves by buying them for $400 apiece. With the South out of the Union this measure was futile. Now Lincoln used the Proclamation as a war move.

Published in September—five days after Antietam—the proclamation declared that on January 1, 1863 (the New Year coming up) all the slaves in any State at that time warring against the Union would be freed *without* compensation to the owners. Lincoln knew this move would win the approval of powerful Liberals in England. He also hoped that the Confederates, jolted by Antietam, might sue for peace and compensation, rather than risk losing all their slaves for nothing.

But the Confederates refused to give in. Some of their leaders raged that Lincoln was trying to explode a slave uprising in the South. The long-dreaded slave insurrection did not occur, however. One of the odd angles to the Civil War (and greatly to the credit of the Negroes) is the fact that the slaves continued to labor quietly in the fields, patiently waiting for liberation while their owners were away at the front. Meantime the immediate effect of Lincoln's proclamation was to stiffen Confederate resistance, becoming hard as granite at Fredericksburg.

Burnside opened the battle in December. Lee brought up heavy artillery and let Burnside charge. Bayonets couldn't beat cannon, and after desperate assaults costing 12,000 men, Burnside retreated.

As the year rolled into 1863, Lincoln replaced Burnside with General Joseph (Fighting Joe) Hooker. Hooker talked a big fight, but in May came up against a bigger one than even he could chew. Chancellorsville. The Union army was camped around this town not far from Fredericksburg. Jeb Stuart struck in from one side and Stonewall Jackson from the other. Hooker had been sampling some "mountain dew." Stuart, Jackson, a hangover, and a spent cannon-ball hit him simultaneously. The Union camp, surprised, went to pieces. Hooker lost his artillery, his supply wagons, Chancellorsville, and his command. He retreated to the Potomac with 16,000 casualties.

Chancellorsville was a tremendous victory for the South. It seemed to cancel the losses on the Mississippi and trump Lincoln's gains in foreign diplomacy. It shrouded the North in indigo and caused gloomy New York newspapers to wonder if the Union could last out. Yet this victory was costly for the Confederacy. For Stonewall Jackson was accidentally killed by his own troopers during the battle. And the northern gloom misled Lee into launching a great drive into Pennsylvania—an invasion he hoped would sink the North's morale completely and force the Union leaders to sue for peace.

So in June the Confederate columns were marching—north by the Shenandoah Valley—on past Hagerstown, Maryland. Jubal Early's gray cavalry raided all the way up to Harrisburg, Pennsylvania, while Jeb Stuart feinted east toward Washington. Lee's main army continued north on a line which paralleled the Monocacy River—a little stream leading toward the small Pennsylvania town of Gettysburg.

Meantime General George Gordon Meade had been put in charge of the Union's eastern army. Meade was no Pope nor Hooker. His staff included such battling field commanders as Reynolds and W. S. Hancock and three sharp young cavalry leaders named Farnsworth, Kilpatrick, and Custer. On Cemetery

Ridge, a long highland flanking Gettysburg, Reynolds ordered his troops to stop Lee's advance. Firing began July 1, 1863. For three days the blue and gray armies surged around Gettysburg under a tempest of lead, fighting the greatest land battle of the Civil War. Here, there, everywhere Lee's army charged. Reynolds was killed. So was Farnsworth. But the blue lines held.

Finally in a desperate infantry charge led by General Pickett, the Confederates were literally blown from the field by Meade's concentrated artillery. Cemetery Ridge was rightly named. 23,000 Confederates lay dead or wounded on the battle-ground alongside 18,000 boys in blue. Gettysburg was Lee's first major defeat— a disastrous one for the Confederacy. Gone was the hope of breaking the North's hold on the vise.

Then the Union came through with another victory. The very next day—July 4th—Grant's forces ended a siege begun that spring by Farragut's gunboats, and Vicksburg fell. Gone was the Confederacy's hope of keeping any hold on the Mississippi.

For the Confederacy there was one last hope—holding out. If Joe Johnston could defend the deep South—if Lee could continue to hold Richmond—there was still a chance for the Confederate Navy.

Smoke on the Water

How about the Confederate Navy? Well, between the summers of '62 and '63 its chances had considerably improved. Although blockaded, the big Carolina seaports of Charleston and Wilmington had continued working overtime, sending out swift blockade runners and building *Virginia*-type ironclads. Cotton still sailed out of Mobile. At sea Confederate commerce raiders were hitting the North's merchant marine so hard that Yankee skippers were wailing over high insurance rates and transferring their vessels to foreign registry. And on January 1, 1863, the Confederacy put a hole in the blockade by regaining the Texas port of Galveston.

Galveston illustrates the rough time the Union had in holding that long Southern coastline. Having fallen easily to Farragut's blockaders, the port was held through the autumn of '62 by a Union regiment and a five-ship squadron under Commodore Renshaw.

In December along came Confederate General Magruder with a couple of rickety cotton-clads and a crowd of Texas riflemen not so rickety. This flotilla celebrated New Year's by waiting for an ebb tide to strand the Union gunboats in Galveston harbor, and then attacked at 0300. The light cotton-clads sneaked in, the Texans boarded, and the fight was a whing-ding. *U.S.S. Harriet Lane* was taken, and her heavy guns turned on Renshaw's *Westfield*. Renshaw ordered abandon ship, then was killed as her magazines exploded. Lieutenant R. L. Law, becoming senior officer, lost his nerve and fled with the remaining U. S. ships. The marooned Federal regiment could only surrender.

Law was immediately court-martialed by Farragut, who sent *U.S.S. Brooklyn* with six more gunboats to blockade Galveston.

Dusk of January 11, 1863, *Brooklyn* sighted a sail on the horizon, and signalled gunboat *Hatteras'* Captain F. B. Blake to investigate. An old side-wheeler, *Hatteras* waddled out into the Gulf to overhaul the distant craft. It took her all night to catch up. Then in the dawn's early light she found herself within trumpet-distance of a long, low, rakish vessel that had steam and metal under her canvas.

"What ship is that?" Blake hailed.

"Confederate steamer Alabama!" came the reply, echoed by a roar of big broadside guns that knocked *Hatteras* into a mess of junk.

Brooklyn heard the explosion and ran out to pursue the stranger, but she never came close to Alabama. For the skipper of this Confederate ship was Captain Semmes—remember?—Raphael the Raider, whom you last saw smoking cheroots in Liverpool. And *Alabama* was that secret vessel built for the Confederacy by Lairds—mysterious "No. 290."

The British built two of these cruisers for the "Italian Navy" —meaning the Confederate States of America. The first went to sea under the name *Oreto*. Somehow in mid-Atlantic she turned into *Florida*, and there were Stars and Bars at her gaff when she finally raced into Mobile. Lincoln's ambassador to England, Charles Francis Adams, raised the roof about this dish of camouflaged spaghetti. While he was raising it, "290" steamed out of Liverpool—and showed up in the Azores as *C.S.S. Alabama*, Captain Semmes.

Sinking ships right and left, Semmes was only beginning when he appeared off Galveston and sank *Hatteras*. From there he took *Alabama* down to Brazil, then on a zig-zag rampage over Cape of Good Hope. A flock of Union warships gave chase, but it was easy to play hare-and-hounds across the ocean in those days before wireless and radar.

In this story of your Navy you've seen ships go from sail to steam—seen improvements in gunnery and navigation—the development of turrets and armor. But communications? Communications were still limited to eyesight, hearing, and Lady Luck—a matter of beacons, telescopes, hails, and flag-signals, exactly as in the time of Chris Columbus.

Shortly after the Federal set-back at Galveston, the Union Navy was thrown for another loss. This happened at Charleston where the Confederates had finally completed two *Virginia*-type ironclads —*C.S.S. Palmetto State* and *C.S.S. Chicora*. On January 31, 1863, the iron pair came ramming out of Charleston harbor and caught the Federal blockaders by surprise. Down went U. S. gunboat *Mercedita*. Twin broadsides smashed her sister, *Keystone State*. The two gray rams might have smashed up the whole wooden U. S. squadron if one hadn't ruptured her engines, and a big Union ironclad hadn't been in the offing.

This last was *New Ironsides* built by Merrick & Sons of Philadelphia—a bulky wooden frigate coated with iron plates and armed with batteries of 11-inch Dahlgren guns. Just the report

of her presence was enough to keep the Confederate rams moored in the security of Charleston harbor. At the same time the rams were a standing threat to the blockade. So "Uncle Gideon" ordered the Navy to "go in and get 'em."

This meant a full-dress attack on Charleston, and the job was up to Flag Officer DuPont. DuPont wasn't sure about it. He wanted monitors (the original *Monitor* had foundered in a storm the previous winter) and he worried about the Charleston forts. "Uncle Gideon" sent him seven new monitors, plus *Keokuk* which had two stationary turrets These along with *New Ironsides* made up the Union's most powerful fleet.

While this task force assembled, word came that a new British-built "Italian" cruiser named *Nashville* was flying the Confederate flag off the coast of Georgia. John Worden, original *Monitor* captain and now commanding the monitor *Montauk,* volunteered to go after her. Late in February, Worden, his eyesight fully recovered, spied the Confederate cruiser in a river-mouth near Savannah. Ignoring land batteries, Worden ran *Montauk* inshore and began punching shells into *Nashville*. After a dozen punches the cruiser blew up.

This encouraged the Navy Department to think monitors could conquer anything, and DuPont was ordered to hurry it up at Charleston. On April 7 he pushed in to the attack. Steaming through the harbor entrance, the whole task force came under the gun-sights of Forts Gregg, Wagner, Moultrie, and Sumter. *Weehawken,* leading monitor captained by John Rodgers, encountered a nest of underwater snares and torpedoes. The line stalled and got a blistering from the forts.

All afternoon the warships banged away at the forts, but in the mined harbor there was no chance for DuPont to repeat his Port Royal maneuvers. *New Ironsides* was pounded from larboard to starboard. The monitors were hammered like horseshoes in a blacksmith shop. *Keokuk,* riddled, rolled over and sank. She was the only serious loss, but DuPont called off the attack at dusk, and carefully withdrew.

"Uncle Gideon" thought him too careful, and ordered John Adolphus Dahlgren to take over the Charleston job. The damaged monitors had to be repaired, and it was summer before the task force was ready again. Meanwhile Dahlgren took time out to send several monitors down the Georgia coast to sink *Atlanta,* another new-born Confederate ironclad. But even Dahlgren and his famous "soda bottles" couldn't knock out Charleston. Laying siege, they volleyed and thundered throughout the summer of '63. They shot up Fort Wagner and levelled Sumter, but Charleston remained to be had.

That was the summer of Gettysburg and Vicksburg, and the Union, cheering these great victories, was inclined to leave Dahlgren all at sea. Naval reinforcements were refused, and finally Dahlgren was ordered to abandon siege. So Charleston was a left-handed Confederate victory—one that encouraged the Confederate Navy to make a big seventh-inning try.

This naval try was as astonishing as anything launched since the Revoluntionary War. But before the Confederates launched it, something happened in another quarter—a strange and unexpected event—one which proves that the Past is often a crystal ball for the Future. Did you know that in the summer of 1863 the United States was at war with Japan?

So Sorry, Please

It wasn't a declared war—on that point the formal Japanese have always been peculiarly informal. It didn't even make a headline in the newspapers. And you probably never read about it in your schoolbooks. But exactly nine years after signing their first treaty with the United States, the rulers of the Sons of Heaven smilingly tore it up. Whereupon Jap guns proceeded to fire on the American mail steam, *Pembroke*, as she left Yokohama for Shanghai by way of Shimonoseki Strait. Dodging the shore batteries, little *Pembroke* ran into a trio of Jap gunboats, and the U. S. mail didn't arrive in Shanghai according to schedule.

So a few weeks later *U.S.S. Wyoming*, under David McDougal, turned up. *Wyoming* had been chasing *C.S.S. Alabama* in a foggy tag-game across the Indian Ocean. Well, *Wyoming* lost track of *Alabama* out in the East Indies. As a matter of fact—to show you what communications were like—she herself was mistaken for the foxy Confederate raider. Anchoring off Singapore, Captain David McDougal, USN, was surprised to receive from the port authorities a basket of flowers and congratulations addressed to his rival, Captain Semmes, CSN.

Thanking the British for the tip, McDougal dumped the flowers and congratulations overboard, and rushed *Wyoming* seaward to waylay the expected *Alabama*. Semmes must have smelled smoke, for he veered off toward Japan, then doubled back. McDougal missed him again, but while scouting in Japanese waters he heard

Pembroke shooting. Decks cleared, he made a bee-line
[Sh]imonoseki Strait.

[He] took *Wyoming* through the Inland Sea, and on July 16,
1863, the guns were going in Shimonoseki. Jap batteries poured
a fierce fire from the bluffs, but not so fierce as the fire poured
back by *Wyoming*. The warship had a close call, however. Zigzagging in the uncharted channel, she went aground. Out pounced
the Jap gunboats which had ambushed *Pembroke*. But *Wyoming*
was no defenseless mail packet. Her sharpshooting gun crews sank
the Jap attackers. Her engineers backed her off the snag. And
once more she steamed through the strait, delivering broadsides
that blasted the Jap shore batteries.

In a war that lasted just seventy minutes, Nippon's blossoming
ambitions were nipped in the bud. Jap leaders blamed it all on
the Japanese militarists—the princely Choeu Clan. Mr. Mikado
said it happened without the blessing of the Tokyo Government.

"So sorry, please."

David and Goliath

They christened the little craft *David*, after the sturdy
shepherd boy in the Bible. And they sent her north to tangle
with Goliath. Goliath, in this particular instance, was the giant
Union ironclad *New Ironsides*. And *David* was the world's second
military submarine (the first being Bushnell's Revolutionary War
Turtle).

In the Confederate Yards at Charleston she looked like a
swordfish—a huge boiler-plated swordfish with iron fins and a
long spar-like snout. She carried a crew of ten men in a space
that would have crowded ten sardines. But that was enough to
keep her swimming along semi-submerged, thrusting ahead that
long spar which carried a 65-pound contact bomb. *David* had
quite a punch. She was the Confederacy's newest secret weapon
—their big hope for the seventh inning.

David was a shining example of Confederate ingenuity and
drive—the same sort of drive that put the South out in front
with anchored mines electrically fired from shore positions. In
the North, Mr. Colt, famous inventor of the revolver, constructed
an electrically-fired mine, and blew up an old ship in the James

River to show Congress how it was done. But as usual there were sleepy-heads who thought it an unworkable dream. In the South, however, there were scientifically-awake men like Matthew Maury. Early in the war a Torpedo Bureau and a Naval Submarine Battery were set up in Richmond under Maury. (By the end of the war, they were laying one-ton electrical mines, and Confederate mine fields had blasted 28 Union ships out of the picture.)

David was also an example of Confederate guts. As a seven-inning hope she was a mighty precarious pinch-hitter. But it was now or never with things the way they were at Charleston.

Dahlgren had called off the siege, but his Union squadron was lying there on blockade. On the night of October 5, 1863, the watch aboard *New Ironsides* saw something that resembled a giant marlin swimming out across the star-lit water. While the lookout was wishing he had a harpoon or at least some cut bait, the marlin veered around and came straight at the stern of *New Ironsides*. Glawk! the lookout swallowed his cud of tobacco. That wasn't a fish! It was some kind of boat and—

"What ship is that?" the O.O.D. hailed.

For answer there was a shotgun blast that dropped the watch officer in the scuppers. Then wham! *New Ironsides* reeled over on her beam, rocked by an explosion that ruptured her stern plates three feet below the waterline.

The Union Goliath was only wounded—in fact, the blow did almost as much damage to plucky *David*. But the explosion dented the Northern giant's shield ($4\frac{1}{2}$-inch armor backed by 27 inches of oak) and started serious leaks that laid her up in drylock for months. *David* limped back to home base to win acclaim as a naval hero—the Civil War grandfather of your modern submarine.

Strictly speaking she was a torpedo boat, but her "sub" profile showed the shape of things to come. What came next was Mark 1, Mod 1—the submarine *C.S.S. Hunley*. Designed by the Confederate inventor of that name, *Hunley* was rushed through the yards at Mobile. Her hull was a cylindrical boiler 48 inches in diameter, 25 feet long. Encouraged by *David's* remarkable performance, the Confederates went all out this time—gave *Hunley* diving fins to take her below the sea. Two water tanks could be filled or emptied by means of valves. Iron castings fastened to the keel by bolts could be detached when the sub wanted to surface. Bulky engines were eliminated in favor of a hand-driven screw—the propellor shaft turned by eight men working a crank. This device harked back to the original Revolutionary War *Marine Turtle*. But unlike the old *Turtle*, or her sister *David*, she towed her torpedo on a long line astern, the idea being for her to dive under an enemy vessel and catch its hull with the explosive charge on the trolling line. The diving apparatus made her a true submersible.

As it turned out, she submerged entirely too successfully. Surfacing, it seemed, was something else again. Ventilation was another troublesome factor, and trial runs on *Hunley* were experiences nobody lived to write home about. Five test crews were suffocated under water. Hunley, himself, was smothered, and she was nicknamed "C.S.S. Floating Coffin," before her diving fins were corrected. The trolling torpedo was also replaced by a bomb on a 22-foot spar—a "spar torpedo" of the *David* type. Four months after the *New Ironsides* bout, *Hunley* was on hand as another David ready to do battle with the Union Goliaths at Charleston.

Now land lubbers and brass hats could shrug their shoulders, but Flag Officer Dahlgren had been worried by the first *David* challenge. Hearing that more "Davids" were on the way, he circularized a letter through the Union fleet, warning the officers to maintain sharp lookout. Booms and outriggings were suggested as defense against the spar torpedoes. Unfortunately some of the old line officers thought the *David* story hot air. It was a day when everyone quoted bushels of Scripture, yet no one aboard the steam sloop *U.S.S. Housatonic* seemed to remember the Old Testament legend, much less *New Ironsides*. Their thoughts were elsewhere on the night of February 17, 1864.

The hour was 2100. Green water and cloudy sky. Watch Officer Crosby halted at *Housatonic's* rail to peer at what looked like a slab of driftwood on the tide. Maybe it was, and maybe it wasn't. Crosby delayed too long—found out too late. He cried the alarm, and the engine room was signalled "Hard astern." But before *Housatonic* could back up or bring a gun to bear, she was torpedoed by *C.S.S. Hunley*.

Get a picture of that little 25-foot sub cruising out to stab her spar into that big Union warship. The men sweating over the hand-cranked propeller shaft. The captain at the awkward steering wheel. No coal fumes and heat as aboard steam-driven *David*, but the air was plenty thick—you can be sure. And plenty chill. Five crews had died in that iron hull. Five times she had gone like a stone to the bottom. Now every man aboard her was a volunteer—five seamen and her commanding officer, Lieutenant G. E. Dixon, of the Alabama Infantry. True, they had orders not to attempt a dive. But they knew the cranky sub might readily disobey such orders.

Slam-bam! The spar torpedo jabbed into the Union warship, sending up a thunderous fountain of water. Holed amidships, *Housatonic* went over on a drunken list, then staggered upright and sank in the shallow channel while her men raced up the masts to save their lives. The top-masts remained above water, and the survivors clinging in the crosstrees stared wildly about for a glimpse of the enemy.

But they saw no enemy. Swamped by the explosive tidal wave, *C.S.S. Hunley* had dived for the last time, taking her crew down with her in history as all-time members of the "Silent Service."

Last of the Seventh

While little Hunley went down in history as the first submarine on record to sink an enemy warship, the grim fact remained that she went down. She did her share. But it takes more than one swallow to make a spring. And it took more than one sinking to make a hole in the Union blockade that spring of 1864.

A hole in the Union blockade—a hole big enough to slip through—that was the Confederacy's desperate objective. Her raiders were chasing Yankee merchantmen off the ocean. Her cotton-clads had won Galveston. Her shore forts held Charleston. Her sharp mine fields made strong harbor defenses at Wilmington and Mobile. But defense wasn't enough. Raiders weren't enough. That hole in the blockade—a shipping lane for Southern cotton—that was the need.

Hunley had made only a small puncture. The Confederates couldn't repeat the submarine performance (it wasn't repeated until years later in 1914). Best chance for the Confederate Navy seemed its ironclad rams. Despite the sad showing of *Nashville* and *Atlanta*, the Richmond naval leaders gave these ironclad-types a high priority. If they couldn't torpedo a hole in the blockade, they might be able to ram one through. While the subs went out as an experiment, Southern shipyards worked night and day to launch a fleet of ram-nosed blockade busters.

Meantime—*Housatonic* to the contrary—the Union Navy had not become a "sitting duck." It had some star pinch-hitters, too, for this touch-and-go "seventh inning." From the first its strategy had been defensive. Now, in 1864, it determined to take the offensive. Here was the overall program:

Plan No. 1—cut off Texas (and Galveston cotton) from the South.

Plan No. 2—knock out the Confederate ocean raiders.

Plan No. 3—get those blockade-buster rams before they got started.

Plan No. 4—knock out Confederate shipping at Wilmington and Mobile.

"Uncle Gideon" gave the go-ahead, and on March 11, plan No. 1 got going. This was the Red River expedition—an amphibious operation shared by Army General Nathaniel Banks and your Navy's David Dixon Porter.

The Red River branches west from the Mississippi, crosses middle Louisiana, and goes cow-boying for miles along the Texas-Oklahoma border. As any Texan can tell you, it's a shallow stream full of snags and sandbars, navigable only during spring flood. Hardly a waterway you'd expect to find the U. S. Navy cruising in, but in Civil War times it was an important transport line. Cotton and cattle flatboated on the Red. So did Confederate supplies coming up through Texas from Mexico. Now General Magruder, CSA, was gathering a Texas army along the Red. Obviously he planned to transport these troops eastward to reinforce the armies of the Old South. Something must be done about Red River, and the Union amphibious forces were there to do it.

Or, rather, the Navy under Porter was there. He had six of the veteran Pook gunboats, four fairly new ironclads, three new river monitors, and seven little old "tinclads." He also had crews of veteran bluejackets who were rarin' to go. Heading west into the Red River, this naval force was on mark. It was joined by 10,000 Union troops, and the expedition captured the first objective, Fort de Russy, in a breeze.

But the breeze died down. General Banks, supposed to be on hand with the main Union Army, was late. Porter fumed, for the river was unseasonably low and he had to take every advantage of the channel. When Banks arrived two weeks behind time, the river was even lower.

Time and tide wait for no man, but that fact failed to hurry General Banks. A red-tape artist, he handed Porter another delay. The troops under Banks were from Tennessee—a detachment from the armies of one William Tecumseh Sherman. These weather-beaten troopers didn't please fussy Banks who complained that Sherman had sent him "a pack of ragged guerillas." Porter, who knew all about time and tide, had to fume like a smokestack for another week while Banks put his troops into new uniforms.

The big amphibious drive finally started on April 3, with Porter determined to move, come hell or high water. Hell came along without the water. The heavy ironclads couldn't navigate the then drying channel, and Porter had to push in with two monitors, the light gunboat *Chillicothe*, and a couple of weak tinclads. Unreeling more red tape, General Banks trailed along the river-bank, carping and crabbing.

With the supply ships left behind, Porter's advance force ran out of fuel. The Confederate scouts, who saw what was coming, had plenty of fuel. On both sides of the river they set fire to the cotton fields, choking the valley with a sea of smoke. Bullets began to whistle around the Union vessels while the bluejackets had to fight their way blindly ashore in search of fence rails for firewood.

Meanwhile General Banks blundered into a place called Pleasant Hill. Confederates rose up on all sides to attack like gray fury. Sherman's "ragged guerillas" managed to keep the retreat from becoming a massacre as Banks went into a fast reverse. This unpleasant news from Pleasant Hill reached Porter on April 7. Realizing he was up the creek with his neck out, he immediately turned back.

But now the river seemed to drain away under him. Porter put the heavier monitors in the lead and followed in the rear with the three tinclads—*Cricket, Fort Hindman,* and *Juliet.* Racing the ebbing channel, the Union vessels floundered back the way they'd come. The Confederates, meantime, had rushed up field pieces and rifle squads to block every river-bend. The leading monitor, *Osage,* went aground and was ambushed by an entire brigade. Her crew took refuge in the turret where her commander, Lieutenant T. O. Selfridge, USN, rigged up an amateur periscope so the gunners could see in all directions. Confederate artillery hammered the monitors' turret almost square, but the Navy gunners beat off the attack, and with the help of a tinclad the monitor got off.

Then *Eastport,* an ironclad won from the Confederates two years before, slammed into a mine. Good-bye *Eastport.* Two days later the Confederates ambushed and sank two of the tinclads. These were part of the flotilla Porter had left with Banks. Fighting down-stream to the rescue, his vessels scraping channel-bottom, Porter ran a gauntlet of fire with *Hindman, Juliet,* and *Cricket.* At one turn *Cricket* was riddled. Nineteen shells went through her, killing pilot, gun crew, and engineer. Porter took the helm himself, and piloted the craft downstream while bullets combed his hair and parted his beard.

On April 28 he caught up with retreating General Banks. This was at the place where he'd left the heavy ironclads and gunboats—at the head of a series of rapids. Now the river had fallen so low that a squadron of frogs could hardly go down the rapids, much less a squadron of ironclads. Confederate armies were closing in. What to do? Banks proposed immediate retreat —desert the stranded warships—blow them up! But those war-ships were half of the Union's inland fleet. See them stuck in the mud and scuttled? Porter was fit to be tied.

Then up stepped a man from the Army Engineers—Jim Bailey. A former Wisconsin lumberjack, Bailey suggested building a log-jam. Dam up the river's trickle, and when the water was high enough, blow the dam and let the warships shoot the rapids on the flood. Porter cheered. Bluejackets and soldiers rushed into the forest to cut logs. Cry of "tim-berrr!" echoed above the crackle of rifle fire as Sherman's "ragged pack" held off the Confederates while the boys in blue chopped wood.

Working like beavers they built the dam. Slow-ly the water-level rose. May 8, ahead of time, part of the dam gave way, sending a rush of water down the rapids. Quick as emergency, Porter gave the word, and four gunboats shot the rapids then and there. When the water gave out, Bailey promptly rebuilt the dam, and three days later the rest of Porter's squadrons got through. Banks immediately retreated after it, and so the operation was over.

The Navy got out with minor loss—two gunboats and an iron-clad. But the Confederacy still held Texas, and Galveston would have to be captured later. Between Banks and the river, Porter's expedition ended in the Red.

But the Red River failure was only a momentary set-back. While it cleared the way for Magruder's forces to lunge east, Union gunboats still held the Mississippi River, and the men in gray would have a tough time crossing. A far more serious threat to the Union was developing on the Atlantic seaboard.

This threat was the Confederate ram, *Albemarle,* a *Virginia*-type ironclad that grew up out of a Carolina cornfield on the banks of the Roanoke River. In a cornfield, yes. The keel laid among the furrows, and the iron casemate rising above the stalks.

That the Confederates could build any ship there at all was a miracle. Their plant consisted of a blacksmith shop and a few sheds. Raw material consisted of iron rails uprooted from the local railway line. But metal shortage was made up by the iron in the men themselves—iron muscles, iron determination, and the iron will of Lieutenant J. W. Cooke, CSN, in charge of construction. Ransacking the countryside for every door-knocker and piece of scrap he could lay his hands on, he became known as the "Ironmonger Captain." And after months of desperate labor, there in the corn was *Albemarle.*

But there was nothing rural about this Confederate battle wagon. 122 feet long with 45-foot beam, twin screws, a casemate 60 feet in length and octagonal in shape, she mounted two 100-pound, rifled guns that could swivel to fire broadside, fore, and aft. Her railroad-track armor was 4 inches thick backed by 10 inches of Southern pine. Iron Man Cooke took over as captain, and she had an iron crew.

The blacksmiths were still working on her when she slid down a mudbank in April, 1864, and set out on her maiden mission. Her mission? To ram that hole in the blockade—blast out that shipping lane so urgently needed by the Confederacy.

You can see the strategy. An outlet to North Carolina, the Roanoke River opens into Albemarle and Pimlico Sounds. In 1862, "Abe Lincoln's Soap-box Navy" had gained control of these sounds and plugged the river-mouth with Union gunboats. Built 80 miles inland in Confederate territory, *C.S.S. Albemarle* now came snorting down the river to smash these blockaders into bits and clear an opening into the Atlantic for Carolina cotton.

Now Federal agents had reported the Confederate ironclad when her hull was just a shuck among the corncobs. Appeals went to the Washington War Department urging an expeditionary drive inland to plow the warship under before it ripened. But nothing was done by War Secretary Stanton, while even less was done by General Benjamin Butler, in charge of Army operations in that area. Former commandant of Union troops occupying New Orleans, Butler had been unable to cope with a lady on a balcony who dumped a bucket of slops down on his head. How could he cope with this North Carolina giantess who might shower his brass hat with 100-pound shells? So he left her alone in her cornfield, and a small force of Federal troops which held the mouth of the Roanoke River was not even reinforced. Well, *Albemarle* was launched and steaming, and it was up to the Navy to stop her.

Torpedo mines in the river-mouth. A line of piles spiked across the channel. Two wooden gunboats anchored along either bank with a chain stretch between them to bar the passage. That was all the Union had ready on the night of April 19 when the big Confederate ironclad came down stream.

High water took *Albemarle* over the mines and spikes. Outsmarting the underwater chain, Captain Cooke veered shoreward and rammed the first gunboat, smashing it as though it were a peach basket. Dragged alongside by the sinking chain, the second gunboat fired furiously at the ironclad without making a dent, while a shell fragment rebounding from *Albemarle's* casemate killed the Union commander. Badly battered, the little gunboat cut away and fled.

With *Albemarle* holding the river-mouth, Carolina troops charged down the banks and captured the Federal beach-heads. Now the Confederate threat was a full-blown menace. The Union ships on blockade duty in the outer sounds were left-overs from the "Soap-box Fleet." Old wooden steamers and ferryboat double-enders, armed to deal with light blockade runners, but so many wash tubs to a buster like *Albemarle*. Captain Melancthon Smith, commodore of this eight-ship squadron, knew the odds. But he prepared to stop *Albemarle* with everything he had, and stood in to await the attack.

It came on May 5—*Albemarle* and two small escort craft striking out for the sounds. The Union squadron charged, and a wild scrimmage followed with the wooden gunboats milling around the ironclad like mongrels barking around a mastiff. Gunboat

Miami tried to jab with a spar torpedo. *Mattabesset* rushed in firing futile shots, then tried to foul the ironclad's propellors with a net. *Wyalusing* caught a shell, and retired with her foredeck ablaze. Star of the action was *Sassacus,* an armed steamer side-wheeling forward in an attempt to ram the horn-nosed ironclad. This action was on a par with a Coney Island excursion boat attacking a modern DD. Flags flying, guns banging, the wooden steamer slammed full tilt into *Albemarle* jarring her to her teeth. But the jar hurt *Sassacus* more. *Albemarle* backed, wheeled, swerved her big guns. A thundering 100-pounder hit *Sassacus* in the boiler, exploded her engine-room, and reduced her to wreckage.

Yet *Albemarle* failed to sink the wash tub squadron. For two hours the gunboats hung on. Then daylight waned and, surprisingly, the ironclad retreated up the Roanoke River. Her steering gear was injured and one of her big rifles had cracked. So the blockaders still held the outer sounds.

They did more than that. Commodore Smith strung a fresh batch of torpedoes across the river-mouth to lock the ironclad in. She came nosing down a few days later to sweep the mines aside, but she didn't come out.

Next, some sailors from gunboat *Wyalusing* volunteered to go up-river and get her. Charley Baldwin, Johnny Lloyd, Allen Crawford—there were three bluejackets for you. Toting 100-pound torpedoes and electrical exploding gear, they crept up the wooded Roanoke Valley, through the Confederate lines to a point opposite *Albemarle's* anchorage. Baldwin and Lloyd swam the river at night, and rigged a cable to haul the torpedoes across. Crawford, a fireman, waited with the sparking gear. Baldwin was just creeping forward to attach a torpedo cable to the ironclad's stern when the guards sighted him. Dodging rifle fire, he swam up-stream. Lloyd also swam the river under fire. They picked up Crawford, and spent four days in the woods and swamps eluding hot pursuit. There weren't any armchairs for the Navy boys on the line in those days, either.

But the wooden ships couldn't blockade an ironclad forever, no matter how great the courage of the crews. *Albemarle* would get out sooner or later. This menace scared Washington's arm-chair brigade, still shaky from the memory of old *Merrimac*. Departments and bureaus wrung their hands and ran about, but again "Uncle Gideon" had an answer up his sleeve.

Ever since the Confederate submarine-torpedo attack at Charles-ton, the Navy heads had been doing some high-pressure thinking. Now at New York Navy Yard the engineers were building three launches—little fellows with big engines, capable of carrying a seven-man crew, a lot of steam, and a powerful spar torpedo at the prow. Here were the world's first P. T. boats—invented back then in the Civil War. Yes, sir, they were to be the Navy's answer to that Confederate "seventh inning" threat, *Albemarle*.

Meantime, while the New York Yard sweated through the spring of '64 building this surprise—while *Albemarle* hung back like a bogie in her lair up the Roanoke—the Union Navy scored in an unexpected quarter.

Cherbourg, France. *Parlez-vous?* Well, maybe you don't, but the crew of a certain Confederate cruiser in harbor there was picking up the language fine. And certainly the cruiser was picking up coal and ammunition and French supplies.

Then—curses!—there off the breakwater was another silhouette —another steam cruiser with rakish masts and gleaming guns along her rail. She was *U.S.S. Kearsarge*, down from Holland under Captain John Winslow. The Union Navy had at last caught up with *Alabama* and Raphael the Raider.

Cherbourg was a neutral port—the French ordered *Kearsarge* to keep out. On the other hand, international rules being what they were, they couldn't keep *Alabama* in. Lincoln's Ambassador was raising a storm in Paris, anyway, about French friendship for the Confederacy. And with Winslow likely to open fire in a temper, the best thing was for *Alabama* to leave.

So it was delicately suggested that the Confederate cruiser go out and fight a duel with the Union cruiser—a contest of "honor." That was all Captain Semmes, with his code of the Old South, needed. Sparks in his eyes, he sent a challenge out to Winslow. The Union captain promptly accepted. Field of honor was arranged—the English Channel directly off Cherbourg. Date was set—Sunday coming, June 19.

So the two ships stripped down to shoot it out like two gentlemen. Semmes had much to lose, considering *Alabama's* value as a commerce-destroyer. But the risk seemed worth it. His cruiser's English guns outweighed the Union warship's—his men were keen—he was tired of chasing merchantmen—and victory over a Federal cruiser in French waters would encourage more French aid to the Confederacy. Winslow, on the other hand, swore to stop this raider that had played havoc with Yankee shipping all over the globe.

Sunday morning, true to promise, *Alabama* came steaming out of Cherbourg with her colors flying. She was escorted by a big French ironclad who was to act as referee and see that the duel took place beyond the three-mile limit. News of the fight had spread, and thousands of people had come on excursion trains from Paris to line the Cherbourg bluffs and watch the spectacle.

They saw the Confederate cruiser go out proudly like a ship on review. They saw the Union cruiser, eight miles off shore, head suddenly in to meet the adversary. *Alabama* opened fire first—white puffs like cotton-blossoms bursting from her distant guns—then the echo—bang, bang, bang—coming in from the sea. *Kearsarge* answered the fire with slower volleys. And then the two ships began to move down the Channel, swinging around each other in wide circles.

Alabama got in the first shot—a projectile that crashed into *Kearsarge's* stern, but luckily for her, failed to explode. Although out-ranged, Winslow found he had a faster ship, and forced steam to close in on the Confederate. At shorter range, the Union guns had better chance. And now, as with every duel in history, it was marksmanship that told.

Firing deliberately, smoothly, and accurately, each gun crew working like an oiled machine, the hard-drilled Navy gunners on *Kearsarge* began to shoot the Confederate cruiser full of holes. *Alabama's* rigging went. Her funnel tumbled. One shell after another struck her deck. Finally an 11-incher tore through her engine room, she exploded internally, the sea poured into her fire-room, and she turned back for shore, badly listing. *Kearsarge* kept after her, hitting her with every shot. Sinking, Semmes struck his colors.

So went down the fierce raider that had, practically single-handed, driven America's merchant marine off the seas. As a somewhat sour aftermath, Captain Semmes escaped to London on a British pleasure yacht which Winslow had allowed to come out and pick up survivors. But the destruction of the Confederate cruiser was enough. Now the Union Navy could concentrate more fully on the blockade, and bear down on such Confederate threats as ironclad *Albemarle*.

The Eagles They Fly High

You may wonder why one Confederate ironclad up a river remained such a problem when the Union Navy had monitors, powerful cruisers, and warships seemingly to spare. Well, the blockade from Norfolk to Galveston was stretched like a thin rubber band. Remove warships from one sector to reinforce another and the rubber band was likely to part at the weakened sector. And the Navy had other fish to fry besides the blockade. Cruisers like *Kearsarge* had to remain overseas to keep an eye on foreign ironclads being built for the Confederacy. The Navy was also launching attacks against those big Confederate home ports, Wilmington and Mobile. So there were no extra men-o'-war to send against *Albemarle*. That explains the rush orders on those three little P. T.'s in New York Yard.

Then in July came news that the South was building another ironclad in Carolina—a sister to *Albemarle*. The Navy Department's hair went up. Two Carolina bugaboos! Not only did they menace the Union Navy's program—they threatened the whole Union Army time-table. To understand why, you need another glance at the overall war picture.

Gettysburg, you remember, threw Lee back into Virginia in the summer of '63. Vicksburg, shortly after, ended Confederate hopes on the Mississsippi. After Vicksburg's fall, Grant's army followed through with a drive on the Confederate base at Chattanooga, Tennessee. Union General Thomas won fame as the "Rock of Chickamauga" by holding off terrific counter-attacks at Chickamauga Creek. The boys in blue went on to storm Missionary Ridge and climb Lookout Mountain. Chattanooga was won that November. The Confederates lost their hold in Tennessee, and Abraham Lincoln had found the General he'd been looking for—Ulysses (Unconditional Surrender) Grant.

Appointed General-in-Chief of the Union Armies, Grant came to Washington in March '64. His campaign hat was dusty, but it somehow outshone all the local brass. And his ideas were the brightest Lincoln had heard in a long time. For, despite Gettysburg and the western victories, things had been going badly in the North. The people were war-weary, shabby, down at heart. There were strikes and walk-outs. Profiteers gouged. Anti-Lincoln politicians threw mud. And "Copperhead" appeasers urged desertion in the field and sabotage on the home front.

An Ohio politician named Vallandingham praised the Confederacy and urged a Northern revolt. When Federal agents imprisoned the Copperhead, Lincoln freed him and shipped him to Richmond, R.F.D., but had to put the North under martial law.

"Unconstitutional!" howled the anti-Lincoln press. "King Abe is a dictator!"

Lincoln answered, *"Must I shoot a simple-minded soldier who deserts, while I must not touch a hair of a wily agitator who induces him to desert? And is it possible to lose the nation and yet preserve the Constitution? By general law, life and limb must be protected, yet often a limb must be amputated to save a life. But a life is never wisely given to save a limb."*

To strengthen the Army, Lincoln put through the North's first draft. Conscription was met with open violence. In New York City, a large body of immigrants, who failed to understand the struggle, staged a week-long riot—1,000 people killed. There were riots in Chicago and elsewhere. The law, messed up by politicians, permitted a draftee to buy himself out of the service for $300. Finally the Union had to offer bonuses to enlisted men.

It didn't help to know that conscription had gone equally sour in the South where anyone owning a dozen or more slaves was excused from army duty. Jeff Davis wasn't facing an election. In the North, 1864 was an election year—McClellan planned to run against Lincoln and campaign for a negotiated peace.

So Lincoln was glad to see a general on a war campaign. Grant's ideas were as blunt and powerful as a sledge-hammer. Briefly, he proposed to move the Union Army of the Potomac straight at Richmond. While he attacked Lee on this front, the Union armies in the west would cut east through the Confederacy's heart to Atlanta and the sea, and then come up-coast to take Richmond from the rear. The general to lead this Georgia drive? An officer who thought war was hell, and so would fight like blue blazes to end it in a hurry. William Tecumseh Sherman.

As Lincoln dryly put it, Grant proposed to "hold the leg while Sherman took off the skin." But the Confederate tiger would fight like all get out—a wounded tiger—gaunt and flaming with desperate courage. The Union armies were two hunters closing in for the kill. The Union Navy was the unbending trap. The hunters would have to maneuver with perfect team-work, for any break in the trap might well prove fatal.

In May, Grant started the drive on Richmond. Simultaneously Sherman pushed out of the west, on his march through Georgia. A lot of water has run under the bridge since then, and today any grown-up American can look at Sherman and appreciate his soldierly job. To begin with, he was entering enemy territory—mountainous, part wilderness, and fiercely hostile. He was up against Joe Johnston, a military leader rated with Lee. To keep Grant's time-table he had to move fast, and this meant discarding wagon trains, baggage carts, even mess gear—pruning his infantry equipment down to the last spare button. No other army in history ever cut away from its base in such fashion

It did damage—war is hell, and no man hated the job more than Sherman. He grew old on that march, and you could see it in his eyes. But foot by foot, with expert tactics, he drove Johnston through the mountains before him. Incidentally, the song "Marching Through Georgia" was written several years after the war was over. But there wasn't any "bring the good old bugle, boys," about the fighting around Atlanta. A lot of boys in blue as well as boys in gray died in that desperate advance.

And now it's mid-July, with Grant hammering at Richmond, and Sherman in Atlanta—the pincer movement already half closed. Do you see the importance of that ironclad, *Albemarle*, there in the Roanoke River?

Well, it lies there athwart Sherman's intended path up the coast, preparing to smash the Union Navy's trap at a moment when everything must hold. How about the other Carolina ram? Washington, D. C. doesn't know. Maybe it's only a rumor. But it seems that *Albemarle* is waiting for this partner, holding back. So the Union Navy must by-pass Carolina in this war of nerves.

Go down to Mobile on the Gulf and you'll find smoke on the horizon. Scout ships probing in. July of 1864, Farragut's fleet was gathering.

For a long time he'd urged the Mobile attack. After the fall of New Orleans this big Alabama port became the Confederacy's main shipping point, an outlet for cotton, an inlet for supplies. Railroads and two large rivers linked the town with the interior. Up one of the rivers, at Selma, was the South's largest remaining navy yard. Its narrow channel protected by three strong forts, Mobile Bay defied penetration. At the same time its shallows—too shallow for heavy warships—made a fine playground for speedy racing boats which continually ran the blockade.

Besides being a nest for blockade-runners, Mobile was hatching some more Confederate ironclads—rams that would make the *Albemarle* threat look puny. One of these, the *Tennessee*, had already been launched at the Selma yard, and her builders were calling her "the most powerful warship afloat." Once her sisters came down the ways and joined her, it would be curtains for Farragut's wooden fleet in the Gulf. It was time to go in and cut Mobile out of the Confederacy's map.

Go in—that was Farragut's way, and at Mobile the only way. He'd have to take his ships up that long, narrow channel right through the fire of those three great forts. But he figured that with monitors and a landing force of troops he could manage. Monitors? Word came that Dahlgren needed them at Charleston and off the James where (great thunder!) the CSN had built two more ramming ironclads. Troops? The Army couldn't spare any.

This delay gave the Confederates time to mount the guns on the *Tennessee* and get her down into Mobile Bay. Farragut steamed inshore one day for a spy-glass look at her. She had a smaller casemate than *Merrimac*, but report said her armor was much thicker and her guns colossal. Farragut reported monitors absolutely necessary against her.

Finally four arrived—brand new ones from the Northern yards. And Sherman, wanting a diversion created, sent 2,000 men. But the monitors would never take *Tennessee*, said the glooms. The wooden ships would never make it past the channel forts in the first place. Entering Mobile, Farragut would be sticking his head into the tiger's mouth. Mobile was no lackadaisical New Orleans.

Farragut knew it—the South had been fortifying the bay for many months. Their chief of naval operations was Franklin Buchanan, and he was commanding the *Tennessee* in person. No matter. It was time to go in. Farragut signalled the fleet to gather and gave the plan of attack to his captains.

"As to being prepared for defeat, I certainly am not," he wrote to his wife. *"Any man who is prepared for defeat would be half defeated before he commenced."*

Unprepared for defeat, then, he set zero hour as dawn, August 5. As at New Orleans he piled his decks with sandbags, shielded the engines with chains. Tactics called for the ships to advance in two columns—monitors slightly in the lead—wooden *Brooklyn* and *Hartford* heading a gunboat parade. The big steam sloops had gunboats lashed alongside to keep them moving if they were disabled.

The plan: broadside the stuffing out of the forts while the monitors held off Buchanan's ironclad. Get by the forts at any odds, then concentrate on the big ram.

By 0530 the ships were under way. Forts Morgan, Powell, and Gaines let go a typhoon of fire as the monitors came within range. Across the channel smoke rolled like a low-hanging fog. Farragut, aboard *Hartford*, climbed in the shrouds to see ahead, and a Quartermaster raced up to lash him to the rigging, fearing the Old Man might be struck and fall overside.

Straining forward, Farragut saw *Tennessee* come plowing down the bay with an escort of gunboats to attack *Brooklyn*. Union monitor *Tecumseh* steamed out of line to attack the ironclad. Against orders! Farragut had commanded the monitors to keep column formation in the channel. And the thing he feared happened. Wham! *Tecumseh* struck a mine.

In a whirlpool of smoke and water the monitor swiftly sank. Her young commander, Tunis Craven, may have misread his orders—no one knows. He went down with his ship, stepping aside to allow the pilot to go topside ahead of him.

Now men shouted from *Brooklyn* to warn Farragut that the channel was a death-trap of torpedoes. So the Navy was given another of Farragut's sayings—

"Damn the torpedoes! Full speed ahead!"

Damning the torpedoes, the ships went forward at full steam. Right through the tempest of cannister, grape, and shell. Right past the forts. Right by the torpedoes that scraped their keels and somehow failed to go off. Right into Mobile Bay.

There were dead and wounded aboard *Hartford* and *Brooklyn*. Two of the monitors had been damaged. Altogether the forts had given the ships a savage pounding. To Franklin Buchanan, peering through *Tennessee's* casemates, the Federal ships must have looked like easy marks.

Or perhaps Buchanan, sent to Mobile as a last-ditch post, saw Farragut's entry into the bay as the last straw. At any rate, instead of keeping under the cover of the forts, he threw caution overside and drove *Tennessee* on a wild charge at the Union warships.

Like a maddened bull, the ironclad thundered across open water to attack *Hartford*. Remarking, *"I didn't think old Buchanan was such a fool,"* Farragut ordered his squadron to let go at the ironclad with everything. *Tennessee* ran into a tremendous concentration of fire. Risking anything to sink Farragut's flagship, Buchanan drove alongside, and set *Hartford* briefly ablaze with a broadside. Gunboat *Lackawanna* was rammed in the melee. But the monitor *Chickasaw* began to slam the ironclad hard. An exploding shell struck an open port, and a flying fragment broke Buchanan's leg—same leg and same place it had been broken when he commanded the *Virginia*.

Catching Hail Columbia from the Union gunners, the ironclad seemed to fall apart. Her funnel went over like a snowballed top hat. Her steering chains cracked up. One after another her guns gave out. And her iron plates were coming off like shingles blown from a roof, when down came her flag.

Farragut and his bluejackets had won. The eagles, they flew high in Mobile.

Eighth Inning

"I propose to fight it out on this line," Grant wrote to Lincoln, *"if it takes all summer."*

It was taking all summer. Right at the start Lee struck Grant's army a devastating smash at Cold Harbor—in half an hour 14,000 Union casualties to 1,000 Confederate. However, unlike the previous generals Lee had encountered, Grant refused to call it a day.

Instead of retreating back to the Potomac, he hung on. In the Shenandoah Valley he had a new cavalry leader, Phil Sheridan, who was beating off Jeb Stewart. Meantime, deep in the South,

Sherman was marching into Atlanta, Georgia. Such was the situation when the word reached Richmond—Farragut had captured Mobile.

It was a stunner for the Confederates. Buchanan a prisoner of war—Mobile in Union hands. They'd made a great "seventh inning" try, but the Union had stolen another base. Now with Charleston bottled up and Galveston isolated, they had that one last big seaport—Wilmington, North Carolina.

Out of Wilmington must go the cotton that paid the bills. Into Wilmington must come the medicine, guns, and foreign-made munitions for Lee's army. Obviously the Confederacy must hold Wilmington. Just as obviously, the Union Navy must take it.

At the mouth of the Cape Fear River the place looked easy to take—on the map. But like the shallows at Mobile, the Cape Fear shoals held off heavy men-o'-war while providing a fast field for the blockade-runners. These craft were skimming in and out like gulls, racing down to the Bahamas and speeding back with tons of army supplies which were rushed through Wilmington to Lee. Determined to hold this base, the Confederates sent every gun and man they could spare to Fort Fisher, a mammoth earthworks on a peninsula flanking the harbor entrance. Fisher's battlements were twenty-five feet thick. A log palisade with loopholes for riflemen topped the parapet. Mine fields and terraces of trenches protected the land approach. Aimed seaward, the coast artillery batteries totalled 44 heavy guns. Fisher was considered the strongest fort in the Confederacy.

To blast this coastal colossus, occupy Wilmington, and cut Lee's maritime supply line, the Union called on the Navy. The Navy sent for David Dixon Porter. He came east in September, studied the project, and saw it would take a fleet with a large landing force. "Uncle Gideon" gave him the strong Atlantic squadron at Hampton Roads, including *New Ironsides*. Grant offered an army of 8,000 men. But the Army command went to General Ben Butler. Porter's whiskers bristled. After the Red River foozle he was in no mood for tin-soldier monkey business. Grumpily he protested to the War Department. Then while the paper work went on, he saw something else—that old ironclad menace, *Albemarle*, still lurking in the Roanoke River, waiting for completion of her sister ram.

Huh! He couldn't send troop convoys down the Carolina coast with this bogie prepared to charge at them from ambush. Where were those three torpedo boats promised from New York?

Well, heading down for Hampton Roads, one had gone ashore on the Virginia coast and had been captured. One had been sunk by high seas. The third had reached the Roads by the skin of its teeth—or rather, the teeth of young Lieutenant W. B. Cushing, commander of the launch flotilla.

Porter liked twenty-one-year-old lads who got things done. When Cushing offered to take his torpedo boat single-handed up the Roanoke after the *Albemarle*, Porter was all for him. Wait. An order from the Department of State—Cushing must appear for trial—some red-tape violation of rules while he'd served on a blockader. Porter fixed the ticket, got Cushing off, and sent him packing to beard the Confederate ram in its den.

October 27—a night of dark drizzle. Fifteen men sardined in a little launch with dynamite in its bow. In tow, a cutter crowded with fighters in case there was a chance to board. The little launch prowled up the Roanoke River unseen. Were they heading into a trap? Would they meet one enormous ironclad, or two? They slipped past a guardship, shadows in the murk. Eight miles up-stream, Cushing, standing lookout, spied the *Albemarle*.

She was lying at a wharf, a silhouette black as midnight. Cushing steered inshore and was preparing to land the cutter's crew for a try at boarding, when the sentries woke up and challenged. A pistol banged. Guards shouted. Ordering the cutter off to attack the guard ship, Cushing circled back to mid channel and readied his spar torpedo for a rush at the ironclad.

Alarm fires began to blaze along the shore. A volley of rifle bullets swept the river. The firelight that exposed the launch also showed to Cushing a barrier of heavy booms floating in the water around *Albemarle*. Anticipating torpedo-boat attack, the Confederates had moored the ironclad behind a fence of huge logs.

Cushing threw his brain and the launch into immediate high gear. Reasoning that the booms had been in the water a long time, and would therefore be slippery, he sent the torpedo boat forward in a headlong charge. Zip—whop! Like a surfboard the launch hurdled the water-logged barrier. There was a great splash, then a blinding explosion as the spar torpedo slammed into the *Albemarle's* side.

At the same time one of *Albemarle's* big guns fired point blank at Cushing. But the launch was capsized by the torpedo blast. Cushing and his boys were in the water. The cannon-shot missed them by a hair.

Albemarle quickly sank. Several of the launch crew drowned; the remainder were captured. Cushing alone swam the river with bullets splashing like skipped stones around him. In the swamps down stream he managed to escape. He found a rowboat, spent a day on the river, and finally rowed out to the Atlantic where he reached a warship on blockade. You can take your hat off to Cushing and the bluejackets in that torpedo boat any time you want to. For ending the long-standing *Albemarle* menace, Cushing was given command of the flagship taking Porter down to Wilmington.

News of the *Albemarle* sinking was black crepe to the Confederate Navy Department. Now they had more bad news, datelined October 7, from Brazil. *U.S.S. Wauchusett* had captured Confederate raider *Florida* at Bahia. One by one the Confederacy's naval hopes were going down.

In November Porter's troop ships were steaming off Cape Fear. *New Ironsides* and the warship squadron were closing in on Wilmington. At the last minute, Butler had wire-pulled himself into Army command by promising to reduce Fort Fisher at one whack. How? Give him an old ship crammed with gunpowder. Have a monitor tow it close to the fort. Touch it off, and say goodbye to Fort Fisher.

Porter thought the plan wasn't worth the powder. But to please the General, 235 tons were packed into a condemned gunboat and run up to Fort Fisher on December 23. The fleet stood back to see the fireworks, and the time bomb went off the day before Christmas. The blast that followed killed fish for miles, but failed to kill Fort Fisher. Some of the men in the underground bomb proofs thought they heard a corporal drop a shoe. As for damage to the fortifications, Butler might as well have touched off a firecracker.

If the demolition plan proved a squib, Butler's land attack

on the fort was a worse botch. All day following the futile blast, Porter's warships bombarded the fortress. Then, Christmas morning, Butler landed his troops down the peninsula to attack the outer works. The boys in blue were storming the gray trenches when Butler suddenly lost heart and called off the assault. When this message reached the fleet, Porter went through the overhead. Political influence or not, he demanded Butler's recall.

News that Sherman had captured Savannah for Christmas cheered the Union boys. Then, after a three-weeks' delay, General A. H. Terry arrived in Butler's place, and the soldiers were ready to go. A fighter, Terry resumed the attack at once, and drove through Fort Fisher's land defenses. Porter's ships steamed in to crush the coast artillery batteries with deadly fire, *New Ironsides* and the monitors shooting at point-blank range. Once again naval guns proved superior to land artillery, and the great fort crumbled.

But the Confederates in the underground bombproofs held on. Then, landing right under the fort's palisade, 1500 sailors and marines fought up to the parapets through homicidal fire. Dozens fell in the desperate charge, but at nightfall the fort was captured.

So Wilmington was taken by the Union.

Last Inning

Lincoln sent orders to Grant and Sherman to give generous terms if the Confederates offered to surrender. The time was getting close. Wilmington's fall had cut Lee's munition supply to almost nothing. Sherman's army, doing the impossible, was driving up through miles of bottomless Carolina swamp to pin the dwindling forces of Joe Johnston. In February, '65, one month after Wilmington's loss, the Confederates evacuated Charleston. In March, Grant's army trained its artillery on Richmond.

The Confederacy was at rope's end. Its paper money was good only for starting fires in kitchen stoves. Foragers had stripped the land Food prices were sky high—$40 for a pound of coffee —$1000 for a barrel of flour. Bread lines stood in market places, and farmers hid their scrawny cattle. The great plantation mansions were unkempt with weedy lawns and broken windows.

Shoes cost $200 a pair. Only the profiteers could afford new clothes.

The army in the field was half barefoot, clad in rags. A Confederate soldier wrote that you could tell a man's rank by the condition of his uniform—a captain had one hole in the seat of his pants, a lieutenant had two, and a private had no seat in his pants to have a hole in. Equipment was equally dilapidated. Transport wagons were worn to the hub, and railroads were mere skeletons. Big guns, munitions, steam engines—all the machinery vital to modern warfare lacked replacement. The Confederacy was hungry and breaking down. The naval blockade had cut off all foreign supplies.

Still the Richmond government clung to a threadbare hope for foreign assistance. Again the Union Navy barred the way to Europe and stood as a seawall, ready to defend the Monroe Doctrine. As for cotton to pay for foreign aid, the blockade had finally sealed it up like a moth in a cocoon. King Cotton, smothered, was "dying on the vine."

Up the James there remained three ironclad rams. In a last desperate foray, this remnant of the Confederate Navy came down the river—and into *U.S.S. Onondaga*. A new double-turret monitor, *Onondaga* sailed into the three armored rams with salvos that battered open their casemates. Faulty engines—the curse of the Confederate ironclads—sang the swan-song of these three; they retired up the river to be scuttled.

Lee still had strong forces at Richmond—some 60,000 men ready to fight for him to the last ditch. But the boys in blue, with good leadership at last, were just as ready to go.

Grant said in a brief word to Sheridan, *"I now feel like ending the matter."*

The blue lines shoved forward. Lee tried to break Grant's center with a bold counter-drive, hoping to stall the Union push and gain time to move his army southward to join Johnston. But Sheridan cut in on his flank, crippling the action. On April 2 the Confederates evacuated Richmond.

April 9, surrounded by Union divisions at Appomattox, Lee surrendered. American history was made at a small farmhouse where Grant, in weather-beaten private's blouse with stars on his shoulders, returned the jewelled sword of the tall general in faultless dress uniform, and told him his men could take their horses home for the spring plowing.

Five days later Lincoln was murdered. Throughout the war his life had been in peril, nearly every mail bringing some anonymous letter (many written in the North) threatening him with destruction. Once a Confederate agent, a woman in widow's veil, entered the White House and embraced him in an attempt to infect him with smallpox! Now on April 14 (Good Friday), attending a theater in Washington, Lincoln was shot and killed by the fanatical leader of a spy ring—John Wilkes Booth. You can still see the theater in Washington, and the house across the way where the tired, homely President died.

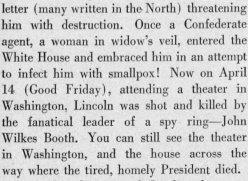

Surrending his trapped Carolina forces to Sherman on April 26, General Johnston said Lincoln's murder was the hardest blow yet dealt the South. Johnston's surrender put the official end to the war which had raged almost four years to the day. Skirmishing went on in remote parts of the country where the news was slow in arriving. It remained for the Navy to occupy Galveston on June 2. Six

months later (November 6, 1865) the Confederate cruiser *Shenandoah* surrendered in a British port, and the Stars and Bars came down for the last time.

The Civil War was over.

U. S. A. and U. S. N.

It had been a terrible conflict—the most devastating America had known. Nearly 600,000 men had died in the fighting, some 60% of them for Union. Thousands of men on both sides returned home sick, blinded, or maimed. Around 5 billion dollars had been spent in the war effort, divided between North and South at 3 to 2. In the South where most of the fighting took place, property damage was beyond accurate estimate. Completely bankrupt, the Confederacy left most of its citizens with nothing but worthless bonds. Although Northern industry had boomed, it had profited but little. The American merchant marine, world's second at the start of the war, had been reduced to the vanishing point.

For the United States of America total disaster had been close. The threat of foreign power—especially Maximilian in Mexico—had hovered over the American continent like a vulture waiting to grab a dying eagle. Imagine what might have happened if the North had lost, the Union had been divided, and the North and South as two nations had lain weakened and exhausted and disunited.

Now, with the nation reunited under one Federal government, the foreign threat evaporated. With a U. S. Army in the field, Napoleon III suddenly remembered the Monroe Doctrine, and pulled out of Mexico. With a strong U. S. Navy at sea, Maximilian could obtain no foreign support from anybody, and his parasite empire popped like a gaudy soap bubble.

The great warship *Stonewall*—an armored giant built for the Confederacy in France—was quickly sold down the river. So were two heavy monitors and a cruiser which the Union Navy had kept penned up in England. Once more the United States of America, a Republic of, by, and for the people, was ready to go forward.

To those bluejackets and boys in blue, officers and men who gave their lives to save the Union—a salute! Because of them the nation had a "new birth of Freedom"—the states remained the UNITED STATES. American democracy was nearer a reality, and all men in the land were given the same right to life, liberty, and the pursuit of happiness.

To the loyal Union Navy—another salute! You've seen the part it played in the war—judge for yourself the share of credit it deserved in the victory.

In England, where the outcome of the war pleased the democratic British liberals, the magazine Punch published a cartoon. This pictured two gladiators at the end of a desperate battle. One—the South—with helmet and Roman sword lay defeated. The victor—the North—stood upright, brandishing a trident and a net. Any sailor could tell you that the victor wore the costume of Neptune, and the net and trident represented naval power.

DAMN THE TORPEDOES, FULL SPEED AHEAD

War With Spain (and Some Others)

Do you like melodrama? Gripping, seat-edge melodrama full of action, mystery, secret papers, underhanded villainy, and the sheriff arriving just in time to save the day? Do you like moon-lit island scenery? European palace intrigue? Conspirators whispering in a waterfront bar? Knives in the dark? Bullets at dawn? A smashing climax in a wild tropical hurricane?

If you do, you'll like this chapter—as a melodrama, it's got everything. What's more, the show may answer some questions you've had in mind. Such as: When did the Stars and Stripes first fly over such Pacific islands as Samoa? How did Uncle Sam come to take over the Philippines? Why did America fight a war over Cuba?

Get set for some old-time dramatics rivalling anything out of Hollywood. You're in the World Theater; the stage is set; here's the programme:

THE INTERNATIONAL PLAYERS PRESENT
A MELODRAMA IN TWO ACTS

ACT I—"BLOOD AND IRON"

Scene I

The time: back in the 1880's. The scene: The German Chancellery in Berlin. On stage: Otto Eduard Leopold von Bismarck, the Prussian Chancellor of Imperial Germany (pacing). With him a group of Admirals and Generalstabsoffiziers.

As the curtain rises you hear a band outside the balconied window playing *Ein Feste Berg Ist Unser Gott*—"A Mighty Fortress Is Our God."

Bismarck crosses the room impatiently to draw thick curtains and shut out the music. Then he turns and points to an enormous wall-map of the world.

"*Achtung!* Do you see that island, Herr Grand Admiral?"

"*Ja*, Excellency. I see it."

"Good! I have decided to take it. The Emperor has been informed accordingly."

"But, Excellency, that island and all that island group are under the protection of Great Britain and the United States as well as Germany. You are aware that you are pointing at Samoa?"

"Did you think I was pointing at a fly-speck? Certainly I point at Samoa. It is soon to become German territory."

"The natives may protest—"

"A handful of natives in grass skirts? Protest to Imperial Germany?"

"But what of the treaty with Great Britain and the United States providing for a three-way trusteeship?"

"Am I one to be stopped by a stupid treaty? I am Bismarck, Chancellor of the German Empire—builder of the German Empire. Did I not smash the will of Austria when she protested my uniting of the German states?"

"*Ja*, Herr Excellency."

"Did I not crush Denmark when she protested German annexation of the province of Schleswig-Holstein?"

"*Ja*, Herr Excellency."

"When France protested further German expansion did I not shatter her in the War of 1870?"

"That is so."

"Germany needs more colonies! Germany needs more living space. The march to the East—our *Drang Nach Osten*—goes forward. We must therefore gain bases in the Pacific."

"But if England and America do question the conquest, Excellency—"

"It means nothing! Britain has her hands full elsewhere,

and at Samoa she has only a consul and a mailboat. As for the United States, they do not even have the mailboat. A nation too busy building railroads to think of anything else, and a President who used to be a small-town sheriff. You have our intelligence reports on the American Navy?"

The admiral fumbles in a dispatch case.

"We have the reports, Excellency. The American Navy has deteriorated considerably since the Civil War."

"For the benefit of my staff, outline the situation in brief."

"Immediately after the Civil War, all naval building and naval training was brought to a stop. Many warships were sent to drydock or sold. Such vessels as *Onondaga* and *Dunderberg* were sold in Europe. *New Ironsides*, lost by fire, was not replaced. When Admiral Farragut died in 1869, the nation seemed to lose interest in the Navy.

"During President Grant's administration, it was allowed further to decline, although a few of the seagoing monitors were completed. Grant's Naval Secretary, A. H. Borie, resigned. He was replaced by Naval Secretary George Robeson, a New Jersey lawyer who became involved in the Philadelphia ship-repair scandals. Under Robeson, Admiral Porter had his hands tied. No new warships were built. Robeson forbade the use of steam-power save in harbors or calm water. He also reduced steam-power by replacing the four-bladed propeller with the older two-blade design."

Laughter from the German naval officers. The Grand Admiral shuffles his notes.

"However, in 1869 the Americans did develop the cruiser, *Wampanoag*, which logged twenty-three knots with Isherwood engines. Similar engines were installed in some other naval vessels

327

which remain in commission but are unarmored and lack fire power. Throughout the 1870's, the decade just past, their Navy ranked twelfth in sea power, behind those of China and Denmark. By 1881 the U. S. Navy did not possess a single armored ship. Cruises were being made on side-wheelers and the old sailing frigate, *Constitution*."

More laughter from the German staff officers. The Grand Admiral shakes his head.

"Wait—the Americans now attempt to remedy this situation. The naval secretaries succeeding Robeson, and the present Secretary Whitney, have put through constructive programs. The navy is considerably strengthened by the new White Squadron."

Bismarck frowns. "What of this so-called White Squadron?"

"It consists of the cruisers *Atlanta, Boston, Baltimore, Chicago, Charleston, Newark*—all new. They average around nineteen knots. *Atlanta, Boston,* and *Chicago* carry the new eight-inch

guns, and all employ the new armor and turrets. They are a formidable advance over the hybrid frigate-cruisers. However, they do not match our German warships in cruising range. Information indicates they were designed primarily for American coastal defense."

"So!" Bismarck smiles at the Pacific expanse on the globe. "America thinks in terms of her coasts. Germany has wider vision."

"*Ja*, Excellency, but there is danger in this American Admiral Luce, who just established the Naval War College. Also in the theories of a young Commander Mahan who is lecturing on naval strategy. New bills will soon be introduced to the American Congress. And three new armored battleships are proposed— *Indiana, Massachusetts,* and *Oregon.* Our agents have learned the designs call for eighteen-inch belt armor and thirteen-inch turret guns!"

"Therefore we must not delay!" Bismarck snaps. "While Britain is busy elsewhere—while the Yankee battleships are still on paper—we must move! I have already drawn up a plan of action for Samoa. An incident has been arranged. Now is the time to strike!"

He gestures dismissal. The officers salute and retire. Bismarck studies the map, squinty-eyed. Then he wheels to the window and whips aside the portieres.

A blare of music comes from the square below. The band is playing *Deutschland, Deutschland Uber Alles*—"Germany, Germany Over All."

The curtain falls.

Scene 2

The time: March, 1887.

The scene: The harbor of Apia, the island of Upolu in the Samoan group. Upolu, the largest of the Samoan Islands, and Apia, the principle port, are under German control. Tutuila with its harbor of Pago Pago has been under U. S. protection since 1872. The smaller islands are under the British. And, as previously mentioned, the three nations are joined in a three-way trusteeship which permits self-government for the Samoans.

At Apia you see a fine harbor fringed with palm trees. Grass-roofed native huts are bunched along the shore. There is a wharf with the usual tin-roofed warehouse, the usual tin-roofed customs house, the usual water-front bar. Outrigger canoes and a small lugger flying the British Jack are tied up at the wharf.

A crowd of fuzzy-headed Samoan natives are on the wharf, gesturing and pointing. A lugger is making ready to sail. However the natives are not concerned with the lugger—their gestures are aimed at a gray warship. There, against the sky tropic blue, fly the black eagles of Imperial Germany.

699197°—46—22

Two figures advance through the natives on the wharf, and pause at the lugger's gangway. One, the schooner captain, fans his face with a salty seacap. The other, a lean Englishmen wearing white ducks and a wide-brimmed straw hat, extends his hand.

"Good luck to you, Captain. A fair wind and a following sea."

"Thank you, Mr. Stevenson."

"And you'll take good care of my manuscript, won't you?"

"Right here," the captain pats his coat. "We always take good care of the British mails, Mr. Stevenson. Especially when it's one of your stories."

The slim Englishman smiles, then, gazing seaward, alters the smile to a puzzled frown.

"That warship out there. You don't suppose the Germans intend to use force around here, do you?"

"What else do they ever use? Especially when there's no one around to stop them?"

"But they can't maltreat these poor natives," Mr. Stevenson protests. "This great thundering row over a few bunches of bananas is ridiculous."

The skipper grunts. "I saw Becker, the German Consul, talking with Brandeis, the plantation manager, over at the bar a while back."

Mr. Stevenson nods. It is a common sight, of late—the German consul and the German planter with their heads together.

"It began a little over a year ago. A couple of stems of bananas were stolen from the German plantation, and Brandeis came raging into Apia as if the natives had filched his entire crop. There's no proof the natives stole the bananas. But Becker summoned poor old King Malietoa and threatened to jail him if the robbers weren't apprehended."

"All over a few bunches of bananas."

"Exactly. Then just this past winter a few more bananas were stolen. Poor old King Malietoa was hauled into court again, and the German consul demanded reparations. Our British consul and the American consul from Pago Pago sat in on the case. They voted against the reparations. Of course the German consul is furious. And now you see a warship out in the harbor."

The skipper boards the waiting schooner, and a few minutes later the lugger, with the British mail flag aloft, is standing out to sea. The Englishman on the wharf watches her dip her flag to the German cruiser in passing. Then he turns and hurries away from the wharf.

In the doorway of the waterfront bar two men in tropic drill and sun helmets are also watching the departure of the mailboat. They speak together in German, and one, short and stocky with a red face, laughs. A couple of uniformed German sailors emerge from the bar-room and stand with them. When the mailboat is hull down on the horizon, the stocky man nods to his companions, and produces an official-looking paper from under his coat.

"Nun los! Immer feste druff!"

The sailors sling rifles to shoulder, and the party tramps past the wharf to the compound fronting the warehouse. Halting before a bulletin board where steamer sailings and other official announcements are posted, the stocky German tacks up his paper. The natives gather to read the announcement which causes a flurry of excitement.

Evening shadows are dimming the beach, the crowd at the billboard grows, several natives depart, running, and presently, somewhere beyond the village, there is the low thump of an island drum.

As the curtain falls you hear the sound of the island drum.

There is a brief interlude of several days.

In the Interlude

You saw the Englishman hurrying away, for he had some distance to walk to his hillside bungalow.

Yes, it was Stevenson, the famous novelist, author of *Treasure Island* and *Dr. Jekyll and Mr. Hyde*. Again the scene is imaginary and the dialogue dramatized, but from here on out the rest is history.

With the British mailboat gone, the German consul immediately

331

published his demands, summoning King Malietoa to court, ordering the arrest of the unknown banana thieves, and asking reparation from the Samoans to the tune of $12,000 for the stolen bananas. If Malietoa failed to raise the money, he would promptly be deposed in favor of Tamasese. Such was Becker's official proclamation, although the British and American consuls, supposedly sharing the authority, were not advised about it.

The plot thickens. The curtain rises again at Apia.

You are looking, now, into the bar room—a typical waterside joint with mud floor, wooden benches and tables, the usual shelves of bottles, sweaty bartender, and beachcomber parrot. Prominent behind the bar is a calendar displaying the date 1887—March 22.

Sprawled on benches and crowding the tables are German sailors, grass-skirted island girls, natives, white traders—Herr Brandeis among them.

Brandeis sways to his feet, gesturing his glass. *"Hoch!"* he is shouting in German. "Come on, everybody. *Hoch der Kaiser!"*

Everybody whistles, stamps, pounds the table, and hochs.

"Sing!" Brandeis bawls. "The 'Watch on the Rhine!' We show Apia we Germans know how to celebrate the Emperor's birthday."

The sailors lunge to their feet . . . Brandeis leads the chorus. " 'A peal like thunder calls the brave'—"

Then a shouted oath. A scuffle. Somebody has jostled somebody. Or one of the natives, who doesn't realize the Kaiser's birthday is to be taken as an international holiday like Christmas, has failed to stand up. Or perhaps he didn't just "hoch" loud enough.

At any rate, a native is knocked down. In a twinkling the room is a fighting uproar. Glasses, fists, oaths, bottles are flying.

And then Becker, the German consul, appears in the doorway. In his fist he clutches a service pistol. His voice bellows into the bedlam.

"Achtung! What is the meaning of this riot!"

A native tries to explain. The German sailors shout him down, and there is planter Brandeis, front and center, shouting accusations.

"These Samoan boys started it. Refused to hoch the Kaiser. They're Malietoa's men! They mean to start an insurrection!"

"Insurrection?" Consul Becker thunders. *"Himmelherrgott!* It will be stamped out immediately! It is time we showed these Samoans how we Germans can rule. We will teach Malietoa to defy the Emperor on his birthday! Hereafter Tamasese is king!"

There is a clatter of hobnails as the police guard arrives. Several of the Samoan boys are hustled off to the stockade. The brawl is over. The Germans resume their drinking, hoching, and singing.

This is the big insurrection—the episode recorded in history as "the Affair of the Emperor's Birthday"—officially described by Becker as *the trampling upon of the Kaiser by Malietoa.*

And no one, of course, can trample on a German ruler. As you will see after a brief lowering of the curtain to indicate an interval of four months.

The date is now August 1887 as the curtain rises on Apia. Where a single warship had been before, there are now five gray warships strung across the roadstead. Flying against the sky, a whole flock of black German eagles.

A native crowd swarming on the waterfront mutters ominously. Fishermen come running in from the beach to join them. A young beach boy, shaking his fist above his head, begins a

speech. Abruptly he breaks off. The crowd is suddenly still as Brandeis, the German planter, enters the scene. The German planter no longer wears a sun helmet and tropical drill. Marching forwards, he appears in the uniform of a Prussian artillery officer, complete with medals. He is followed by a squad of natives in German uniform. Waving a pistol, he scatters the Samoans with a shout. Then he marches his squad to the warehouse where he runs up the German flag.

His men tramp across the compound and begin to tack up posters and proclamations in German. These are headed, *"Achtung!—Verboten!—By the authority of the Imperial German Government!"*

Now you hear a distant drum. It is echoed by another. Off-stage somewhere there is a rifle shot. The insurrection is on.

Officer Brandeis orders his men into the warehouse. And as the curtain falls, they reappear, dragging behind them a small field gun.

There will be another brief interlude to permit a change of scene.

Scene 3

The time: a few months later. The scene: Washington, D. C. On stage: President Cleveland and his cabinet.

Stout, with thinning hair and untrimmed gray moustache, this one-time Sheriff of Buffalo, N. Y.—so kindly a sheriff that he couldn't bear to see a man hanged—this American who chews tobacco and wears suspenders, is quite a contrast to such a fellow as Bismarck.

"A public office is a public trust." That's Grover Cleveland.

A kind-hearted sheriff, yes. But today, conferring with the members of his cabinet, his eyes are stern. He is discussing the situation in Samoa.

He shows the report from the American consul at Pago Pago. Points to the news from Berlin. The Germans have arrested King Malietoa and are holding him prisoner aboard a warship. The German Pacific Squadron is steaming for Apia. A Samoan beach boy named Metaafa is raising a guerrilla band to oppose German occupation What can those islanders with clubs and fish-spears do against German naval guns? Here is another note from Bismarck proclaiming Apia German territory. There is fighting in Samoa.

The President's cabinet members listen gravely.

Then the Secretary of State points out that the Germans, breaking the three-way Samoan agreement, are trying to put over what diplomats call a *fait accompli*—"an accomplished thing." (This is a fancy way of saying, "Now that I've done it, it's too late for you to do anything about it.") As far as America and Britain are concerned, this is a deliberate breach of trust. Samoa has great strategic value as a naval base, and the Germans obviously intend to seize the islands. Great Britain, however, is keeping hands off. Bismarck's attitude is threatening. Any action on America's part may start a war between the United States and Germany.

Cleveland nods. The German move is cleverly timed. It is an American election year. And with the public eye on the Presidential race and the administration slated to change, it is no time for a war in the Pacific. What of the American Navy? Is it prepared?

Secretary of the Navy Whitney informs him there are several warships at Pearl Harbor in Hawaii. On maneuvers in the Pacific are *Trenton, Vandalia,* and *Nipsic* under Rear Admiral Kimberly—out-dated wooden vessels of the steam-and-sail type. The warship nearest Samoa is a small gunboat, the *Adams.*

Grover Cleveland, President of the United States and Commander-in-Chief of the U. S. Navy, makes his decision with firmness.

"Our warships will proceed to Samoa."

The curtain lowers for the setting of the final scene.

Scene 4

The time: December 1888. The scene: the island of Upolu in the Samoan group. You see a panorama of the islands—the Port of Apia with its semicircular bay and harbor-mouth flanked by coral reefs—hilly interior, and several miles of palm-fringed beach.

Cruising along the coast are three German men-of-war—*Olga*,

Eber, and *Adler*—their decks stripped for action. The tompions are out of their gun-muzzles now.

A salvo booms across the water and echoes through the hills like a thunderstorm. Crump! Smoke swells up among the thatched native huts and drifts sluggishly over the palms. Crump! Crump! Crump! The warships are shelling the beach.

Now tenders loaded with German sailors are advancing through the surf, heading for shore. The oars quicken as the tenders draw in. But just as the landing parties reach the sand, a sharp volley of gunfire roars from the palm thickets. Another volley. Then a shower of darts and spears. The sailors break, reform their lines, and charge the thickets, shouting.

Firing from ambush, the natives drive them back. The Germans charge again and again. Finally, the Germans ebb back to their warships leaving behind their dead and wounded. The Emperor has been "trampled upon" to the extent of fifty casualties.

By way of reprisal, the warships steam into line, and begin an indiscriminate bombardment of the island. Native huts blaze up like bonfires. Soon the whole jungle will be aflame

Then the German lookouts are surprised to see a smear of smoke come around a distant point of land. The smudge grows. A warship traveling under forced draught!

And here comes *U.S.S. Adams,* Captain Leary, full speed into the battle scene! The Germans signal the American to stay clear. Not Leary. He takes his signals from Washington. Right on course he stays, driving the little gunboat on a bee-line between the German squadron and the shore.

Down the line goes *Adams* while the German captains sputter and hold their fire. Then, as the German guns open up again, *Adams* circles hard about and comes back.

Down the line Leary takes the gunboat. Right in the groove. He knows the Germans won't dare put a shot through the flag flown by *U.S.S. Adams.* Knows they won't take the risk. Leary has his orders, and he carries them out

And the German naval bombardment dies out. The German officers, too, have their instructions. Bismarck has not yet decided to tackle America.

Guns silent, the warships troop back to Apia.

The curtain lowers to indicate a lapse of two months. And now when it rises again on the harbor of Apia there are more naval vessels on the scene. The date is March 15, 1889.

Anchored in mid harbor, the German warships, *Olga*, *Adler*, and *Eber*, are all but surrounded. At anchorage off *Olga's* stern lies the American cruiser, *Nipsic*. Lying off *Adler's* port bow, and blocking the channel ahead of *Eber*, is *H.M.S. Calliope*. And in the harbor mouth, at anchor, are the American cruisers *Trenton* and *Vandalia*.

No gunfire shatters the shore line now. Once more the Samoan Islands are under a three-way "trusteeship." Apia is quiet. Perhaps too quiet. The stillness is like a drawn breath. There is something in the atmosphere, something electric. Things can happen in this hush.

In Washington, London, Berlin the newspapers talk of war clouds—the "Samoan Crisis." Will Bismarck back down? No one knows the Iron Chancellor's intentions. He has been weighing the situation, balancing German sea power against that of his opponents. *Olga*, *Adler*, *Eber* are powerful vessels—*H.M.S. Calliope* is small.

But the climax that breaks is one beyond even Bismarck's calculations. Darkening skies. Wind from the sea. A scudding rainsquall. Waves piling over the coral reefs. Apia is struck by a hurricane without precedent in island history.

All day and all night the terrific tempest blows. And in the morning *Eber* is lodged on a reef, *Olga* is dragging her anchor toward a pounding shoal, *Adler* is high on a shelf of coral. The American cruiser *Nipsic* is on the rocks, *Trenton* and *Vandalia* are dragging their anchors, drifting shoreward. *H.M.S. Calliope*, steam up in new engines, is fighting to buck the hurricane and escape seaward.

The Yankees cheer as the Britishers work *Calliope* out through the coral jaws of the harbor. No such escape is possible for the Americans. Titanic seas are booming in, and the elderly ships are unable to make headway. *Vandalia*, her engines gasping, is driven down the bay and forced ashore not far from *Nipsic* where the surf threatens to break her back. Floundering in this melee of wind and water, *Trenton* loses her rudder and both propellers, then is rammed by the German, *Olga*.

Restored calm sees the three old American vessels on the rocks; only the German cruiser *Olga* remains afloat.

Plunging into the sea, the Samoans are rescuing many exhausted survivors. Thanks to these dauntless natives, and the resourcefulness and courage of *Trenton's* men, the American fatalities have been limited to fifty-three.

Ninety-one Germans are drowned. Drowned, too, is their Pacific squadron and Bismarck's plot to seize Samoa.

However, the Samoan natives, so recently bombarded by the German Navy, are making a human chain out into the surf to rescue the German sailors.

Curtain!

Between the Acts

The hurricane which wrecked the antiquated American squadron at Samoa gave the whole U. S. Navy a shake-up. Make your navy a first-class navy, for a second-rate navy is no navy at all —only a risky bluff too likely to be called, inviting quick defeat and disaster. This was the advice of Captain Alfred T. Mahan who, throughout the 1880's, was lecturing at the new Naval War College. A writer and a student of naval warfare, Mahan, in 1890, published his famous book, *The Influence of Sea Power Upon History*. The work had historic influence.

For one thing, it called attention to the Navy's needs. It also aroused the Navy, emphasizing the value of mental as well as physical training. Mahan's work marked the final transition from sail to steam, not only in naval construction but in naval thinking. No longer would the Navy be regarded as a shore-hugging shield for coastal defense, or an arm for raids on enemy commerce. The best time to stop an attack was before it arrived on this side of the ocean—the Navy must go out and "meet it half way." These were some of the conclusions to be drawn from Mahan's writing.

So the building program begun under Cleveland went forward. America began to look out across the Pacific and Atlantic.

The Navy had been operating around Midway Island as early as 1870. Five years later a treaty was negotiated with the natives of Hawaii. In 1884 Pearl Harbor was granted the U. S. as a naval station. These islands were stepping stones to China and Australia, where American commerce was thriving.

Trouble developed in Hawaii in 1893 when a native princess assumed power and disputed the American treaty rights. Benjamin Harrison was President at this time, and his minister in Hawaii encouraged American residents to back a local revolution with the idea of annexing Hawaii to the United States. But Grover Cleveland, elected President for another term, canceled this scheme. It was a little too "imperialistic" for the forthright mind of Cleveland. But when the Hawaiian government, established under Cleveland's guidance, soon failed, annexation became the only practical solution. Similarly there was one practical solution in the case of Cuba and the Philippines, long troubled by the tyrannical misrule of Spain.

And this brings you up to Act II in this drama of sea power. The Spanish-American War—

ACT II—BLOOD AND SAND

You can now watch a drama that begins in 1870, but historically goes back to the time of Christopher Columbus.

Spain ruled Cuba with the hand of the despot. Old-world inefficiency and corrupt domination in the Caribbean gave Americans grave concern. Cuba turned and twisted and struggled in anguish, appealing for liberty, and as early as 1850 there were many Americans who believed it would be a neighborly act to set the island free. In 1870 the Cuban troubles worsened, and the American Government protested. There was no reason for Spain to keep this Caribbean island in an uproar. No reason for the Spaniards to rule Cuba as they ruled her in 1500.

From 1868 to 1878 the island was bloodied by savage warfare between Cubans and their Spanish overlords. An American schooner, *Virginius*, was seized by a Spanish gunboat off Havana. Arms were found aboard, and the schooner was pronounced a gun-smuggler. Perhaps she was. But, swearing they had no knowledge of the ship's cargo, eight American sailors were shot dead by a Spanish firing squad. President Grant threatened immediate intervention unless the Spanish government revised its quick-triggered policy.

Promise was given, but not kept. The plantation of an American was seized by the Spanish Army. In Havana other Americans were beaten up. Then two American tourists, lost in the Cuban jungle, were shot as "spies" by the Spaniards—apology with bows, but nothing more. Meantime Morro Castle and other prisons were crammed with Cuban patriots.

In 1895 Spain sent General Weyler to chastise the island. Concentration camps were set up, plantations confiscated, and firing squads worked overtime. When American property was seized, President William McKinley protested to Madrid, and the odious Weyler was recalled. But his successor, Blanco, was no less harsh. Spaniards in Havana incited anti-American riots. In January, 1898, the American battleship *Maine* was ordered to Havana to protect American citizens.

It wasn't the time for DeLome, the Spanish Ambassador in Washington, to write a letter to an editor in Madrid describing McKinley as a cheap, vacillating politician. The letter was uncovered, quoted in the New York press, and caused a lot of indignation. DeLome resigned as tension grew.

Then, just as the situation seemed quieting, came the explosion.

On the evening of February 15, 1898, *Maine* was swinging around the hook at her anchorage in Havana harbor. Taps echoed through the dusk. Captain Sigsbee was writing a report in his cabin.

Then, suddenly, the cabin wall buckled at Sigsbee's elbow, and a blood-smeared sailor stumbled blindly along the outer passage. Captain Sigsbee staggered out on deck. The battleship's fore-end was blown to rubbish, smoke poured from her hatchways, and she was sinking.

Taps for *U.S.S. Maine.* Among her 353 men there were 305 casualties.

Remember the Maine!

Madrid sent a board of inquiry. The Spanish officers boated out to the wreck, scrutinized the hulk through an underwater glass, and quickly announced the blast was "internal." That meant that *Maine's* powder magazines had blown by accident, and the disaster was due to improper stowage or faulty munitions. America's responsibility.

The American commission brought divers. They examined the submerged wreck on the bottom. Worked for a month. Came up with the decision that *Maine* had been blasted "externally" by some sort of submarine mine. Spain's responsibility.

A mine? The Spanish officials were horrified. Impossible!

But *Maine's* forward magazines, which had been blasted, contained only an old type of brown powder, a type chemically stable. There was no instance on record of such powder exploding by itself. High explosives in *Maine's* after magazines did not go off. Also the buckled plates on the ship's bottom indicated an external blast, whereas an internal blast would have blown them outward.

Then, cried the Spanish, the mine was planted by Cuban insurrectos—deliberately—to bring America into war.

Far-fetched. The shabby, ill-equipped Cubanos, watched closely by the Spanish, could hardly have towed a large mine into Havana harbor and sunk it close to *Maine*, under the eyes of the American watch. Yet the American naval commission, still bending backwards, refused to blame the Spaniards for planting the mine. (Mine explosion was established beyond doubt in 1912 when the ship was raised, re-examined, towed out to sea, and sunk with military honors.)

But the explosion had finished something more than an American battleship. It had finished America's tolerance for Spanish tyranny in Cuba. A Spanish mine or not, it was touched off by the violence with which Spain had ruled Cuba. On April 19, 1898, Congress voted Cuba an independent state, and on April 25th the United States declared war.

Dewey Goes to Manila

European "experts" thought America was bound to lose. They spoke of poor American gunnery, a fleet designed for coastal defense, battleships second-rate—and only four of them, at that. They totalled 86 American warships as against Spain's registered 137. Spain had culture, pride, centuries of experience. Americans were undisciplined, used slang, and chewed cut-plug—said the "experts."

The "experts" overlooked Mahan and the new naval strategy. They didn't know Sampson, Schley, and Commodore George Dewey. They hadn't heard of that energetic Assistant Secretary of the Navy, Theodore Roosevelt.

Singing "Hot Time In the Old Town Tonight," American troops in khaki and blue entrained for Florida.

In far-off 'Frisco, *U.S.S. Oregon* began a race around the Horn that was to break all existing Navy records.

Rear Admiral William T. Sampson, leaving a reserve force called the "Flying Squadron" under Commodore Winfield S. Schley at Hampton Roads, directed the Atlantic Fleet out of Key West. Reports had it that a Spanish fleet under Admiral Cervera had just left the Cape Verde Islands and was coming across the Atlantic to shoot America's eastern seaboard into submission. Sampson proposed to intercept this armada head-on.

Meantime in the far Pacific, Commodore Dewey awaited orders at Hongkong. His Asiatic squadron—cruisers *Olympia, Raleigh, Boston, Baltimore,* and gunboats *Petrel* and *Concord*—stripped for action. Orders came. He was to find and destroy the squadron of Admiral Montojo based in the Spanish Philippines.

Mild-mannered, with fatherly white moustache, Dewey didn't give the appearance of a hard-hitter. Never mind. He'd trained under Farragut, and he could hit when necessary, as he'd proved twelve years previously as commander of *U.S.S. Pensacola.*

There'd been mutiny up forward, and Dewey, wearing two pistols, had faced the men to call the roll. John Johnson, the first name called, refused to answer.

"Johnson, I see you," Dewey announced. *"I'll call your name once more, and if you don't go on deck you'll be a dead man."*

Again Johnson's name, and no response. Dewey shot at once, and the man fell. Then roll-call went on, and everyone answered.

No, the European "experts" didn't know Dewey. But his men did, and he knew them. He also knew the Spanish. In the year he'd been on Asiatic duty, he'd studied every book, chart, and news item he could find concerning the Spanish Navy and the Philippines.

Spain was boasting of her prowess in Asia. Montojo's squadron was touted, and the Spanish-Philippine defenses loudly advertised. Manila Bay was planted with mines. Land fortifications would blast Dewey's squadron to bits. Montojo's fleet would wreck the "Yanqui fools." At Manila the Spanish Captain-General issued a proclamation calling the Americans "too contemptible to fight." And the Archbishop of Manila issued a statement in the churches declaring that the United States had begged the Pope to intervene and save the Americans from Spain's vengeance.

Midnight, April 30, Dewey's squadron was off El Fraile rock at the entrance to Manila Bay. Forward went the squadron in pitch blackness, Dewey thinking of his training under Farragut —damn the torpedoes.

When all but the rear ships were past the rock, El Fraile fired one futile shot that passed between *Petrel* and *Raleigh*. *Raleigh* answered with a 5-incher, and the Spanish battery was silenced. Safe inside Manila Bay (no torpedoes as yet) the American squadron calmly anchored, and the gunners slept by their guns.

At 0500 Manila came to view in morning mists, and in a few minutes the Spanish batteries at Cavite opened fire. Montojo was at the end of the bay, and Dewey sailed straight for the Spanish ships, keeping his gunners ready.

Spanish shots were falling wild, but as *Olympia* drew on, a few rounds splashed off the bow. Impatient, the Yankee gunners set their teeth.

At 0542 Dewey turned to *Olympia's* captain with that famous remark, *"You may fire when you are ready, Gridley,"* and Gridley was ready. *Olympia's* guns boomed a broadside. Broadsides from *Raleigh, Boston,* and *Baltimore.* Fire from *Petrel* and *Concord.* All in line the ships let go, moving calmly down the bay, then circling and coming back up-bay, like a parade.

Five times the maneuver was repeated while the Spanish ships fired furiously and wildly in return. On the third round, the Spanish warship *Don Juan de Austria* came rushing out on a desperate attempt to ram *Olympia. Don Juan* got shot to pieces for the pains. Then the Spanish flagship *Reina Cristina* made a similar frenzied attack, only to get a terrible blasting from Dewey's 8-inch guns.

By 0700 the thing was absolute carnage. *Reina Cristina, Don Juan, Isla de Cuba, Castilla*—all the heavy Spanish ships were knocked out. Dewey steamed out of range and calmly ordered breakfast for his men.

One Spanish ship remained—*Ulloa*—hiding behind Sangley Point. Dewey's gunners sank her after breakfast.

During the morning the desperate Spaniards scuttled their few remaining ships. There was some ineffective fire from the forts. At 1230 it was all over.

To this day the score remains unbelievable. The Spanish had lost every ship at Manila. Out of 1200 men, 381 were killed or wounded. Not a single American vessel was damaged. Not a man under Dewey was seriously hurt. One American—an engineer—had died of heat-stroke.

The Battle of Santiago

Oregon, under Captain George Clark, raced around South America to join Schley's "Flying Squadron" at Hampton Roads. Hers was a fireroom saga—a story of the men below-decks, of new marine engines, new and highly-trained engineers.

Off Rio, she picked up the old gunboat, *Nitcheroy*, and word of the battle in the Philippines. The Brazilians were sad about the reports just in from Spain. Montojo had won at Manila. Dewey's squadron had been massacred. And Cervera was on the Atlantic with a giant fleet, threatening to destroy the U. S. Navy.

Her up-and-downs hammering, *Oregon* raced on. At Barbadoes, halting for stores, Clark learned Cervera was in the Caribbean, seeking battle. *Oregon* went racing through the West Indies, dodged into Key West, and there learned the truth. Dewey had won. It was the U. S. Navy that was going places!

The "scare-head" news heard at Rio was typical war reporting of the time. Madrid, of course, was one source. Another was a New York "yellow journal" which faked a Sunday extra featuring a great battle in mid-Atlantic. Dewey's tremendous victory at Manila made these scare-sheets a laughing stock, and the one which faked the Atlantic battle became nicknamed the "one-cent liar."

Cervera's sea force consisted of four armored cruisers, three torpedo-boat destroyers, three smaller vessels, and an auxiliary. The cruisers were *Infanta Maria Teresa* (flagship), *Vizcaya*, *Almirante Oquendo*, and *Cristobal Colon*. Modern ships with six-inch belt armor, they seemed formidable enough. But *Colon*, the newest, was typical of the Spanish Navy. In her forward and after turrets the gun-ports were vacant. Someone, it seemed, had forgotten to install her big guns.

This was the armada that came steaming across the Atlantic to be joined by the old cruiser *Reina Mercedes*, waiting in Cuba. *Mercedes*, however, was unable to make rendezvous. Her engines were too rusty to move her.

Instead of rushing north to attack the American coast, Cervera took his men-o'-war south to the Dutch island of Curacao where coaling arrangements had presumedly been made. Arriving in Curacao, the Spanish admiral was shocked to discover that Madrid had failed to make the arrangements—no coal. This forced him to go to Santiago, Cuba, where fuel might be obtained. There in Santiago harbor he was sighted by the scouts of Schley's "Flying Squadron" which had come down to Cuba for a look-see.

Cervera couldn't have sailed into a better snare. With its long, bottleneck entrance and hill-surrounded bay, the harbor of Santiago made a perfect trap, and the Spanish ships were shut in. Schley's squadron rushed to plug the bottle-mouth with a tight blockade. Sampson, advised of this incredible catch, raced the main body of the American fleet to join Schley's force. Cervera was netted. All that remained was to take him out of the trap and put him in the bag.

But the narrow entrance was heavily mined and guarded by fortifications. Sampson decided to cork the bottle-neck by sinking a hulk in the channel. On June 3rd, after four days of blockade, Naval-instructor Hobson with seven volunteers took the collier *Merrimac* into the narrows under cover of night. But moonlight betrayed the enterprise, and the Spanish batteries opened fire.

The Spanish marksmanship was so foul that fourteen of their own gunners were slain in the cross-fire, and not a man on *Merrimac* was hit. The collier's rudder was struck, however, and she drifted too far down-channel. Hobson sparked the explosives, nevertheless, and pulled away on a raft with his men to surrender to Cervera. It was a daring exploit which inclined Cervera to a mood of pessimism.

So Cervera sat inside, and Sampson and Schley sat outside—waiting. For a month the stalemate continued. Then the Americans determined to break it. It was decided that the Army, arriving under General Shafter, should land at Daiquiri, a few miles east, and circle behind Santiago to take the harbor from the rear. The troops gained the beachhead and advanced rapidly, only to be stopped in Santiago's outskirts by desperate Spanish resistance. Teddy Roosevelt led his Rough Riders in a fierce charge up San Juan Hill, but there the campaign bogged. Fever and poor supply hampered the Americans as much as enemy fire. General Shafter, a man of enormous girth, became ill and discouraged, and informed the Navy that his troops were stalled.

Had Cervera decided to sit it out, the story might have run a few more installments. Instead, the Spanish admiral made one of the worst blunders in military history.

On the morning of July 3rd, a Sunday, Admiral Sampson aboard his flagship, *New York*, steamed out of the blockading line and moved four miles down the coast to hold conference with Shafter. Ranged off Santiago, the rest of Sampson's fleet was in semi-circle—battleships, *Indiana*, *Iowa*, *Oregon*, *Texas*, Commodore Schley's cruiser, *Brooklyn*, and gunboat *Vixen*.

Sunday services were in order. Inspection. Then, a little after 0930, *Iowa's* lookout sighted a Spanish warship emerging from the narrows. Cervera's flagship was coming out!

General alarm rang through the *Iowa*. Her captain, "Fighting Bob" Evans, raced out on the bridge. Once, with one ship, he had faced (and offered to take on) the whole fleet of hostile Chile in the harbor of Valparaiso. But he'd never seen a sight like this.

Her battle-flags hoisted, her ensign flying red-and-gold, out of Santiago's harbor mouth steamed *Infanta Maria Teresa*. Behind her came *Vizcaya*, *Almirante Oquendo*, and *Cristobal Colon*, all in line. It was fantastic. Incredible. Like a sea-going circus procession. And plain suicide! For every American warship could see the advancing Spaniards, and every American sailor raced to his battle station.

What induced Cervera to make this move? An order from

Madrid? The "heat" on Santiago? Some silly idea about his Spanish "honor!". Doubtless all these factors were involved, but Cervera was aware of impending doom.

Teresa's Captain Concas requested the Admiral's permission to open fire. Cervera nodded, and bugles trumpeted the order.

"My bugles were the last echo, a signal that four centuries of greatness was ended," Captain Concas mourned afterward. *" 'Poor Spain!' I said to my beloved and noble Admiral, and he answered by an expressive motion."*

So Don Quixote, the mad Spanish knight, once rushed out to duel with windmills. But the American warships were no windmills. Thundering salvos answered *Teresa's* fire. The Spanish ships turned west, moving at forced draught. Closing in at tangent, the American ships raced to cut them off.

In the smoke-haze and excitement *Brooklyn,* trying to head off *Teresa,* cut across *Texas'* bow and was nearly rammed. For a moment it looked as if the Spaniards might get away. But deadly American gunnery found range and stayed on target, and hits began to stagger the Spanish ships.

Teresa, with wooden decks, was first to go, bursting into an inferno of flames. After a six mile run she veered in and went ashore, a total wreck full of dead and dying. With boats smashed, those able, including Cervera, swam dolefully in to the beach.

Then *Oquendo,* pounded by *Iowa,* was beached in a shroud of flames.

Vizcaya, overhauled by *Brooklyn, Oregon,* and *Iowa,* was soon another molten furnace. She tried to fight, but her guns jammed, firing mechanisms failed, breechblocks refused to close, and a boiler in the fire-room burst. She fired one shot at *Brooklyn*, which killed a seaman. Then she foundered.

Colon, newest and fastest, was last to die. Pursued by *Brooklyn*, *Oregon*, and *Texas*, she ran fifty miles before she fell under range of *Oregon's* 13-inch guns. With her own big guns somewhere in Spain, she was an empty holster. Her captain headed shoreward and rammed her into the beach.

It was early afternoon. Spain's Navy was no more.

Remember the words of Admiral Dewey, *"It was the ceaseless routine of hard work and preparation in time of peace that won Manila and Santiago."*

Grand Finale

Santiago fell on July 17th. After Cuba and her sister island, Puerto Rico, meant only a mop-up operation.

The Philippine Islands were not that easy. Dewey blockaded Manila with his squadron while Generals Merrit and Otis landed 10,000 men to occupy Luzon. Spanish resistance ended on August 13, 1898, when Madrid sued for peace. Then warfare continued against the savage Moros and the Filipino guerilla-leader, Aguinaldo.

This proved a long and difficult struggle. On March 31, 1899, General Arthur MacArthur captured Aguinaldo's capital in the interior, but the Moros were not put down until 1902. (General MacArthur, by the way, found time to raise a son named General MacArthur. Recognize the name?)

So the Philippines came under the Stars and Stripes, but there was a moment when they were shadowed by another flag. Your Navy had seen this flag before at Samoa.

It came over the horizon in mid-June of '98, at the time Dewey was blockading Manila and awaiting the arrival of American troops. The black eagles sailed into the scene, and there, without so much as a pleasant "good day" was a German squadron under Vice Admiral von Diederichs.

Now there are certain international rules which govern waters under blockade. Neutral ships, particularly warships, are supposed to respect them. British, French, and Japanese warships

349

were at Manila when the Spanish-American War began, and these retired to outer anchorages, respecting Dewey's declared blockade.

Von Diederichs snapped his fingers at the rules. With German cruisers *Irene* and *Cormoran*, and his flagship, *Kaiserin Augusta*, the vice admiral coolly anchored between Dewey's ships and the shore.

Dewey paid the German an official call to remind him that Manila was blockaded. Von Diederichs' answer was gruff.

"I am here by order of the Kaiser, sir."

Dewey, who took his orders from the U.S.A., advised Von Diederichs to anchor elsewhere. Instead of that, the Germans began to signal to the Spanish forts at night and steer their launches in the way of the American patrols. Finally they openly sent supplies to the Spaniards.

Dewey tossed a verbal message to the German admiral's aide.

"Tell the Admiral I am blockading here. I am tired of the character of his conduct. Make no mistake when I say it will mean war. You may tell him that if he wants a fight he may have it right now."

The admiral's aide delivered the message. Von Diederichs sent a query to Captain Chichester, commander of the British squadron on hand, asking what the English would do if the Germans defied Dewey. The English commander made frank reply. He simply moved his British warships to an anchorage between the American and German ships, and then the British bands played "The Star Spangled Banner."

This concert was too much for Admiral von Diederichs. His black German eagles folded their wings, and *Irene*, *Cormoran*, and the *Kaiserin* quietly stole away. Once more the U.S.A. had called Germany's bluff.

The Spanish-American War gives you another exhibit of forward-marching American democracy. Despite demands for annexation from some quarters, despite a few who wished to profit from the victory, the American people demanded that the Cubans and Filipinos be allowed to build their own self-governments.

Cuba was set up as a Republic. American military missions co-operated with the Cuban leaders, and the work of the medical commission, in which a group of enlisted men volunteered to risk their lives in experiments to uncover the source of yellow fever, resulted in ridding the islands of that murderous disease. Freed of Spanish misrule and "Yellow Jack," Cuba was truly liberated.

The Philippines, too, were promised complete independence. But events intervened to delay the date. Out-faced by Dewey, the Prussian war lords did not tear up their plans. Rather, they tore up another treaty, calling it a "scrap of paper."

In the next chapter you will see how American democracy, with the Navy as its spear-head, frustrated this tyrannical move.

HARD WORK AND PREPARATION WON

World War I

Someone once said victory depends on what has been done before the fight begins. With sea fights as with prizefights, the winner is the combatant who has kept in condition and has had superior training.

The kayo delivered by your Navy in the Spanish-American War clearly illustrates the point. In weight, the contestants were fairly matched. But the Spanish Navy was like a former champion gone soft. The Spaniards lost every round because they were out of condition and hadn't trained.

By contrast, the U. S. Navy was ready to go at the bell, trained to a hair. Doubt about the outcome may have been cherished by the Old World "experts," but there was no doubt at all in the mind of Admiral Stephen B. Luce, USN. He knew. He had trained that fighting Navy.

He began it early in the 1880's. In that era of side-wheelers and side-whiskers, Luce was as forward-looking as a telescope— one of the few Navy officers to see that ships which operated by steam needed sailors who could use their heads as well as their hands.

In the old days any bucko who would pull a rope could learn seamanship. Any Jack capable of lighting a match could learn gunnery. A sailor might learn his lessons the hard way at "rope's end," or he might learn simply by watching his mates. But steam navigation and the new high-powered guns demanded head-work. This called for training methods of high caliber. Mental agility could not be acquired "monkey see, monkey do."

So Luce launched a bluejackets' training program. He established schools for enlisted men aboard ship, introducing courses in English, math, geography. He organized training cruises and devised war games, certain that the seamen as well as the officers would surely get a kick out of sham battles and competitive maneuvers.

All work and no play made Jack a dull sailor, so Luce campaigned for sports in the Navy and went all out for fencing matches, baseball, boxing. Convinced morale was vitally important, he gave the men good books for sparetime reading, installed bands aboard warships, and sponsored minstrel shows and song fests.

The Navy soon recognized the value of this kind of training, and Luce was given a free hand. The question is: How did it suit the enlisted men?

Well, back in the old days a Navy seaman was a pretty rough, tough customer. In battle he was as brave as they came, but he seldom knew or cared what the war was about, and he was apt to manufacture his own in the first port of call. Ashore he was either spending his last dime or flopping around like a fish out of water.

For milder recreations he skipped rope and danced the hornpipe. Socially speaking he ate with his knife. And literally. As late as 1864 a sailor sat cross-legged on deck with an oilcloth apron in his lap, munching his hard tack and salt horse.

Now Luce changed the picture. Sailors began to think—and act accordingly. Spare time went into reading, study, self-improvement. Spare money went into the bank. Sailor manners (and sailor morals) improved. Laying the foundation for the fine educational program you enjoy in the Navy today, Luce turned Jack into a better sea fighter, a better citizen, and a better man. And the Navy, stepping out of its 1870 decline, was able to knock the enemy in '98 harder and colder than a frozen catfish.

But Old Spain was not in good condition. What would happen if the Navy came up against a harder-boiled opponent?

The Navy made the most of the time remaining before the next big fight—World War I. And by 1914 your Navy had made many improvements.

Brains + bravery + brawn—if anything takes that combination, it's the submarine service. In the slump which followed the Civil War, the Navy forgot about submarines. But in 1887 naval engineers began to dust the cobwebs off the idea. After all, little *David* and *C.S.S. Hunley* had put two warships out of action. Moreover, European navies were experimenting with undersea boats.

Consequently the Navy Department advertised for bids on the construction of "one submarine, complete with torpedo appendages." Specifications called for a vessel capable of 15 knots on the surface, 8 knots submerged, a diving depth of 150 feet, and security for at least three hours' stay under water.

Twelve years later the U. S. Navy had its first submarine, *U.S.S. Holland*. Built in Baltimore, she more than met the requirements, and carried one torpedo tube. Her first CO was Lieutenant H. H. Caldwell, USN. Used for training at Annapolis, she performed successfully, and seven more submarines (120-tonners) were added to the Navy by 1903.

Twenty larger submarines, the biggest a 400-tonner, were completed by 1911, and the Navy's "Silent Service" was fully launched. Volunteer crews manned this submarine flotilla, which had as its head an up-and-coming young lieutenant destined to be known all over the sea as well as under it. His name? Lieutenant Chester W. Nimitz, USN.

Meantime the surface fleet was getting some brightening. Decisive as was the kayo delivered Spain in '98, the operation at Santiago had not been flawless. *Brooklyn* had almost rammed *Texas*, and some of the shooting could have been better. An unfortunate dispute developed between Admiral Sampson and Commodore Schley. A court of inquiry criticized Schley. Then Theodore Roosevelt, who had become President after the assassination of William McKinley, decided after reviewing the evidence that there hadn't been complete cooperation at Santiago and that the battle had turned into an old-style "captain's fight."

Obviously the fleet needed more schooling in the new tactics and strategy. Deplorable as was the Schley-Sampson controversy, it showed that the Navy as a national organization was not above public criticism nor disposed to conceal flaws from itself.

Of course, the speaker who criticizes should know his stuff, and offer constructive criticism—something beyond mere fault-finding or complaint. Such a critic was Lieutenant William S. Sims, a young officer out on China Station in 1901.

Previously a naval attache at Paris and St. Petersburg—and in charge of secret service in Spain, Russia, and Italy—Sims had become acutely interested in naval gunnery. Comparison of records convinced him that American gunnery was not yet up to par, and while in China he devoted much study to the matter.

The North Atlantic Fleet, out for target practice, had made a shabby record firing at a range of 2800 yards. Young Sims, reading the report out in China, was surprised to notice that it went unremarked. He had written several letters to the Navy Department on the need for improved ordnance and marksmanship, and now he wrote another. Like the others it was ignored. Finally Sims could stand it no longer, and risking his naval career on the certainty that he was right, he sent a letter direct to the President.

This letter, written in November 1901, caused a storm. But Sims had the courage of his convictions, and his convictions were 100% right. Furthermore, he suggested means of improvement. Teddy Roosevelt, demanding that he be given all of Sims' reports, ordered the fleet out for another target practice.

This showing was equally poor, only 13 hits per hundred when the Royal Navy was scoring 80 to 85.

"Cable to China and have that young man come home at once!" T. R. ordered. *"Give him entire charge of target practice for eighteen months. If he doesn't accomplish something in that time, cut off his head and try somebody else."*

Was Sims "decapitated"? For over six years he held the post of inspector of target practice, and in that time American gunners scored the world's record in marksmanship. Still the 90's weren't high enough for Sims. He wanted the score at 100. Detecting structual defects in the design of guns and battleships, he began another improvement campaign which called for dreadnaught-type ships to equal those of Britain. Soon after, dreadnaught construction was begun.

Meanwhile, the Navy was being readied for a big peace-time

venture—the world cruise of 1908. In December 1907, the fleet
set out under Rear Admiral (Fighting Bob) Evans.

Starting from Hampton Roads, it rounded the Horn to 'Frisco,
then cruised to Hawaii, Australia, the Philippines, Japan, the
China coast, and back home via the Mediterranean. The sixteen
battleships maneuvered expertly. No fleet had ever accomplished
such a cruise, and the whole world was impressed. Visiting Italy,
the American warships arrived at Messina just after a terrible
earthquake had devastated the city, and the bluejackets worked
valiantly to aid the stricken Italians.

Also impressed (but in another manner) were the rulers of
Germany and Japan. There had been pugnacious talk in Nippon
where the Sons of the Rising Sun were feeling their oats. And
now, having just dealt the navy of decadent Czarist Russia a
colossal defeat (after surprise attack in an undeclared war), the
Japanese militarists of 1907 were looking for other worlds to
conquer.

The German leaders, too, were seeking other worlds to conquer.
Germany now owned large African colonies. Making money
hand over fist, the German industrialists were prospering and
the nation was as well off as any in Europe. But the Junkers
weren't satisfied. They wanted Germany to be Mr. Big and
run the world.

Storm Warnings

With Germany on a military bandwagon, the other European
nations also began to arm. So began an armament race that

piled up guns and munitions all over the continent, with some of the arms manufacturers selling happily to everybody. In this military free-for-all, the national leaders maneuvered a series of secret treaties and alliances. Germany, Austria-Hungary, and Italy had formed the Triple Alliance under Bismarck in 1885. So France and Russia allied themselves in the 1890's. England, fearing the expanded German Navy, made an alliance with France. Jammed in south central Europe, the Balkan kingdoms were pressured into the rival camps, everybody choosing sides like boys in a sand lot going fist-over-fist up a baseball bat.

Despite a long-standing treaty with Belgium, German army engineers had deliberately built a number of military rail lines straight to the Belgium border. Similar railroads had been aimed like spears at Russia. German arms factories were working over-time. Thousands of reserves were being trained. And it was known that the German General Staff had devised a plan, known as the Schlieffen Plan—the plan of the "Swinging Door"—intending Belgium to be the hinge of a great invasion that would slam through France.

It was also known that Von Tirpitz, building a huge naval force, was concentrating on submarines. The North Sea approaches to Bremen and Hamburg had been mined. Big guns were installed at Helgoland. And while the Americans had been digging the Panama Canal, the Germans were working like beavers on the Kiel, or "Kaiser Wilhelm Canal"—a great canal system which connected Kiel and Wilhelmshaven. This canal was to make of the Helgoland-Bremen-Hamburg area a mammoth naval fortress. Certainly Germany was more than defensively prepared. It seems evident today that the Kaiser was only waiting for a signal, and Germany was ready to go.

In the American Navy, now including a force of 21 battleships and 15 armored cruisers, technical developments were being made. By 1903 a British officer had invented the "dummy loader;" the Navy was quick to adopt this device. To the Royal Navy the Americans were indebted for still another invention—the "dotter" which Yank gunners called the "ping-pong." If you never heard of it ask your gunner's mate pal about it. It works a little like those airplane-target gadgets you see in the penny arcades.

Telescopic sights, range finders, and centralized fire control were other innovations developed by the American Navy at this time. Many of these improvements were sponsored by Captain Sims, and they gave the Germans something to think about.

America had her eyes turned south rather than westward. With the Panama Canal a going concern, Uncle Sam had a special interest in the stability of Central America. There was trouble in Nicaragua in 1909 when hot-headed revolutionists executed two Americans. In 1912 a naval force was sent to Nicaragua to restore order.

UNCLE SAM—THAT'S A LIVE WIRE, GENTLEMEN!

Mexico, too, was suffering internally at this time. In 1911 the peons overthrew the aged dictator, Porfirio Diaz, and tried to set up a liberal government. Many Americans, sympathizing with the Mexican peons who had been living like penniless serfs, approved the revolution which intended to break up the great landed estates of the hidalgos. The revolutionary leader, Francisco Madero, a poetic idealist, was unable to put over these reforms. In 1913 the old ruling class, led by General Huerta, overthrew the liberal government. Madero was murdered.

Woodrow Wilson, newly elected President of the United States, refused to recognize Huerta's dictatorship. The Huerta reactionaries sneered at American democracy. Huerta's officers refused a salute to the flag, and in April 1914, an American Navy shore party, going about peaceful business in Tampico, was set upon and arrested.

A former college professor and a staunch liberal, Woodrow Wilson had been cartooned as a "pacifist." He did hate war— as any sensible, humane man would hate it—but now an aggressor had attacked. He immediately ordered the blockade of Mexican ports and the occupation of Vera Cruz. On April 21 the American fleet arrived at that hot spot, and Rear Admiral Fletcher sent a landing party to seize the port.

Sailors and Marines went in smartly; after four days of sharp fighting Vera Cruz was taken. Three South American countries offered their services as mediators to judge the situation and arrange a peaceful settlement. Wilson quickly accepted the offer, on condition the Americans could occupy Vera Cruz for six months. This cut off Huerta's forces from their main source of munition supply, and a little later Huerta fled the country.

Leader of the Mexican liberals, Carranza then became President, and was recognized by the American Government. But he had hardly taken office when one of his lieutenants, Pancho Villa, turned bandit and started a series of raids along the Mexican-American border. A skillful guerilla, as pesky as the cockroach of his bandit song, "La Cucaracha," Villa set out to plague Uncle Sam. American headlines featured the Rio Grande.

Then while this Mexican trouble was cooking, something happened in Europe.

In the Balkan city of Sarajevo, June 28, 1914, Gabriel Princip, a young Serbian student, inflamed with nationalism, assassinated Franz Ferdinand, the Austrian Crown Prince.

The bomb in Sarajevo blew the lid off Europe. Its fragments ricochetted as far east as China, as far west as Seattle. If that explosion in the Balkans did one thing, it proved that an event far off in a tiny corner of the globe could affect the lives and destinies of people thousands of miles away.

Americans didn't realize it, then. To most Americans the Balkans were as remote as the mountains of the moon. Whatever the trouble was, many Americans were sure it would blow over.

It didn't.

The Serbian Government denied responsibility for the slaying of the Austrian Archduke. It denounced the assassin as an irresponsible terrorist, and agreed to arrest any Serbian conspirators. But, pointing out that the slaying took place on

THE NEW YORK TIMES

NEW YORK, MONDAY, JUNE 29, 1914—EIGHTEEN PAGES.

**HEIR TO AUSTRIA'S THRONE IS SLAIN
WITH HIS WIFE BY A BOSNIAN YOUTH
TO AVENGE SEIZURE OF HIS COUNTRY**

Francis Ferdinand Shot
During State Visit
to Sarajevo.

TWO ATTACKS IN A DAY

Archduke Saves His Life First
Time by Knocking Aside
Bomb Hurled at Auto.

SLAIN IN SECOND ATTEMPT

Lad Dashes at Car as the Royal
Couple Return from Town Hall
and Kills Both of Them.

LAID TO A SERVIAN PLOT

Heir Warned Not to Go to Bos-
nia, Where Populace Met
Him with Servian Flags.

AGED EMPEROR IS STRICKEN

Archduke Francis Ferdinand and his Consort the Duchess of Hohenberg
Slain by Assassin's Bullets.

Austrian territory, Serbia, backed by Russia, refused to do more. Austria's first answer was mobilization, to punish the Serbian nation.

The vast Russian Army began to mobilize. This meant that if Austria attacked Serbia, the Russians would go to the help of their Slavic cousins by attacking Austria. So, Austria appealed to her ally, Germany. The Germans mobilized. The Kaiser's Government told the Czar's Government that any Russian move to aid Serbia would mean war between Germany and Russia. While the continent sweltered in the heat of July, 1914, millions of troops stood under arms, and Europe was on the brink.

Then, 28 July 1914, Austria declared war on Serbia.

Germany gave Russia twelve hours to demobilize, and when the ultimatum was disregarded, Germany declared war on Russia (August 1, 1914).

699197°—46—24

As France was bound in alliance with Russia, Germany declared war on France on August 3rd.

War's Beginning

Sir Edward Grey, British Foreign Minister, sadly remarked, *"The lights are going out all over Europe."* He was right. The Germans, according to plan, immediately attacked neutral Belgium, the German Chancellor scornfully calling the Belgian treaty a "scrap of paper." But the English, calling it a contract, held to their pledge. On August 4th, Great Britain declared war on Germany.

Note that Italy jumped the Triple Alliance and joined the Allies in 1915. Rumania joined the Allies a year later, after Bulgaria came in on the Germanic side (the Central Powers). In all Europe only Holland, Switzerland, the Scandinavian countries, and Spain managed to keep out of World War I.

The German generals never counted on the war's lasting until 1916—much less '17 and '18. They figured their immense army, their crack officers, and their scientific equipment, including newly invented machine guns, would make it a short war. That was their first miscalculation.

Their second miscalculation was a hitch in the "Swinging Door" plan. They figured they could invade Belgium without much opposition, swing rapidly down along the English Channel, and then slam the door on Paris before the French could successfully mobilize But the Belgians resisted stubbornly. They resented German troops trampling their fields, German shells smashing their villages, and German Uhlans sabering the villagers. For several weeks the Belgian border forts of Liege and Namur held out under a terrific pounding. King Albert's little army fought with great valor all through August. The gray German horde was delayed, giving France time to set up a defense.

A third miscalculation of the German War Lords was the strength of the French Army. Despite the handicap of red-legged trousers and old-fashioned guns, the French poilus put up a terrific fight to hold back the German invasion.

Again, the Kaiser's generals underestimated Britain. To begin with, they didn't think the English would fight. Then they didn't expect an English Army to get across the Channel. When British troops did reach France, the Kaiser referred to them as a "contemptible little army," which won them the nickname of "Old Contemptibles." They were only a few battalions, but they fought with a valor that caused the German generals to pull another boner. Racing through Belgium, the huge army of General Von Kluck could have gone straight to Paris like a steamroller. Instead, the High Command did an about-face and overestimated the British. Von Kluck swung over to the Marne to enflank Paris. There he ran into

the famous "taxicab army" of General Gallieni and the brave "Red Legs" of Papa Joffre. The "swinging Door" jammed and stuck.

Before the Germans could get it moving again, the Russians in the east broke through. Making one of the longest forced marches in history, the Czar's armies crashed over the Austro-Hungarian border like an avalanche.

On the south, the Austrians had already bogged down in Serbia. Poor leadership and lack of training muddled the Austrians. And the Serbs were fighting like tigers.

The war of maneuver was now slowed to a sparring match while Germany piled up reserves to meet the Russian onslaught in East Prussia. 1914 ebbed away into autumn and winter. Then Ludendorff, guiding genius of the Kaiser's war machine, put General Hindenburg into command of the eastern line. In February 1915 the Russian armies attacked. Hindenburg decoyed the advancing force into the Masurian Lake district, and there in a snare of swamps the charging mammoth was trapped. The Czarist officers fled the field. The Russian high commander committed suicide. Crack German artillery slew the leaderless and helpless Slavs by the thousands in a massacre almost beyond count. Finally the Germans allowed the few remaining Russians to surrender at Tannenberg.

The disaster broke the back of the Russian Army, and Czarist Russia never recovered. Hindenburg quickly threw his forces against France. But the Allies had been given the chance to dig in, and the war became a vast stalemate from Belgium to the Alps, and from the Alps to the Dardanelles. Intrenched across Europe, mighty armies struggled in death-grip. Throughout 1915 and 1916 the continent shook to the thunder of guns and writhed in a belt of flames. Thousands upon thousands of men died in Flanders, in Picardy, in the Balkan Mountains, holding the Germans back.

Then the Germans tried to break the dead-lock. At sea. With SUBMARINES.

War At Sea

When the war broke out in 1914 Great Britain with 39 dreadnaughts was the world's strongest sea power. Germany had achieved second place with only 17. (Neutral U. S. had fallen back down the list with 12.)

The difference between the Royal Navy and the German Navy was not so great as it seems, however. Britain had to keep many of her warships patrolling the Empire's sea lanes, while the German fleet could remain more or less compact. Although a strong French fleet joined the British, it was canceled somewhat in the Mediterranean by the Austrian Navy. In the Baltic the Russian Navy was negligible. Most significant of all was the great flock of German submarines—no one knew how many— operating out of hidden bases on the North Sea.

Great Britain's main naval problem was to guard the British Isles, to transport armies across the Channel to France, and to keep open the oceanic sea lanes which were the supply lines feeding England.

Germany's main naval problem was to guard the German North Sea coast, to stop Britain's Channel transport, and to cut the supply lines feeding England.

As previously described, Germany's North Sea approaches were guarded by the Helgoland-Wilhelmshaven naval fortress, the most powerful fortification of its kind. From behind this iron sea wall, the Kaiser's fleet sailed out to test British sea power late in January 1915. Off Dogger Bank the German dreadnaughts ran smack into the British Grand Fleet under Admiral Jellicoe. The Britons gave the Kaiser's warships a pounding, and the German fleet turned tail and fled back into its fortress.

The German fleet made one more attempt to get out and fight—this time heading northward in May 1916. Again the Royal Navy caught the Germans. Fought above the Danish Peninsula, the ensuing Battle of Jutland was the greatest fleet engagement of World War I. The British lost 14 major warships, the Germans 11. Results were considered indecisive. There was criticism of Jellicoe's tactics and of his failure to destroy completely the German High Seas Fleet which managed to escape back to Wilhelmshaven.

However, the German fleet was dealt a serious blow, and it made no attempt to gain the Atlantic thereafter. So long as its maneuvers were confined to the Kiel Canal it constituted no more than a threat. The Royal Navy stood on "offshore watch," and at sea as on land the war seemed stalemated.

Here was where the Germans pulled their rabbit punch. Submarines! The U-boat was the big secret weapon of World War I.

Up to 1914, the modern submarine had never been tested by warfare. The French, British, and other navies had built a few, but many naval experts considered them expensive toys. To the public they were in the realm of Jules Verne, on a par with that fantastic novelty, the airplane.

But the submarine had come far since the *Marine Turtle* of David Bushnell and the fatally floundering *Hunley*. In June 1914, British Admiral Sir Percy Scott had startled England by publishing in the London Times a letter predicting that submarines and aircraft had made surface navies obsolete. The letter was derided. Then in September 1914 the German sub U-9 sank three British cruisers within an hour. From that hour on the Allied navies realized they were up against something.

There was a rush to build destroyers and to perfect the depth bomb. Too late. Built in great secrecy before the war, the German U-boats were at sea, and the submarine menace was a nightmare established.

Now in 1915-1916 the German subs set out to cut those vital

sea lanes that were arteries pumping life-blood to England. One British merchantman after another went down. Despite frantic countermeasures, the torpedoings increased. Dogger Bank and Jutland looked fine in headlines, but the Royal Navy's Admiralty knew the fatal truth. Like a giant tourniquet, the submarine blockade was tightening, closing off one supply artery after another.

On land the deadlock remained. In November 1914 Turkey had joined the German side, encouraged by German agents to start a Moslem "holy war" which the Germans hoped would spread eastward to India. Although the religious war failed to spread, Turkish control of the Dardanelles cut the Allied supply line to Russia. In April 1915, attempting to open the Dardanelles with an amphibious operation at Gallipoli, French, Australian, and British troops were all but massacred by the German-armed Turks.

This disaster was partially countered by Italy's join-up with the Allies in May 1915. The Italians hoped to regain the great seaport of Trieste and other territory lost to Austria some years before. But the feeble Italian effort proved more of a handicap than an aid to the Allies. The Rumanians, too, gave little support when they joined the Allies in 1916 to take on the Bulgarians, who had sided with the Central Powers. Serbia had finally fallen, giving Germany control of the Balkans. But these eastern German successes had not broken the Western Front stalemate—the submarines were doing that. The Allies were losing at sea, and the Germans were winning the war.

Already Germany's ruthless attack on Belgium had turned American opinion anti-German. Baseball and business had taught Americans to believe in sportsmanship and in keeping a contract. The German Chancellor's cynical reference to the Belgian treaty as a "scrap of paper," and the savage treatment of Belgium's civil populace had shocked Main Street and Broadway.

"What the devil do those Uhlans mean, shooting up helpless refugees?"

"Only brutes could set fire to that beautiful city of Louvain!"

Sure, atrocity stories were played up by the British, and a new word had entered the dictionary of warfare—PROPAGANDA.

Admit the Czar's Cossacks were as cruel as the Kaiser's

Uhlan's. Admit that England, early in the war, had stopped American ships and cargoes on the high seas, claiming they were Germany-bound. (1812 all over again, Americans had cried!) And the English and French were wrong about many things. Admit all that!

It still didn't justify Germany's attack on Belgium. Or the German policy of "frightfulness," military terrorization deliberately sponsored by the Kaiser's generals. It didn't erase Germanic ambitions, or cancel Germany's announcement that all waters around England were closed to neutral shipping.

Then there was the *Lusitania*.

She sailed out of New York in April 1915—a great British passenger liner with hundreds of civilian travelers, including many Americans, aboard. On May 7th, off the Irish coast, she was torpedoed by a U-boat. Nearly 1200 men, women, and children (over 100 of them Americans) were drowned. Yes,

the Germans stated they had warned her not to sail from New York. And declared she was carrying munitions. Admit that, still it was a barbarous sinking. General Public glared in outrage at the headline and began to form his own opinion.

President Wilson wrote letters to the German Government. America was "too proud to fight," but these attacks on defenseless passenger liners and American shipping must stop. They didn't stop.

Meantime the Mexican troubles came to a head. On the night of March 8, 1916, the bandit leader Pancho Villa crossed the frontier with about 500 guerillas and attacked the town of Columbus, New Mexico. Pitched battle with border guards cost the lives of 14 American cavalrymen and 10 civilians. This looked like full-dress warfare, and Wilson mobilized the Army on the Mexican border, ordering the troops to follow and capture Villa.

This was the first large-scale American Army operation since the Civil War. General John J. Pershing had the field command, heading some 170,000 regulars and National Guardsmen. Only 10,000 regulars moved across the border, but for a few days war with Mexico seemed impending. Then the Mexican Government, although hostile, disclaimed Villa. Pancho, himself, evaporated with his bandit army somewhere in the Mexican mountains, to become a legend and later a movie with Wally Beery.

However, this chase through the cactus was a little something more than a horse opera. Germany wouldn't have been sorry to see Uncle Sam at war with his peppery southern neighbor. Did you ever heard of the Zimmerman Letter? While trouble in Mexico went on, this letter was unearthed by British Intelligence and handed over to the U. S. State Department. In brief, it was a note from the German Government to the Mexican Government urging Mexico to declare war on the United States, promising German aid, and suggesting California and Texas as a reward. Berlin denied the letter, declaring it a British fraud. The British declared it a genuine piece of business (admitted by the Germans after the war). Was it possible Pancho Villa had German money in his jeans? At any rate, the letter didn't turn America pro-German.

Neither did the "Black Tom" dock explosion which shook Jersey City on July 30th that year. Two Americans were killed in this $22,000,000 munitions blasts touched off by German saboteurs. If this wasn't war on America, what was it?

Now in January 1917, the Germans announced a vast submarine zone extending far into the Atlantic. And on February 1st they opened a campaign of unrestricted submarine warfare, threatening to sink all shipping in this zone, neutral or otherwise.

This was the final act that forced America to a decision. On April 2, 1917, Woodrow Wilson made a fighting speech to Congress. There would be no peace if the Germans won. The free and self-governed peoples of the world had to combine, he said, *"to make the world safe for Democracy."*

Congress voted that a state of war existed between America and Germany.

America In the War

They sang "Tipperary" and "Pack Up Your Troubles"—British songs. And "Madelon," borrowed from the French. And "Long, Long Trail," "Good-bye Broadway, Hello France," "Keep the Home Fires Burning," and those star-spangled tunes by George M. Cohan, "Yankee Doodle Dandy" and "Grand Old Flag" and "Over There."

Who did? Why, your Dad and your Uncle Johnny, maybe. Perhaps your grandfather, even. And maybe that old Chief over there, with so many hashmarks he'll soon have to wear 'em down his pantleg. And that gray-haired man in the neighborhood with one arm (He never advertised it, either, and you didn't hear about his Croix de Guerre.). They did.

They sang those songs as they lined up at recruiting offices, as they marched off to training bases, as they drilled and turned to and learned to handle their deck gear and guns just like you today. They piled into Portsmouth and Norfolk, Brooklyn and Newport, and they sailed out into the blue. Like the boys in khaki they sang, "We may not know what the war's about, but y'bet, by Gosh, we'll soon find out." And they found out.

The war was about submarines. They manned big, fast, sea-going destroyers to beat those submarines. (Big destroyers were a feature of the U. S. Navy at the time, and that was lucky.) They sailed on "mosquito boats" and transports, on cruisers and battlewagons, on mine layers and cargo carriers—all out to beat those submarines.

For the Navy's main problem was to get troops and supplies to England as soon as possible, and the crux of the problem was beating the German U-boat. "Impossible!" the Germans thundered. "Our U-boats control the seas! The *verdammt* Americans can never transport an army across the Atlantic to Europe!" Even British Admiral Jellicoe had seen no possible answer. But Sims had seen an answer, and given it to the British and the Navy Department in Washington.

"Convoys!"

Why not? Sail the merchant ships in fleets protected by war-ships just as in the old days. Make a prowling sub attack a whole crowd of destroyers instead of just one DD and a slow merchantman trying to creep through the danger zone.

"Sorry," the British said, "but we've already considered it. A fleet of cargo ships trying to zigzag without lights would surely collide. Inexperienced merchant captains can't keep up with naval maneuvers. And we've too few destroyers—"

Never mind. Sims urged the British Admiralty to try it, and cabled Washington to send a destroyer squadron at once to the British Isles.

On the ready at Boston, six new destroyers under Commander J. K. Taussig sailed at forced draught for Queenstown, Ireland. Arriving on May 4th, Taussig reported to British Vice Admiral Bayly.

"How soon," Bayly asked anxiously, *"will you be ready to go on patrol?"*

He expected the American to ask them for a refit after a forced-draught Atlantic run. Taussig's reply astounded him— and set up a U. S. Navy slogan for World War I.

"We are ready now, sir."

A trial convoy made a test run, Gibraltar to England. No collisions. No torpedoings.

The first American convoy reached the French port of Brest on July 4th, 1917. No hits, no subs, no errors.

Admiral Sims had said "can do," and the U. S. Navy was doing it again. American troops and supplies were landing in France. Incidentally, the first American fighting force to land in France was a detachment of naval aviators.

Navy Men Aloft!

You might say NAVAL AVIATION began when the Frenchman, Louis Bleriot, flew the first airplane across the English Channel in July, 1909. The plane crossed 32 miles of water in 37 minutes.

When World War I broke out, aviation—especially naval aviation—was still wet behind the ears. Planes were called "flying machines," and they looked like combination box kites and bicycles. Flyers were called "aeronauts." They wore their caps backward, and dressed in goggles, gauntlets, and leather leggin's. When they were about to take off, friends would shake hands earnestly and say, "So long." When they got back it made a headline in the papers.

The Wright Brothers had made America air-minded by 1914, but flying was still a dangerous novelty. In Europe the few warplanes did not seem to prove Admiral Scott's grim predictions. At first their military use was confined to scouting. Then some German in an Albatross fired his pistol at a Frenchman in a Bleriot, and the next Frenchman that took off carried a machine gun mounted on his nacelle. Flying machines went armed from there on up, and became combat planes.

These were shortly followed by bombers when German pilots began dropping grenades, then heavy hand-bombs on Allied ground forces. By 1917 the types of planes were fairly well established, and the sky over the Western Front was roaring with German Fokkers, French Nieuports and Spads, and British Camels and DH9's. Within the dizzy rush of three years the rickety flying machine had become a deadly 100-mile-an-hour battle plane, gunning down the sky to strafe an enemy with machine guns synchronized to fire through propellors. The aeronaut was now an expert pilot—an ace in the RAF or the Lafayette Escadrille, fighting Von Richthofen's Flying Circus.

During the decade prior to World War I, obtaining aviation funds from the U. S. Government was like pulling teeth from the Great Stone Face. In 1910, however, Captain W. I. Chambers, USN, was assigned by the Navy Department to make a study of aeronautics, report on its possible value to the Navy, and instruct Navy personnel in the subject. Chambers was a lucky choice. He had sailed on Arctic exploration, and his horizon wasn't limited. He had an engineer's mind and a scientist's vision. Like Sims, when it came to improvements, he wasn't stopped by red tape.

Foreseeing the airplane's value as a naval scout, he soon recommended the purchase of hydroplanes for the Navy. But such planes were still in the experimental stage. Land planes, then, and devise some means of launching them at sea. But how could a plane take off from a ship, much less land on one?

In November, 1910, Chambers showed the critics. Obtaining the services of Eugene Ely, a daring test pilot formerly employed by the Curtiss Company, he also obtained use of the cruiser *Birmingham*, then at Norfolk. If *Birmingham's* crew wondered why the devil they had to stay aboard Sunday and build a wooden platform on her foc's'le, they soon found out. A plane was going to fly from their ship. Didn't those bluejackets get a kick out of that? *Birmingham* steamed out into the Chesapeake, and fly Ely did—with 57 feet of runway for the take-off! It certainly looked like another bubble when Ely's plane belly-whacked down over the water and the propellor actually splashed the tops of the waves. But Ely got her up, somehow, and the first take-off from a warship had been made.

Two months later (January 1911) Ely did it again—this time in reverse. Taking off from an aviation field on San Francisco

Bay, he landed on the fantail of *U.S.S. Pennsylvania,* rigged with a platform for the purpose. The photograph above gives you an idea of the hazards. It also gives you an idea of the vision and foresight of Captain Chambers.

Unfortunately Ely was killed in a crash the following autumn. Twenty-five years later, Congress, recognizing his contribution, awarded him posthumously the Distinguished Flying Cross. But Navy heads at the time remained cautious, and Government heads skeptical. In 1911 the Navy was awarded $25,000—which might be used to purchase one airplane.

That same year Glenn Curtiss, laboring to develop the hydro-plane up on the Finger Lakes, was training a military class which included two Navy volunteer flyers—Lieutenants Jack Towers and "Spuds" Ellyson. Ellyson, who qualified as a licensed pilot under the rules of the Aero Club of America, was the Navy's first pilot. So the Navy had an aviator, but did not own a single plane for him to fly. How long ago was this? In 1911!

But in October, 1911, three planes were delivered—one Wright and one Curtiss land plane, and a Curtiss hydroplane, a two-seater with a top speed of 57 miles an hour. Lieutenant John Rodgers completed the original pilot roster, and the Navy air arm was launched.

Under the air-minded drive of Captain Chambers and the tutelage of Glenn Curtiss, a training school was set up near San Diego in 1912, and in 1913 four more aircraft were added to the Navy's force. A program calling for 400 pilots and 200 planes was urged by Chambers. The Secretary of the Navy asked Congress for 50 planes. The following year the Navy got 10.

With radio entering the picture, the idea of radio-equipped naval scouting planes excited flyers and radio bugs alike. But aircraft radio remained a "gadget" throughout World War I, and many old timers continued skeptical of naval aviation.

When the United States entered the war in 1917, the Navy air arm consisted of 54 airplanes, 38 pilots, and 239 crew men. Not a single plane was suitable for service use! And this at a time when the British were flying regular North Sea patrols, the Germans and French were operating some 2,000 planes each, and the Italian Navy had so good an air force that it was offering to train U. S. Naval pilots in Italy.

Defeat in Russia

In other respects the United States did not realize the job at hand in April 1917. Unfamiliar with trench warfare, the American Army faced a monster German war machine schooled in all the tricks. The Germans had introduced liquid fire, the saw-tooth bayonet, gas. Tanks, the British secret weapon, had made but a slight dent on the Somme front where Ludendorff was massing for a gigantic drive. And just before America entered the war, something happened that added a colossal reserve force to that drive.

This something was the Russian Revolution. The blood of more than one massacre was on the hands of the despotic Czar Nicholas II. Russian Socialists, driven underground, were organizing for revolt. The army's defeat at Tannenberg set off the revolution. The cabinet of Alexander Kerensky, a moderate Socialist, could bring no order—neither at home nor at the front.

The government was taken over by the Bolsheviks (the word means "majority men") headed by Lenin and Trotsky. They favored a "people's dictatorship," with the abolishment of the landed aristocracy. They acknowledged that Russia had lost the war with Germany, and began to negotiate for peace.

In March 1918, the Russian leaders signed peace with Germany—the Treaty of Brest-Litovsk. It was a tough peace. The Russians were made to pay a huge indemnity. They were forced to surrender Poland and the Baltic provinces of Latvia, Estonia, and Lithuania. Above all, Russia was knocked out as an Ally.

The loss of Russia was a staggering blow to the Allied side. Something like a million German troops were released for action on the Western Front where American troops had hardly arrived. They poured like a cement river to reinforce the Hindenburg Line.

It was the spring of 1918, and Ludendorff was ready to start his Juggernaut offensive.

They Shall Not Pass!

When Von Kluck's first drive across Belgium had threatened to crash through to Paris, the French at the Marne had cried, *"They shall not pass!"* Now, four years later, facing another colossal steamroller, British Tommies and French poilus were repeating the slogan.

But it wasn't enough for the American doughboy moving up to the Western Front. The Yanks under Black-Jack Pershing were going to crack this Hindenburg Line as if it were so much peanut brittle. Sure. Like football players, they themselves were goin' to do the passing.

America's Navy men had the same attitude. That attitude can be summed up in the phrase, "Go get 'em!"

No use sitting around on your ashcans waiting for this German U-boat drive to cross the Atlantic. Sail out to where the U-boats are, and drop your ashcans right down their periscopes. Take your convoys right smack through the sub zones. More! Go right up into the mouth of the North Sea and lay a mine blockade that'll bottle up the Heinies like medical exhibits pickled in alcohol.

While the Germans planned their own drives, the U. S. Navy launched this three-part program. How did it go?

Well, dropping ashcans down the periscopes of German subs was a very tough job. Army Intelligence, examining a wrecked German Zeppelin, managed to pick up a German naval code book which made good reading for the USN. The U-boats swarming around England and off the French coast had a habit of surfacing at night and locating each other by radio. With the code in their possession, American destroyer-skippers had an ace.

But by the time a DD, racing at thirty knots, reached the spot where the U-boat radioed, the sub had dived, and the spot was only an area. You could cover a wide area with ashcans, but then you never knew. Maybe oil came up, and maybe it didn't, but even if it did (no sonar in those days) you never knew. Case of the American freighter, *Luckenbach*, was typical.

October 19, 1917, at 0830, *U.S.S. Nicholson*, DD, picks up an S.O.S. "*J. L. Luckenbach. Being gunned by submarine. Position 43.08 N, 9.31 W.*"

Off starts *Nicholson*, her firemen working like Vulcans, her Old Man calculating that *Luckenbach's* enemy is the sub U-62 known to be hunting the convoy in that area.

Luckenbach's call repeats at 0940.

"*How soon will you arrive?*"

"*Two hours*," replies the DD. "*Don't surrender.*"

"*Never*," Sparks on *Luckenbach* sends back. Then, "*On fire. Look for boats.*"

However, *Luckenbach's* crew neither surrendered nor took to the boats. Squaring with the highest traditions of the Merchant Marine, the crew fought fire and sub alike to hang on. Outgunned, their ship a-blaze, those seamen beat off the U-boat for two hours. Just in time *Nicholson* reached the scene. Then down dived the sub, with the DD after her, dropping the cans.

Four hours later, the near-by convoy was under torpedo

attack. *Nicholson,* hopeful of finding U-62, had raced to rejoin the escort. Now she turned the ocean inside out with depth charges. Hurrah! Up came a big spew of oil, a lot of rubbish, and a German officer's cap.

But that night the wireless officer hears a German sub on the radio. "*Sank two ships. Attacked with depth bombs. Escaped. Hashagen.*"

Hashagen is U-62. You never can tell with ashcans.

So the Navy built sub chasers with Y-guns to throw the ashcans farther, and more big DD's, and set to work on an electrical listening device. *Nicholson* caught a sub, anyway, that November.

In December a U-boat sank the destroyer *Jacob Jones* in the Channel, and the Americans redoubled the anti-sub drive. By the spring of 1918 there'd been a mutiny at Kiel. A phrase had become too common at U-boat Headquarters. The phrase, "*sperlos versenkt,*" meaning, "sunk without trace."

Part two of the Navy's program—convoys to Europe—was even more successful. By March, 1918, there were four American divisions on the Western Front, three behind the lines, and more coming up.

Freighters, converted yachts, tramp steamers, and giant ocean liners like the *Leviathan* (German vessel caught at Hoboken at the start of the war) served to transport the A. E. F. And your Navy escorted this vast transport. A few cargo carriers were torpedoed—for example, the *Westover* in the summer of '18, trapped when she dropped out of convoy with broken engines. But the doughboys were getting across. And the Germans early saw the handwriting on the wall.

Late in March, fearful of this growing American power, Ludendorff attacked. The main push hit the British lines, and practically destroyed the British Fifth Army. In this sector the Germans advanced 30 miles.

Doughboys In Action

Another such break-through would take the Germans to the Channel port of Dunkerque, and cut off Belgium from France. The Allied leaders voted to make French Marshal Foch supreme commander of Allied forces, and General Pershing placed the American Army at his disposal.

On April 9th the Germans struck again. But this drive got mired in the spring mud, and Ludendorff failed to reach his objectives.

Now some eighteen American divisions had reached France. In desperation the Germans struck again, this time smashing the French line on the Aisne and pushing through to the Marne. There, at Chateau-Thierry, they were stopped by a division of U. S. Regulars. This was their first full-dress battle with American doughboys, and the Germans learned something about Yankee marksmanship. That is, if 3,000 dead Germans could learn anything.

On June 4, 1918, another American division counter-attacked at nearby Belleau Wood. The assault was spearheaded by two regiments of U. S. Marines. This terrific battle lasted a week. The Heinies retreated, and the Yanks made their first big gain.

The Kaiser's generals knew their goose had begun to cook. Three million Americans were being trained to come overseas. Desperately the German leaders appealed to their Navy to stop these transports. But the German fleet was in its lovely Wilhelmshaven fortress, sealed up by the British and the American battle fleet outside. And the U-boats were now unable to sneak out of the North Sea as they had before.

So you come to part three of the Navy program—the mine barrage. Early in 1917 the Navy Department had suggested to the British Admiralty that a mammoth mine field be sowed between Scotland and Norway to shut up the mouth of the North Sea. Impractical, said the British. It would take 400,000 mines—more than could be manufactured in a generation. And mine layers for such a project weren't available.

But Admiral Earle of the Navy Bureau of Ordnance thought otherwise. American industry could manufacture 20,000 mines a month if put to it. And Commander Fullwinder of the BuOrd mining section had just received the invention of a Down-Easter named Browne. This device was an electrical firing mechanism which, attached to a long antenna-wire, might be adapted for mines. Might be? Admiral Earle decided it should be.

The ordinary contact mine was an iron sphere with little trigger-knobs jutting from its surface a couple of inches like warts. In other words, to explode it required contact. In this respect it was not much different from David Bushnell's early torpedo, famous in the "Battle of the Powder Kegs." But suppose these antenna-wires were attached to the triggers to trail out like the hair on a mermaid—or longer, like the tentacles of an octopus—or—

Long copper filaments trailing under water with a mine at the business end. Metal contact sends an electric current through the filament. Bang! And underwater pressure crushes the guts out of the unlucky submarine. That was the Navy's new mine.

And as the long filaments covered a wide area, 400,000 weren't necessary. Two over-age cruisers, *San Francisco* and *Brooklyn*, were converted into mine layers. Special crews went into training. May, 1918, the mine flotilla sailed quietly for Europe, Captain R. R. Belknap in command. June, the mine barrage was under way.

Working their arms out at the elbows, the sweating bluejackets, aided by a few British tars, put down 68,000 mines in about four months. That summer one U-boat after another vanished in the mouth of the North Sea. In September the submarine sailors at Wilhelmshaven mutinied.

So the U-boats were licked, and the A. E. F. arrived full force overseas. By mid July, 1918, there were 29 divisions in France. Trying another push that month, the Germans were thrown for a loss all down the line. Generalissimo Foch now decided to uncork a major counteroffensive. To Pershing's army he assigned the St. Mihiel sector near Verdun.

The offensive opened well—British, French, and Yanks going over the top all down the line. With Ludendorff's troops in Belgium reeling under the British charge, Foch shifted American weight to the Argonne Forest on the Meuse.

It was a nasty sector, knifed through with jagged ravines. The Yanks went over on September 26th. After a month of terrific fighting they broke through and shattered their end of the Hindenburg Line. The Germans began to retreat twenty miles a day. On November 6th the Yanks were at Sedan.

Ludendorff and the Junker generals decided to call it quits.

The German Navy mutinied.

The Kaiser fled to Holland to saw wood.

And on November 11, 1918, World War I was over.

Armistice

The Germans signed the Armistice in a little railway car in the French forest of Compiege, and the world sat down, exhausted, to think it over. It had been a tough war! The Kaiser had been beaten at last. Now everybody could go home.

But the U. S. Navy didn't have much time to sit. On Broadway there was a popular song—

> *"Though the Army is in clover,*
> *'Twas the Navy took them over,*
> *And the Nay-vee will bring them back!"*

That was another transport job for the bluejackets.

Did the Navy do it? Ask your Dad. Altogether the boys in blue did a bang-up job in World War I, and the Navy chalked up another record. Although the Atlantic fleet did not fight a major battle with the enemy, it was "over there" all set and ready for action. By November, 1918, some 300 American warships manned by 75,000 officers and men were in European waters on the job.

Only two major warships were casualties—the old cruiser *San Diego*, sunk by a German mine planted off the American coast, and the veteran battleship *Minnesota*, damaged by another. One destroyer had been torpedoed, and two lost through collision. Two small armed yachts were sunk by tin fish in the Mediterranean. Those were the U. S. Navy's losses.

In turn the Navy had set up a winning convoy system, chased the U-boats out of the mid-Atlantic, beaten them with a whale of a mine barrage. Perhaps its greatest feat was transporting 2,079,880 American soldiers to France WITHOUT THE LOSS OF A SINGLE MAN. Darn right, those sailors were proud!

Won War—Lost Peace

The Treaty of Versailles, signed on June 28, 1919, was mild, considering. Alsace-Lorraine (lost to Germany in 1870) was returned to France. German had to give up her colonies. Territory was granted Poland and Belgium. The German Army was reduced to 100,000 men. Germany was ordered to destroy her fortifications, and given thirty years to pay reparations to the Allies.

Yet the Germans squealed like stuck pigs. The treaty had named them the aggressor responsible for the war's outbreak. *Nein*, the Allies were more responsible! Pay reparations? *Ach*, we spent all our money for guns! Disarm? *Ja*, we will see about that.

Wilson tried to set up a League of Nations, hoping the countries of the world would eventually get together as the states had once joined hands in America. But many Americans at home were against a world organization. Politicians campaigned to keep the United States out of the League. Without American participation, the League was bound to fail, and Wilson returned from Europe sick and empty-handed, convinced the Allies had won the war but lost the peace.

However, shocked by the murderous cost of modern warfare, the American people insisted that armaments be somehow reduced. At America's invitation a conference of world powers gathered in Washington in 1921. (The Soviet Union was not invited.) The United States leading, Great Britain, France, Italy, and Japan agreed to prune down their standing navies. They also agreed to keep hands off China in the East, maintaining the policy of the "open door" by which all could trade freely with China. And to show her sincerity, the United States began a battleship-scrapping program.

Meantime Britain and America tried to help a German Republic get started. Both countries made huge loans to the new German leaders whose intentions at the time seemed good. But hell was paved with good intentions. The war had destroyed the Kaiser's government. It had killed a couple of million German soldiers. But it hadn't destroyed such industrialists as Fritz Thyssen and the Krupps. It hadn't killed the German Junker generals. And the intentions of these latter? Pretending to "go into retirement," they laid low while the industrialists, out in front, aided by Allied loans, got the German gun factories running again.

While this was going on, American eyes were turned suddenly East. The Washington Naval Limitations Conference hadn't worked. The U. S., Britain, and France had kept their pledges, and in the four years following the naval treaty had built but six warships among them—one British light cruiser and five French submarines. (Note Uncle Sam, still dismantling the fleet, building none.) But the Jap naval leaders had gone in for warship production to the limit, building thirty-two.

This was hardly a peaceful gesture after a conference aimed to bring on world disarmament. What were the Japanese aiming at? It was soon apparent they were aiming at poor old China, struggling to get along as a republic since 1912.

The Japs had come in as an ally of Great Britain in the World War, but their aid had been mainly confined to seizing the German-owned Chinese port of Kiaochow. Their total losses in the war amounted to 300 men. As a reward for this meagre help they were granted control of the Caroline Islands. Now, with the Nipponese Navy building full blast, Britains and Americans began to regret this grant. China, troubled by civil wars, regarded Tokyo with anxiety.

Yet the Orient is a long way off. And most Americans, after a glance, forgot about it. There couldn't be another war. No mad-dog leader would dare start one.

However, war had already flamed out again in Europe with Poland fighting Soviet Russia and the new republic of Czecho-slovakia over boundaries. Poland also fought a brief war with Estonia, and Marshal Pilsudski emerged as a dictator.

In Italy an ex-newspaperman, Benito Mussolini, had seized

the government with his Black Shirts, and was shouting, "Italy must revive the Roman Empire!"

In Spain military leaders were in the saddle, plotting a dictator-ship.

In South America war was brewing between Uruguay and Paraguay.

To Main Street and Broadway, these border wars seemed like remote skirmishes, while the idea of a modern Roman Empire was a laugh. A major war? Not with casualty lists still in memory. Not with bombing planes on the horizon. Why, one of these days someone was going to fly the Atlantic.

Someone did. "Putty" Read, commanding officer of the U. S. Navy flying boat NC4. In May, 1919, Read and his crew took off from Halifax, bound for Lisbon. American destroyers were standing by like stepping-stones in the Atlantic as station ships. The plane hopped to the Azores, and on to Portugal. The Navy flyers made it, and the Atlantic had been spanned for the first time by air.

NC4's flight should have taught certain parties something. First, that Uncle Sam was no longer tail-end Charley when it came to aviation. Second, that a lot of any future war was going to be fought in the air. American Navy men were on the beam now. In 1922 the old collier, *Jupiter*, was undergoing a strange transformation. When she put to sea in October she was like no other vessel afloat, her superstructure nothing but a wooden platform. She was now *U.S.S. Langley*, affectionately nicknamed "The Covered Wagon"—your Navy's first aircraft carrier.

Early in the 1920's the German Junker generals decided they hadn't lost the war at all. It had been lost, they decided, not by their own miscalculations, but by the stupid people at home. And because Italy jumped alliance. And if they'd only exploited the Russian Ukraine, and kept America out of it, why, they could have won hands down.

The Junkers called in their friends, the German industrialists. They had a plan.

First thing to do was to smash the German Republic before Democracy got a foothold. How to smash the republic? Inflation. Ruin everybody. That was up to the money wizards like Herr Dr. Schacht.

With the Republic smashed, Nationalism could be revived. Bring in a hero—a man who could stir up the mob and promise to lead the people to glory. Revive the old "master race" story. Blame the lost war on the Jews—that was it! Start a campaign against the Jews, who couldn't fight back because they were far in the minority.

Then start rearming. Slowly at first. On the quiet. Buy up iron and steel supplies with this money loaned by the fool Allies. And if they protest? Easy. Tell the world Germany arms against the Russian menace—to save the world from Bolshevik Communism!

Next, rig up an iron-bound blood-pact with Mussolini in Italy. Then win over Spain for a henchman on the Mediterranean.

If England kicks? Let her kick! The British are sick of war. Decadent. So are the French. Meantime sow mistrust between English and French. Stir it up all over Europe. Revive religious prejudices, old grudges, race hatreds.

Next? Take over Austria. Buy up Hungary, and undermine Czechoslovakia. No trouble winning control of the Balkans. Assure them the war will be aimed at Russia. And then—

Turn west and smash at Britain and France. Make it a surprise attack—thousands of planes to jump the Maginot Line.

If America makes trouble? Make trouble for America in the Pacific. Work up an alliance with Japan. Bound to be a row between Washington and Tokyo, anyway, with Japan planning to grab all China. A Japanese-American War! That would keep the U. S. Navy out of the Atlantic. American Democracy was stale at best. *Deutschland uber alles!*

In 1923, General Ludendorff and an obscure zealot named Adolph Hitler marched from a beer hall in Munich to launch a revolt against the German republic. Exactly ten years later Adolph Hitler became Chancellor, and the German republic vanished. Within five years Germany, Italy, and Japan had formed the Rome-Berlin-Tokyo Axis. Spain, under Franco, had become an Axis partner. The League of Nations had collapsed like a house of cards. Race riots, religious persecution, hate, and mistrust were sweeping every country in Europe. Russia mistrusted the world, and the world mistrusted Russia. Isolationists were calling on fellow Americans to "stay out." China was fighting for her life against Jap invasion. Arms factories were working overtime. Britain had sent Chamberlain to Munich, and Austria belonged to Germany. Fanatical Nazi troops were chanting—

"Today we own Germany—tomorrow the whole world."

But Franklin D. Roosevelt and 130,000,000 Americans were going to have something to say about that. So was the U. S. Navy.

WE ARE READY NOW, SIR

World War II

Nazi Germany and Samurai Japan—two nations with the same enormous idea: the conquest of the world. For the present they were allies, since they had their respective portions of the globe to beat into submission. Suspicious as they were of each other, there was no reason for conflict between them while Hitler concentrated on the enslavement of Europe and Premier Tojo lashed 150 million people into his Greater East Asia Co-Prosperity Sphere. But the Germans believed themselves supermen, destined to rule the world. And the Japs? They were the children of heaven; obviously the world must belong to them.

Fantastic? It seemed so to most Americans. They couldn't take it seriously, this world conquest business. But a number of Americans changed their minds on 1 September 1939.

It was then Hitler unleashed his Wehrmacht. His panzer legions swept across the broad plains of Poland; his Luftwaffe swarmed black in the sky. Poland, heroically fighting this undeclared war, was doomed. France and England came in too late, and Warsaw fell in four weeks. Here it was, then—World War II.

And for those who still couldn't see Hitler's design of conquest, the next year, 1940, made it bloodily plain. The Germans seized Denmark and Norway. Their blitzkrieg armies pounded into Holland, Belgium, France—countries tragically unprepared to fight this lightning war. On June 22 France signed an armistice; and Germany gathered her strength to knock out England.

The Nazis missed. This was the first big hitch in the swastika scheme of victory—England refused to go down. Instead, her vastly outnumbered RAF went up day after day, night after night, to shoot up the vaunted Luftwaffe. England was pounded, blasted, broken; but England wasn't knocked out.

In Central Europe and in North Africa the Nazis continued to spread the new German empire. Then, on 22 June 1941, Hitler made his second move that was destined not to work out according to plan—Germany invaded Russia. The German war machine seemed to roll on unchecked at first. But the Russian retreat was too orderly to be a Nazi victory, and that winter the retreat turned into a Russian offensive.

The United States had become the "Arsenal of Democracy," sending arms and supplies across the perilous Atlantic to the men still fighting for freedom over there. Maybe Uncle Sam could keep out of the shooting war. It looked bad in Europe; but weren't the British still fighting, and the Russians? Things were getting worse all the time in the Orient; but hadn't Japan sent a special "peace envoy" to Washington? Maybe—

Pearl Harbor

The 7th of December, 1941—a bright Sunday morning at Pearl Harbor, with the great Pacific Fleet lying at anchor, ready for emergency orders but surely secure in this Pacific bastion. Captain H. M. Markin, CO of the Kaneohe Naval Air Station, was at breakfast when he noticed planes making a right turn into the entrance of the bay—a prohibited maneuver. His son pointed out a strange thing about those planes—they wore the insignia of the Rising Sun. The time was 0748.

For an hour and fifty minutes the Japs kept coming. This was no crazy banzai charge from the sky. It was a carefully planned attack, executed with great skill. First it struck the air stations and the Army Air fields; then, seconds later, the big ships lying in Battleship Row. In the thunder of exploding bombs and torpedoes, in the smoke and flame of wrecked ships and shore installations, the peacetime U. S. Navy became a Navy at war and fought back with a magnificent valor that you and every other American remember.

But valor could not prevent a grim disaster. By 0945 that Sunday morning—

> *Arizona* was sunk, broken in two.
>
> *Oklahoma* had completely capsized.
>
> *West Virginia* had settled in shallow water at her berth.
>
> *California* was sunk at her berth.
>
> *Nevada* had been run aground to prevent her from sinking.
>
> The old *Utah*, a training ship now, was sunk, bottom up.
>
> *Pennsylvania, Maryland, Tennessee* had all been damaged by bombs.
>
> Three light cruisers and three destroyers had been damaged.
>
> And, most tragic of all—aboard ship and ashore, 2,628 Navy officers and men had been killed and many more were to die in the hospitals.

Luckily—very luckily—not a single carrier was in Pearl Harbor that Sunday.

Three hours after the attack Japan declared war on the United States. And later that week war was also declared by Germany and Italy. Uncle Sam was in the shooting.

On the same fateful day of 7 December, the bulk of the American air power in the Philippines was wiped out; and three days later the Japs surged ashore in the Islands—to be met by the heroic but hopeless resistance of General MacArthur's American and Filipino troops. Everywhere the Jap warlords were making swift capital of their treachery, seizing Guam and Wake Island, invading Malaya and Borneo, sinking two of Britain's most powerful warships off Malaya, conquering Hong Kong.

So now the United States was not only an arsenal, but an armed camp for a two-ocean war. To fight the enemy, Americans would have to cross thousands of miles of ocean patrolled by enemy ships and planes. Clearly that meant Navy—big Navy, the biggest any nation ever owned. A Navy with the biggest job any Navy ever faced.

This Navy would have to fight simultaneously on two oceans, over tremendous distances. Men, ships, planes—the Navy needed them quickly; and she needed bases thousands of miles from home. She must perfect new fighting methods, for this wasn't old-fashioned naval war. In this one the Navy was to carry the Army and the Marines into vast combat theaters, delivering the soldiers on hostile beaches in the most difficult of all military operations. She also had the task of protecting the supply lines so vital to the Allies and to American forces overseas.

Yes, it was a new kind of war, requiring a changed Navy. But the new Navy couldn't be built overnight, and meanwhile the United States would have to fight with whatever she had.

Guts and Not Much Else

The Navy didn't have the men, the ships, or the planes to stop the Japs from seizing an empire. By May 6, when Corregidor fell, the Japs had accomplished exactly that—capturing the Philippines, Malaya, the Dutch East Indies, and Singapore. This empire contained the world's finest supply of rubber, tin, and quinine. Strategically, it controlled the trade routes to the Far East.

But in those terrible early months the Navy proved that she had the most valuable commodity of all, the essential secret weapon—plain fighting guts. She had it in that tiny Marine garrison on Wake Island which fought off an enormously larger Japanese force from the 8th to the 23rd of December. She had it in Patrol Wing 10 in the Philippines, a few battered PBY's, piloted and serviced by miracle men. She had it in Lieutenant John Bulkeley's Squadron 3, a half-dozen PT boats, racing out on torpedo missions night after night in Lingayen Gulf, slipping through the mine fields around Corregidor, and navigating largely "by guess and by God" to carry General MacArthur away from the Philippines. These Marines and flying boat crews and PT men had the same essential courage earlier seen on the *Bonhomme Richard* and the *Constitution*.

It was the same kind of unequal fighting in the South Pacific when the Japs carried the offensive there, into Malaya and the Dutch East Indies, threatening Australia. Admiral Thomas G. Hart's Asiatic Fleet was composed of the CA *Houston*, the CL *Marblehead*, 13 overage destroyers, 29 submarines, and the remnants of Patwing 10. Augmented by a few Army planes and the small fleet and air force of the Dutch, the Asiatic Fleet had to oppose a powerful Japanese offensive built around air power.

The Java Sea campaign opened with an engagement which destroyer men will be talking about for a good many years to come. On a black January night Commander P. H. Talbot led four tincans into Makassar Strait—and into the center of a huge Jap convoy. First a force of enemy destroyers swept by, without seeing the Americans in the blackness. Then Commander Talbot ordered his four-stackers to open their throttles all the way, and the little force went charging into the convoy. There were plenty of torpedo targets that night and the boys made the most of them.

Before the Japs could decide what was hitting them, the old tincans had executed a 180-degree turn and were coming down the line again. With Japanese shipping blowing up all over the place, Commander Talbot turned for a third run. This time the destroyers exhausted their supply of torpedoes, so they opened up with the guns. The Japs had finally concluded that they were being attacked by a surface force, but there didn't seem to be much they could do about it—Talbot's destroyers were moving too fast.

In fact, the Japs never did do much about it; they landed only one shell on an American ship during the entire engagement. The proof of Commander Talbot's success lies on the bottom of Makassar Strait.

From then on the Java Sea campaign was a series of raids by U. S. and Dutch ships, which slowed the Jap advance but could not stop it. American ships were battered and broken, and a number of them went down, in battles that may never get into history books because no one was left to tell the story. It was a doomed campaign, which could not have been fought more gallantly.

Gallant was the word for the light cruiser *Marblehead*. When Jap bombers caught her in the Java Sea on February 4, they landed a bomb aft which jammed her rudder hard over so that she could only move in circles. And the bombers kept coming; for three hours they kept coming. Another bomb struck forward, a third was a damaging near miss; *Marblehead* was on fire; her

plates were sprung, and she was listing badly. Yet in spite of the wreckage, the fires, and the jammed rudder, Captain Arthur G. Robinson continued to maneuver his ship. By racing first one propeller and then the other he varied the size of her turn; and that queer, spinning course saved her from another bomb.

When finally the Jap bombers quit, a damage control party managed to secure the rudder amidships. It couldn't be operated, however. With her rudder set and water pouring into her so fast that her pumps had to be augmented with bucket brigades, *Marble-head* limped to port, first into Tjilatjap and then to Ceylon. She was still taking water when she put out for South Africa, where she was dry-docked. From there it was a 9,000 mile cruise to home in the States. This was a crew, the Navy said, *"that does not know the meaning of the word 'abandon'"*

With the Java Sea bottled up and the Asiatic Fleet ·shattered, the Japanese admirals undoubtedly were telling each other that the war was almost won. They must have been unpleasantly surprised by a couple of incidents occurring early in 1942. January 31 of that year is a date for the Navy to remember. On that day the Pacific Fleet, commanded by Admiral Chester W. Nimitz, struck its first offensive blow of the war. Vice Admiral William F. Halsey, Jr., led a task force in raids on the Gilbert and Marshall Islands. Then Admiral Halsey paid a damaging visit to Wake Island; and Vice Admiral Wilson Brown raided New Guinea with the carriers *Lexington* and *Yorktown*. While the Tokyo high command was recovering from these disagreeable interruptions, bombs started dropping outside Hirohito's window. The carrier *Hornet*, commanded by Captain Marc A. Mitscher, had brought Jimmy Doolittle's Army medium bombers within range of Tokyo. No, Hon. High Command, the war wasn't over yet.

Japanese strategy in that spring of 1942 was to cut the lifeline to Australia and isolate the continent for eventual invasion. But as the Japs moved southeast, the U. S. Navy stepped into their path. Commanded by Rear Admiral Frank J. Fletcher, a task force containing the *Lexington* and the *Yorktown* fought a five-day battle in the Coral Sea which introduced several "firsts" into

naval history. This was the first battle between American and enemy carrier forces; and the planes that radioed back *"Scratch one flat-top!"* sank the first Jap carrier of the war. When the Coral Sea battle was over and the Japanese southern offensive had been stopped, Admiral Fletcher's force had carried out the first major engagement in naval history in which surface ships did not exchange a single shot.

To make so much history in a few days is always costly, and the Navy paid a heavy price in losing the *Lexington*. The Japs had thrown fifty-four planes against the great flat-top, nineteen of which she had brought down. Thirty torpedoes had been launched against her. When the assault was over, she had a six-degree list and was burning below decks, but she was still able to receive her returning planes. Eventually the damage control crews extinguished the fires and patched and trimmed the ship, so that she was in shape to cruise when the damage control officer wound up his report to the skipper by saying: *"I respectfully suggest, sir, that if you have to take any more torpedoes you start to take them on the port side."*

Then, when it looked as if the *Lex* would return to fight again, a series of explosions started below decks—apparently caused by ignited gasoline fumes. For five hours the crew fought fires and tried to repair the havoc, but those thundering explosions became too great a menace. On the ravaged deck, waiting their turns to abandon ship, the men passed the time by eating up the ship's supply of ice cream!

Air Power and Midway

How had the Japs won their swift victories at Pear. Harbor and in the Dutch East Indies? By the strength of their naval air arm. Long before Pearl Harbor the U. S. Navy had foreseen how the growth of air power would change the ways and means of naval warfare. So the fleet had some planes and carriers, but not enough, not nearly enough; some had already been lost and more would go down. That was one big reason why the shipyards and factories of the nation were working at such desperate speed—to furnish the fleet with more flat-tops, more planes.

In the old days a naval force was built around its heaviest guns. But the task force of World War II was a different kind of outfit in which the heart of power was often the carrier, with battle-wagons for escorts. Remember that in the Battle of the Coral Sea the surface ships had not exchanged a shot. There was another, even more important battle coming which would restore the balance of power in the Pacific by means of the air.

What were the Japs planning now, in the early summer of '42? Here, very briefly, was the way Admiral Nimitz and his colleagues figured it. Since the Japs knew that most of our carrier and cruiser strength was in the South Pacific, this would seem to them like a good time to strike in the central or the northern parts, hoping to cut the American lines of communication. Figuring this way, CinCPac summoned carriers and supporting ships to the Central Pacific, so that the total strength on hand was 3 carriers, 7 heavy cruisers and 1 CL, 14 destroyers, and about 20 subs. Divided into two task forces under the command of Rear Admiral Raymond A. Spruance and Rear Admiral Fletcher, these ships patrolled in the neighborhood of Midway Island. It turned out that the admirals had done some very accurate reading of the Japanese mind.

The first attack on the Jap task force approaching Midway was carried out by land-based Army, Navy, and Marine planes on June 3. These attacks must have impressed the Japs considerably because they apparently began to withdraw. Then, on June 4, the American carriers went into action.

Do you know the story of Torpedo 8? You should, because that squadron of fifteen Douglas Devastators will live in history. Sent out from the *Hornet*, they were the first to locate the Jap force. But when they did spot three (and later four) enemy carriers, the Devastators were practically out of fuel. So, radioing back the discovery, Lieutenant Commander John C. Waldron asked permission to withdraw for refueling.

In a matter of minutes, then, Rear Admiral Spruance had to make one of those terrible decisions that are a part of war and victory. He knew that Waldron's request was urgent. He knew, also, that four Jap carriers meant the balance of power in the Pacific; that they were far distant now and might soon escape entirely. The order that went to Torpedo 8 was: "Attack at once."

Without fighter protection, the planes attacked, with a devastating effect worthy of their name. But from that attack not one

395

plane returned; and the only man to survive was Ensign George H. Gay, who was able to pancake his blasted Devastator into the ocean. He got free of his plane, although he was wounded, and he clung to a life raft. Floating there, he had a fish-eye view of the Battle of Midway.

What Torpedo 8 started so brilliantly the other squadrons carried on. By nightfall of June 4, the Navy tally looked like this: 4 Jap carriers out of action; six other surface ships damaged, including 2 battleships; 1 destroyer sunk. And the Battle of Midway continued for two days more, the Japs in flight and the Navy pursuing. When the remnants of the Japanese force had finally vanished and the Navy checked losses, the heaviest one, outside of the losses in planes, proved to be the sinking of *Yorktown*.

She had seen a lot of war, for just before Midway she had concluded a combat cruise of 104 days, one of the longest in naval history.

At Midway the Japanese Navy received its first major and decisive defeat in three hundred and fifty years. At Midway the danger of attack on Hawaii and the West Coast was ended, and the balance of power was restored in the Pacific. At Midway the course of the war in the Pacific was changed.

Guadalcanal

The Central Pacific had proved unpleasantly hot for the Japs, so later in the summer of '42 they turned their attention southward again. For renewed attack on American supply lines to Australia and New Zealand, they began to build an airfield on an obscure island which few Americans had ever heard of. It was named Guadalcanal.

The day the Marines went ashore on Guadalcanal and neighboring Tulagi they took the Japs by surprise, and in twenty-four hours they had control of Tulagi and of the airfield on "Guadal." That was the comparatively easy beginning to one of the most fiercely fought and exhausting campaigns in any war. Besides the furious land fighting, it included seven distinct naval battles and innumerable raids. Because the Americans had to hold or have their supply lines destroyed, because the Japs came back again and again, the name Guadalcanal became as familiar and important a word to every American as Bunker Hill or Gettysburg.

In the first naval battle of the Guadalcanal campaign, occurring off tiny Savo Island, the Navy took a beating. An American force was caught by surprise in the early morning, and between 0145 and 0215 the cruisers *Quincy, Vincennes, Astoria,* and *Canberra* (Australian) were so badly smashed that they later sank, and three more ships were damaged. If the Japs had known how severe U. S. losses were, they could have made more capital of it than they did in the months to come.

The Japs did not pull off one of those surprises again. Their cruisers and battlewagons were banged around so smartly in the next engagement, off the Eastern Solomons, that the ships hurriedly retired. But in spite of raids on their shipping, the Japs continued to supply Guadalcanal, coming in with such persistent regularity that the Marines named the system the Tokyo Express.

In the protection of Uncle Sam's supply lines, the great carrier *Wasp* was sunk. Three torpedoes rammed into her, starting gasoline fires that flared a hundred feet into the air. Topside was ablaze, rattling and blasting with explosions, as the armed bombs in the planes, the machine-gun ammunition, and the charges in the gun trays went off, flinging shrapnel around. For an hour the crew struggled to save the *Wasp,* and then the order came from Captain F. C. Sherman to abandon ship. The men lined up their shoes along the deck and went over the side.

In October, 1942, Vice Admiral Ghormley's forces had their opportunity to repay the Japs in full for the surprise defeat of Savo Island. Repayment was made at the Battle of Cape Esperance, won by means of cruisers and surprise. Catching a Jap force at midnight as it moved toward Guadalcanal, the gun crews of the *San Francisco, Helena, Boise,* and *Salt Lake City* taught the enemy a short and lethal lesson in gunnery. *Salt Lake City* and

Boise sank a heavy cruiser, two destroyers, and an auxiliary, and damaged another CA and a CL—in the first twelve minutes. *"It was,"* said Captain Ernest G. Small of the *Salt Lake City*, *"a hell of a melee."*

There was no pause for rest in the Guadalcanal campaign. A few weeks after Cape Esperance the fighting took to the air, in the Battle of Santa Cruz Island. The Japanese force contained two carriers and so did the U. S. force—*Hornet* and *Enterprise*. It is estimated that the two American flat-tops were attacked by a total of 180 planes; that anti-aircraft fire brought down 56 of them. In that remarkable AA performance, one ship accounted for 32 of the planes—a type of ship that some of the armchair experts had decided was obsolete. That was Captain T. L. Gatch's famous "Battleship X," the new *South Dakota*. The men on the carriers at Santa Cruz would not have agreed that the battle-wagon was obsolete.

While the anti-aircraft gunners were tearing holes in Nipponese air power, the men upstairs were busy on the same task. Flyers knocked down another fifty attacking Jap planes. One of the flyers, Lieutenant Stanley Vejtasa, disposed of five Japs in one engagement, having brought down two others and possibly three earlier in the day. Afterwards he remarked: *"Just think—if only I'd had more ammunition!"*

The Santa Cruz Island battle temporarily eliminated two enemy carriers from combat, but the Navy lost one flat-top permanently. *Hornet* had been so battered that she had to be abandoned and sunk.

On October 26 Major General Vandegrift's Guadalcanal Marines killed 2,200 Japs in one engagement. Those statistics convinced the Japanese high command that if they did not throw another and even heavier force into the campaign, it would be lost. At the same time Admiral Halsey, who had assumed command in the South Pacific, was determined to bring in urgently needed supplies. The two decisions, American and Jap, met each other in an explosion known as the Battle of Guadalcanal.

November 13—the moon was blacked out that night as Rear Admiral D. J. Callaghan led his ships up "the slot" between Guadalcanal and Florida Island. The American force moved toward the Japs in single column—4 destroyers, then 5 cruisers, then 4 more destroyers. It was nightmare duty for the lookouts, straining to penetrate the darkness. But before the Japs were aware of what was coming, *Helena* had located them, and the American ships had steamed closer—so close that when a Jap searchlight blazed, the two forces were almost colliding. Then the guns began.

Searchlights were quickly shattered. But within one minute a Jap heavy cruiser had blown up and the glare showed how powerful the enemy force was, stretched out on each side of the Americans. The flagship *San Francisco* tangled with a battleship at such close range that the Japs could not depress their big guns to fire at the hull. Instead they smashed the *San Francisco's* superstructure, killing Admiral Callaghan, the skipper, Captain Cassin Young (hero of the *Vestal* at Pearl Harbor), and the executive officer. Lieutenant Commander Bruce McLandless, Jr., the OOD, assumed command and kept his ship fighting although he was wounded twice. As a destroyer threw torpedoes and shells at the *San Francisco*, one of her five-inch mounts was being manned by three wounded men—one missing an arm, another a leg, the third with a hole in his belly.

This is what the battle was like: *Atlanta* crippled and out of control, with Rear Admiral Norman Scott dead on board, ninety seconds after the action began; the destroyer *Cushing* trading machine-gun fire with a battle wagon; another DD, *Laffey*, using her only remaining gun to sink a Jap ship; *Helena* knocking out a cruiser with her main battery, then a destroyer with her secondary. That was the way it went, until the Japs were firing at each other and the action was over. The entire action had lasted twenty-three minutes—*"one of the most furious sea battles ever fought,"* in the words of Admiral King.

And the Battle of Guadalcanal wasn't finished. The next day the BB's *South Dakota* and *Washington* went into action, along with destroyers and bombers. The third day the destroyer *Meade* had a field day all by herself, moving leisurely up and down the Guadalcanal coast and blasting away at beached Jap shipping.

That three-day battle won control of the sea and the air in the southern Solomons. The Japs made a last challenge on November 30, off Tassafaronga—a challenge that cost us one heavy cruiser and serious damage to three more. But the Imperial Japanese Fleet had been stopped dead in the water; and five weeks later the Marines had won their campaign on Guadalcanal.

Amphib

In the thunder and fury of the Guadalcanal campaign it is easy to neglect an important fact: Guadalcanal was the first American beachhead of the war. The Marines had studied and practiced ship-to-shore operations for years; now they carried out the first in World War II. But from a look at the map of the war zones it was clear that sooner or later millions of soldiers would have to establish beachheads on enemy soil; and it was one of the Navy's tasks to bring them safely to those beaches. Ship to shore—that would become the bridge to victory. So a new outfit was born in the Navy—the Amphibious Force.

Military experts call amphibious invasions the most difficult of all military operations. Hitler and Hirohito hoped they would prove impossible for us. Certainly they couldn't be accomplished without special and rigorous training, special and rugged ships. So the Navy set to work to supply both.

From the shipyards came peculiar, unlovely craft which were designed to do exactly what seamen for centuries had been using all their skill to avoid. These vessels were intended to run up on the beach. With their shallow draft, their tubby lines, their bows that dropped open, and their ramps, they would have horrified an old frigate man like John Paul Jones. But these ugly ducklings were essential in the bridge to victory.

To handle the landing craft, large and small, men were especially trained at bases on both coasts. They were taught how to maneuver boats in any kind of surf, how to cope with the tactical, communication, and gunnery problems of amphibious operations. Above all, they were trained to work in perfect coordination with the Army. For without teamwork, invasion would fail.

A main purpose of amphibious operations was to gain bases. The Marines and the Army seized the territory, but specialists were needed to bring supplies ashore, to repair, and to build. They had to be specialists who knew how to fight. That need

brought another new outfit into the Navy, recruited from construction men and mechanics, commanded by engineer officers. The Seabees.

At Guadalcanal the Seabees started their reputation for performing miracles by having Henderson Field ready for use in an amazingly short time. They took for themselves the motto: "Can Do, Will Do—Did." And they weren't fooling. In every amphibious operation they went ashore in the first waves. They built, and fought the enemy while they were building. On New Guinea in 1943 they chopped an airfield out of the dense tropical jungle in thirteen days. During the first eleven days there was sixteen and a half inches of rainfall. Were these Seabees rugged? Off Sicily ninety survivors of a bombed ship were pulled out of the water by four Seabees. Were they fast? General Vandegrift reported that his Marine officers said of the Seabees: *"They build roads so fast that the Japs are using them for avenues of escape."*

Amphib was getting ready for something big, the biggest thing of its kind in military history. It came on 8 November 1942, when an allied armada of 500 transports and supply ships and 350 warships swept down on North Africa. Running in size from trawlers to liners, these ships had to move across 3,000 miles of sub-infested waters and arrive at the right spot at the right minute. Until the actual landings began, there was only one casualty—the torpedoed transport *Thomas Stone*. And the troops from her boated 150 miles to Algiers in the *Thomas Stone's* landing craft.

The North African invasion, commanded by Lieutenant General Dwight D. Eisenhower, was divided into three main operations —two of them in the Mediterranean at Oran and Algiers; the third on the Atlantic coast of French Morocco, around Casablanca. The Royal Navy gave support to composite British and American landing forces in the Mediterranean; but the Moroccan invasion was entirely U. S. Navy business, directed by Rear Admiral H. K. Hewitt. And here the invasion met the bitterest resistance.

The Moroccan attack was split three ways, with the main force hitting the beach at Fedala, 15 miles north of Casablanca. This rock-bound shore is known as the "Iron Coast," always dangerous to mariners and particularly dangerous to amphibians. They were lucky to have a smooth sea that morning, but as the Army waded out of the surf, the French opened up with vicious machine-gun fire. *Augusta* and *Brooklyn*, with covering destroyers, stood inshore and threw some big stuff at the shore batteries. It was a busy day for the cruisers, for the French sent a cruiser and half a dozen destroyers out for action. They got it; all the enemy ships were either sunk or beached. The two other Moroccan landings, at Safi and Port Lyautey, did not meet serious resistance.

Islands on the Road to Tokyo

Back at the time of Midway, the Japs had stretched a long arm northward and seized the Aleutian Islands of Kiska and Attu. These barren, wind-swept islands, wrapped in the gloom of endless fog, sat in the northern route to Tokyo, and in the Japanese northern route to North America. They were, therefore, important.

They were also one of the most difficult battlefronts in the world. Day is like night up there; the seas run high; and there are continual squalls swirling out of the storm factory of the Bering Sea. To make it worse, at first the Navy had little to fight with except the Catalinas of Patwing 4. These PBY's weren't suited to this type of bombing duty, but the Patwing 4 flyers did it anyway.

Then bases built by the Seabees on the tiny islands of Adak and Amchitka enabled Army bombers to set to work on softening up the Japs. It went on for months, in spite of snow, ice, sleet, and rain. On 11 May 1943, an amphibious force led by Rear Admiral F. W. Rockwell descended on Attu, landed, and annihilated practically every Jap on the island in savage fighting. After that the amphibs were prepared to claim they could take any island, anywhere, any time. Three months later they climbed ashore on Kiska, but the Japs did not want any more. They had gone away, and the Aleutian campaign was over.

More islands—far to the south. More landings, on New Guinea and New Georgia, and later on Bougainville, in the slow, bloody progress toward Tokyo. When the Marines had taken Munda airfield on New Georgia and the Seabees had put it in shape, Uncle Sam's grip was firm on the Central Solomons.

In the last days of the Tokyo Express the South Pacific Force fought the two battles of Kula Gulf. They closed that traffic route to the Japs, but in the first of the engagements the Navy lost a great ship. She was *Helena*, repaired after Pearl Harbor and a veteran of thirteen engagements in eleven months of war. Tokyo knew about her, for after one of her bombardments the Jap radio announced that the Americans were using "a new secret weapon—a 6-inch machine gun." The secret weapon, of course, was the speed of *Helena's* gun crews. Through twelve battles and innumerable raids *Helena* had lost just one man.

Nowhere did the news of her sinking strike harder than aboard the destroyer *O'Bannon* who had been her battle companion and was called the *"Little Helena."* The beautiful way those two ships worked together, the way *Helena* "looked after" the little ship, had become legendary in the South Pacific. When the cruiser sank, the *O'Bannon* crew, to a man, requested permission to go on a suicide search for *Helena* survivors. *"They are our buddies,"* the crew's spokesman said.

Island Road to Rome

It looked like a floating city, the fleet of ships stretched across the skyline. And yet this was only a part of the whole, a unit of the enormous Allied force that invaded Sicily from newly conquered Tunisia in July of 1943. Coming from different bases within the Mediterranean on a staggered time schedule, 3,266 American and British ships took part in the invasion— half of them ships of the U. S. Navy.

And they had rough going. For a month before, the Mediterranean had been smooth as a bathtub, but now she began kicking up. One of the first American waves was transported entirely by landing craft, escorted by PC's and SC's. The little vessels heaved and rolled, showing half their bottoms; the seas ran so high that postponement was considered by the Allied command. But the invasion wasn't postponed, and the little ships got there.

Vice Admiral Hewitt's American forces struck the south coast at Scoglitti, Gela, and Licata. That third landing was particularly tough; it was there that the U. S. Navy battled against tanks. The enemy had launched a tank counterattack before the Army could establish anti-tank fire on the beach, and that counterattack threatened to smash the beachhead. Solution: cruisers and destroyers moved inshore, opened fire, and drove back the enemy tanks, saving the American landing force.

Two months later, when the Allied troops had crossed Messina Strait and moved up the Italian Peninsula, another huge amphibious operation was carried out at Salerno. Here the Nazi troops were dug in solidly in the hills above the beach. The LST's and the LCI's had to run in to the beach under withering German fire in order to reinforce the Army. If anybody still had doubts about those little amphibs, the doubts ended at Salerno.

The last amphibious assault of the Italian campaign struck at Anzio on 21 January 1944. Again the Nazis fought savagely and with skill; and Anzio became one of the bloodiest beachheads of the war. But with the thundering support of cruiser and destroyer guns the Allied ground forces began to inch forward on the road to Rome.

Beachheads In the Central Pacific

Because the Japanese offensive threat in the South Pacific was ended, and because the nation's production lines had strengthened the Pacific Fleet in an amazingly short time, Admiral Nimitz was able to acquire some land in the Central Pacific. There he created a Central Pacific Force, placing it under command of Vice Admiral Spruance. The new force did not wait long for action.

On the morning of 20 November, after delivering a terrific bombardment and air bombing, the Central Pacific Force invaded the Gilbert Islands, landing Marines on Tarawa and soldiers on Makin. Tarawa—there had been nothing in the Pacific war to equal this battle. At one point on the island the bodies of

105 Marines were counted in a space covering twenty yards. Into seventy-two dreadful hours the Marines crammed a whole war of fighting, losing more than a thousand men, killing more than four thousand Japs. *"Guadalcanal,"* one veteran said, *"was a picnic."*

In the Makin operation the Navy lost a great combat flyer who had already become a legend. Back in 1942, Butch O'Hare had saved the old *Lexington* almost single-handed by shooting down five enemy bombers and damaging a sixth in a matter of minutes. That had earned him the Congressional Medal of Honor. At Makin, Lieutenant Commander Edward H. O'Hare, now an air group commander, failed to return from a night battle with Jap torpedo planes. Once again Butch O'Hare had prevented disaster, for Rear Admiral Radford said: *"O'Hare, with accompanying planes, saved my formation from certain torpedo hits."*

The Central Pacific Force moved on, toward Tokyo. Vice Admiral Spruance opened the year 1944 with the greatest operation, so far, in the Pacific war. With forces larger than the entire Navy at the time of Pearl Harbor, he launched an attack on the Marshall Islands, held by Japan since 1914. Thirty years had given the Japs plenty of time to fortify the atolls; but the Central Pacific Force attended to those fortifications.

By the time the troops had gone ashore, a total of 15,000 tons of bombs and shells had been unloaded on the atolls of Kwajalein, Rio, and Namur. Did those explosives do the necessary job? Well, Rear Admiral R. K. Turner's amphibious force met some stiff resistance; but the Japs did not use a single large gun or a single plane. Their guns and planes had been obliterated.

Kwajalein was conquered in a week—Uncle Sam's first conquest of pre-war Japanese territory. Vice Admiral Spruance had not lost a ship. So, while the guns were still firing in the Marshalls, he refueled many of his carriers, battleships, cruisers, and destroyers, and executed a devastating two-day raid on Truk, the Japanese Pearl Harbor. Nineteen enemy ships were sunk and 201 planes destroyed, chiefly by the flyers from Rear Admiral Marc A. Mitscher's fast carrier force (to become so renowned as "Task Force 58"). Announcing the blow at Truk, Admiral Nimitz said: *"The Pacific Fleet has returned at Truk the visit paid by the Japanese Fleet on December 7, 1941, and effected a partial settlement of the debt."*

Five hundred planes attacking—two hundred aircraft destroyed —in these vast engagements the statistics sometimes obscure the separate, heroic acts which fit together in the pattern of victory. The Truk raid, for instance, produced the story of William J. Moak, AMM2c. The TBF in which he manned the turret was attacked fifteen times by three Jap fighters. Early in the fight, flying glass and metal splinters wounded Moak in the right arm and temporarily blinded his right eye. Then the ammunition feed of his gun began to jam. He was holding the ammunition with his good hand and operating the gun with his wounded one when he discovered that the TBF had caught fire. Climbing down from the turret, he dragged a wounded radioman out of the fire, beat at the flames, and then returned to blast at the Jap fighters. But the fire wasn't extinguished; he went back twice to fight it. When the heat began to explode the ammunition for the tunnel gun, he pulled out the exploding cartridges with his bare hands, heaved them out of the plane, and returned to his gun again. It was after the pilot had brought the TBF back to her carrier in a crash landing that Moak learned he had shot down one of the Japs. That satisfied him.

Anti-Sub, Atlantic

No war can be won without supply lines—Hitler knew that. He knew that if he could prevent supplies from reaching England and Russia, American troops from reaching Europe, he would be free to arrange the continent according to his own design. So he gambled on U-boats, on undersea "wolf packs" to cut the Atlantic chain of supply. And his gamble very nearly proved good.

Those U-boats were blasting ships in the Atlantic long before 7 December 1941. The moment the U. S. entered the war the subs came prowling into American coastal waters, torpedoing ships before they were well underway, laying mines to seal the harbors. There were brief periods in 1942 when New York harbor and the Chesapeake Bay ports were closed by German mines. To fight this battle so close to home, the Navy set up sea frontier commands from Maine to the Caribbean and armed them with rugged little patrol vessels, with patrol planes, and lighter-than-air craft. It was a tough, silent battle, but gradually the patrol tightened into a protective sea wall. The U-boats retired from American shores.

In the Atlantic, however, they increased in menace, sinking fifty, sixty, and seventy ships a month in 1942. The convoy system had been established, for if the merchant ships straggled out alone into the Atlantic they were easy prey. To give these convoys fighting power, the Navy called for new types of ships. Called for escort carriers, which could serve in convoy duty as efficiently as their bigger sisters. For destroyer escorts, small fast ships armed with depth charges. The first of these joined the fleet early in 1943, and as they grew in size, in numbers, and in effectiveness, Hitler's U-boat war began to look like a bad gamble for him.

The Navy also invented a new outfit to fight the anti-submarine war The Armed Guard, it was called, an organization specializing in fighting against heavy odds. These small Navy gun crews, each commanded by a naval officer, went aboard every merchant ship. They fought U-boats, and on the terrible "Murmansk Run" to Russia they fought land-based German planes.

There were hundreds of episodes proving how vital a part the Armed Guard played in the Battle of the Atlantic; here is one of them—In a week-long battle with Nazi subs and planes the Armed Guard crew of the Liberty ship *William Moultrie* shot down eight bombers and damaged twelve others with hits, drove a U-boat away with gunfire, and with the accuracy of their marksmanship exploded an approaching torpedo before it reached the ship.

The Navy could not beat the U-boats by efficient convoys alone; it had to go out hunting. This was the task of Admiral Royal E. Ingersoll's Atlantic Fleet—to cover the whole breadth of the Atlantic in search of submarines. The way the fleet accomplished its task is well illustrated by the story of Task Group 21.14, awarded a Presidential Unit Citation for destroying more U-boats than any other naval team in history.

The unit was composed of the escort carrier *Card*, Squadrons 1 and 9, containing Avenger torpedo bombers and Wildcat fighters, and three old destroyers of 1917 vintage—*Barry*, *Goff*, and *Borie*. In a three-day period late in 1943 this team accounted for at least five U-boats, and *Borie* fought one of those subs in hand-to-hand combat.

On a night foray the *Borie* neatly disposed of one U-boat and proceeded in search for more. She found her second, all right—at such close quarters that there was only one thing to do and the *Borie* did it: she rammed her prow over the bow of the U-boat. The Nazis came up on deck, the *Borie* crew came on deck; and one of the queerest battles of the war was on.

One *Borie* gun crew couldn't depress their gun enough because of the shield, so they cut a hole in the shield and fired through it. The executive officer blazed away with a tommy-gun; others fired shotguns, pistols, even signal pistols. The gun captain started heaving empty shell cases at the Nazis, and another man threw his knife and knocked a German overboard. After ten minutes of this hand-to-hand battle, the U-boat broke away. She rammed the destroyer. By then, one engine room crew was neck-deep in water and topside was a mess; but the *Borie* kept on fighting. She fired until the U-boat blew up. But the old destroyer had been so battered and her machinery was so fouled with water that she didn't live long after her remarkable victory. She was abandoned the next day in the North Atlantic.

But new, heavy, hard-slugging destroyers were joining the fleet, and Admiral King could announce in March of 1944 that the U-boats had *"changed status from menace to problem."*

Subs, Pacific

Three cruisers and four destroyers were unusually heavy escort for only three transports, making the mission of the submarine *Seawolf* all the more important and hazardous. She slipped into the harbor of Christmas Island where the transports were unloading, and took her aim and fired. Within a couple of minutes after the explosion of the torpedoed Jap vessels, the depth charges started coming. They came so fast that one detonation was indistinguishable from the next, merging in one steady, seemingly endless explosion. Under the blasting impact, the sub sprang several leaks; but Lieutenant Commander Frederick B. Warder got her out of the harbor safely.

There was more work to be done in the neighborhood of Christmas Island. That night the sub spotted an enemy light cruiser and sank her. Destroyers appeared, depth charges dropped; but the submarine crew was getting accustomed to having a noisy time down below. And there was still work to be done. The next day the sub went back into Christmas Island harbor, where the four Jap tincans and two cruisers were on hand. The sub picked out the largest cruiser and sent torpedoes to their destination. Again the torpedoed ship's explosion was swiftly followed by the boom and smash and shudder of depth charges. It kept on and on, until the air down there was almost unbreathable from long submergence. Until the only hope of survival lay in some kind of miracle. And then the miracle occurred. The sub struck a deep current that carried her out of the harbor and sufficiently far away so that she could surface, take a long breath, and head for her base.

These submarine men went places where only Japs were supposed to go in the early days of the war. Lieutenant Commander Thomas B. Klarking torpedoed a couple of ships so close to the home island of the Rising Sun that his sub was fired on by the shore batteries. Later, on a quiet Sunday afternoon, his crew had a periscope view of a horserace at a Japanese seaside track. The men made bets and they were annoyed when they weren't able to find out which horse won. Yes, the submarine men liked to keep in touch with things on Japan.

There was no sea hideaway for the Japs that was safe from American submarines. Commander Eugene B. Fluckey, skipper of the submarine *Barb*, had suspected for some time the existence of a secret Jap harbor; and one day he found it. Tankers, freighters, and ammunition ships lay in the concealed anchorage, the entrances guarded by screen of warships. If the *Barb* went in, she would have to cruise on the surface of shallow, heavily mined waters. Commander Fluckey figured that she wouldn't be able to submerge for at least an hour after the attack. That meant the pursuit would have a comparatively easy target, and Commander Fluckey knew there would be plenty of pursuit. But the *Barb* went in that night.

She slipped through the darkness to an attack position. She sent her torpedoes into the massed enemy shipping and it disintegrated in flame, smoke, and explosion; ship after ship blowing up and then blending into one vast fire. On the *Barb's* bridge, Commander Fluckey could not pause to study results. The moment after firing, he headed his ship at flank speed toward the rocks strewn in the harbor. That was the plan of escape he had previously worked out—to take the *Barb* through uncharted waters filled with rocks, where the Jap escorts might not dare follow. Lying in the escape route of the *Barb* were dozens of fishing junks; the sub dodged and twisted among them, with shells from the Jap escorts falling close by. But as Commander Fluckey had hoped, the fishing junks confused the pursuit; as he had figured, the escorts did not follow him among the rocks. By dawn the *Barb* reached open water, undamaged and with a magnificent achievement behind her.

These episodes illustrate something that was routine in the battle of the Pacific—the unrelaxing vigilance, the skill, and the matter-of-fact daring of the submarine service. Submarine men do not sit around talking about "heroism" and "devotion to duty," but if they wanted to give an example of both, they would undoubtedly tell the story of Commander Howard W. Gilmore, captain of *Growler* when she fought a surface engagement with

a Japanese gunboat. In the exchange of gunfire the Japs wounded Commander Gilmore and so seriously endangered *Growler* that it was urgent to make a quick dive. Only the commander was on deck now, too badly wounded to get below without help; and the safety of ship depended on instant action. *"Take her down!"* Commander Gilmore ordered. He was there on deck when his ship submerged.

Without a large merchant fleet, the Japs could not supply their advance bases, or bring home the raw materials from their temporary empire. The Japanese merchant fleet did not remain large for long—because of the Silent Service.

Ready to Rampage

You could not put your finger on a date in the calendar; you could not say—here, this was the day the change came. But you knew when the change had come. When the Navy proved herself with such huge achievements as the invasion of North Africa and the Marshalls, when she was carrying out her own plans with perfect assurance and always with superior force, then the change had come. Then the Navy was ready to rampage. The next chapter is the story of her rampaging.

SIGHTED SUB: SANK SAME

Seapower Spells Victory

1944—the whole U. S. Navy was on the offensive. That's a big word, a headline word with the ringing sound of victory. But an offensive does not just happen like an explosion; it requires meticulous planning and intricate organization for a fighting force the size of the U. S. Navy in 1944. Where was the nerve center controlling this American naval power?

That nerve center was the Navy Department in Washington, D. C. There Fleet Admiral Ernest J. King held the Navy's two highest commands: Commander-in-Chief United States Fleet (Cominch) and Chief of Naval Operations (CNO). The broadest aspects of strategic planning, however, could not be carried out without close teamwork between the Army and the Navy, and so the basic, major decisions were made by a board called the Joint Chiefs of Staff. These men composed the joint board: Fleet Admiral William D. Leahy, Chief of Staff to the Commander-in-Chief of the Army and Navy; General of the Army George C. Marshall, Chief of Staff of the Army; Fleet Admiral Ernest J. King, Cominch and CNO; and General of the Army Henry H. Arnold, Commanding General Army Air Forces. And even these high officers could not act without the approval of higher authority—the Commander-in-Chief of the Army and Navy, Franklin D. Roosevelt, President of the United States.

The Navy Department in Washington, a complex structure of bureaus and offices, was the core of the vast shore organizations necessary to the fleet. What the Navy achieved at sea had its origin on land: in the Navy Yards, the operating bases, the training centers, the air stations, the gun factories, the laboratories. Naval warfare had come a long way since the cutlass-and-cannon days, and victory was born in the mathematicians' calculations and the experiments of the scientists. Radar, sonar, degausing, rockets, jet propulsion—these were a few of the scientific achievements that speeded the Navy toward victory.

Because the States-side Navy had to be so huge, a new outfit joined the service. The official designation was Women Accepted for Volunteer Emergency Service—which means the WAVES. As Yeomen, Storekeepers, Pharmacist's Mates, Radiomen,

Aviation Machinist's Mates, and Aviation Metalsmiths, they took over countless shore details, releasing men for sea duty. Women in the Navy! It was the beginning of the end, some of the old-timers muttered. They quit muttering soon enough when they saw the girls doing their jobs as well as and better than the men had done them. Fleet Admiral King said that Navy shore efficiency in many cases had increased with the arrival of the Waves.

The Longest Pipeline in the World

The scientist in the Naval Research Laboratory and the Wave Y3c in BuPers had the same fundamental purpose—to serve the fleet, to keep the Navy in fighting trim. Perhaps no part of that service to the fleet posed so many and such staggering problems as the task of supply. If you've had duty in the Pacific, you realize the difficulty of that task, for you know how enormous the distances are out there. Bases located half the world away and ships operating thousands of miles from any base had to be supplied. They needed everything from potatoes to high-capacity ammunition, and they needed a lot of it all.

The Japs counted on an operational limit for the American fleet. Before World War II a naval force did not attempt a lengthy mission over great distances because there was always the hazard of exhausted supplies. This seemed to promise safety to the Japs. They did not see how the U. S. Navy could ram an offensive down their throats. They were rudely awakened from this deep dream of security when Admiral Spruance's Fifth Fleet arrived at the Marshalls and then at Truk and Guam —a cruise of some eight thousand miles. That just wasn't in the book.

But the U. S. Navy had added another chapter to the book. The Navy had developed the train, or more properly the Service Force, to a degree where it possessed all the magic potency of a secret weapon. The Service Force amounted to a complete base that could follow the warships wherever they went. Food, water, oil, ammunition—the auxiliaries had them ready for immediate delivery. Repairs—any damaged ship still floating could be patched sufficiently well so that she could return to her base, and often so well that she did not have to return. Thirty-six types of auxiliaries composed the Service Force, 17 of the classes new with this war. There were floating dry docks, many of them—and right where needed. With the support of this enormous "A" fleet, combat ships remained at sea for

months at a time, operating over virtually unlimited distances. The Japanese brand of isolationism had proved untenable. No wonder one high Jap official remarked sadly: *"Our island bases in the Pacific are unsinkable, but they are not very maneuverable."*

To Keep the Men at the Guns

"To keep as many men at as many guns as many days as possible"—that is the slogan of the Navy Medical Department. How well these men and women lived up to their slogan makes one of the finest stories of the war. Ask a wearer of the Purple Heart about the skill of the Navy doctors, nurses, and corpsmen. Read their record of achievement in this simple statement: of

the wounded who lived long enough to receive medical attention, 98 out of every 100 survived.

The Navy developed new methods of medical care. Mobile hospitals were organized and trained as units in the States, then sent overseas. Surgical landing craft, fully equipped, hit the beaches with the first waves of amphibs; and jeep ambulances brought the wounded to the medical stations. Among the most important of the new techniques was the evacuation of the wounded by air, which saved thousands of lives.

There were new treatments. The sulfa drugs, penicillin, improved burn treatments, insect control to combat malaria—they served the Navy well. But most doctors, if you asked them to name the greatest single factor in the success of war medicine, would probably answer you with one word: PLASMA. Here was a lifesaver which every corpsman could administer as soon as he found a wounded man lying on the beach. It was simple, like most miracles.

For the doctors and the corpsmen it was combat duty in every way but one; they did not shoot back. On the decks and the beaches they took whatever the enemy was throwing while they

went about their work. Kids just out of high school, men from banks and factories, the corpsmen joined the fleet or the Marines after a brief specialized training, and they accomplished things that would have called for a medical consultation back home. In a Guadalcanal fox-hole a Pharmacist's Mate amputated the leg of a wounded Marine and saved his life by the operation. In a submarine another Pharmacist's Mate performed a successful appendectomy without medical guidance or proper instruments. With skill and daring the corpsmen kept their shipmates at the guns.

Normandy: Hitler's Fortress Falls

Fortress Europe, Hitler called it; he boasted that the shores of his conquered empire were impregnable. But he must have known that some day the Allies would challenge him; and he must have realized why ships were massing in the English ports through the winter of 1943 and the following spring. The allies were coming. But where, when?

Where? The Allied High Command had to select a spot fairly close to English airfields and serviceable English ports, a spot not too ruggedly fortified. The choice was Normandy. When? Weather and tide affected this decision, for the long days of late spring or early summer would give the most opportunity to the air forces; and a spring tide would carry the landing craft far up on the beaches at high tide and expose beach obstacles at low water. The choice was the first week in June.

Again General Eisenhower held supreme command. The Allied Naval Commander-in-Chief was British Admiral Sir Bertram H. Ramsay. Under him there were two great task forces—the Eastern, composed of British ships and British and Canadian soldiers; the Western representing Uncle Sam. Commanded by Rear Admiral A. G. Kirk, the American armada consisted of two assault forces and a follow-up force, scheduled to strike Normandy in two places called "Omaha Beach" and "Utah Beach." In all, 2,479 ships of the U. S. Navy took part in the invasion of Normandy.

By 3 June the troops had been loaded on the ships and briefed. D-day was scheduled for 5 June, but a forecast of bad weather caused a postponement. D-day: 6 June, 1944.

The minesweeps came first. British and American, they carried out the greatest minesweeping operation in history. As they cleared the seas, the Allied Air Forces operated a lethal shuttle system between England and Hitler's already tottering fortress. Then the big Navy guns began to thunder in the dawn. Here were the three oldest battle-wagons in the U. S. Fleet slugging away like youngsters—*Arkansas*, *Texas*, and *Nevada*. They smashed at the beaches, the cliffs, and guided by specially trained Shore Fire Control parties and by planes, they threw their shells far inland at enemy troops and tanks. Indeed, this heavy fire from battleships and cruisers proved so powerful and accurate that the Nazi military commentators remarked on it afterward over the air. The "floating batteries," the Germans said, "enabled the invaders to achieve overpowering artillery concentrations at any point along the coast."

Of the two beaches assaulted, "Omaha" turned out the tougher —very tough indeed. There was a choppy sea. The bombers had been prevented by bad weather from doing a thorough preliminary job. And entirely by accident a German division happened to be holding exercises nearby and joined immediately in the defense. The landing craft and the wading troops had to make their way through a vicious tangle of underwater obstacles of iron, wood, and concrete. As the troops reached the beach, the Germans caught them in a cross-fire from artillery, machine-guns, and mortars. But they clung to those first few yards of liberated Europe, and destroyers moved in daringly close to shore to pound the Nazi defenses. By 1330 that day the American troops were advancing up the slopes of the beach.

At Utah Beach the first waves went in with less difficulty. The seas ran heavy, but the amphibious tanks rode them successfully to the beach where enemy fire was weak. Later on, the coastal batteries, temporarily silenced by air attack, began to operate again. Here once more the shore fire control parties proved invaluable, directing the big guns of *Nevada* and *Quincy*, blasting away at the Nazis and their guns. In the first 12 hours at Utah Beach, Force U landed 21,328 troops, 1,742 vehicles, and 1,695 tons of supplies.

The assault was only the first step in the invasion. The Navy had a second, in some respects even more complicated task—

to reinforce and supply the beachhead fast enough to build an army larger than the enemy's. Because the large French ports had been so heavily fortified, the Allies had not launched the invasion against them; but now, to support the great expeditionary force, the Navy needed the protection and facilities of harbors. So in one of the most remarkable engineering feats of the war, the Navy brought its own harbors to the beaches of Normandy.

Small boat shelters, given the code name "Gooseberries," were formed by sinking old warships and merchant ships in shallow water. That was a simple operation compared with "Operation Mulberry." Two of these complete artificial harbors had been constructed in England, part by part, with the greatest secrecy, and a fleet of British and American tugs towed the Mulberries, part by part, to the French coast. With characteristic speed the Seabees sank hollow concrete caissons for a breakwater, secured floating pierheads, and connected them with the beach by a pontoon roadway and two sunken causeways. The Mulberry operation was proceeding on schedule—until a raging storm hit the coast. Not even the Seabees can secure a storm. When fair weather returned after three days of wild seas, three hundred ships lay stranded on the beach, many of them shattered; and the Mulberry had been wrecked. Since the storm had treated the British Mulberry far more gently, it was repaired with parts from the American one, and the Omaha Mulberry was abandoned. "Gooseberries" and pontoon causeways served as harbor protection at Utah and Omaha Beaches.

When the Army had fought its way into position, General Eisenhower clamped a squeeze on the great port of Cherbourg. Again those three ancient but far from decrepit battlewagons, *Arkansas, Texas,* and *Nevada,* swung into action, accompanied by the American cruisers *Tuscaloosa* and *Quincy,* two British cruisers, and 11 destroyers. During the three hours that they bombarded Cherbourg they were under continual, accurate fire from the Germans' twenty shore batteries; and almost every heavy ship was hit. But the floating artillery accomplished its mission: two days later Cherbourg had been captured.

One month after Normandy D-day, Cherbourg was operating as an Allied port and the Army was driving far inland. As the invasion armada had steamed toward France a month before, Admiral Kirk had said to his men: *"I await with confidence the further proof in this, the greatest battle of them all, that American sailors and seamen and fighting men are second to none."*

Proof had been given.

Conquest of the Marianas

It was a cheerless spring for the Japanese Empire. In April, General MacArthur's Southwest Pacific Forces had carried out landings in the Hollandia area of New Guinea, with the support of the redoubtable Task Force 58, that swift and powerful force of carriers, battleships, cruisers, and destroyers commanded by Rear Admiral Mitscher. The Hollandia landings had very nearly finished up the New Guinea campaign. After Hollandia, Task Force 58 had stopped by at Truk long enough to destroy more than a hundred planes trying to defend that insecure bastion.

Now, in the middle of June, Japanese weather became even stormier. Admiral Spruance brought against the Marianas an invasion force of more than 660 ships, more than 2,000 aircraft,

and 300,000 soldiers, sailors, and Marines. Conquest of the three key islands—Saipan, Guam, and Tinian—would provide Uncle Sam with bases within bombing range of Tokyo. It would also seal off the outposts of the Japanese empire, Truk among them.

Objective No. 1 was Saipan, which the Japs had held since World War I and had strongly fortified. After seven hours of battleship bombardment, after the minesweeper and Underwater Demolition Teams had cleaned the waters and the beaches, Vice Admiral R. K. Turner's amphibious force put the Marines ashore. With a blaze of rockets, being used on a large scale for the first time, the amphibians pushed their way in. But enemy artillery was good and there was plenty of it. The Marines met immediate and savage resistance.

As the landing craft carried their cargoes to Saipan on that first day of the invasion, Admiral Spruance received the sort of news that the Navy kept hoping for: the Japanese Navy was coming out to fight. The size of the approaching enemy force posed a threat to the whole Marianas operation; but the size of it also gave the Fifth Fleet a chance at a major victory.

Postponing the assault on Guam and Tinian, Admiral Spruance sent out some of his fast carriers and battleships to meet the enemy—not so far out, however, as to leave the Saipan operation unprotected.

The Japs, apparently, intended their carrier planes to refuel and rearm on Guam after they attacked the Fifth Fleet on 19 June. Jap aircraft arrived in strength, expecting to find the Americans unprepared, planning to smash the fleet and then fly on triumphantly to Guam. It didn't work out that way. The startled Japs ran smack into the ready and waiting air power of Task Force 58. That was bad enough for the enemy. Even worse, the Nip flyers who did succeed in reaching Guam found their airfield wrecked and more American planes waiting for them. It was a turkey shoot. By the end of that day Vice Admiral Mitscher's flyers had destroyed 402 Jap planes—with the loss of only 17. The next day TF 58 went in search of the Jap fleet.

The Jap commander, however, had been unpleasantly impressed by the activities of the previous day, and he had decided to

retire. It wasn't until afternoon that American search planes located the hurriedly retreating Jap ships, far distant now from Task Force 58. If Mitscher's flyers went out to attack, they would be tackling one of the most hazardous missions in flying history because of the great range and the approaching darkness. But if they did not attack now, a powerful Japanese force would escape entirely.

The airmen attacked.

Just before dusk, plunging through heavy anti-aircraft fire, they struck the wildly maneuvering Japanese ships. Three TBF's from Air Group 24, without accompanying fighters or dive-bombers, set the standard of the operation by sinking a 28,000-ton flat-top. That standard was maintained; the mission was accomplished. But the flyers' supply of fuel was running low, and now thick black night descended over the Pacific.

In the perilous return to the task force, 73 planes were lost because of exhausted fuel and landing crashes in the darkness. Most of the crews were rescued. Calculated by the grim arithmetic of war, far greater losses would have been justified by the results achieved on 20 June—2 carriers, 2 destroyers, and 1 tanker sunk; 3 carriers, 1 battleship, 3 cruisers, 1 destroyer, and 3 tankers severely damaged.

That ended the engagements which are now called the Battle of the Philippine Sea—a battle as costly to Japan as Midway. Admiral Spruance returned to his primary task, the conquest of the Marianas. And the Jap navy didn't appear again.

On Saipan the slogging battle continued, with the Japs dug into caves and fighting until they died. When the Marines smothered a banzai charge on 7 July, organized resistance on the island was virtually finished. Meanwhile preparations had begun for the reoccupation of Guam, the first U. S. territory seized by the Japs in the war. The airmen plastered the island; and every day for three weeks it was bombarded by heavy naval guns. When the amphibians assaulted the beaches at the end of July, the landscape of Guam had been altered by American explosives, but there were still Japs, ready to die fighting. The Tinian campaign, opening on 24 July, progressed more easily; and by the second week in August Uncle Sam had secured control of the three islands of the Marianas. No doubt Tokyo realized that bombers were scheduled to arrive soon.

Did you notice the mention of "Underwater Demolition Teams" in the invasion of Saipan? Their designation was UDT, and they were one of the most closely guarded and remarkable naval secrets of the war. First at Sicily and at the Marshalls, then at Normandy, the Marianas, and the Carolines, and later at the Philippines, Iwo Jima, and Okinawa, the Underwater Demolition Teams spearheaded the invasion.

They swam to enemy beaches ahead of the invasion barges, to clear away the explosives and barriers planted in shallow waters. These officers and men were all volunteers, picked to meet exacting physical standards and trained in greatest secrecy. The battle dress of an underwater demolition man was a pair of swimming trunks. His weapons were a knife and as many high-explosive charges as he could strap around his waist. And he worked under the muzzles of enemy guns. Dangerous? At Omaha Beach, Normandy, three out of every five underwater demolition men were casualties. But in two days they removed 85% of the German traps; and afterward every physically fit survivor volunteered for similar duty in the Pacific.

At Guam, when the first wave of Marines hit the beach, they found this sign:

> "Welcome to Guam, U. S. Marines.
> USO two blocks to the right.
>
> (Signed) Underwater Demolition Team Four."

Big Job Finished, Bigger Jobs Ahead

To his intense distaste, Adolph Hitler had been compelled to learn the potency of amphibious operations. Probably he was sick of the subject, but he received another lesson on 15 August 1944.

Down in the Mediterranean, where enemy activity was mild by now, Vice Admiral H. K. Hewitt, Commander Eighth Fleet, assembled a Western Task Force. From Naples and many other ports the ships set out for southern France—American, British, French, and Greek ships. They struck in three areas east of

Toulon, after a sea and air bombardment that paralyzed the strong Nazi fortifications. Paralyzed was the only word for it, because the landings went off with remarkable ease. The troops under Major General A. M. Patch swept inland so rapidly that the Navy's big problem was to keep the supplies coming fast enough.

Two weeks after the landings, the great ports of Toulon and Marseilles had surrendered. These ports were speedily made usable by the Seabees and the Army engineers. And here in southern France, one phase of the war had come to a close. It was the Mediterranean phase that had begun at North Africa. The Italian campaign had bogged down, it is true. But the concerted advance to the German frontier was now well under way.

In the Pacific, however, even bigger business for the Navy lay ahead. First of all, Admiral Nimitz had several essential details to clean up. preparatory to the major business; and so did General MacArthur. In the Western Carolines Admiral Halsey, now Commander Third Fleet, led a force against the Palau Islands. Timed with it was General MacArthur's assault on Morotai, under the naval command of Vice Admiral D. E. Barbey.

To support these operations, Vice Admiral Mitscher conducted his fast carriers, battleships, cruisers, and destroyers on a whirl-wind tour of Jap localities. Chichi Jima—Haha Jima—Iwo Jima—Yap—the Palaus, they all received a thorough pasting. While the Japs meditated on this display of air power, the air arm struck the Philippines, first in Mindanao, then in the central islands. These blows, destroying more than a hundred enemy planes on the ground, met unexpectedly light opposition—a fact of such importance that Admiral Halsey immediately boarded a plane and flew to confer with General MacArthur. The Japs learned their decisions later on. Too late.

Beginning on 15 September, the Third Fleet amphibious force under Vice Admiral Wilkinson carried out landings first on Peleliu, then on Angaur, and finally on several smaller islands. With the Palaus now in American hands, the Tokyo warlords found themselves pretty much out of touch with their empire to the south. Furthermore, General MacArthur's forces had landed on Morotai the day of the assault on Peleliu. And Morotai, as anyone can see on the map, is close to the Philippines.

Return to the Philippines

Radio Manila was playing "Music for Your Morning Mood" the morning of 21 September 1944 when American planes roared down the sky in the first carrier attack of the war on Manila and Luzon. As the Jap radio announcer interrupted the morning mood to scream an air raid warning, did he and his countrymen realize that history had reversed in a very unpleasant way? The time before it was the Japs who had struck Manila from the sky.

The American airmen hit Manila again, and other targets on Luzon. They raided the central islands—Leyte, Samar, and the western Visayans. Then the carrier force withdrew, only to make ready for even more important operations. Admiral Halsey's report on the weak air defense in the central Philippines had caused a change of plans, a speedup of the march back to the islands. Leyte would be the point of first assault, on 20 October (this time called A-day).

On A-day a powerful Central Philippine Attack Force, commanded by Vice Admiral Thomas C. Kinkaid, would land four Army divisions on Leyte. Scheduled to support the attack,

Admiral Halsey's Third Fleet began the preliminaries in the second week of October. The fast carrier force created another of those whirlwinds so disastrous to the Japs. It caught the enemy by surprise on Okinawa. It ravaged Aparri on northern Luzon. Then, invading the enemy backyard, the carrier force struck Formosa with such fury that 915 enemy planes were smashed. The Formosa battle lasted for several days while the Jap radio trumpeted about the huge American losses. The amazing thing was that the Japs apparently believed their own propaganda, for an enemy naval force put out to destroy the remnants of the allegedly shattered American fleet. Finding the Halsey fleet large as life and full of fight, the Japs promptly turned around and headed for home. Actually the damage to Third Fleet ships amounted to two cruisers hit but still afloat. And, on A-day minus 2, the carrier force (which the Japs had sunk over the radio) began a concentrated attack on the central and northern Philippines.

The Japs expected an eventual invasion of the Philippines, but they did not expect it at Leyte. The troops went ashore there on 20 October without meeting heavy opposition. Then, when the beachhead had been firmly established, the Japanese Navy threw everything it had.

Battle of Leyte Gulf

By driving in with three strong naval forces, the Japs attempted to crush the Leyte operation. Up through the Sulu Sea toward Surigao Strait came a southern force containing two battleships. A much stronger central force, composed of 5 battleships, 10 heavy cruisers, a couple of CL's, and about 15 destroyers, moved east through the Sibuyan Sea, heading for San Bernardino Strait. Finally, a northern force built around 4 carriers approached from the home islands. These three forces, according to Jap planning, were to execute a power play.

The Battle of Leyte Gulf developed into three distinct battles; but before they took shape, the enemy had been discovered and attacked. Two submarines caught first sight of the central force and proceeded at once to sink two cruisers. Then, on the morning of 24 October, carrier planes went after both the central and southern forces, inflicting particularly heavy damage on the enemy in the Sibuyan Sea. There the airmen sank the battleship *Musashi*, pride of the Japanese Navy, as well as a cruiser and a DD. The Japs retaliated with their land-based planes which fatally damaged the light carrier *Princeton*. Fires on board reached the magazines; the flames and explosions grew so fierce that the *Princeton* had to be abandoned and sunk by American gunfire. She was the first fast carrier to go down since the *Hornet* in 1942.

Those first-round blows brought blood, but they weren't knockout punches; the slugging lay ahead. So the Americans made ready. Vice Admiral Kinkaid held his Seventh Fleet in the waters near the Leyte beachhead; Admiral Halsey arranged the Third up and down the east coast of the Philippines. On the morning of 25 October the Philippines seas threshed in the turmoil of three full-scale naval battles.

The BATTLE OF SURIGAO STRAIT was the kind of sea fighting that admirals dream about. To prepare a reception for the

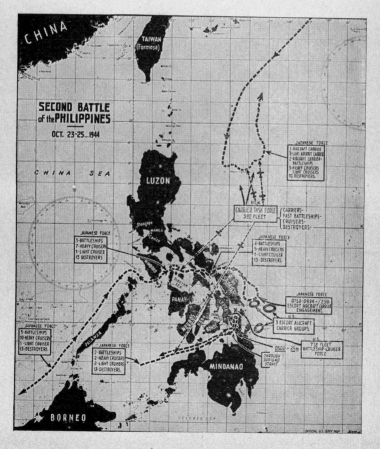

approaching Jap southern force, Admiral Jesse B. Oldendorf had sealed off the upper end of the strait with a line of old battleships—ships which Japan claimed to have sunk at Pearl Harbor. On each flank Admiral Oldendorf had arranged his cruisers and destroyers. Then he and his men settled down in the early morning to wait for the enemy.

PT boats, lurking at the lower entrance of the strait, made contact with the Japs at 0130, but Admiral Oldendorf let the enemy come on. They advanced in rough column formation, a force of 2 battlewagons, 1 heavy cruiser, and 2 destroyers. When they had steamed directly into the trap, the American destroyers opened the attack, rushing in from each flank to fire their torpedoes and then slipping out of range. Still the Japs kept moving minute by minute toward disaster. At a range of 16,000 yards Admiral Oldendorf ordered his battleships to open fire. According to the Admiral, *"Every damned salvo landed right on!"* For forty minutes the venerable battlewagons pounded away, and then the battered, burning Jap ships began to turn tail and retreat. Here, neat as a diagram on the blackboard, was a perfect demonstration of the classical naval tactic known as "crossing the T." Turning ships offer splendid targets, and the American gunners made the most of their opportunities. *"We really gave them hell on the knuckle,"* the Admiral said. *"So badly shattered were those ships that the brains of their commanders must have been shaken up as well. They kept coming in column, singly, like ducks in a shooting-gallery chain."*

In that early morning battle the Japs lost two battleships and three destroyers. The escaping cruiser was sunk by aircraft the next day.

But the BATTLE OFF SAMAR was no tactician's dream; in fact, it bore a much closer resemblance to a nightmare. To maintain patrols and support the land fighting, Vice Admiral Kinkaid had stationed three groups of escort carriers, with their destroyer and destroyer escort screens, off Samar. They hadn't the strength to tangle with a powerful surface force. But that was exactly what they had to do.

Air raids had banged up the Japanese central force, and some of the ships had turned back. But not all of them. Four battleships, 5 cruisers, and 11 destroyers had changed course and slipped down the east coast of Samar, unobserved. In the dawn of the 25th the escort carrier group commanded by Rear Admiral C. A. F. Sprague sighted the pagoda masts of Japanese battleships. Pagoda masts meant 16-inch guns, and Admiral Sprague had 6 escort carriers, 3 destroyers, and 4 DE's, with no guns larger than 5-inch and virtually no protective armor.

A running fight was the only chance; and running is a slow process for CVE's. As the big enemy ships drew within range, Wildcats and TBF's from the escort carriers lunged again and again at the Japs through heavy anti-aircraft fire. When their ammunition ran out, the planes executed dummy attacks simply to divert the enemy fire from the carriers. The DD's and DE's laid smoke screens and made gallant, suicidal sorties. Damaged, steered by hand, the destroyer *Hoel* launched her tin fish so effectively at a cruiser that the ship had to be abandoned. Then *Hoel* went down, after being struck by some forty shells. Also lost in that action, *Johnston* dueled for two hours with cruisers, often at point-blank range. The DE *Samuel B. Roberts* made a successful torpedo run and then traded fire with cruisers before she was sunk.

This valiant fighting by the planes and the little ships slowed the enemy, sinking two heavy cruisers and a destroyer. But the situation looked desperate for Rear Admiral Sprague's group. The enemy sank the CVE *Gambier Bay* and damaged other ships, and it was only the poor marksmanship of the Japs and the skillful way the American ships maneuvered that had saved the group from total destruction. The Japs were closing now to 12,000 yards. Then, to the amazement of the embattled CVE's, the Japanese warships suddenly swung around and began to withdraw at top speed, trailing oil from their injuries. Why did they quit? Your guess. Perhaps the Jap commander had received the news of catastrophe in other engagements.

The Battle off Samar wasn't finished, though. Now land-based enemy planes descended on the escort carrier group, eventually sinking the *Saint Lo*. And the Jap central force didn't escape without further attention, for in the afternoon Third Fleet carriers arrived in a hurry from the north. The enemy lost three more cruisers and his battleships took a pounding. When Rear Admiral Sprague's battered but unbeaten escort carriers reached safety at last, they received this tribute from Vice Admiral Kinkaid: *"Your performance was one which could have been expected only of CV's!"*

On the 24th, air reconnaissance of the enemy's southern and central forces had reported plenty of battleships and cruisers, but no carriers. Admiral Halsey reasoned that in a major enemy operation, as this clearly was, there would be carriers somewhere. He ordered a special search to the north; and the results proved very interesting. Four carriers, 2 BB's with flight decks, 5 cruisers, and 6 destroyers were approaching to throw their weight into the Battle of Leyte Gulf.

Vice Admiral Mitscher's fast carrier force headed out to meet this third Japanese contingent—to strike before the enemy could escape after pulling off one of those long-range operations attempted in the Battle of the Philippine Sea. The BATTLE OFF CAPE ENGANO opened in the early morning of the 25th; but that morning, too, Admiral Halsey received word of the unequal Battle off Samar. Promptly he dispatched carriers and battleships at top speed to the aid of the escort carriers.

Admiral Mitscher's flyers caught the enemy by surprise off Cape Engano. The Japs had pulled off a long-range operation the day before, and many of the planes hadn't yet returned to their carriers. That simplified the task of the Third Fleet airmen. They came down so suddenly on the Japanese northern force that antiaircraft crews were strafed from their guns before they could loose an effective barrage. From 0840 to 1800 the flyers methodically worked over the enemy. In the afternoon the absent Nip planes began to return, only to find a most unhappy situation. There seemed to be no decks to land on. However, they didn't have long to worry about it; they were soon shot down. At the close of the long air attack, Third Fleet surface units struck at the crippled and fleeing Japs to add to the victory statistics. Those statistics satisfied everyone but Tokyo: all 4 carriers sunk, as well as a CL and a DD; severe damage to the battleships.

The next day Third Fleet aircraft chased the Japs until the remnants of their fleet were out of range. The Battle of Leyte Gulf was over. It was ready for the history books, where it would be written down as one of the decisive battles of the world.

The Leyte campaign went forward on schedule. Meanwhile, Third Fleet fast carriers, commanded by Vice Admiral John S. McCain, ripped at Japanese shipping and air power; and the Seventh Fleet carried out two more landings—at Ormoc Bay on Leyte and on Mindoro Island 300 miles northwest. Far more damaging than Jap resistance was the typhoon that battered our fleet, sinking three destroyers.

Then the Japs were fooled again by another major amphibious operation. Vice Admiral McCain's flyers had pounded so hard at Manila Bay that the enemy expected the next assault there. Instead, Vice Admiral Kinkaid sent an 800-ship convoy into Lingayen Gulf to unload its cargo of fighting men and machines on the south and southeast coasts. Thus, on 9 January 1945 Americans returned to the battlefield where Americans and Filipinos had fought so valiantly thirty-seven months before. This was the second battle of Bataan.

The Japanese Navy did not put in an appearance. But Jap

air power came out in considerable strength, harassing the invasion convoy as it steamed up the coast, striking at the bombardment group that shelled the shore defenses for three days before the landings. On board the lead bombardment ship Rear Admiral Theodore E. Chandler received severe burns when his flag bridge caught on fire. He remained there, helping to man a hose, until his chief of staff forced him to go below to sickbay. The Admiral went walking, without aid. The next day he died from the burns.

The bombardment and the blistering rocket fire from landing craft cut down resistance on the beaches of Luzon. The Japs could not send reinforcements by air or sea because Admiral Halsey's Third Fleet continually got in the way. Starting operations well before Luzon D-day, the carrier-borne planes blasted Manila, Formosa, the Ryukyu Islands. Then, after the landings in Lingayen Gulf, the Third Fleet fast carrier force charged right into the South China Sea which was supposed to be strictly Japanese property and no trespassing allowed. Admiral Halsey trespassed for 3,800 miles, raiding the Indo-China coast and then descending on the great China ports of Hong Kong, Amoy, Swatow, and Canton. All this time no Jap aircraft was able to approach the U. S. carriers closer than twenty miles.

Next, with the Army closing upon Manila, the Navy invaded Manila Bay. The fire power of cruisers and destroyers kept Corregidor so occupied that landings on Bataan and Corregidor itself went off with complete success. In less than half the time it had taken the Japs, General MacArthur followed their bloody road of 1942. And one reason for this swift liberation was the powerful concentration of floating artillery offshore—Navy guns to blast the way for the Army.

Greetings to Tokyo

"THIS OPERATION HAS LONG BEEN PLANNED AND THE OPPORTUNITY TO ACCOMPLISH IT FULFILLS THE DEEPLY CHERISHED DESIRE OF EVERY OFFICER AND MAN IN THE PACIFIC FLEET."

Those were Fleet Admiral Nimitz's words when he announced that carrier forces had again raided Tokyo. February 16, 1945, was the Navy airmen's day. Attached once again to Admiral Spruance's Fifth Fleet, the great carrier task force commanded by Vice Admiral Mitscher approached the coast of Japan under cover of bad weather, and caught Japan off guard. For two days the flyers distributed their greetings and best regards, destroying 500 planes as well as ships, factories, airfields. In the smoke and fire and explosion of those two days, Tokyo became acquainted with the United States Navy. The acquaintance would be renewed.

(Do you remember that when Brigadier General Doolittle's bombers raided Tokyo in 1942, they took off from *Hornet*, commanded by Captain Marc. A. Mitscher?)

The Tokyo raid also served as a strategic covering operation for the primary mission of the Fifth Fleet—assault on a small, desolate, volcanic island called Iwo. This bleak island had two great values for Uncle Sam: it possessed airfields, and it was situated only 750 miles from Tokyo. Iwo Jima would provide a base for fighter planes to accompany the B-29's from Saipan on their trips to Tokyo, as well as a base for medium bombers aimed at Japan.

Iwo had natural defenses, a large garrison, and only two beaches possible for assault. So it could not be seized by surprise; victory depended on overwhelming power. For seven months planes and surface ships had blasted away at the island; and now, on the day of the Tokyo raid, Admiral Spruance opened a terrific pre-invasion bombardment. He had brought 800 ships to the little island; brought 60,000 Marines commanded by Lieutenant General Holland M. Smith, veteran of Saipan and the South Pacific, a pioneer in amphibious warfare. At 0900, 19 February, the Marines stormed the beaches.

It was terrific fighting. It was inch-by-inch fighting against fanatical Japs equipped with excellent weapons, stationed on strategic heights, and entrenched in pillboxes and caves. It was such bloody fighting that the Marines renamed Mount Surabachi "Mount Plasma." It was a battle that General Smith called *"the toughest we've run across in 168 years."* But on 14 March the United States flag was raised over Iwo Island, 750 miles from Japan.

Passing of a Friend

On 12 April 1945 the Allied world was saddened by the death of President Franklin D. Roosevelt. His passing came on the eve of the great victories he had planned for with brilliance and foresight. The Navy felt the loss to a man—for President Roosevelt had been one of the Navy's best friends. Vice-President Harry S. Truman succeeded Mr. Roosevelt, vowing to prosecute the war with equal determination.

V Stands for Victory

On 7 May 1945 Germany surrendered unconditionally to the Allies—and one half of World War II was over. As the guns fell silent in Europe, the Pacific front blazed with the battle of Okinawa. Day after day Navy ships ringed the island. Destroyers and destroyer escorts took their picket stations, keeping close radar guard, instantly warning the land forces of the approaching Jap air attacks. Heavier ships were on day-or-night call for precision shore bombardment. Transports and supply ships fought their way into the beaches and out again. All the vessels in the area were exposed to the fanatical Jap airmen, aiming their planes—often in flames and carrying a 500-pound bomb—for the bridge of the target ship. For 82 days the battle raged, with heavy casualties in American ships and men because of the suicide air attacks of Japan's last "secret weapon," the Kamikaze corps. But when Okinawa fell at last, Uncle Sam gained sea, air, and ground-force bases on Emperor Hirohito's doorstep.

Every day the big B-29's battered Jap cities. Roaming close to the shores of Japan, Admiral Halsey's Third Fleet methodically smashed to pieces the last remnants of the Imperial Navy. Clearly the knockout was coming soon. Yet when it did come, the knockout blow staggered the world, for it was struck with a fantastically powerful new weapon—the atomic bomb. Two of these bombs, in the development of which Navy experts had played a vital part, leveled the Jap cities of Hiroshima and Nagasaki. On 14 August 1945 President Truman announced that Japan had surrendered.

Japan signed the surrender terms on 2 September (Tokyo time) on board the great battleship *Missouri*, lying in Tokyo Bay. She and her comrades of the fleet had come a long, perilous way since the Japs fired the first shot—the shot that backfired 'round the world.

FIGHTING MEN SECOND TO NONE

Epilogue

OPERATION CROSSROADS! Thus the Navy aptly named its atomic bomb tests at Bikini in the Pacific during the summer of 1946. Mankind may well be at a portentous cross in the roadways of its recorded history. And, even as you read, the Navy makes history.

It is history in the making with the most colossal weapon ever devised by man—the A-bomb. At Hiroshima and at Nagasaki it proved itself a weapon capable of destroying a fair-sized city at one blow.

The atomic bomb is in its infancy. Its present stage of development is comparable to the muzzle-loaded cannon, the submarine *Turtle*, or the first rickety airplane. Many nuclear scientists apprehend a day when atomic power, fully developed, may bring forth a weapon more deadly than the present A-bomb.

On the brighter side, it is to be expected that the principles behind "atomic fission" may well be turned to uses that will benefit mankind. Already scientists are at work, exploring the uses of atomic energy in the field of medicine, and anticipating commercial possibilities. In testing at Bikini the effects of atomic power on ships and on living things, your Navy forwards a scientific research program that may immeasureably advance the welfare of mankind in peace—"Navies are not all for war."

Is it possible to hope that the foreboding implications of the atom bomb may convince the peoples of the world that war— as a means of settling national differences—is out-dated? Already the cost of war in lives and fortunes is almost beyond humanity's capacity to pay. With the cost of World War I still burdening the earth, the added bill for World War II will surely impoverish many nations for generations yet to come. Once the idea of atomic power convinces all people that peace is the only answer to survival, then the atom bomb and those who developed it have indeed made history.

Meanwhile, your peace-time Navy continues to mount guard—to further the advance of the ideals of Independence, Liberty, Justice, and Democracy. The Navy will protect those rights defended by American sea power from the time of the Revolutionary War to the close of World War II—ideals which may be summed up in the simple term, "the Rights of Man."

To the Navy men of the past
To the Bluejackets of the present
To the Navy men of the future:
This book is sincerely dedicated.

Reading List

A History of Sea Power. William Stevens and Allen Wescott. New York, 1943

History of Naval Tactics. Samuel Robison. Annapolis, 1942

Makers of Naval Tradition. Carroll Alden and Ralph Earle. New York, 1942

John Paul Jones. Lincoln Lornz. Annapolis, 1943

We Build a Navy. Lt. Cdr. Halloway Frost USN. Annapolis, 1940

Rise of American Naval Power. Harold and Margaret Sprout. Princeton, 1933

Sea Power and the Machine Age. Bernard Brodie. London, 1942

Navy Wings. Harold Miller. New York, 1937

Life of David Glasgow Farragut. Loyall Farragut. New York, 1897

The War At Sea. Gilbert Cant. New York, 1942

Torpedo Junction. Robert Casey. New York, 1942

Layman's Guide to Naval Strategy. Bernard Brodie. London, 1942

The United States Navy. Carroll Alden and Allen Wescott. New York, 1943

The Navy—A History. Fletcher Pratt. New York, 1943

Sea Power in Conflict. Paul Shubert. New York, 1942

Queen of the Flat-Tops. Stanley Johnston. New York, 1942

The Destiny of Sea Power. John Cranwell. New York, 1941

Sea Power. Capt. Russell Grenfell USN (Ret.). New York, 1941

Your Navy. Capt. Claude Mayo USN (Ret.). Los Angeles, 1942

The Navy Reader. Edited by Lt. William Fetridge USNR. New York, 1943

Battle Report—Pearl Harbor to Coral Sea. Walter Karig and Welbourn Kelley. New York, 1946

Battle Report—Atlantic War. Walter Karig. New York, 1946

History of the Modern American Navy. Donald Mitchell. New York, 1946

Index

447

Index

Index

Index

Index

Index

Index

U. S. GOVERNMENT OFFICE: 1946—699197